AF352607

André Gide and the
Second World War

ANDRÉ GIDE AND THE SECOND WORLD WAR

A Novelist's Occupation

JOCELYN VAN TUYL

STATE UNIVERSITY OF NEW YORK PRESS

Published by
STATE UNIVERSITY OF NEW YORK PRESS
ALBANY

© 2006 State University of New York

For information, address
State University of New York Press
194 Washington Avenue, Suite 305, Albany, NY 12210-2384

Production, Laurie Searl
Marketing, Susan Petrie

Library of Congress Cataloging-in-Publication Data

Van Tuyl, Jocelyn, 1964–
    André Gide and the second World War : a novelist's occupation / Jocelyn Van Tuyl.
       p. cm.
    Includes bibliographical references and index.
    ISBN-10: 0-7914-6713-9 (hardcover : alk. paper)
    ISBN-13: 978-0-7914-6713-8 (hardcover : alk. paper)
  1. Gide, André, 1869–1951—Political and social views. 2. World War, 1939–1945—
Literature and the war. I. Title.

PQ2613.I2Z84 2006
848'.91209—dc22

                                                                              2005014627

                    10   9   8   7   6   5   4   3   2   1

To the memory of Hélène Vitet

Contents

Acknowledgments

Numerous individuals and organizations supported the completion of this project, and they all have my most sincere thanks.

The inspiration for this book grew out of a National Endowment for the Humanities Summer Seminar on "War and Memory: Postwar Representations of World War II and the Occupation in France" held at Harvard University. Seminar leader Susan Rubin Suleiman and my fellow seminar participants offered valuable advice and feedback in the early stages of this project.

Financial support came in the form of a National Endowment for the Humanities Fellowship for College Teachers, a University of South Florida International Travel Grant, numerous research and travel grants from the New College Faculty Development Fund, and the generous assistance of the New College Division of Humanities.

Research for this book took me far afield. I wish to thank the librarians and staff of the Bibliothèque Littéraire Jacques Doucet and Fonds André Gide, the Bibliothèque Nationale de France, the Public Record Office in Kew, England, the British Library, and the Harvard and Yale University Libraries. Above all, the entire staff of Sarasota's Jane Bancroft Cook Library has my deepest gratitude.

I am indebted to Catherine Gide, who graciously granted me permission to consult manuscripts from her personal collection as well as those held by the Bibliothèque Littéraire Jacques Doucet. I also thank Pierre Masson and Martine Sagaert, who generously sent research materials across the Atlantic.

An earlier version of chapter four was published in *André Gide's Politics: Rebellion and Ambivalence*, edited by Tom Conner, © Tom Conner. Grateful acknowledgment is made to the original publisher, Palgrave Macmillan.

Further thanks go to the *Bulletin des Amis d'André Gide* and *Francographies*, which also published early versions of some material in this book.

This project could not have come to fruition without the practical, scholarly, and emotional support of a host of friends and colleagues. I would never have begun this book were it not for the advice and assistance of Suzanne Janney. I would never have completed it without the help of Helen Rees, who tirelessly read endless drafts, offering encouragement and unerring guidance. The international community of Gide scholars provided unprecedented career support at a critical juncture and I owe them all endless thanks. I am also grateful to Pat and Freddie Rees, who welcomed me to their home while I did research in London, to Geneviève and Pierre Masson, who provided a timely rescue during a French transit strike, and to the extended Vitet-Pellé clan, who have given me a home and family in France for the past quarter century.

Additional thanks go to Christine Latrouitte Armstrong, the late Holly Barone, Maribeth Clark, Glenn Cuomo, Laszlo Deme, John Burt Foster, Pamela Genova, Maegan Henderson, Jennifer Herdt, Jason Jacobs, Andrew Jaffee, Ken Krauss, Hélène Lowe-Dupas, Claude Martin, John Moore, Brigitte Muller, Walter Putnam, Amy Reid, Marie-Claire Rohinsky, Naomi Segal, Liz Temkin, Michael Tilby, and Miriam L. Wallace. Many apologies to anyone I may have forgotten.

Finally, I wish to thank my entire family, especially my daughter Mileva, who demonstrated patience beyond her years while I was writing.

Abbreviations

G/Sch	André Gide and Jean Schlumberger, *Correspondance 1901–1950*
G/Ster	André Gide and Thea Sternheim, *Correspondance 1927–1950*
G/V	André Gide and Paul Valéry, *Correspondance 1890–1942*
I.I.	André Gide, *Imaginary Interviews*
IID	André Gide, *If It Die*
J I	André Gide, *Journal 1887–1925*
J II	André Gide, *Journal 1926–1950*
J 2	André Gide, *The Journals of André Gide*, vol. 2
J 3	André Gide, *The Journals of André Gide*, vol. 3
J 4	André Gide, *The Journals of André Gide*, vol. 4
J 39–42	André Gide, *Journal, 1939–1942*
LE	André Gide, *Littérature engagée*
NRF	Claude Martin, *La* Nouvelle Revue Française *1940–1943*
OC	André Gide, *Œuvres complètes d'André Gide*
PJ [A]	André Gide, *Pages de Journal, 1939–1941* [Algiers]
PJ [NY]	André Gide, *Pages de Journal, 1939–1942* [New York]
R	André Gide, *Romans, récits et soties, œuvres lyriques*
SBI	André Gide, *So Be It, or The Chips Are Down*
SV	André Gide, *Souvenirs et voyages*
TL	André Gide, *Two Legends: Œdipus and Theseus*

Introduction

ARGUABLY THE MOST influential French writer of the early twentieth century, André Gide is a paradigmatic figure whose World War II writings offer an exemplary reflection of the challenges facing a leading writer in a time of national collapse. Tracing Gide's circuitous "intellectual itinerary" from the fall of France through the postwar purge, this book examines the ambiguous role of France's senior man of letters during the Second World War. Eschewing simplistic or partisan readings that summarily label the writer as either collaborator or resister, this study of Gide's neglected wartime writings focuses on the author's profound political ambivalence and his unacknowledged efforts to reinvent himself over the course of the war. With the exception of the early wartime *Journal*, Gide's publications during France's "dark years" have received scant critical attention. *André Gide and the Second World War* scrutinizes the entire wartime oeuvre in depth, tracing the evolution of Gide's political views and, most important, reading the wartime texts against each other. For it is the interplay among these texts that reveals the full complexity of Gide's political positionings and the rhetorical brilliance he deployed to redress his tarnished image. From late 1941 until after the Liberation, I argue, Gide made a systematic effort to conceal objectionable or ambiguous statements made during the early months of the war. The author's strategies range from outright deletions in the *Pages de Journal* to the subtler reworkings of the "Interviews imaginaires"—a series of literary essays in which Gide revisits infelicitous observations, giving them a new, resolutely patriotic flavor. Through careful editing and judicious placement of wartime texts in periodicals associated with the resistance, Gide created the impression that his thinking followed a neat trajectory from unavoidable defeatism to appropriate patriotism.[1] Reading the published works against Gide's diary, however, exposes the author's persistent political ambivalence. This book challenges Gide's characterization of his political evolution as a straightforward march from "darkness into light" (J 4)[2] and shows how methodically the author constructed his narrative of redemption.[3] Gide's intricate maneuverings ultimately offer privileged insights into three issues of broad significance: the relationship of literature and politics in World War II France, the repressions and repositionings that continue to fuel controversy about this period, and the role of public intellectuals in times of national crisis.

WARTIME FRANCE: THE DRIFT OF PUBLIC OPINION

An individual who amply documents his life in diaries, correspondence, and published writings leaves a reasonably clear record of his evolving viewpoints. A politically diverse nation of forty million is another matter—especially when the complications of censorship, propaganda, and a division into two administrative zones make it difficult to assess what most citizens knew at any given time. Consequently, the historical précis that follows gives only a general sense of the predominant trends in public opinion during the Occupation of France.

In the years following the First World War, the scarred French nation wished only for peace. During the 1930s, the government adopted a policy of non-intervention vis-à-vis the Spanish Civil War and the growing threat of Nazism. Most citizens applauded the 1938 Munich Agreement, in which France and Britain averted war with Germany by condoning Hitler's annexation of the Sudetenland. When Germany invaded Poland in September 1939, France and Britain reluctantly declared war on the Reich. A six-month period known as the "drôle de guerre" (phony war) ensued, but, when the attack came, it was crushing. In May 1940, German armies swept through Belgium and the Netherlands, pierced the French frontier at Sedan, and marched into Paris on 14 June. Just days later, Premier Paul Reynaud resigned in favor of World War I hero Marshal Philippe Pétain, who immediately sued for peace. With the signature of the Armistice on 22 June, France was divided into a German-occupied zone in the north and along the Atlantic coast and an unoccupied zone in the south, where citizens were free of direct German control but had to face the authoritarian policies of the Vichy government (established in early July 1940) as well as that regime's increasing collaboration with Germany.

The Armistice was greeted with despair but also with relief, since France's prompt surrender spared the lives of thousands of French soldiers. There seemed no other course of action given that the United States declined to intervene and England seemed likely to fall in France's wake. To make matters worse, Britain ceased to be a potential savior and began to look more like the "hereditary enemy" she was in the eyes of many Frenchmen: on 3 July 1940, British warships attacked and sank the French fleet, then anchored at the Algerian port of Mers el-Kébir, to prevent its coming under

German control. Public opinion shifted by the autumn, however, becoming pro-British and anti-German as the initial impression of the occupiers' gentlemanly behavior was tarnished by acts of brutality and the promise of life as usual was belied by increasing food shortages (Jackson 274–76).

At this stage, liberation from within seemed impossible. As Julian Jackson has aptly observed, "[b]efore it could be joined, resistance had to be invented. So did the very concept of resistance." Although isolated incidents of defiance and sabotage occurred during the first months of the Occupation, "they petered out at the end of the year because, without any organized Resistance movement to give them a purpose, they were futile, dangerous, and led nowhere" (406, 286–87). Moreover, the Vichy and Free French leaders alike discouraged acts of rebellion: from Vichy, Pétain condemned armed resistance; from London, de Gaulle warned against such actions for fear they would bring about heavy reprisals (Ferro 127). The people's aversion to the German occupiers and, later, to the Vichy regime "did not necessarily lead to active opposition or support for the emerging Resistance: caution and fatalism prevailed" (Jackson 281).

Prudent acquiescence seemed easier than rebellion, especially in the southern zone, where the figure of Marshal Philippe Pétain, head of the new État Français (French State), made collaboration palatable to many citizens. As "the subject of an extraordinary personality cult," Pétain lent the regime far more coherence and credibility than it would otherwise have enjoyed (Jackson 278). Much of the marshal's popularity can be attributed to his rivalry with his minister of state, Pierre Laval, who took greater initiative toward collaboration with Germany. Laval's overtly pro-German stance fostered the myth of the "double jeu" (double game)—the widespread belief that Pétain was collaborating under duress while secretly negotiating with the Americans. Jealous of his minister's political maneuvering, Pétain dismissed Laval on 13 December 1940, briefly placing him under house arrest. Explaining Laval's ouster to the French people, Pétain claimed that the minister was viewed unfavorably by foreign governments—meaning the British. In a letter to Hitler, however, Pétain presented Laval as an obstacle to collaboration, insisting that his dismissal did not in any way suggest that Pétain had gone back on his resolution to collaborate loyally with Germany (Ferro 42, 46–48). To the French, who knew nothing of Pétain's actual dealings with Germany, Laval's departure only increased Pétain's prestige. When Laval returned to power in April 1942, assuming the office of premier, the halo effect persisted—all the more so since Pétain's public restraint vis-à-vis Germany contrasted sharply (and positively) with Laval's June 1942 declaration that he hoped for Germany's victory.[4]

If Laval's reinstatement in the spring of 1942 marked a turning point, the end of that year—described by Winston Churchill as "the end of the beginning" (6693)—brought a decisive shift in public opinion. Germany had invaded the Soviet Union in June 1941, and the United States had joined the war in December. It was only a year later, however, that the effects of these developments became obvious, with the first German defeats at Stalingrad and El-Alamein and the Allied invasion of Morocco and Algeria in the fall of 1942.

Paradoxically, these German defeats translated into increased repression in France: in response to the Allied landings in North Africa, the German army invaded the southern zone, extending the Occupation to the entire French territory; because of the financial costs of the doomed Eastern offensive, Germany increased its demands on French industry and required additional French manpower in German factories (Ferro 96–97). In 1942, the *relève*—the program whereby one French prisoner of war was liberated for every three workers who volunteered to work in Germany—gave way to the Service du Travail Obligatoire (S.T.O.), for which thousands of young Frenchmen were conscripted. Many of these young men turned to the armed resistance units known as the *maquis* rather than travel to Germany, and many citizens helped conceal and protect the *réfractaires* (conscription resisters). By turning "law-abiding citizens into outlaws," the S.T.O. "not only helped the Resistance win new recruits, it also discredited Vichy even among its hard-core supporters" (Jackson 480). Where there had been quietly circulated resistance papers and scattered acts of sabotage, from the summer of 1942 onward there was resistance en masse (Ferro 126–27).

With increased resistance came more frequent executions of hostages and *résistants*. This further appalled the French, as did the simultaneously worsening persecution of France's Jewish population (Ferro 99). Although Vichy's first anti-Semitic laws dated from October 1940, repression escalated after the January 1942 Wannsee Conference, at which Germany consolidated its plan for systematic extermination of the Jews. Numerous anti-Semitic measures followed immediately in all occupied countries. The yellow star was instituted in France, deportations began, and massive roundups marked the summer of 1942.

The remaining years of the Occupation were brutal, but there was growing cause for hope. Resistance movements were increasingly consolidated by 1943, and it seemed clear to most Frenchmen that Germany would eventually lose the war. By the time the Allies landed in Normandy in June 1944, the Forces Françaises de l'Intérieur were prepared to join battle from within France, while Charles de Gaulle's Free French fought alongside the Allied liberators. August 1944 brought the invasion of Provence and the liberation of Paris, though complete liberation of France's Atlantic coast would be delayed until Germany's total capitulation in May 1945.

This final phase of the war was one that Gide experienced only at a remove. Having spent the early war years in the south of France, he left for French North Africa in May 1942. Instead of the events of metropolitan

France, Gide experienced the occupation and liberation of Tunis, then witnessed the Gaullist consolidation of power in Algiers. Throughout the war,
however, the evolution of Gide's political viewpoints closely parallels that of
the average Frenchman.[5] This finding is somewhat surprising, for André Gide
was far from average.

ANDRÉ GIDE: LIFE, LETTERS, AND LOVE

André Gide was born in 1869 to a wealthy Protestant family of considerable
intellectual achievements.[6] His upbringing was quite rigid—even puritani-
cal—especially after the death of his father when André was eleven years old.
Emancipation came during an 1893 journey to North Africa, where the bud-
ding writer discovered his homosexuality and had his first sensual encounters
with young boys. Two years later, shortly after the death of his mother, Gide
married his first cousin Madeleine Rondeaux. Their marriage gave way to
partial estrangement in 1918 when Madeleine learned of Gide's relationship
with his protégé, sixteen-year-old Marc Allégret. Though Gide's marriage to
Madeleine remained unconsummated, the writer did father a daughter,
Catherine, born in 1923 to Élisabeth Van Rysselberghe, the daughter of
Gide's close friend and chronicler Maria Van Rysselberghe.[7]

Gide's vast and varied literary oeuvre is so well known that it does not
bear recapitulating here. Two aspects of his literary efforts are of particular
relevance, however. The first is the *Nouvelle Revue Française (N.R.F.)*, the
prestigious and immensely influential literary journal that Gide cofounded in
1908. The *N.R.F.*, read around the world, published France's finest and most
up-to-date literary and political writing throughout the first half of the last
century. Moreover, the literary and cultural endeavors associated with the
N.R.F. group—the Gallimard-N.R.F. publishing house, the Vieux-Colombier
theater, and the intellectual gatherings known as *décades* held each summer
at Pontigny—were among the most influential and successful cultural insti-
tutions of their day.[8]

The second literary trend of interest is the thematic omnipresence of
homosexuality in nearly all of Gide's fiction as well as in his memoirs and the
1924 essay *Corydon*, which Alan Sheridan has described as "the first serious
attempt by a homosexual to defend the practice of homosexuality to the general public" (626). Many well-known writers of Gide's era were gay, though
with varying degrees of openness.[9] Gide distinguished himself from his contemporaries through his willingness to tell the truth about his sexuality—and
to do so in his own name. By speaking in the first person, Gide was defying the
admonitions of both Oscar Wilde and Marcel Proust, who warned that one
could say anything so long as he never said "I" (J I: 1124; J II: 44; Gide, *Prétextes* 248). He also eschewed the gender-bending codes of writers like Henry
de Monthlerant, who used "female pseudonyms" for his young male partners

and described "pedophilic acts [. . .] in language customarily used for hetero-sexual intercourse" (Krauss 146–47).[10] He strongly disapproved of Proust's use of a similar code in À *la recherche du temps perdu*, for the author's decision to "transpose '*à l'ombre des jeunes filles*' all the attractive, affectionate, and charm-ing elements contained in his homosexual recollections" meant that "for *Sodome* he [was] left nothing but the grotesque and the abject" (J 2: 267).[11] To Gide's mind, the *Recherche* represented a missed opportunity for a great gay writer to depict homosexuals sympathetically, and ran counter to his own pro-ject of portraying "normal homosexuals" (O'Brien, *Portrait* 253–54).[12]

In his quest to normalize homosexuality in the eyes of the reading pub-lic, Gide swiftly denounced as degenerate those homosexuals whose sexual practices differed from his own. In his 1918 *Journal*, Gide outlines a taxon-omy of homosexuals distinguishing among the "pederast" who desires young boys, the "sodomite" who loves adult men, and the "invert" who assumes the receptive or "female" role (J I: 1092). Inverts alone, he asserts, deserve the accusations of "moral or intellectual deformation [. . .] that are commonly addressed to all homosexuals" (J 2: 247).[13] Whereas Gide usually uses the term "pédéraste" to refer to "an adult male lover of adolescent boys [. . .], for the French reader, this term [. . .] was synonymous with 'homosexual'" (Sheri-dan 378). However, the distinction was crucial to Gide, who used the classi-cal conception of pederasty to understand and justify his sexual morality.

Attracted to adolescent and prepubescent boys, Gide would today be called a pedophile. Yet our modern lexicon elides the civic and cultural virtues with which Gide surrounded his view of pederasty. In Alan Sheridan's words, Gide's homosexuality was "'Hellenic', in an earnest, idealized way" (117). To support his theory that a mentor's love could help cultivate his protégé's finest qualities—both as an individual and as a member of society—Gide turned fre-quently to the classics and to pederasty's honored place in ancient Greece and Rome (Gide, *Corydon* [Fr.] 126–27, 122).[14] "Mostly, but not exclusively, the province of highborn males," Naomi Segal explains, classical pederasty:

> depended on a specific balance of similarities and differences. Theoretically, the relationship was between an older and a younger partner, *erastes* and *eromenos*, sometimes translated simply as "lover" and "beloved", with the clear distinction of subject/object, active/passive which those terms imply. The age-difference was not fixed and might be very small [. . . .] But the cen-trality of this model of older/younger is absolute, because it sanctifies the difference between a senior and a junior on which the whole structure depends. In the loves of adult men, the "other" could belong to any of a variety of inferior groups: women, slaves, foreigners and children. (13–14)[15]

Power imbalances were thus a constituent element of the classical model around which Gide built his sociosexual philosophy. Yet Gide was unable to acknowledge pederasty's inherent inequalities.

Gide's single-minded focus on defending his version of homosexual morality led to an arguably skewed viewpoint that sometimes short-circuited his thinking on other political issues. His first overtly political work, *Voyage au Congo*—a travelogue denouncing the abuses Gide witnessed in French Equatorial Africa—is a case in point. In a diary entry excised from the published text, Gide narrates his traveling companion's unsuccessful attempt to seduce a terrified young girl brought to him by their "interpreter-procurer." Having heard that Africans never dared refuse a wife or daughter to anyone willing to pay for her, Marc Allégret had requested a tryst with the interpreter's youngest wife. The realization that the interpreter had "chosen and sacrificed" the young girl in order to spare his own wife led Gide to a series of painful insights about Africans' alleged lasciviousness—clearly a myth—and Europeans' cynical exploitation of that myth. Rather than follow through to a conclusion about the power imbalance underlying the sexual commerce between colonizer and native, Gide makes this an occasion to tout "the advantage of homosexual leanings, which at least never bring about this kind of distress and involuntary cruelty."[16] Here Gide is duplicitous to say the least, for he, too, used the African journey as an opportunity for sexual tourism.[17] In this instance, Gide's idealization of homosexuality blinded him to the abuses of power in his own sexual conduct. The "blind spots" of Gide's sexual politics will be crucial to our understanding of Gide's wartime experience.

As this brief biographical sketch suggests, Gide was, paradoxically, both an insider and an outsider to French society. As a Protestant and homosexual, he was in the minority, yet both these groups were powerful: many prominent intellectuals of the day were gay, and French Protestants have historically exercised considerable influence in government and business. His not-too-shabby "outsider" status gave Gide the luxury of independence, the privilege to critique—as did his inherited wealth, which enabled him to pursue a life of letters, underwriting the publication of his early works and helping to launch the *N.R.F.* Throughout his life, he was a staunch defender of individualism, an opponent of all forms of totalitarianism (be they religious or political, from the right or from the left), and an often provocative proponent of individual liberties of all kinds—intellectual, sexual, and civic. Yet what is astonishing is the degree to which Gide's political trajectory over the course of the Second World War followed that of the "average" Frenchman. As a critic writing in the immediate aftermath of the war observed, Gide's opinions so neatly dovetailed with those of his compatriots that mass opinion had obviously exerted a strong influence on the writer's political viewpoints (Béguin).[18]

Like the majority of his compatriots, André Gide moved from initial shock and *attentisme* (a "wait and see" attitude) toward a stance more critical of Vichy and the German occupiers, arriving finally at wholehearted approval of the Gaullist resistance. Because Gide so cherished sincerity, he made no attempt to camouflage the twists and turns of his political opinion in his private diary. Yet the famous Gidian principle of sincerity never guaranteed any coherence of opinion. "How can anyone rival André Gide's sincerity?" asked Jean Prévost: "We have only one [. . .] and he has twelve. [. . .] Hypocritical? Not at all. Sincere at every instant, for an instant."[19] In the wartime *Journal*, those successive "instants" reveal doubts and profound grief, but also fairly frequent insouciance. These day-to-day shifts are highly revealing and thoroughly understandable.

Yet the editing of the manuscript diary for publication—the alterations and omissions that Gide (or those who claimed to represent him) made in accordance with the political mood of the moment—calls for a much more complex and nuanced understanding of Gidian "sincerity." On the one hand, we see modifications and claims that make published versions of the *Journal* less-than-accurate reflections of Gide's actual statements. On the other hand, we find an uncontrollable sincerity, a stubborn resolve on Gide's part to speak his mind publicly, regardless of the personal or political consequences of his statements.

The continued exercise of his much-touted sincerity reveals Gide's failure to comprehend the impact of his words and actions, and this failure was especially damaging because Gide was the archetypical public intellectual. Writers, scholars, and thinkers enjoy considerably greater influence in France than they have ever attained in North America and Britain. Intellectuals are routinely thrust into the spotlight: poets are expected to comment on politics, and their opinions—informed or not—find listeners. As a prominent intellectual, Gide was co-opted to serve strikingly different political agendas during the Second World War. As a homosexual, champion of individualism, and self-proclaimed *inquiéteur* (disturber), Gide was denounced for his "demoralizing" influence on the youth of France in the months following the Armistice. Later, both collaborationist and resistance editors tried to claim the author for their causes: even when André Gide the writer remained silent or withheld permission to publish his work, André Gide the cultural property was pressed into service. Thus, Gide's case exemplifies the role writers play in the collective imagination and the ways in which they are used to serve political ends.

PREWAR POSITIONS

At the outset of the Second World War, Gide's highly varied political and social views led to considerable speculation about his probable political alignment. Would his staunch belief in individual freedoms and the virtues of the French Republic make him an opponent of the Occupation and collaborationist regime? Or would his history of anti-Semitism, pacifism, and internationalism incline him in favor of the German occupiers? Throughout the war and its aftermath, every aspect of Gide's prewar writings—from the overtly political to the purely literary—would come back to haunt him. The author took a political beating from almost every faction at some time or another: during the shameful months following the defeat, conservatives condemned his supposedly decadent influence on interwar France, linking this influence to the nation's defeat; after the Liberation, communists nursing a grudge about Gide's 1936 critique of the Soviet Union accused him of abetting the enemy, or, at best, of remaining unforgivably above the fray. A brief overview of Gide's prewar politics will elucidate the political baggage the writer brought to the Second World War and underscore the complexity of the issues he would have to negotiate once his nation fell to the Germans in 1940.

Gide's experience of the First World War serves as a useful interpretive template, revealing thoughts and actions Gide would reexperience—or seek to replicate—during World War II. At the onset of both wars, Gide chose to devote himself actively to humanitarian causes and to abandon writing.[20] In 1914, horrified at his vision of Europe entering "a long tunnel full of blood and darkness" (J 2: 48)[21] but medically exempt from military service, Gide dedicated himself to aiding refugees from Belgium and northern France, serving as vice-chairman of the Foyer Franco-Belge throughout the first sixteen months of the war. During this period, Gide wrote no fiction, and even neglected his diary for nearly a year (Sheridan 280, 282–83). His silence can be attributed to his anguished feelings about the war and the heavy demands of his work of the Foyer, but it can also be interpreted as a political choice: as Martha Hanna has argued, "Gide chose to serve the war by abandoning, rather than exploiting, his intellectual vocation" (20).

While Gide did decline an invitation to contribute to a Swiss publication calling for "international conciliation"—largely because the proposed journal was to be published in German and he was "reluctant, after having kept silent for so long, to enter the debate in the language of the enemy" (Hanna 20)—he soon resumed work on his *Journal* and the private "green notebook" that would appear after the war as *Numquid et tu. . . .* These intimate writings reveal paradoxical right-wing leanings that would resurface during the Second World War. An outspoken individualist and defender of France's republican values, André Gide would seem an unlikely supporter of the authoritarian, ultranationalist Action Française movement. At the turn of the century, Gide had argued very publicly with Action Française leader Charles Maurras, vehemently contesting his extreme nationalism. Gide continued to read Maurras with interest, however (Léger 61), and it may have been "Gide's insistent attention to the opinions of his adversaries and his dialectical pursuit of truth" which account for his interest in Action Française in the years preceding the Great War (Hanna 13). This same passion for understanding the other's viewpoint—an impulse inspired by Gide's sense of fairness as well as by his conception of the novelist's craft—would, decades later, cause Gide to give serious credence to the collaborationist viewpoint and imagine dialogues with Hitler.

Gide expressed his concurrence with Action Française's values in a 1915 letter to the movement's leader. Transcribing passages from the last writings of his friend Pierre Dupouey, a pro-Action Française naval officer killed in action in 1915 (Léger 62), Gide informed Maurras: "I copy these lines with a deep emotion and all the more gladly since I most heartily associate myself with them" (J 2: 158).[22] Gide authorized Maurras to publish his letter in the group's newspaper *L'Action Française* and included payment for a subscription to that paper, where his letter appeared on 5 November 1916.[23] In a second letter, which he never actually sent to Maurras (Léger 65–66, 62), Gide declared that, in spite of the frequent and venomous attacks on him from the Action Française camp, he had "always remained, despite you and despite your followers, very close to your thought" (J 2: 158).[24] If Gide leaned toward the right-wing nationalist movement during the turbulent war years, it was largely because he saw it as the only viable alternative to socialism. In a 1918 *Journal* entry, Gide describes a lunch with Lucien Maury, who worried about "the wave of socialism he feels rising, which he foresees as submerging our old world after we think the war is over." Gide replied that Action Française's "resistance organization" represented *"the only"* hope for those opposing a socialist Europe (J 2: 226).[25] Gide's attitude toward the movement was always ambivalent, however, and he soon reversed his position: after 1920 he broke definitively—and bitterly—with the group (Hanna 2), becoming, in François Léger's words, a sort of "anti-Maurras" (68). A decade later, he became an enthusiastic supporter of the socialist movement he had so feared during the First World War.

Personal anxieties combined with Gide's political apprehensions to fuel his brief attraction to the Action Française. Throughout 1916 Gide chronicled a "profound spiritual crisis in which he struggled to come to terms with his sensuality, his understanding and acceptance of the Christian tradition, and his understanding of his national (and his nation's) identity" in both his diary and the notebook that would become *Numquid et tu . . .* (Hanna 17). Plagued by self-loathing—"I get up with a horrible disgust of everything and of myself"—Gide declared that: "[e]verything in me calls out to be revised, amended, re-educated." What needed correcting was clearly sexual in nature: Gide's biggest struggle was with his "sensual curiosity," and he even found "[t]oo much sensuality [. . .] constantly slipping into [his] charity" when he visited refugee families in connection with the Foyer Franco-Belge (J 2: 121, 117, 128).[26] Moreover, his *Journal* for this period contains numerous "scarcely veiled references to masturbation and his attempts to resist it" (Sheridan 288). Martha Hanna has argued that Gide's longing for sexual discipline and self-restraint also manifested itself in the political sphere (18). Thus, one could see a projection of Gide's own anxieties about self-indulgence in his June 1918 critique of the French people and nation: "that *Liberty* we claim to represent and defend is most often but the right to have our own way, to please ourselves, and would be better named: insubordination. All around us I see nothing but disorder, disorganization, negligence, and waste of the most radiant virtues—only falsehood, politics, absurdity" (J 2: 232).[27] Although Gide is not explicitly calling for German discipline as a corrective to French self-indulgence, the fact that he wrote these lines while the German army was at Château-Thierry, a mere fifty-five miles from Paris, gives his criticism a disturbing edge. The man who called for discipline during the First World War—going so far as to express support for monarchy, or even despotism[28]— would envisage the benefits of dictatorship during the Second World War. In both instances, the threat—or reality—of German conquest would make Gide's statements seem highly unpatriotic.

Although Gide's calls for national discipline persisted, the Second World War found the writer in a state of greater sexual self-acceptance. Between the wars, he had published the autobiographical *Si le grain ne meurt*, which recounts his early homosexual experiences, and *Corydon*, a treatise in defense of homosexuality. The publication of these works in the 1920s followed one of the most significant love affairs of his life—an idyll that shook him out of the mental crisis depicted in the World War I-era *Numquid et tu. . . .* Young Marc Allégret (who was sixteen years old to Gide's forty-seven when the relationship began in 1917) exerted such a "curative effect" that Gide's friend François-Paul Alibert succinctly reinterpreted the nature of the writer's previous torment: "Don't you realize that what you took to be self-hatred and self-disgust was merely your inability to renew your joy and happiness?" (qtd. in Sheridan 297–98).[29] Gide and Marc spend four idyllic months in England during the summer of 1918, and the older man's sexual and political torment abated in the face of this new love.[30] Gide's relationship with Marc found an echo—or, more properly, a reverse image—in his World War II-era interactions with another adolescent boy, François Reymond. Confronted this time with a young man who was not amenable to his advances, Gide had no hope of using sex or love to dispel the anxieties provoked by the war. Instead of a diversion from the war, his relationship with Reymond would provide Gide with an opportunity to comment on current events and a platform for his recurring exhortations about the need for individual and national discipline.

The authoritarian leanings expressed in his World War I-era writings help explain Gide's periodic statements, during World War II, about the benefits of German Occupation for "undisciplined" France. One aspect of the Occupation that he did not approve was the persecution of France's Jews. The anti-Jewish actions of Germany and Vichy would, however, force Gide to revisit his own long-standing anti-Semitism. Gide's opinions on the "Jewish question" are particularly revealing because they highlight the confluence of literary and political concerns at the heart of his thinking. Moreover, they reveal the conflict in Gide's mind between racial bias and humanitarian impulses. Throughout his life, Gide evidenced the "cultural anti-Semitism" so common to Frenchmen of his class and era (Lottman, *Left* 121). His aversion manifested itself primarily in the literary sphere. To Gide's mind, the works of French Jewish authors represented a threat to "true" French literature: "I do not deny, indeed, the great worth of certain Jewish works," he wrote in January 1914, "[b]ut how much more naturally I should admire them if they [. . . came] to us [only] in translation! For what does it matter to me that the literature of my country should be enriched if it is so at the expense of its significance" (J 2: 5).[31] In his often provocative *Histoire de l'antisémitisme*, Léon Poliakov compares this diary passage to Joseph Goebbels's assertion that "[w]hen a Jew speaks in German, he is lying!"[32]—conceding only that Gide's style was more refined than that of the Nazi propaganda minister. As his actions during the infamous Dreyfus Affair attest, however, Gide never let his personal views stop him from defending what was morally right. Privately protesting his antipathy and mistrust in a letter to avowed anti-Semite Eugène Rouart—"I don't like Jews any better [. . .] on the contrary I have never believed them to be more dangerous"[33]—Gide nevertheless signed *L'Aurore*'s petition in favor of the accused Jewish officer and his famous supporter Émile Zola.[34] Gide's public show of support for Dreyfus, while undoubtedly sincere, also provided a useful alibi in later years: when charged with anti-Semitism, Gide was invariably quick to point out his pro-Dreyfus stance of the 1890s.

Gide's "unconscious or culturally-acquired prejudices" against Jews were shared by enough core contributors to the *Nouvelle Revue Française* to earn the journal an anti-Jewish reputation in some readers' eyes. Yet the opposite view was even more widely held, especially among right-wingers. Many considered the *N.R.F.* "a haven for influential, subversive, war-mongering Jews"—despite the fact that prominent contributors like Julien Benda, Benjamin Crémieux, and André Suarès "wrote as assimilated Jews, eschewing Zionism and other extreme forms of nationalism." Perhaps the best-known exponent of such views is Louis-Ferdinand Céline, who had the *N.R.F.* group in mind when writing his 1937 work *Bagatelles pour un massacre*, a denunciation of the Parisian intellectual establishment that conflates Jewishness and homosexuality (Cornick 178–79, 172). Céline directs much of his venom at the person of André Gide: "I know with certainty that Gidian art, after Wildian art, after Proustian art, is part of the implacable continuity of the Jewish program. Lead all the goys to sodomize each other thoroughly. Carefully rot their elite, their bourgeoisie, by justifying all forms of inversion."[35] Gide is not the only target of Céline's screed, however: among the "raffinés" who rouse his ire, Céline cites Benda, Duhamel, Colette, and Valéry (Céline 11). Yet it soon becomes clear that Céline's categories are far from literal: as

Julian Jackson puts it, "Céline's list of 'Jews' is so eccentric—Stendhal, Racine, Picasso, Roosevelt, the Pope, Neville Chamberlain—that the designation seems to have become a free floating term attached to everything Céline hated" (106).

Gide, for one, did not take Céline's anti-Semitic screed seriously. On 11 March 1938—ironically, the day German troops invaded Austria—he formulated a rather dismissive appraisal of the *Bagatelles*: "it has no bearing on the Jewish question." By the following day, when he had learned of the *Anschluss*, Gide radically revised his assessment: "Numerous considerations on the Jewish question. Gide is not far from thinking that this is the most important [question] of all," reports Maria Van Rysselberghe.[36] Though shifting events caused him to reassess the book's timeliness, Gide persisted in dismissing Céline's rantings as a literary joke: Céline "does his best not to be taken seriously," Gide maintained in his April 1938 essay "Les Juifs, Céline et Maritain."[37] Certain that many readers would be amused by the *Bagatelles*, Gide cautioned that others might find this "literary game" with potentially "tragic consequences"[38] rather tasteless.[39] Though his approach was profoundly incommensurate with the inflammatory manifesto's potentially tragic political consequences, Gide did not share Céline's extreme beliefs. Rather, as Hannah Arendt later put it, Gide "rejoiced in [. . .] the fascinating contradiction between Céline's bluntness and the hypocritical politeness which surrounded the Jewish question in all respectable quarters," and his pleasure in this "unmasking of hypocrisy [. . .] could not even be spoiled by Hitler's very real persecution of the Jews, which at the time of Céline's writing was already in full swing" (335).

Gide's failure to acknowledge the connection between Céline's text and current events is, in retrospect, one of the most striking blind spots of "Les Juifs, Céline et Maritain." As Martyn Cornick has observed, Gide's myopic emphasis on the literary and stylistic aspects of the *Bagatelles* led him to neglect the crucial and contemporary reality of anti-Semitic violence in Nazi Germany. Moreover, the essay's treatment of Catholic philosopher Jacques Maritain's *Les Juifs parmi les nations* focused on the origins of the "Jewish question"—which Maritain thought to be "socially and historically derived rather than racially determined" (Cornick 179, 173)—to the exclusion of Maritain's most timely and prescient statement: "There are, in Europe today, those who desire the extermination of the Jews [. . .] and who, underneath the stupid apparatus of racist scientism or forged documents, conceal [. . .] the mad hope for a general massacre of the race of Moses and Jesus."[40] Ignoring the urgent contemporary resonances of Maritain's argument, Gide instead berated the philosopher for failing to investigate the positive contributions of a "heterogeneous element" such as the Jews; rather than seeing minorities solely as "troublesome elements,"[41] Gide argued, one should acknowledge that "this trouble can become salutary, all the more useful and premonitory as the tendency toward uniformity grows more extremist."[42] Here, then, is another facet of the role Jews played in Gide's mental universe: as "minorities"—aligned, in his mind, with individualists and dissenters—they represented a useful challenge to totalitarianism.

It was his own opposition to fascism and human rights abuses that led Gide to speak out against Hitler's anti-Semitic policies despite his own privately held biases. Whereas in the spring of 1938 he was able to minimize the potential political consequences of Céline's *Bagatelles pour un masssacre*, he took quite a different stance by the end of the year, when Nazi violence had sharply escalated. In the wake of the November 1938 pogrom known as *Kristallnacht*, Gide was one of the leading intellectuals asked to "comment on the Jewish question" in the pages of *La Revue Juive de Genève* (Cornick 174). In his heartfelt "Déclaration" of December 1938, Gide expressed his "profound indignation before a collective crime whose ferocity, treachery, and cowardice go beyond what one might fear from an oppressive regime," and lamented "the mediocrity of reactions, in France, to such abuses of power."[43] Gide's protest earned him a reputation as a defender of Hitler's victims—a reputation that caught the attention of Paul Léautaud, the literary and social gossipmonger of interwar Paris. In the spring of 1939, Léautaud affirmed that Gide had made a similar declaration to a Hungarian reporter: "Gide is rather anti-Semitic [. . . .] And yet, when *La Revue de Hongrie* came recently to interview him about the Jews in Germany under Hitler's dictatorship, he gave the review a sort of protest, signed by him, against the misfortunes inflicted on those poor people."[44] Though no trace remains of Gide's alleged protest,[45] defending the victims of Nazi oppression would certainly have been in character, as Gide's secretary Lucien Combelle—the alleged source of Léautaud's anecdote (12: 246)—pointed out. "In this period of European anti-Semitism, Gide is listening to his heart. And he declares that his sympathy goes out to all of those unfortunates. [. . .] Ah, yes, his heart! He should be careful, though," Combelle opined, alluding to Gide's earlier infatuation with Soviet communism: "It was his heart which led him to Moscow."[46] Combelle's assessment was lucid, for Gide's heart and mind were in perpetual conflict, his humanitarian impulses at war with his "rational"—though often prejudiced—judgments. These opposing tugs would dictate the abrupt twists and turns of Gide's political engagement throughout the interwar period.

The positions Gide took on key European political issues of the interwar years—Franco-German relations, the Soviet experiment, and the Spanish Civil War—were characterized by a steadfast defense of internationalism, a fierce determination to act independently rather than enroll in political parties and movements, and an often unpopular sense of right that caused him to critique his own side's moral lapses more harshly than those of the opposition. Complicating these principles was Gide's idiosyncratic way of slicing up the world: his political views were articulated in relation to "culture" and colored by a predominant strain of intellectual elitism.

In the immediate aftermath of the First World War, Gide framed his views on Germany in terms of intellectual values. Refusing to reject the German nation or German thinkers, he instead denounced those—be they French or German—who were hostile to culture and individualism. In his 1919 essay "Réflexions sur l'Allemagne," Gide vigorously opposed those Frenchmen who would reject Nietzsche, Wagner, and Goethe; the latter, Gide asserted, would have abhorred the "monstrous" 1914–1918 war (37). Moreover, "the best of German thought rises up against Prussia, which is leading Germany to combat."[47] Failing to acknowledge the diversity of German opinion could be fatal, Gide warned: "how can you fail to understand, you who want to reject Germany outright, that by rejecting Germany outright you are working toward her unity?"[48] In the decades following World War I, Gide proved a lucid judge of France's responsibility for ultranationalist developments in the defeated nation. He disapproved of France's intransigent refusal to modify the humiliating terms of the Versailles Treaty,[49] and went so far as to applaud the "excellent" May 1933 speech in which Hitler condemned that treaty as the source of Germany's economic and social crisis. "If Hitlerism had never made itself known otherwise, it would be more than merely acceptable," Gide declared. "But it remains to be seen where the real face ends and the grimace begins" (J 3: 270).[50]

Hitler's "true face" was swiftly revealed, and Gide was quick to speak out against the abuses of the Nazi regime. Following Hitler's election as chancellor in January 1933, the Weimar Constitution's freedoms of press and assembly were suspended, pacifist or antinationalist books were banned, and the police, exercising their newfound right to arrest and intern at will, imprisoned thousands of communists, socialists, and Jews in the wake of the February 1933 Reichstag fire. Presiding at the Association des Écrivains et Artistes Révolutionnaires (A.E.A.R.)'s March 1933 protest rally against the alarming developments in Hitler's Germany, Gide lamented the silencing of that portion of the German population that was most likely to resist the Nazi regime.[51] He also reacted to the German crisis in the pages of the communist paper *L'Humanité*, declaring on 6 March 1933 that extreme nationalism such as Germany's was always accompanied by oppression and inevitably led to war.[52] Only class struggle and the dismantling of imperialism could help avert the cataclysmic hostilities Gide foresaw on the horizon (LE 21).

While the vocabulary of class struggle had crept into his speeches during the 1930s, it cohabitated with the typically Gidian language of individualism and literary values—a lexicon that often put Gide out of step with the communist organizers behind the scenes of many left-wing political manifestations of that period.[53] Presiding at the A.E.A.R.'s October 1934 meeting— convened as a forum for reports on the First Congress of Soviet Writers held that summer in Moscow—Gide delivered an opening speech that offered an unorthodox take on the topic "Littérature et Révolution." "Literature has no obligation to put itself in service to the Revolution," Gide declared: "An enslaved literature is a debased literature, however noble and legitimate the cause it serves."[54] Addressing the first Congrès International des Écrivains pour la Défense de la Culture the following summer, Gide chose to focus on individualistic rather than collectivist values: "it is by being the most singular that each being best serves the community."[55] Having turned toward social and political causes in the late 1920s, Gide nevertheless retained his former values, and his contributions to the political debates of the 1930s were invariably idiosyncratic.

A highly visible though tentative participant in the communist-inspired meetings and manifestoes of the 1930s, Gide oscillated between engaging fervently and keeping his distance, lending his considerable authority to numerous left-wing causes while vigorously asserting his independence. A curious and sympathetic fellow traveler, he declined to join the Communist Party. Though he presided at the 1933 and 1934 conventions organized by the Association des Écrivains et Artistes Révolutionnaires, Gide chose not to enroll in the organization, arguing: "I believe that my cooperation [. . .] can be most truly beneficial to your (to our) cause if I give it freely and if people know me to be *unenlisted*."[56] At times the authority conferred by his signature was not entirely voluntary: systematically refusing to sign any declaration that he had not drafted himself (J II: 416), Gide occasionally found that his name had been used without his consent, as in the case of the European Anti-Fascist Congress of June 1933 (Lottman, *Left* 52). Though he might protest privately, he generally allowed his name to stand for fear that a retraction would harm the political cause in question (LE 47).

Gide's involvement in the antifascist activities of the 1930s went beyond speeches and signatures. He intervened actively on behalf of the Bulgarian and German communists accused of setting the February 1933 fire that destroyed the German Reichstag—a fire actually set by Nazi agents provocateurs. Following their trial in Leipzig, defendants Dimitrov, Tanev, Popov, and Torgler were acquitted but not released from prison (LE 20). Gide voiced his support for the Leipzig defendants in the pages of *L'Humanité*, and in January 1934 he accompanied André Malraux on a mission to Berlin to lobby Propaganda Minister Goebbels on behalf of Dimitrov and his co-defendants. Though Goebbels was unable or unwilling to meet personally with them, the French representatives of the International Dimitrov Committee delivered a letter urging the defendants' release. Dimitrov was eventually freed on 27 February 1934 (LE 41, 44).

Another journey marked the most decisive step in Gide's flirtation with communism. Like many Western intellectuals before him, Gide accepted an invitation to travel to the Soviet Union in 1936.[57] Much has been written about Gide's trip and his subsequent condemnation of the Soviet regime. The aim of this brief discussion is to examine that voyage and the works that grew out of it—the 1936 *Retour de l'U.R.S.S.* and 1937 *Retouches à mon retour de l'U.R.S.S.*—as they relate to the coming world war. To begin with, there are the famous photos of Gide's departure, which show Gide on the tarmac at Paris's Le Bourget airfield and framed against the doorway of the plane that would take him to Berlin and then to Moscow. What the viewer may not realize is how carefully each shot was composed so as to conceal the giant swastika emblazoned on the tail of the German aircraft.[58] That hidden insignia is highly symbolic: it represents the looming threat of Nazi expansionism, against which the Soviet Union seemed to offer the only defense. Gide's great transgression on coming home would be to express his disenchantment with Moscow in a manner that many feared would facilitate Berlin's conquests.

Throughout his Soviet tour, Gide was fêted and congratulated; he was taken to view an exhibit on his life and works at Moscow University and enticed by a swimming pool filled, for his benefit, with handsome young Red army soldiers. Gide, however, saw through the red-carpet treatment extended to him and his party. With great lucidity, he observed the repressions of Stalin's regime, including the government's harsh stance on homosexuality, to which he particularly objected (Lottman, *Left* 111–13). On his return to France, Gide denounced Soviet totalitarianism through an explicit comparison with Nazi Germany: "I doubt whether in any other country in the world, even Hitler's Germany, thought be less free, more bowed down, more fearful (terrorized), more vassalized" (*Return* 42).[59] He even observed privately that Stalin's use of fascist practices seemed to "justify" Hitler (J II: 590).[60] In the fall of 1936, with Gide's negative views of the Soviet Union leaked to the press and the publication of *Retour de l'U.R.S.S.* imminent, the book's implications for the delicate political balance between the U.S.S.R. and Europe's fascist nations made for alarmed reactions from Gide's communist associates. Those who sought to block or delay the publication argued political expediency, and warned that a public denunciation of the Soviet Union would merely play into Hitler's hand.

A more pressing argument against immediate publication of the *Retour* concerned the 1936–1939 Spanish Civil War, which was in some respects a microcosm of the world war to come. Since July 1936, the democratically elected Spanish Republicans had been fighting Franco's forces. Whereas Germany and Italy were providing men and materiel to Franco's rebels, France had opted for neutrality (LE 150–51). Gide was among those who protested France's policy of nonintervention—a policy that would, in the end, facilitate Franco's victory.[61] The Soviet Union, on the other hand, was providing considerable support to the Republicans. Soviet agent Ilya Ehrenburg visited Gide in October 1936 to argue against publication of the *Retour de l'U.R.S.S.* on the grounds that the timing would be detrimental to the Spanish Republican cause. Since September, Gide had been receiving enthusiastically pro-Republican letters from Dutch communist Jef Last, who was in Spain fighting for the Republican cause. Last encouraged Gide to travel to Spain as an intellectual figurehead opposed to fascism, and his urging was seconded by an invitation from the Spanish Ambassador (CAG 5: 558, 566, 563). Over the course of the following weeks, Gide and Pierre Herbart—who was eager for opportunities to show Gide in a good light and demonstrate that he remained "on the same side of the barricade"[62]—recruited members for a politically diverse delegation of French intellectuals and clergy. Herbart obtained airplanes, visas, and funds from Prime Minister Léon Blum, but the plan fell apart in late November and the funds were returned to the Ministry of Foreign Affairs (Masson 320). While the voyage was being mooted, Gide listened to the admonishments of Ehrenburg and Herbart and briefly delayed publication of his Soviet chronicle (Lottman, *Left* 114). At the last moment, he was also moved to soften the blow by adding two sentences about Soviet aid to the Spanish Republicans to the final page of his book.[63]

Despite this eleventh-hour addition, the *Retour* and subsequent *Retouches* caused irreparable damage to Gide's standing with the communist intelligentsia. A further twist of the knife, from the communists' point of view, came when Gide joined Georges Duhamel, Roger Martin du Gard, François Mauriac, and Paul Rivet in protesting the Spanish Republican government's treatment of political prisoners in Catalonia (LE 197; Rubenstein 170). Writing in the pages of *Izvestia* on 3 November 1937, Ilya Ehrenburg denounced Gide in no uncertain terms. Outraged that Gide dared to criticize the Republicans' conduct while saying nothing of Franco's abuses, Ehrenburg condemned the so-called protest by "'the new ally of the [Spanish rebel army] and the Black Shirts,' the 'wicked old man,' the 'Moscow crybaby'" (qtd. in Lottman, *Left* 118).[64] Gide later explained his conduct by stating that he expected ignominious behavior from a declared adversary, but could not accept similar actions from the antifascist side, which was resorting to the most despicable of fascist tactics (LE 198). Gide's consistent and vigorous criticism of his own side's less than admirable actions—as well as the animosity engendered among French communists by his prewar stance on Spain and the Soviet Union—would lead to vicious attacks on Gide during and after the Second World War.

GIDE'S "AFTERLIFE"

To read many biographical and critical studies, one might almost think that Gide died after his Soviet odyssey—or, to put it more accurately, that he merely slipped into silence, into his dotage, into the oft-touted "serenity" he evinced on his deathbed in 1951. The triumphant and somewhat self-satisfied *Thésée*, the luminous and typically provocative *Ainsi soit-il* are read as the sole landmarks of what might almost be dubbed Gide's afterlife—at least as far as politics are concerned. The same might be said of Gide's place in the

French "republic of letters." The dean of French letters at the outset of the war, Gide found his influence eclipsed by a new generation at the war's end. The soon-to-be superstar of this generation was Jean-Paul Sartre; the generation's political identification was largely communist. The transition was to be expected considering Gide's age and his devotion to moral and aesthetic values that went completely out of fashion in the firebrand years following France's liberation. Yet one must also ask how the choices Gide made during the war may have hastened this transition, and how the aging writer attempted to maintain favor by polishing his image to suit the times—times in which the "resistance myth" was the dominant narrative.

With an eye to both the political and the literary, then, this cultural and political study could be deemed the story of Gide's afterlife. The chapters that follow trace Gide's meandering political and literary itinerary from the eve of the Second World War through the postwar purge and Gide's deathbed revisionings of his own war story. The first chapter explores Gide's reactions to the phony war and the fall of France, considers the attacks on Gide during the "querelle des mauvais maîtres" (the debate about deleterious intellectual influences which followed the Armistice), then looks at Gide's response to those who blamed literature for France's defeat. Chapter two traces Gide's involvement with the wartime *Nouvelle Revue Française*, which was taken over by fascist writer Drieu La Rochelle in 1940. This chapter focuses particularly on Gide's efforts to tailor his diary to fit the *N.R.F.*'s collaborationist tone, then examines his abrupt withdrawal from the journal and rejection of his early accommodationist position. The book's third chapter interprets the 1941–1942 "Interviews imaginaires" as both a vehicle for coded messages encouraging resistance and an opportunity to revise and revisit opinions expressed in the 1940–1941 *N.R.F.* articles—opinions that the intervening months had led Gide to regret. A fourth chapter concentrates on Gide's experience of the 1942–1943 siege of Tunis, reading the *Journal*'s account of his domestic situation as an allegory of the war, and using François Reymond's subsequent refutation to raise questions about the link between politics and sexuality. Chapter five explores Gide's efforts to clean up his image and associate himself with the literary resistance via savvy and somewhat duplicitous editing of excerpts from the wartime *Journal* and through the 1944 fiction *Thésée*, which I interpret as a tribute to de Gaulle and an allegory of victory over Vichy. A sixth chapter examines attacks on Gide during the postwar purge, when old animosities about his rejection of communism resurfaced. After exploring the personal, political, and literary aftereffects of the war, this chapter concludes with an analysis of Gide's efforts, in the posthumous *Ainsi soit-il*, to sketch a myth of resistance by proxy. An epilogue examines Gide's wartime experience in relation to that of his peers, and hypothesizes that Gide's fall into relative obscurity after the mid-twentieth century was, in part, a consequence of the war.

ONE

From Munich to Montoire

National Crisis and the Man of Letters

A SENSE OF FINALITY pervaded André Gide's personal and professional life on the eve of the Second World War. The writer was nearing age seventy. His major literary works (with the exception of *Thésée*) were behind him, and he had sworn off political involvement following the publication of his 1936 *Retour de l'U.R.S.S.* and 1937 *Retouches à mon retour de l'U.R.S.S.* His wife Madeleine—partially estranged, but still a major interlocutor in Gide's emotional and intellectual life—died in April 1938.[1] The following year saw the publication of Gide's *Journal, 1889–1939* and of the fifteenth and final volume of his *Œuvres complètes*. Yet the book was not closed, for the approaching war forced Gide to take political positions even as it plunged him into the greatest political confusion he had ever known.

On 30 September 1938, the leaders of France, Britain, Italy, and Germany signed the Munich Agreement, thus condoning Germany's annexation of the Sudetenland. To many Europeans, the pact meant to secure "peace in our time"[2] came as a welcome relief. Roger Martin du Gard subscribed to this view, and Gide initially shared his friend's opinion, believing that reason—if not justice and right—had prevailed (G/MG 152; J II: 625). Gide soon revised his assessment, however, on receiving a letter from Jef Last, the young Dutch communist with whom he had traveled to the Soviet Union two years before. Last saw the Munich Agreement not as a victory but as the triumph of violence, injustice, and cowardice—as democracy's "suicide" (G/Las 59–60).[3] War had been averted for the moment, Last wrote on 1 October 1938, but by yielding to a dictator the signatory nations had taken a giant step toward the massive conflict that "Hitler predicted and wished for in his book *Mein Kampf*: Germany's holy war to annihilate France."[4] Gide swiftly came around to Last's position (albeit with some of his usual wavering and hesitation); Martin du Gard changed his views only after Hitler annexed the remainder of Czechoslovakia six months later (Martin, "Ce fou" 119). Though his correspondence reveals Gide's acute attention to the Munich crisis, the *Journal* is silent on this topic. Utterly preoccupied with the events of October 1938, Gide abandoned his diary for two full weeks. When he resumed writing, it was to note that his silence did not indicate lack of interest in "public affairs";[5] rather, his thoughts on political events seemed out of place in the diary. Moreover, his silence revealed the depth of his shock and bereavement (J 3: 404). This reaction set the tone for the *Journal* in the coming years. Throughout the phony war and early Occupation, Gide's literary production consisted almost entirely of this war-inflected diary with its alternating silences and outpourings, its attempts to ignore then to understand.

This chapter examines Gide's political and intellectual trajectory from Munich to Montoire—from the 1938 pact that paved the way for Hitler's expansionism to the 1940 encounter that set France on a course of collaboration with Germany. After discussing Gide's decisions about how best to give of himself as the war approached, I trace his reactions to the war, examining the bewildering shifts in his political opinions and the stylistic evidence of his internal struggle to understand and judge what was happening around him. Next, I turn to several attempts to press Gide into political service—both to support and contest the aims of Germany and Vichy. The chapter concludes with a discussion of the many vicious attacks on the author during the "querelle des mauvais maîtres" that followed the Armistice as well as Gide's robust refutation of the argument that literature had weakened the nation.

THE PHONY WAR: ENGAGEMENT BEHIND THE SCENES

Immediately after the declaration of war, newspapers and the airwaves were filled with patriotic exhortations by some of France's most prominent intellectuals. Gide's friends Jean Schlumberger and Georges Duhamel put considerable effort into patriotic writings during this period,[6] and Duhamel, André Maurois, and Paul Valéry[7] addressed the nation over the airwaves (CAG 6: 151). Like many other readers, Gide found these patriotic essays rather ineffectual (G/MG 192, 202–04); he reacted even less favorably to the self-congratulatory tone of many radio broadcasts, lamenting French reaction even more than the events themselves.[8] Gide noted, with a touch of false modesty, that "a few crackpots" (notably Duhamel) had attempted to persuade him that his eloquence would suffice to "calm the troubled waters."[9] However, close friends who were well acquainted with Gide's political malleability dissuaded him from speaking publicly and succeeded in keeping him away from Paris, where the pressures to do so would undoubtedly be too strong for Gide to resist (CAG 13: 476).[10] For the time being, at least, silence seemed to be the best policy—both because Gide wished to retain his independence[11] and because he clearly perceived the risks of taking a public stance on a rapidly evolving situation: "I do not want to have to blush tomorrow for what I should write today" (J 4: 5).[12]

Wary of appeals to serve as a cultural or political figurehead, Gide instead chose to involve himself in a more personal and humanitarian way. During the First World War, he had eschewed political debates and devoted the bulk of his time to helping refugees through the Foyer Franco-Belge in Paris (SV 1057). At the outset of the Second World War, he adopted a similar approach, sparing no effort on behalf of the numerous intellectuals who appealed directly to him for assistance. Gide's involvement began in the spring of 1939, when exiles from Franco's Spain began to fill French refugee camps. From the perspective of his friend Claude Mauriac, Gide approached these visits as something of a dilettante, taking autographed copies of his works to the Spanish Republican refugees and appearing to be drawn primarily by "those laughing dark boys who play pelota [. . .] in front of the [camp] gate" (*Conversations* [Eng.] 157).[13] Gide's efforts on behalf of communist refugees such as Raoul Laszlo and Harry Domela were more effective, and his intervention with the Ministry of the Interior helped secure Domela's release from a camp in Perpignan (G/Las 84; CAG 11: 133–34). In August 1939, Gide went to Pontigny, where intellectuals gathered each summer to debate various literary and political issues, to attend a *décade* devoted to the plight of refugees. His presence provided young Mauriac with an opportunity to praise Gide's "ardent" efforts on behalf of refugees and point out that he had already saved many political exiles from "the wretchedness of the camps."[14]

Among these detainees were numerous exiles from Austria and Germany—most of them Jewish, and all violently opposed to Hitler. In an October 1939 statement in *Le Petit Niçois*, Gide denounced France's indiscriminate incarceration of German and Austrian nationals—even those who had been deprived of their citizenship and were technically stateless—and cited England's more humane approach as a model (Fraysse). Following the article's publication, the writer was inundated with pleas for help from internees (G/P 231).[15] Working closely with André Dubois of the Ministry of the Interior and the Commission de Triage in Nice, Gide managed to secure the release of several prisoners who had given "sufficient proof of attachment to France" (G/Sch 887; SV 1058).[16] Despite his considerable efforts, however, Gide's success was extremely limited (CAG 6: 160). The failure of many of his attempted interventions led Gide to worry that he was suspect, "red-tinted,"[17] in the eyes of the military authorities. Since one of the unspoken fears motivating the internments was apprehension about possible communist propaganda by anti-Nazi Germans, Gide worried that his recommendations might actually compromise those he was trying to help (G/Sch 892, 895–96).[18]

Gide's frustration was underscored by his conviction that general measures—rather than piecemeal efforts on behalf of individual internees—were called for (G/P 232).[19] Above all, he worried that France's "monstrous" mistreatment of German refugees might provide excellent material for Germany's propaganda campaign to keep America out of the war (G/Sch 890, 1070).

Though he deplored the camps' unnecessarily harsh conditions and condemned the lack of discernment in French detention policies, Gide nonetheless agreed with the general principle of internment.[20] His diary entry of 25 May 1940 is a study in ambivalence:

> Concerning [Léon] Blum, you said: a Jew cannot be a true patriot because he has no true homeland. And now [. . .] you say: every German Jew is a German before he is a Jew, and remains German despite the persecutions and massacres. [. . .] That said, I hastily add that I wholeheartedly applaud the decision that has been made to intern all Germans indiscriminately [. . .] and even if there were among them only one traitor per hundred or per thousand, we would be right to act thus: the peril is too great.[21]

With the German army advancing toward Paris as he noted these reflections, Gide's fears outweighed his political and humanitarian convictions. Within a month, however, his nation would fall, and an attempt to rescue Gide himself would put the writer in a position to help other imperiled intellectuals flee occupied France.

In the summer of 1940, the Emergency Rescue Committee (E.R.C.) sent American journalist Varian Fry to Marseille to help orchestrate the rescue of European artists and intellectuals "whose works and words had made them enemies of the Third Reich." Gide was among those the E.R.C. most wanted to evacuate, but, like many other key intellectuals, he chose to remain in France (Fry 3, 140): "I don't want to leave," Gide told Maria Van Rysselberghe, "I want to remain with all of you, all in the same boat."[22] Though he declined help for himself,[23] Gide petitioned Fry and Thomas Mann—an active member of the E.R.C. while in self-imposed exile in America—on behalf of several friends and associates, most of them prominent intellectuals.[24] Among these were the Czech communist Raoul Laszlo, Gide's German translator Ferdinand Hardekopf, and the Jewish Yugoslavian writer Jean Malaquais (CAG 6: 202; Buenzod 246–48; CAG 11: 133–34).[25] Another beneficiary of Gide's efforts was Pléiade editor Jacques Schiffrin, a Russian Jewish immigrant. The editor and his family sailed for Martinique in June 1941, but on arrival their ship was turned back to Casablanca. Gide had the Gallimard firm send Schiffrin money from his own royalties account and helped the family avoid internment in Morocco by lending them his Casablanca apartment. The family managed to sail to America later that summer, eventually making it to New York, where Schiffrin helped carry out a project Gide had mooted in December 1940. Talking with representatives of the Emergency Rescue Committee during that first winter of the Occupation, Gide had proposed the idea of a French publishing company in America that would fulfill the urgent need of writers in occupied France (Lottman, *Left* 131; CAG 6: 254). As predicted, Schiffrin's Pantheon Books became an invaluable outlet for French authors—including Gide himself—during the Second World War.

AN INADVERTANT FIGUREHEAD

As France's senior man of letters at the outset of the war, André Gide would be recruited—with or without his knowledge and consent—by a wide range of political interests. Gide's prestige was so great that even the most unlikely parties pressed his writings into service to meet their political ends. In 1940, Berlin published *Experiences in the Congo: France's Inefficiency as a Colonial Power*, a pamphlet consisting of excerpts in English translation from Gide's *Voyage au Congo* and *Le Retour du Tchad*. While carefully disapproving of the "mystifying and disturbing effect" Gide's fictions supposedly exerted on readers, the pamphlet's introduction nevertheless touts Gide's authority and veracity: "even those who disagree with his tenets do not attempt to deny his uncompromising love of truth." There follow some thirty pages of passages foregrounding France's incompetent and inhumane management of its African colonies, and the pamphlet concludes: "The Congo horrors are merely another example of the criminal inefficiency of the French as colonizers. The methods employed by France in governing her colonies have brought disgrace upon her name" (7, 39). As Walter Putnam has argued, the German propagandists responsible for this pamphlet were presenting Gide's highly critical travelogue as "evidence that the French were unworthy allies of the British and Americans" (93).

The following year, the political-intellectual machine in occupied Paris would also seek to enlist André Gide to bolster the legitimacy of the Académie Française, whose wartime membership included many mediocre but politically "cooperative" writers (Lepape 430). In June 1941, Gide received a cryptically worded interzone card from Jean Paulhan: "P.V. ([Academician Paul] Valéry) sends word to Uncle G. (Gide) that if he wants to return to Paris the Académie would like nothing better than to elect him."[26] Gide, who had no desire to assume an official institutional role, made no reply to this indirect offer.

Even as Germany and occupied France tried to profit from Gide's writings and reputation, their opponents were attempting to recruit the nonconformist writer for the resistance cause. A cautious but highly public appeal came from writer Jules Romains, who, like Thomas Mann, had chosen self-imposed exile in America. In an August 1940 "Message aux Français"—part of a broadcast series relayed to France by the B.B.C.—Romains implored the writers of his acquaintance (including Gide, whom he addressed by name) not to let France be dishonored by her defeat or reject the qualities that had historically constituted her raison d'être in the eyes of the world (38).[27]

Other appeals, made privately, were more concrete. The first came from Max-Pol Fouchet, founder of the Algiers journal *Fontaine*, an early resistance periodical. In July 1940, Fouchet contacted writers whose prestige could help *Fontaine*'s mission of opposition. Foremost among these was André Gide, whose reply proved disappointing: unsure of the course events would take— unsure even of his own opinions—the writer preferred to wait before committing himself (Fouchet 123–24). Gide was still unready to commit in September 1941, when Jean-Paul Sartre came to visit, bearing encouraging news about "the state of mind in that other France"[28]—the occupied zone, where fledgling resistance movements were developing. Sartre, who humorously referred to himself as a "traveling salesman" peddling ideas—dangerous and subversive ones, Van Rysselberghe reported[29]—tried unsuccessfully to persuade the older writer to join the group Socialisme et Liberté. Having failed to convince Gide, Sartre next tried to enlist André Malraux, but again met with failure. As biographer Annie Cohen-Solal points out, Sartre's attempts to recruit Malraux and Gide were premature, for in 1941 most writers preferred "a passive, 'wait and see' attitude"[30] to immediate action (310, 314). Such was Gide's position: watch and wait, stay out of the public eye, and consign any political observations to the pages of his diary.

GIDE'S WARTIME *JOURNAL*

"Weathervane" and "chameleon"[31] are the tropes most commonly used to describe the confused, conflicted author of the wartime *Journal*. Political commentary in the diary runs the gamut, and opposing viewpoints follow each other in quick succession as Gide revises and retracts statements made just days—or hours—before. The disconcerting, even incoherent variety of viewpoints in the wartime *Journal* stems largely from the diarist's own character, and from the intellectual and social habits of a lifetime. First, there was Gide's profound lack of political sense. Pierre Herbart, an intimate and insightful friend, believed that Gide was "amoral" not by choice or provocation, but quite simply because he failed to understand politics. As a result, he often resorted to banal and conventional viewpoints, and was capable of making statements as reactionary as those of the right-wing Action Française group (*Recherche* 35–36). Then, too, Gide had an extraordinary capacity for being influenced—he often found himself subscribing to the opinions of the last person with whom he had spoken, or agreeing with a viewpoint simply because it was well expressed (J II: 705)—and the people who informed his thought during this period displayed a considerable diversity of opinion.[32] Finally, there was Gide's temperament—the mode of thinking of a self-described "creature of dialogue" (IID 234)[33]—and a sort of professional bias that condemned the novelist to see both sides of any argument: "It is not with impunity that, throughout a whole lifetime, my mind has made a practice of understanding the other person,"[34] Gide wrote in January 1941 (J 4: 55).[35] These characteristics made for considerable incoherence in the early wartime diary—a "lack of intellectual rigor [that] reveals the extent of his confusion," in Pierre Herbart's words.[36]

Stylistic artifacts of Gide's internal upheaval abound in the wartime diary. As Yaffa Wolfman astutely remarks, the interrogative mode dominates the pages in which Gide reflects on the coming war (141). Once the catastrophe had occurred, Gide shifted from the rhetoric of interrogation to that of persuasion—or rather, of self-persuasion. To maintain an illusion of control, Pierre Herbart contends, Gide took the initiative of accepting—even approving—France's humiliating defeat in the pages of his *Journal* (*Recherche* 22). But the effort to reach a state of acquiescence left rhetorical traces, and some of the most shocking expressions of "acceptance" in the wartime *Journal*—the passages most often quoted and denounced by Gide's critics—are hedged round by qualifying terms like "I am almost inclined to say" and "I try to persuade myself."[37] These repeated expressions of restriction are the rhetorical remnants of Gide's intellectual and moral struggle.

Gide often referred to his *Journal* as his most important work, and the outbreak of war prompted him to open his notebooks after a six-month silence. His chief source of anxiety at that point was the war's threat to European culture: "Yes, all that might well disappear," he wrote on 10 September 1939, "that cultural effort which seemed to us wonderful (and I am not speaking merely of the French effort)" (J 4: 3).[38] He doubted that even the sacrifice of those he loved most dearly could save the values he cherished (J II: 678). Despite his fears and pessimism, however, Gide did not oppose the war on principle, and he refused to sign pacifist Félicien Challaye's September 1939 petition calling for an immediate and unilateral end to hostilities (Hebey 158).

The declaration of war found Gide in the village of Cabris on the Côte d'Azur, surrounded by the Van Rysselberghe-Herbart family[39] and numerous friends. Despite the "monstrous events," the phony war was, for Gide, a period of "calm felicity among perfect friends [. . .] sheltered from the torment" (J 4: 14–15).[40] Nevertheless, the writer was deeply, anxiously interested in the mounting European conflict. During the summer of 1939, he spoke of living in an "era both exciting and loathsome,"[41] and Maria Van Rysselberghe described him as torn between horror and curiosity. Gide fed his craving for information by listening to whatever radio broadcasts he could receive, in whatever language available; as the clandestine press developed, he avidly read any available news from the occupied zone (CAG 6: 154, 281). Yet Gide's keen curiosity was accompanied by an equally strong capacity for detachment: "the 'events' interest me powerfully, I admit, but as a play [*un spectacle*] would," he told Paul Valéry.[42] Gide found it easy to disengage his mind from events which, he claimed, "in no way affect my thinking."[43]

Those thoughts that were unaffected by and unrelated to the war were the only ones Gide deemed worthy of recording in his *Journal* during the early months of the war. With a nod to Nietzsche's *Untimely Meditations*, he declared: "My unseasonable thoughts, until better times, I will store up in this notebook" (J 4: 5).[44] Gide attributed his own propensity for happiness to the "antihistoricity" of his mind (J 4: 50).[45] In portions of the diary from this period, he seems to be blithely ignoring the ongoing tragedy, making full use of that propensity for happiness. More often, however, this impression proves to be an illusion. It was because current events left him bereft and nearly mute that Gide resolved to focus on the intimate and the abstract: "Through a sense of decency I am concerned in this notebook only with what has nothing to do with the war; and this is why I go for so many days without writing anything in it. Those are the days on which I have not been able to rid myself of the anguish, not been able to think of anything but *that*" (J 4: 18).[46]

Gide's determination to "continue to cover the pages of this notebook *as if nothing were happening*"[47] colors the early wartime *Journal* (J 4: 42). Even when references to events and political opinions creep into the diary, they alternate with abstract intellectual reflections and "untimely" anecdotes that are truly vintage Gide. Given the historical context, such remarks easily give an impression of shocking insouciance. Thus, just two days after Gide mentions the "dismaying news"[48] of Germany's invasion of the Low Countries, we find an entry describing familiar Gidian pleasures: having hoisted a group of children into a cherry tree so they could rob it of its fruit, Gide watched them play for more than an hour, and reflected that his greatest pleasure always came in the company of young children. Then, with a tinge of irony, Gide comments that France is experiencing the same glorious weather it had enjoyed during the summer of 1914: "How, despite the hideous horror of the war, can one help feeling joyful this morning?," he asks.[49] If this passage—suppressed until 1997, undoubtedly because of its "unseemliness"—evokes the sensual pleasures of the *Nourritures terrestres*, there is a reason: recently recovered from the long and debilitating bout of nephritis that had kept him in bed throughout most of April 1940, Gide was again experiencing that fragile exuberance of convalescence he had described in the lyrical 1897 work.

That bout of nephritis—and plans to treat it with a mineral water "cure"—made for one of the oddest and most darkly comical episodes of Gide's war. During his illness in April, Gide wrote to his friend Roger Martin du Gard that he would have to go to Vittel or Contrexéville to take the waters. Ironically, his quest for health and safety led him to that most infamous of French spa towns—Vichy. With the German army advancing, Marc Allégret cabled Gide on 25 May, urging him, in the name of an imaginary Dr.

Dubois, to begin his treatment at Capvern in the Pyrénées immediately. It was obvious that Allégret thought Gide was in danger; it was even possible that he was communicating an unofficial warning from the Ministry of the Interior (J II: 697). Rather than head toward the Spanish border as "Dr. Dubois" had suggested, Gide set off in the opposite direction, accepting a ride from a young Belgian refugee named Vezal who was driving Gide's doctor, Roland Cailleux, to Vichy. On 4 June the party left for Vichy, where Gide planned to see his old friend Arnold Naville, then proceed to the spa in the Pyrénées (J II: 698; Sheridan 541; CAG 6: 177). The twenty-two-hour drive to Saint-Genès-la-Tourette was interrupted some twenty times for verification of identity papers; on arriving in La Tourette, the voyagers learned of the German bombing raid on Paris during the night of 3 June (J II: 699; Sagaert, Notes [J II] 1394). Proceeding to Vichy, the three men were traveling against the tide of the *exode* (Hebey 161)—the mass southward "exodus" of some six to ten million refugees who had been flooding the roads of France since the invasion of Belgium on 10 May (Jackson 119–20).[50]

Gide's *Journal* tells of fleeing families clogging the roads, wandering without a clear destination, of children separated from their families, and of parents desperately searching for those children. During his first night in Vichy, Gide was moved by the distressed cry "Pierre! Pierre!," which he heard three times through his open window. The next morning, Arnold Naville explained that it was not a bereft man seeking a lost loved one, but the night watchman crying "Lumière! Lumière!" ["Lights! Lights!"] each time he saw a lighted window—in this case, Gide's own (J II: 699; J 4: 21). Sensitive to the caller's distress, Gide was nevertheless oblivious to the ways he might be endangering others with his open, lighted window. The window incident, like the entire trip northward to Vichy, is emblematic of the extent to which Gide was out of sync with the rest of the French population during this time of crisis—suffering deeply, but moving, behaving, and often thinking against the grain.

Giving up on the idea of a spa cure, Gide remained in Vichy until 16 June, departing days before the arrival of the German army and not long before the collaborationist government set up shop in the resort town (Sheridan 541; CAG 6: 178). Gide would spend the first two years of the Occupation on the Côte d'Azur, which fell under the jurisdiction of Pétain's Vichy government.[51]

Marshal Pétain's politics—and Gide's reaction to them—form a short but crucial chapter of Gide's wartime *Journal*. "[S]imply admirable"[52] was Gide's assessment of the 20 June 1940 broadcast in which Pétain justified his request for an armistice on the basis of Germany's overwhelming military superiority (J 4: 23). In approving of the Armistice, Gide was in the majority: most Frenchmen—even many who would later resist through their writings or actions—knew that a French victory was impossible and wanted

French soldiers' lives spared. Pétain's speech, which consisted chiefly of military facts and figures, was essentially unobjectionable (Pétain, *Actes* 449–50). There was little of an ideological nature, save the criticisms of interwar France: "Since our victory [in 1918], the pleasure principle has won out over the spirit of sacrifice. We have demanded more than we have served. We wanted to stint on effort; today we are encountering adversity."[53] These comments in fact coincided with Gide's own views on the Third Republic's interwar decadence: "It cannot be better expressed," Gide opined, "and these words console us for all the *flatus vocis* of the radio" (J 4: 23).[54]

As this statement suggests, Gide's assessment of wartime speeches had as much to do with rhetoric as with political positions. Indeed, it was the spin Pétain put on the Armistice that led Gide to withdraw his approval of the marshal a few days later. On 22 June, the day the Armistice was signed, British Prime Minister Winston Churchill addressed the French nation, asking all Frenchmen not under pressure from the enemy to assist with France's liberation. Churchill promised that England would take up the cause of the French people, despite the Bordeaux government's acceptance of the German conditions of armistice (qtd. in Pétain, *Discours* 346–47). Pétain responded the following day: dismissing Churchill as no judge of French interests and honor, he averred that France had chosen to cease fighting "independently and with dignity." With rousing but fallacious patriotic rhetoric, Pétain concluded: "We know that our nation remains intact as long as her children's love for her subsists."[55] This was too much for Gide to stomach:

> Yesterday evening we heard with amazement Pétain's new speech on the radio. Can it be? Did Pétain himself deliver it? Freely? One suspects some infamous deceit. How can one speak of France as "intact" after handing over to the enemy more than half of the country? How to make these words fit those noble words he pronounced three days ago? How can one fail to approve Churchill? Not subscribe most heartily to General de Gaulle's declaration?[56] Is it not enough for France to be conquered? Must she also be dishonored? (J 4: 24)[57]

In later years, Gide would point to this early expression of support for de Gaulle as proof of his long-standing resistance allegiances. What he concealed throughout his lifetime was the retraction, two days later, of the *Journal*'s denunciation of Pétain.

In a speech delivered on 25 June, the head of the État Français implicitly criticized both de Gaulle's decision to leave French soil and his call to rally in England and fight from the empire. Summarizing the battles of the past weeks, Pétain explained that he had sought the double armistice with Germany and Italy to avoid prolonging futile combat (Pétain, *Actes* 452–53). Again returning to the theme of France's interwar weaknesses, Pétain admonished: "Our defeat came of our slackness. The pleasure principle destroys what the spirit of sacrifice has built up. I urge you, first of all, to undertake an intellectual and moral reform [*redressement*]."[58] Here again, the marshal was speaking Gide's language. "Pétain's explanations are clear, reasonable, and are the only ones we had any right to expect," Gide wrote on 26 June: "I yield to his reasons, and cannot keep my mind in the state of protest I felt the day before yesterday. There is nothing to do but submit and accept, alas! what is inevitable, and against which all revolt can succeed only in dividing the French people."[59]

Gide later chose to suppress this diary entry that invalidates the picture of surefooted progress toward resistance sentiments that he sought to present to the world. At the time, however, his approval of Pétain put him squarely in the mainstream of French opinion. In the summer of 1940, the Vichy policies he would come to disapprove had yet to be put in place. Even with the passage of time, however, Gide clung to the hypothesis of the *double jeu* (double game)—the idea that Pétain might be duping the Germans. In October 1942, he worried that he might die without ever finding out "[w]hether Pétain was not, at heart, the most 'Gaullist' of us all" (J 4: 126).[60] This fairly commonplace suggestion is followed by a somewhat more disturbing comment omitted from published versions of the *Journal* until 1997. Like many Frenchmen, suggests Jeannine Verdès-Leroux, Gide disassociated the "good" World War I hero Pétain from the "bad" Pierre Laval, who actively sought to promote the German agenda (272). Yet the October 1942 *Journal* entry reveals Gide's willingness to believe that even Laval was playing a game to France's advantage: "I go so far as to wonder whether Laval himself is not much more clever than he seems [. . .], whether his role, the most thankless of all, is not indispensable, and whether he isn't playing it exactly as he should."[61] Such doubts persisted, and Gide's views on both Vichy and the Free French would waver dramatically throughout the war.

Equally changeable but more compelling to the author were his views on the German leader. Oddly enough, it was Hitler—not Pétain or de Gaulle—who truly captured Gide's imagination. He could not help feeling "an admiration full of anguish, fear, and stupor" for the führer.[62] In the *Journal*, Gide repeatedly laments Hitler's skillful manipulations and his exploitation of France's weaknesses. Gide's rueful admiration reaches its fullest expression in the passages concerning the French fleet. Gide saw plainly that the terms of the Armistice, which did not call for France to turn its naval fleet over to Germany, constituted an invitation to England to destroy France's ships—which it did in the 3 July 1940 attack at Mers el-Kébir. While rejecting Vichy's attempts to define England as the common enemy of France and Germany, Gide grudgingly admired Hitler's "genius" in setting France and England against each other (J II: 708–09, 717).[63] Bitterness colors Gide's admiration here, but elsewhere it is hope—even against reason—that characterizes his assessments. As Maria Van Rysselberghe reported, it was not defeat but the rot it revealed that distressed Gide so greatly. Despite knowing that Hitler opposed everything he valued, Gide believed that the only hope was to rebuild the world. "Perhaps Hitler is the one who is destined to reestablish this new world," he wondered. Speculating that the use of force was perhaps a necessary first step, Gide mused: "Who knows, perhaps we are doing Hitler an injustice by assuming that his ultimate dream is not one of worldwide harmony?"[64]

Many Europeans entertained such thoughts, but Gide's particularly strong sense of *sympathie*, of attempting to understand others' viewpoints, sometimes led him into fantasy and paradoxical thinking. In January 1941, he penned an imaginary dialogue with Hitler—a dramatization of his mental struggle between condemnation and admiration that is characterized by a mix of detachment and sick fascination. In this dialogue, the "voice of hell"[65] points out similarities between Hitler's ideas and Gide's own, even quoting from Gide's writings (J 4: 57). Apostrophizing the führer, Gide writes: "Do not say, Hitler, that I am unable to understand you. I understand you only too well; but in order to approve of you it would be necessary for me to understand only you."[66] In a more rational mode, Gide describes Hitler as the would-be "great gardener of Europe,"[67] calling his program of "pruning" inhuman and predicting that only mourning and devastation would remain on earth if his plan were to succeed (J 4: 57).

To Van Rysselberghe's mind, the "Hitler" in this dialogue could only be a fiction: for Gide, she believed, "Hitler, in short, is a sort of symbol for all the reforms which would make possible a new life, on other bases."[68] Yet the botanical metaphor of Hitler wielding pruning shears has significant resonances with Gide's earliest political writings, revealing a continuity of antifascist opinion in the midst of Gide's wartime confusion. In the January 1941 dialogue, Gide develops his horticultural metaphor to conclude that Hitler's policies may end up strengthening those very values he wanted to suppress: "Indeed, persecutions act like plant-pruning, which precipitates into the remaining buds all the sap that was previously insufficient to nourish the whole shrub" (J 4: 59).[69] The implicit comparison here is with right-wing ideologue Maurice Barrès, whose novel *Les Déracinés*—published at the height of the Dreyfus Affair in 1897—illustrated the deleterious consequences of "uprooting" and "questioned, by implication, the 'health' of uprooted people such as Jews" (Sheridan 3). Invoking his own dual heritage in his riposte—his mother was from Normandy and his father from the Languedoc—Gide called uprooting "a school of virtue"[70] that brings out latent qualities and fosters originality. In the 1903 essay "La Querelle du peuplier," Gide took issue with Barrès for quoting Charles Maurras, the future founder of the Action Française group and "eventual ideologist of the Vichy government" (O'Brien, *Portrait* 130). To Maurras's assertion that a poplar tree cannot stand uprooting, Gide replied with extensive botanical information, challenging Barrès's denunciation of "uprooting" with a positive ethic of "transplantation" (Gide, *Prétextes* 57). Decades later, Gide pointed out the similarities between Hitler's values and those of Barrès and Maurras: shortly after Hitler came to power in 1933, Gide remarked that Barrès would probably approve "Hitlerism"; a year later, he observed that the doctrines Germany was currently espousing were those of Barrès, and that Hitler had made the French ideologue's principle of "opportune justice"[71] his own. Reiterating his long-standing rejection of such doctrines, Gide claimed that it was simple to predict that Barrès's nationalistic theories could easily be turned against France (J II: 404, 465). The portrayal of Hitler as gardener in the 1941 fantasy dialogue was a way for Gide to reassert his earlier arguments against extreme nationalism, though the alternating condemnation and identification tend to obscure the continuity of Gide's political values.

While he held fast to certain core beliefs, Gide was profoundly shaken when France fell, and he remained confused as to his own political viewpoints for quite some time. Given the instability of his political opinions, Gide wisely decided to remain silent during the initial months of the Occupation. It was not yet time to take a public stand, Gide wrote in the June 1940 diary entry reaffirming his approval of Pétain: "For the moment I feel nothing in me but expectation [*de l'attente*]; and hope . . . but I do not yet know of what" (J 4: 26).[72] This familiar Gidian state of expectancy or *attente* effortlessly transformed itself into the political position shared by the majority of Frenchmen: *attentisme*. "Wait and see" was the predominant attitude at the outset of the Occupation. Who knew how the German and Vichy regimes would develop? Despite the anguish and humiliation of the invasion and Armistice, it was just possible, many believed, that the new order would bring about positive changes. Like most of his compatriots during that first summer and fall of the Occupation, Gide reasoned that there was nothing to be done but make the best of the situation: "To come to terms with one's enemy of yesterday is not cowardice; it is wisdom, and accepting the inevitable," he wrote on 5 September 1940: "What is the use of bruising oneself against the bars of one's cage? In order to suffer less from the narrowness of the jail, there is nothing like remaining squarely in the middle" (J 4: 45).[73] Gide's resignation and apparent willingness to cooperate with the former enemy would earn him bitter criticism at the end of the war. In point of fact, though, his views were unremarkable, and the much-maligned diary entry of 5 September should not be construed as a call to collaboration. Rather, as Pierre Assouline has aptly observed, the "center of the cage" represents the position of the silent majority, the *attentistes* (*L'Épuration* 38).

This is not to say that acceptance sat easily with Gide. On the contrary, though Gide described himself as "in no wise inclined toward revolt," the *Journal* at times reflects his palpable effort to coax himself into an attitude of acceptance: "Doubtless it is good, it is wise to be resigned when one cannot do otherwise," he wrote in an entry lamenting Vichy's call for a "return to the soil." Resignation should not come with blinkers, however: "it is bad not to see clearly"[74]—to fail to recognize that the policy conferred a tremendous advantage upon Germany at France's expense (J 4: 47).

Gide also believed it was imperative to see France clearly, without ignoring her less admirable characteristics. Despite his love for his country, Gide could not deny the decrepitude of Third Republic France,[75] and he attributed the defeat both to German "faults" and to French "qualities" (J II: 694, 702, 733). The full force of Gide's sorrow and censure are apparent throughout the month of July 1940. Indeed, entries from this month are among those most often cited by Gide's detractors. In the somber days leading up to the first Fête Nationale of the Occupation—by Vichy decree, a national day of mourning with church services for the dead rather than affirmations of France's republican values—Gide made three diary entries that would later be denounced as attacks on French patriotism. Gide believed that nine out of ten Frenchmen would accept German domination if it guaranteed abundance, and lamented that French peasants cared more about the price of grain than about cultural luminaries like Descartes or Watteau. After all, he concluded on 14 July, patriotic feeling is no more constant than our other loves—which, if we are perfectly honest, do not always amount to much (J II: 711–13).

This last entry in particular would provide fuel for Gide's detractors, not only because it maligned French peasants but also because it implicitly compared their patriotic feelings to Gide's own highly suspect amorous behavior. Gide foresaw the reaction to such comments and observed that zealots reserved special scorn for those who cared less about the political regime than about the right to "think and [. . .] love freely."[76] Provided he retained those rights, Gide himself would willingly adapt to the constraints of dictatorship— a *French* dictatorship, he hastens to add—the only regime that could save the nation from "decomposition" (J II: 712). Two important issues are at stake here, the first of which is Gide's paradoxical leaning toward dictatorship at the outset of the Second World War. Pre-invasion predictions that only a dictatorship could save France[77]—a nation Gide diagnosed as suffering from excessive freedom—would resurface in the diary throughout the war. Yet Gide had long been an ardent antifascist, a believer in France's republican ideals, and a champion of individualism. The second significant issue, Gide's sexuality, was inextricably enmeshed with his deep attachment to individual freedoms, both in his own mind and in the eyes of the reading public. Long an outspoken defender of homosexuality, Gide had good reason to fear that the new regime might prevent him from loving as he chose. Indeed, Vichy legislation would criminalize pederasty in August 1942, some months after Gide had left France for North Africa (Copley 178, 203). Although the 10 July 1940 diary entry juxtaposes Gide's sexual agenda and his pro-dictatorial proclivities in a troublesome way, it would be a mistake to interpret this passage as evidence of homofascist views. While much fine scholarship has been done on the link between fascism and homosexuality, it has little relevance for Gide, an avowed antifascist who, in any case, was drawn to young pubescent or prepubescent boys rather than to macho soldiers or the "beefcake" displays of some fascist iconography.[78] While certain post-Liberation detractors did not hesitate to make this connection, most of Gide's wartime attackers interpreted his sexual orientation as an effeminizing, weakening influence, going so far as to blame this influence for the fall of France.

PERNICIOUS INFLUENCE:
THE "QUERELLE DES MAUVAIS MAÎTRES"

When France fell to the Germans, many Frenchmen urgently sought a scapegoat to blame for the nation's defeat. The culprit many influential politicians and writers lit upon was literature. "Pessimists, defeatists, immoralists and Corydons" filled the bookshelves, André Billy wrote in *Le Figaro*, and these *mauvais maîtres* (negative role models) had "exerted a terrible influence."[79] In the national debate about deleterious intellectual influences—the "querelle des mauvais maîtres"—that followed the fall of France, writers like Gide, Proust, Valéry, and the surrealists were blamed for the nation's "decadence" and defeat.[80] Many articles in the post-Armistice press took up Marshal Pétain's call for intellectual and moral *redressement*, suggesting that literature must be set right in order to promote the nation's recovery. Predictably, the influences these writers condemned stood in direct opposition to the "virile" values Vichy professed.

At a time when Vichy's Minister of Education was announcing a strict program of physical and moral education designed to inculcate the discipline, work ethic, and sense of duty characteristic of "robust" nations, André Gide's influence was perceived as highly undesirable ("La Jeunesse" 1). Gide had used his influence and considerable talents to demolish the values of religion and the family, claimed Camille Mauclair, who lamented the younger generation's idolization of the author (7). It was Gide's influence on French youth that became the focal point for most attacks. "La Jeunesse de France," an anonymous article published in *Le Temps* in July 1940, was among the first to accuse Gide of corrupting France's young people both morally and intellectually:

> One cannot deny the influence of André Gide's works on contemporary literature and on the minds of our youth. It is against this considerable but disastrous influence that we must react today. The seductive author of *L'Immoraliste* and *Le Traité de Narcisse* (sic) has led a troublesome school. He has molded a proud and decadent generation; under the pretext of sincerity, he has brought them up with a perverted moral sense.[81]

Pointing out that his anonymous attacker had apparently denounced him on the strength of his books' titles alone, Gide declined to defend himself publicly against such accusations (J II: 715).[82] In his diary, however, Gide energetically opposed the spirit of attackers like Mauclair, who accused him of "poisoning youth with doubt,"[83] by endorsing the salutary effects of doubt and questioning. Calling the education of youth the most crucial of tasks, Gide stressed the need to develop children's critical faculties: "There is nothing better against 'nazism,'" he wrote on 16 July 1940 (J 4: 34).[84]

To many people in the defeated nation, however, Gide—a self-avowed *inquiéteur* (disturber)—looked like a dangerous mentor. He was singled out for his defense of homosexuality and for his flirtation with communism during the 1930s (Mauclair 7). While many critics denounced Gide by name, others condemned him implicitly with references to "immoralism" or through more or less accurate quotations and paraphrases of his work. Marshal Pétain's personal secretary René Gillouin (Winock, *Histoire* 212) made Gide the chief target of his February 1942 article "Responsabilité des écrivains et des artistes." The centerpiece of Gillouin's condemnation comes from *Un Malfaiteur: André Gide*, a 1931 pamphlet in which Étienne Privaz excoriates Gide, labeling him the most obscene, noxious, and subversive writer of his time (10). The pamphlet features a bereaved father's account of his son, "a young man of great promise, [who] had been perverted, degraded, and finally led to suicide by the influence of André Gide."[85] Like Privaz, Gillouin wonders how many other suicides Gide may have caused (Privaz 26; Gillouin 3).[86] The story trotted out by Privaz and Gillouin was an old one that Gide rejected outright: "From beginning to end that story is a pure (or impure) invention, what the English call 'a forgery'" (J 4: 102).[87]

Whereas Gillouin suggests that Gide's personal influence was to blame for the anonymous young man's death, Privaz quotes the grieving father's assertion that the "pestilential influence of his obscene books"[88] obsessed his son and pushed him to suicide. For many contributors to the debate, it was the literary works themselves—or at least the intellectual atmosphere to which they contributed—that had weakened the French nation. Some rejoiced when book-banning began;[89] others hoped, in somewhat more moderate terms, that readers would abandon the writers who had led to the nation's downfall: "a novelist of immorality who, we hope, will no longer have any readers, set them [his readers] on the road to defeat by teaching them that 'every pleasure is worth snatching up,'" wrote J. Peyrade in 1941.[90] Even discerning critics like Emmanuel Mounier voiced some blame for the "mauvais maîtres." Refusing to detract from the literary value of works like *Les Faux-Monnayeurs* and *À la recherche du temps perdu*, Mounier nevertheless decried the mentality of the interwar period's "frolicsome and decadent intelligentsia":[91] "a certain Gidian climate, a certain Valéryan detachment, a certain Bergsonian pathos, a certain political conformity with opposing polarities, a certain literature of excess contributed to the decomposition of the French soul."[92] Camille Mauclair made a similar argument in more explicitly political terms, declaring:

> Byzantine, evading belief and virtue, at least a part of our literature since 1918 has not been worthy of our ephemeral victory. [. . . It has] contributed to a disaster which was not an unforeseen blow of fate but the inevitable consequence of generalized lack of restraint. Whereas in Germany fanaticized youth renounced the seductions and dissolutions of individualism, and sacrificed them to a collective ideal, our literary stars were wantonly destroying national cohesion.[93]

Again laying the blame at Gide's doorstep, Mauclair blamed the *Nouvelle Revue Française*—so closely associated with Gide as to be considered *his* magazine—for presenting its "more or less clever and putrefying literary production" to the world as the "supreme expression of the taste and aspirations of postwar Frenchmen."[94]

Gide, of course, rejected the notion that literature was to blame for France's defeat (J II: 700, 728). In October 1940—coincidentally, the month Marshal Pétain met with Hitler at Montoire to agree on a program of collaboration—Gide broke his self-imposed vow of silence. He did so with a contribution to *Le Figaro Littéraire*'s series "Que sera demain la littérature?," which featured thirty well-known writers' responses to a survey on the future of literature.[95] In his brief "Réponse à une enquête," Gide responds mainly to the survey's second question: "Was our literature on the wrong track before the turmoil?"[96] Gide, who was blamed more than any other writer for France's prewar "decadence," replies laconically: "It seems to me just as absurd to blame our literature for our defeat as it would have been to congratulate it in 1918, when we were victorious."[97] The essay's final section addresses the survey's request to rank a number of literary genres—the novel, the essay, criticism, and poetry—in terms of their current importance (AQ 25). Gide ranks poetry first, using a biblical simile that he turns into a dig at Vichy rhetoric: France does not need a "return to the soil," says Gide; instead, French culture needs, "like the Gospel seed, to die and renounce itself first. Beyond the grave, 'on the third day,' it will rise again, rejuvenated."[98] Poetry will be the most natural expression of France's rebirth, Gide asserts.[99] Even more daring than the reference to Vichy's policy of "return to the soil" are the essay's remarks on criticism, a mode of thought Gide defines in terms that go beyond the literary. Although poetry may be the genre that will express France's rebirth, says the author, France must never let go of "its principal quality: criticism. I am speaking of criticism not as a 'genre' but as a very rare quality, that quality most indispensable to all real culture, a domain in which France has no equal [. . . .] Criticism, in our time, is the most endangered faculty; consequently, we must cherish our critical qualities and virtues."[100]

As early as autumn 1940, therefore, Gide was taking advantage of a question on literary criticism to encourage a spirit of ideological critique. Within a year, his "Interviews imaginaires" would begin to exploit the possibilities of literary criticism *as* political critique. In the meantime, however, came a period of involvement with the wartime *Nouvelle Revue Française* under the leadership of the Germans' handpicked editor, fascist writer Pierre Drieu La Rochelle.

TWO

Accommodation and Reaction

The Wartime N.R.F.

"THERE ARE THREE great powers in France: the bank, the Communist Party, and the *Nouvelle Revue Française*," German Ambassador Otto Abetz is said to have declared upon arriving in Paris in 1940: "Let's begin with the *N.R.F.*"[1] The *Nouvelle Revue Française*, cofounded by André Gide in 1908, was extraordinarily influential: though primarily literary in nature, the internationally read monthly was also a forum for a diverse range of political opinion. In the years following the First World War, the *N.R.F.* urged rapprochement with Germany, but a deepening schism developed among its contributors after the Nazi Party took power in 1933 (Cornick 98). Some, like Jean Schlumberger, maintained steadfastly pacifist positions, while others, like Gide, considered "*rapprochement* with Hitler [. . .] untenable." The *N.R.F.* decried book-burnings in Nazi Germany and solicited a prescient 1934 essay in which Leon Trotsky warned that "a new European catastrophe"[2] would occur as soon as Germany's rearmament was complete (Cornick 118–20). Yet it also published the pro-fascist writings of Pierre Drieu La Rochelle, a young Frenchman impressed by his contacts with Nazi youth in Berlin and Nuremburg. Despite the inclusion of writers like Drieu, France's extreme right wing considered the *N.R.F.* a bastion of leftist politics and dangerous literary experimentation. At the height of the "querelle des mauvais maîtres" in October 1940, Paul Riche excoriated the journal's leadership as a "team of evildoers," accusing the revolutionaries, surrealists, homosexuals, Jews, and Trotskyites at the *N.R.F.* of contaminating and destroying France's "intellectual inheritance."[3] Although the German occupying authorities also considered the *N.R.F.* to be under the influence of Jews, Freemasons, and communists (Heller 42), they believed that the review could become a valuable tool for Franco-German collaboration under the leadership of their chosen editor, Drieu La Rochelle.

This chapter examines the takeover of the *N.R.F.*, focusing on the difficult choices made by Gaston Gallimard, Jean Paulhan, and André Gide as typical of those facing other publishers, editors, and writers in wartime France. After reviewing the *N.R.F.* leadership's protracted courtship of André Gide and the writer's tortured decision to contribute to the journal, discussion turns to an analysis of the "Feuillets"—the two installments of diary excerpts Gide published in Drieu's *N.R.F.* Next, I examine Gide's showy break with the wartime *N.R.F.* and the writings by Jacques Chardonne that led to the rupture. A look at the fate of the wartime *N.R.F.* and Gide's first, tentative opposition to Vichy concludes the chapter.

THE TAKEOVER

Immediately after France declared war on Germany, Gaston Gallimard moved the operations and personnel of both the *N.R.F.* and the Gallimard publishing house to the Manche department as a safety precaution (G/P 221). The *N.R.F.* appeared as usual through June 1940, but when German bombardments destroyed proofs and other materials for the July issue, the journal temporarily ceased to appear (Cornick 201). Editor Jean Paulhan thought it best not to resume publication immediately after the Armistice, and Gide agreed that waiting would be wisest (G/P 245). As events would have it, the *N.R.F.* would not appear for another six months, and then only under new management.

The journal's new director was to be fascist writer Pierre Drieu La Rochelle. Otto Abetz, the Reich's Ambassador in Paris, first met Drieu La Rochelle during the Frenchman's 1934 trip to Berlin. Drieu spent a week with a group of young Nazis during this journey, returning the following year to attend a Nazi Party rally in Nuremburg. Drieu became increasingly anti-Semitic during this period, although he stayed in touch with Jewish acquaintances, including his ex-wife. This period also marked the beginning of Drieu's commitment to fascism: from 1936 until January 1939, he was a member of Jacques Doriot's Parti Populaire Français. Drieu's relations with the *Nouvelle Revue Française*, to which he was a contributor, deteriorated as the war approached. Although *N.R.F.* writers expressed a variety of opinions on the 1938 Munich Accords, the staunchly pro-Munich Drieu attacked the *N.R.F.* as a "warmongering, Jewish-influenced" journal.[4] Drieu's final break with the prewar *N.R.F.* came in the spring of 1940, when editor Jean Paulhan turned down the second part of his novel *Gilles*—the semiautobiographical tale of a young man's evolution toward fascism—in favor of works by communist poet Louis Aragon and his Russian-born wife Elsa Triolet, whom Drieu suspected of having foreign allegiances (Drieu, *Journal* 176). In his 21 June 1940 diary entry, Drieu swore to have his revenge: "The *N.R.F.* [. . .] is going to grovel at my feet. That heap of Jews, pederasts, timid surrealists, and

Masonic pawns is going to writhe miserably."[5] Less than two months later, on 10 August 1940, Drieu met with Abetz, now the German Ambassador to France, to discuss the possibility of founding a new journal. Abetz soon proposed—indeed demanded—that Drieu instead take over the *Nouvelle Revue Française* (Heller 41; G/P 245).

Once Drieu's directorship was mooted, months of negotiations and internal debates among the journal's prewar leadership ensued. Publisher Gaston Gallimard, editor Jean Paulhan, and many of the journal's contributors had to decide whether—and on what terms—to involve themselves with the new, German-backed *N.R.F.* For Gallimard, the futures of two separate but related entities—the literary journal and the affiliated publishing house known as the Éditions de la Nouvelle Revue Française—were at stake. Gallimard, with his considerable personal fortune, was tempted to let the Germans take over his publishing company and sit out the war in America. He worried, however, about the "possible misappropriation of great works for anti-French ends"[6] and was equally concerned about the magazine's potential as a "precious propaganda tool."[7] Both Gide and Gallimard feared that, if they failed to cooperate, the Germans would take over the journal by stealth, publishing a "pseudo *N.R.F.*" that could easily exploit the title, appearance, and subscription list of the venerable review. If that were to happen, there would be no way to inform readers of the change, and the *N.R.F.*'s former leadership would be helpless to protest (G/P 246; CAG 6: 199).

Gallimard's stable of writers, whatever their political leanings, overwhelmingly urged the publisher to return to Paris, accept the Germans' conditions, and resume operations. Financial concerns were central to this nearly unanimous appeal, for royalties on past publications were at stake—not to mention the possibility of publishing new manuscripts (Assouline, *L'Épuration* 100). Future publications were out of the question, however, for those *N.R.F.* authors who found themselves blacklisted by the September 1940 *Convention de censure*. The *Convention* was a voluntary agreement on self-censorship drawn up by the French Syndicat des Éditeurs a month before Hitler and Pétain's historic meeting in Montoire made Franco-German "collaboration" official. According to the *Convention* of 28 September 1940, each company was responsible for its own publications and agreed not to publish works by any author banned in Germany. The proscription applied to Freemasons, Jews, and any writer deemed anti-German, such as émigré novelist Thomas Mann. Communist writers were later added to the blacklist, which was known as the *Liste Otto* after German Ambassador Otto Abetz (Heller 29, 213–14; Assouline, *Gallimard* 272). The *Convention* was a notably xenophobic document, one that rejoiced that French literature would flourish after being "purified" of foreign writers who had found asylum on French soil.[8] Yet a great many French writers, including André Gide, were to see their works removed from circulation. As early as October 1940, Gaston Gallimard informed Gide that his *Journal, Retour de l'U.R.S.S.*, and *Retouches à mon retour de l'U.R.S.S.* had been banned by the Syndicat des Éditeurs (CAG 6: 198). Gallimard's information was unreliable, as it turned out: Gide's diary was not actually blacklisted, and his two works on the U.S.S.R. did not appear on the *Liste Otto* until July 1942 (Lepape 422). Nevertheless, Gide faced the post-Armistice publishing world with the understanding that his works had been proscribed—an understanding that clearly influenced his conflicting desires to remain silent and to speak at any price.

By early October, the *Convention de censure* had been signed and the initial *Liste Otto* distributed. On 9 October, Propaganda-Staffel chief Kaiser requested that the German military administration temporarily close down four publishers in order to "clarify the situation in terms of ownership [. . .] purify the management [. . . and] cleanse [the firms'] output in compliance with the interests of the German Reich."[9] The Nathan and Calmann-Lévy firms were to be shut down because of their Jewish ownership, the Éditions de la Nouvelle Revue Critique for its anti-German publications. Kaiser's order also included the Gallimard/N.R.F. enterprise: the influence of Jewish directors and editors[10] sufficed to earn the *N.R.F.* an "anti-German" designation, and the presence of 140 Éditions de la N.R.F. titles on the *Liste Otto*—the largest number from any single publisher—made the firm a prime target for "épuration" (purification or purging). Kaiser soon had second thoughts and asked that the closings be delayed, but because of an administrative mix-up his initial order was carried out.[11] On 9 November 1940, a section of the Geheime Feldpolizei arrived at Gallimard headquarters in the rue Sébastien-Bottin, ordered the publishing company to cease operations, and placed seals on the doors to forbid entry (Fouché I: 67, 62, 68–69). Once the mistake was discovered, it was immediately decided that the company should be reopened, but the German authorities imposed a delay of several weeks to avoid losing face. When the building was reopened on 2 December, Gaston Gallimard discovered that the premises had not even been searched (Heller 46).

Though the Gallimard shutdown was the result of an administrative blunder, it was presented as a warning to other French publishers. The story circulated by the Germans explained the forced closure as retribution for Gaston Gallimard's initial refusal to permit German participation in his publishing activities. Gallimard had indeed rejected proposals for commercial collaboration—refusing to merge the Librairie Gallimard with a German publishing firm and turn over fifty-one percent of the shares to the Germans—but his motivations were clearly more financial than political (Assouline, *Gallimard* 281; Fouché I: 72). The official story held, moreover, that the German authorities had consented to reopen the firm only after Gallimard agreed to surrender control of the *N.R.F.* to Drieu La Rochelle. In fact, arrangements for the *N.R.F.* to resume under Drieu's stewardship were already in place before the Gallimard premises were closed on 9 November (Fouché I: 71, 62).

Although Gallimard played up his refusal to capitulate entirely to the occupiers' demands,[12] the actual terms of his arrangement with the Germans were more pragmatic than heroic. Drieu would take charge of the *N.R.F.* for five years, Gallimard agreed, while he himself continued as head of the publishing house. Drieu, however, would have extensive powers over "the firm's 'intellectual and political output'" (Assouline, *Gallimard* 270–71; Fouché I: 73).[13] While there was no question of making the *N.R.F.* submit to German influence, Kaiser assured Drieu, the firm must avoid publishing anything hostile to Germany and should contribute substantively to "the new idea of political coordination within Europe [. . .] and to collaboration between Germany and France."[14] Drieu and Gallimard were both satisfied with the arrangement: the publisher was convinced that Drieu's presence would serve to protect the firm, and Drieu sincerely believed the arrangement to be an experiment in successful Franco-German collaboration. Former *N.R.F.* editor Jean Paulhan, however, thought both men were naïvely optimistic (G/P 245–46).

Though he refused to work officially for the wartime *N.R.F.*, Paulhan discreetly assisted the journal's new director by reading manuscripts and using his connections to solicit material (Assouline, *Gallimard* 307). In this capacity, he acquired a privileged view of planned changes to the journal's list of contributors. Under Drieu La Rochelle, the *N.R.F.* would keep its well-known mainstream writers (Gide, Valéry, Audiberti), eliminate Jewish contributors (Benda, Wahl, Suarès)[15] as well as those deemed anti-Nazi (Claudel, Bernanos, Romains), and add a few "Nazis" (Fabre-Luce, Bonnard, Chateaubriant) (Hebey 130). This approach—facilitated by Drieu's lack of compunction about using manuscripts submitted before the German invasion—made for an interesting mix of contributors, especially in the early issues (Richard 67–68). Apolitical or *attentiste* writers were published alongside those with decidedly collaborationist views, and relatively unknown authors shared the journal's pages with names like Giono, Péguy, and Valéry. The usefulness of these famous names was perfectly apparent to Paulhan: Drieu's *N.R.F.* was attempting to "pass off questionable fish (the articles expressing 'collaborationist thought') thanks to the literary sauce of the greatest French writers."[16] The most important of these writers—the most crucial for the success of the new *N.R.F.*—was unquestionably André Gide.[17]

GIDE'S *N.R.F.* "FEUILLETS"

Considering Gide's participation indispensable to the relaunching of the *N.R.F.*, Gaston Gallimard called on his friend during each of the three trips he made to the south of France in the autumn and winter of 1940–1941.[18] The publisher urged Gide to accept a position on the journal's editorial committee and return to Paris, where "true resistance"[19] would surely take place. Adrienne Monnier, a Parisian bookstore owner who was close to the *N.R.F.* circle, best summed up the hopes associated with Gide's influence: his presence in Paris would surely prevent the *N.R.F.* from drifting in a pro-German direction, she believed (Grenier 179). However, those who knew Gide better feared the opposite scenario. Sensing in Gide "a spontaneous tendency toward collaboration and non-resistance,"[20] Maria Van Rysselberghe urged her friend to stay away from the capital and off the *N.R.F.*'s editorial committee. The rest of Gide's entourage concurred with her advice. Gide saw the validity of his friends' concerns: as he grew older, he had increasing difficulty taking firm positions, especially given the overwhelming nature of the current crisis. Without his friends' counsel, he might well be tempted to "collaborate loyally with Germany," despite his conviction that German appeals for collaboration were a form of "trickery."[21] Van Rysselberghe issued a further warning: "whatever the *N.R.F.* does, if your name is associated with its return, it is you who will be held accountable."[22]

In the end, Gide decided to compromise: while declining to serve on the editorial committee,[23] he offered two installments of *Journal* excerpts as a token of his goodwill toward the magazine. As a precaution, the first installment would end with the words "to be continued"; if Gide disliked the general tone of Drieu's journal, or if the German censor "whitewashed" or "denatured" his text, he would withhold the second installment.[24] Even before the first "Feuillets" installment appeared, however, Gide began to regret this commitment. A November 1940 letter from writer Jean Wahl—excluded from the pages of the *N.R.F.* because he was Jewish, and disappointed in Gide's decision to contribute—opened Gide's eyes to the ramifications of his participation. Shocked to find that his friends Jean Schlumberger and Maria Van Rysselberghe agreed, Gide admitted that he had underestimated "the impact his action could have in the occupied zone."[25]

For a time, Gide's inner struggle focused on a question of semantics. He had agreed to "collaborate" with the new *N.R.F.* in early October, at a time when the verb *collaborer* had only intellectual (and perhaps financial) connotations (NRF xx). However, Marshal Pétain gave the term new meaning by declaring, after his 24 October meeting with Hitler at Montoire: "today I embark on a course of collaboration."[26] "Since I agreed to contribute to [*collaborer à*] the new *N.R.F.*, the word *collaboration* has taken on a general, absolute meaning which it did not have at that time,"[27] Gide lamented, as the political consequences of "collaborating" with Drieu La Rochelle's *N.R.F.* belatedly dawned on him. By late November, Gide hoped that plans to resuscitate the *N.R.F.* would fail, and that the passages "painfully excerpted"[28] from his diary would never be published. The December 1940 issue appeared on schedule, however, with the first installment of Gide's "Feuillets"—diary entries that seemed strangely detached from recent events, yet disconcertingly in step with the new *N.R.F.*'s collaborationist agenda.

Excerpted from the *Journal* of February through November 1940, Gide's *N.R.F.* "Feuillets" are intentionally untimely. Removed from their chronological context and largely purged of political content, these undated fragments read like a series of maxims or meditations. They are dominated by literary observations and personal reflections, for, as Gide determined on rereading recent diary entries in September 1940, "[i]t is only in its timeless elements that thought can remain valid" (J 4: 47).[29] The relative paucity of political commentary reflects the author's uncertainty in the face of calamity, his unwillingness to adopt a single, definable position, and, above all, his refusal to "blow in the direction of the wind" (J 4: 6).[30] Yet Gide's very refusal to be overtly political endowed his "Feuillets" with shades of political meaning: by expunging most references to current events, Gide played into the hands of the Germans, who sought to present the *N.R.F.*, French literature, and France itself as unchanged.

The "Feuillets" are not entirely devoid of political content, however. Focusing on Gide's criticisms of interwar France and his apparent resignation to the Occupation and Vichy regime, I propose to read the "Feuillets" against the *Journal* in order to elucidate the politics of editing that shaped Gide's *N.R.F.* essays.

In places, Gide's views truly mesh with the values of the État Français. Remarks on the French educational system are a case in point: deploring France's lack of unity, Gide declares that the schools could have inculcated young people with the principles of national solidarity, "but the teachers preferred a different curriculum, and were themselves more interested in 'class struggle,' whose payoff seemed more immediate and of greater benefit to them."[31] Here Gide is essentially echoing the opinions of Marshal Pétain, whose August 1940 article "La Réforme de l'Éducation Nationale" denounced the system of secondary education supported by radicals and socialists in the 1930s as "a school of division, of social strife, of national destruction."[32]

Elsewhere, unavoidable self-censorship makes Gide sound far less critical than he really was. One of the most stinging statements in the "Feuillets" is the implication that France deserved her fate. Gide, who had often criticized his nation's harsh treatment of Germany after World War I, added a new twist by declaring: "We shall have to pay for all the absurdities of the intangible Versailles Treaty, the humiliations of those who were then the defeated, the useless vexations [. . .] the shameful abuse of victory. Now it is their turn to abuse." In his diary, Gide goes on to speculate about Germany's probable reaction had France shown a more generous spirit after 1918: "Probably it would have been fantastic to count on 'gratitude,' but the best way of preventing Hitler was not to provide him a justification" (J 4: 25).[33] This implied criticism of Hitler was of course unpublishable in occupied France, so Gide omitted the sentence from his "Feuillets." He made similar cuts in a diary entry about the French State's call for a "return to the soil." Gide saw only "retreat and resignation"[34] in Vichy's shift toward an agricultural economy; those who saw the policy as a source of renewal were deceiving themselves, he believed. The *Journal* passage from which this warning is taken states Gide's lucid assessment of the policy even more explicitly: the "return to the soil" is a step backward, Gide opines, a withdrawal that plays into Hitler's hands; reserving industrial, commercial, and intellectual productivity for Germany, Hitler would reduce France to an agricultural nation, and raid France's "subjugated agricultural production" at will (J 4: 47).[35] In the one instance when Gide risks a public criticism of Vichy, the constraints of censorship obscure the extent of his opposition.[36]

Where outright omissions were unnecessary, Gide altered his wording to conform to the tone of the "occupied" *N.R.F.* At times, however, his original meaning was essentially transformed, as on the final page of the "Feuillets." The passage in question revises the cynical view of French patriotism that Gide had expressed on 14 July 1940: "The patriotic feeling is [. . .] no more constant than our other loves, which some days, if one were utterly sincere, would be limited to very little" (J 4: 32).[37] By November of that year, Gide's views had evolved, and he no longer stood by his comments on "the lapses and intermittences of the patriotic sentiment": "There is nothing like *oppression* to give that sentiment new vigor. I feel it reawakening everywhere in France, and especially in the occupied zone. It assures and affirms itself in *resistance* like any thwarted love" (J 4: 54, emphasis added). Because he thought it important to attenuate the defeatist remarks published in the first installment of "Feuillets," Gide retained the November 1940 passage in his second installment. The wording of the "Feuillets" version differs substantially from that of the diary, however: "There is nothing like *adversity* to [. . .] give [patriotic sentiment] cohesion and vigor. Like any thwarted love, love of country grows strong in times of *trouble* [*dans la gêne*], and repeated blows harden it" (emphasis added).[38] Thus, the conclusion of the "Feuillets" couches its message of hope not in terms of resistance to oppression but in terms of the salutary, hardening effects of adversity and discomfort—terms right in line with Vichy rhetoric.

Astonishingly, Gide's semantic and stylistic alterations sometimes serve to mask the most accommodationist—*not* the most rebellious—statements from his wartime diary.[39] Quoting heavily from Goethe—a practice that may have led some readers to conclude that Gide held pro-German views[40]—the writer counseled acceptance: "'*Untersuchen was ist, und nicht was behagt,*'[41] Goethe says *wisely. If* I feel limitless possibilities of acceptance in myself, it is because they in no way commit my innermost self" (adapted from J 4: 45, emphasis added).[42] Apparently bowing to a German master—albeit a literary one—Gide seems to be making a case for submission. Published just six months after France's defeat, this statement was bound to dismay many read-ers. As disturbing as it might be, however, this "Feuillets" passage is in fact much milder than the 5 September 1940 diary entry from which it is adapted. In the *Journal*, Gide prefaces the Goethe quotation with the obser-vation that: "[t]o come to terms with one's enemy of yesterday is not cow-ardice; it is wisdom, and accepting the inevitable." The quote is followed by an exhortation against resistance: "What is the use of bruising oneself against the bars of one's cage? In order to suffer less from the narrowness of the jail, there is nothing like remaining squarely in the middle" (J 4: 45).[43] Stylistic modifications further attenuate the statement: in the "Feuillets," Goethe speaks "wisely" (*sagement*), not "excellently" (*excellemment*) as in the *Journal*. Moreover, the remark about "limitless possibilities of acceptance" becomes much more tentative when inserted in a hypothetical clause.[44] In a similar vein, Gide made savvy changes to a diary entry on oppression and freedom of thought:

> If tomorrow, as is to be feared, *freedom* of thought [*la liberté de penser*], or at least of the expression of that thought, is refused us, I shall try to convince myself that art, that thought itself, will lose less thereby than in excessive freedom. [. . .] *I try to persuade myself* that it is in non-liberal epochs that the free mind achieves the highest virtue. (adapted from J 4: 38 and J 4: 49, emphasis added)[45]

By adding the phrase "I try to persuade myself," restricting the original refer-ence to "*all freedom* of thought," and eliminating the exclamation "Hurrah for thought held in check!," Gide substantially softened the more forceful word-ing of the original diary entry (J 4: 49, emphasis added).[46] Walking a fine line between German censorship and public censure, Gide eliminated the most submissive as well as the most subversive diary statements from his *N.R.F.* "Feuillets."

Perhaps as a result of Gide's careful self-editing, German censors left the "Feuillets" untouched (NRF xxvi). The first of the conditions Gide had placed on his participation was thus fulfilled. His second condition, that nothing tendentious in the journal's content indicate that the *N.R.F.* was "inspired by the occupiers,"[47] was also met to the writer's satisfaction. "One senses a muffled resistance," Gide said of the first issue;[48] his sole dissatisfac-tion was with his own contribution, which struck him as "wishy-washy"[49] in comparison to the surrounding articles. Gide's assertion that the new *N.R.F.* evinced a spirit of resistance was charitable at best: while the staunchly pro-German tone of the wartime *N.R.F.* had yet to develop, the inaugural issue revealed the lineaments of the journal's collaborationist attitude. Jacques Chardonne's sketch of peasant life in the Charente region idealized dignified submission to the occupier. For Drieu La Rochelle and Alfred Fabre-Luce, Europeanism was the theme of the moment: the European continent will be

America's equal, Fabre-Luce tells his American interlocutor, "and you will no longer feel the scorn which our Balkanized Europe used to arouse in you."[50]

Despite his initial satisfaction with the *N.R.F.*'s first wartime issue,[51] a series of disapproving letters from readers left Gide "deeply tormented"[52] about his association with the journal. Arnold Naville reacted with shame and disgust, and several Jewish readers expressed their sense of hurt, shock, and betrayal at Gide's decision to contribute to the German-backed periodical (CAG 6: 218). Their concerns seemed valid to Maria Van Rysselberghe: "You do not know what a gift you are bestowing upon enemy propaganda," she told Gide: "your collaboration will be presented by them as proof of their liberalism."[53] Though he denied any complicity with the enemy (CAG 11: 188–89), Gide began to worry about appearances: "my participation [*collaboration*] in the *N.R.F.* [. . .] appears to acquiesce to a state of things that I condemn with all my heart. [. . . T]he enemy's propaganda will be able to use this appearance as a weapon, even though it goes against reality."[54] Alarmed by these reflections, Gide resolved to withhold the second installment of "Feuillets" that he had promised to the *N.R.F.* (J II: 743).

In his attempt to woo Gide back, publisher Gaston Gallimard took a pragmatic approach: "for me, too, the easiest solution would be to live as a spectator, to revel in other people's resistance and courage [. . . but] one cannot refuse to join in and at the same time enjoy the financial benefits of an activity one condemns."[55] Since the Éditions de la N.R.F. had stopped sending monthly royalty payments in the fall of 1939, Gide found Gallimard's financial argument rather hollow. Gide also stated that he would have a guilty conscience if his collaboration with the *N.R.F.* were to guarantee favorable treatment for his books (G/MG 225).[56] By this stage, Gide had already formulated the standard of judgment he would apply henceforth to those accused of intellectual collaboration—the notion that guilt began with profit: "in my own eyes, I would suspect myself of accommodating [the enemy] only when I derived some benefit from my actions."[57]

In the end, it was his own prior commitment that caused Gide to set his scruples aside. Since the conditions he had established for his continued association with the *N.R.F.* had been met, Roger Martin du Gard argued, Gide had no valid reason to refuse Gallimard his second set of "Feuillets" (G/MG 230).[58] When Pierre Herbart concurred, Gide telephoned Gallimard to authorize the essay's publication (CAG 6: 213; NRF xxvii; G/MG 230).[59] By January 1941, Gide's compunctions had abated considerably, and he even foresaw a happy consequence of his participation in the wartime *N.R.F.*: "I really don't know any longer whether I should have such regrets about having contributed to [*collaboré à*] La *N.R.F.*; that may even give me more impetus for future resistance."[60] Within months, this prediction would come true.

GIDE'S BREAK WITH THE *N.R.F.*

On 30 March 1941, Gide received two pieces of mail that would lead him to break definitively with the *Nouvelle Revue Française* and its wartime editor, Drieu La Rochelle. The first was an adroitly worded letter in which Drieu urged Gide to return to the capital of occupied France. "Come to Paris, it is indispensable," he wrote, arguing that Gide's presence would help free many Frenchmen from their "delay" in understanding and judging the current situation. Alluding to Gide's public reversal of his position on the Soviet Union, Drieu concluded: "the man who made the journey to Russia owes it to himself to undertake this new journey"—a statement that Maria Van Rysselberghe glossed as meaning "he owes it to himself to disavow his prejudices publicly."[61] Having been led to believe that the goal of the changes at the *N.R.F.* was to preserve the review's independence, Gide was stunned by the policy of undisguised collaboration revealed in Drieu's letter.

This impression was confirmed and reinforced by the second item in Gide's mail: a copy of *Chronique privée de l'an 1940*, the latest book by *N.R.F.* contributor Jacques Chardonne. "L'Été à La Maurie," the lead article in the first issue of Drieu's *N.R.F.*, was reprinted in this volume as the chapter "Été"—arguably the book's most scandalous section (Hebey 177). Recounting his visit to a village in the Charente department during the summer of 1940, Chardonne celebrates La Maurie's peasants, who in his eyes embody the true spirit of France. Although they have no wish to be ruled by the Germans, the villagers bear France's defeat with admirable stoicism. But then, they are used to being governed by enemies, Chardonne claims—those enemies being the Third Republic politicians who sacrificed the French people and their values while waging ideological battles. "From one's own people, one will accept anything,"[62] Chardonne laments.

The story's most politically charged anecdote concerns World War I veteran Eugène Briand. The well-to-do peasant welcomes a newly arrived German colonel[63] with a glass of the precious cognac distilled by his great-grandfather, who fought in the Napoleonic wars. If Briand's ancestor participated in the crushing French victory at Jena, the German colonel points out, "We're even now." Noticing Briand's limp, the German inquires after its cause. Rheumatism? Sciatica? "Verdun," the Frenchman answers laconically. The German, it turns out, also fought in this decisive World War I battle. As the two men companionably sip cognac, Briand declares: "I would rather have invited you. But I can't change the way things are. Enjoy my cognac. I am happy to offer it to you."[64] Though Chardonne would later swear that "L'Été à La Maurie" was documentary in nature and insist that Briand was not a fictional character, the story certainly reads like collaborationist propaganda (*Voir* 11). The "peasant" values whose loss Chardonne laments—work, the home, the village—clearly echo the Vichy slogan "Travail, Famille,

Patrie" (Work, Family, Country) and the regime's call for a "return to the soil." Even the peasant's name may serve the essay's collaborationist agenda, as William Kidd has suggested, for it evokes Aristide Briand, the post-World War I Minister of Foreign Affairs who pushed for reconciliation between France and Germany and received the Nobel Peace Prize in 1926 (40).

Understandably, "L'Été à La Maurie" elicited negative reactions from *N.R.F.* readers, contributors, and the journal's prewar management. Former editor Jean Paulhan deemed the story "abject," and François Mauriac objected so strongly that he rescinded his prior commitment to contribute to Drieu's *N.R.F.* (Guitard-Auviste 210). André Gide said nothing when "L'Été à La Maurie" appeared in the *N.R.F.*,[65] but when *Chronique privée de l'an 1940* was published five months later, it became the catalyst for his definitive break with the wartime *Nouvelle Revue Française*. Chardonne's book went much further than the original essay, making it clear that "L'Été à La Maurie" was not "simply tactless" but "the expression of a clearly declared pro-German position."[66] *Chronique privée de l'an 1940* extols Pétain, praises Vichy's "Révolution Nationale" (92), and argues the merits of "certain regimes which we used to consider oppressive to humanity."[67] This fuller exposition of Chardonne's positions—arriving by the same post as the letter elucidating Drieu's editorial politics—swiftly jolted Gide out of his *attentiste* position.

Gide's surprisingly intense reaction to *Chronique privée de l'an 1940* can be attributed in part to the remarkable similarities between himself and Chardonne. For Gide, Chardonne served as the man in the mirror—a peer whose stance he evaluated objectively, then firmly rejected. Like Gide, Chardonne was an essentially literary writer who had made limited forays into the political before the war—most significantly with the anticapitalist and anti-Semitic 1939 essay "Politique" in the *N.R.F.* Gerhard Heller, head of the Propaganda-Abteilung's literary section, was among the many people surprised by the collaborationist position Chardonne adopted at the beginning of the war, since the writer hardly seemed predisposed to take such a stance (Heller 85). Indeed, in a 1939 work also titled *Chronique privée*, Chardonne declares France's "liberal spirit" to be irreconcilable with despotism. Totalitarian regimes cannot tolerate "that personal freedom we call civilization, nor anything of what constitutes human value for us," Chardonne wrote in 1939, adding: "today, more than one nation is counting on our military strength for its resurrection, or the defense of its liberty."[68] Chardonne's 1940 work differed so radically from his 1939 chronicle that one had to wonder what had happened: "Was the defeat enough to change the direction of his ideas to such an extent?,"[69] Maria Van Rysselberghe mused.

Chardonne's tone changed so markedly after the fall of France that his 1940 remarks on French liberalism were the polar opposite of those he made in the 1939 *Chronique privée*: "Now they are announcing that our society will no longer be liberal. It is better that way, since it has ceased being liberal in any case. Liberalism is not possible in all seasons. Many things must be buried in order to flower again."[70] Chardonne's image of death and rebirth is startlingly like Gide's own published assertion that French culture, like the Gospel seed, must "die and renounce itself first. Beyond the grave, 'on the third day,' it will rise again, rejuvenated."[71] As the shared reference to death and rebirth illustrates, similarities of tone and image underscore the areas in which the writers' political views overlap. Most remarkable of all are the two men's views on censorship. "Censorship will not bother me. It can only prevent me from writing trifles. Yet if I am judged subversive, I will keep silent. A writer's best work grows out of his being stifled,"[72] Chardonne writes, uncannily echoing Gide's provocative "Hurrah for thought held in check!" (J 4: 49).[73] Gide was understandably disturbed to recognize the similarities between his own early wartime statements and those of an avowedly collaborationist writer. He read *Chronique privé de l'an 1940* with "amazement and dismay" (J 4: 62),[74] but was grateful to Chardonne for making his collaborationist position explicit, thereby helping him clarify his own political stance:

> This book provokes a reaction in me, for as I read it I feel clearly that this position is at the opposite pole from the one I must and will take; and it is important for me to declare it at once. My mind is only too inclined by nature toward acceptance; but as soon as acceptance becomes advantageous or profitable, I am suspicious. An instinct warns me that I cannot accept being with them on "the right side"; I am on the other. (J 4: 63)[75]

Despite initial similarities, the two writers' paths soon diverged. Chardonne's wartime activities were consistent with the collaborationist opinions he expressed in his 1940 *Chronique*. He frequented receptions at the Institut Allemand, led the French writers' delegation to the 1941 Weimar conference organized to foster Franco-German intellectual collaboration, and participated in a second Weimar meeting the following year (Heller 88). In 1943, his publishing firm, Stock, put out an unabashedly collaborationist anthology of German poetry.[76] Gide, on the other hand, made a highly publicized break with Drieu's *N.R.F.*, and would soon begin tacitly encouraging opposition to Vichy and the occupier.

Gide's reaction to the Chardonne book was uncharacteristically swift and forceful. On 30 March 1941, the day he received the book along with Drieu's letter urging him to return to Paris, Gide drafted the text of a telegram to the *N.R.F.* editor. Initially, the telegram merely indicated Gide's intention to break with the *N.R.F.*, but Pierre Herbart pointed out that Drieu might use the telegram against Gide unless the latter cited specific reasons for his resignation (NRF xxix). Gide therefore incorporated a reference to Chardonne into the message, which he recorded in capital letters and telegraphic syntax in his *Journal*: "APPRECIATE YOUR CORDIAL LETTER AND REGRET comma AFTER READING LAST PAGES OF CHARDONNE'S BOOK

CLARIFYING YOUR POSITIONS comma HAVING TO ASK YOU REMOVE MY NAME FROM COVER AND ADVERTISEMENTS YOUR REVIEW" (adapted from J 4: 62).[77] Despite the remarkable—even reckless—decisiveness with which Gide reacted to Drieu's letter and Chardonne's book, he began to waver almost immediately. On realizing that he had no address for Drieu, who was temporarily in Lyon, he gave up on the idea of sending a telegram and made do with a simple *carte familiale*—a slower and far less certain means of transmitting his message. Almost simultaneously, Gide resolved to write a review of Chardonne's *Chronique privée de l'an 1940* for *Le Figaro*, and informed the paper's editor Pierre Brisson of his intention. Gide soon regretted contacting Brisson, however, for he realized that he could have made Drieu an embarrassing ultimatum: publish his article on Chardonne or Gide would leave the *N.R.F.* (NRF xxix–xxx).

Gide honored his commitment to *Le Figaro*, however, and in mid-April the paper published the news of his break with the *N.R.F.* alongside his review of *Chronique privée de l'an 1940*.[78] The announcement of Gide's withdrawal gave added weight to the cautious but politically freighted essay "Chardonne 1940," a veiled attack on the values and policies of the new French leadership and on those who acquiesced to the new order. Gide makes his point quietly by stressing how much Chardonne's opinions have changed since the onset of the Occupation. Quoting briefly from the 1939 book *Chronique privée*, in which Chardonne denounced totalitarianism and despotism, Gide expresses his regret at being unable to quote more extensively from that prewar text: unfortunately, "space, and not only space, is lacking."[79] Alluding discreetly to the constraints of censorship, Gide was testing out a technique he would exploit fully in the "Interviews imaginaires": referring readers to works that express or imply oppositional thought.

In "Chardonne 1940," Gide voices his political views through literary allusions and judgments: as Malcolm Cowley astutely observes, the writer "discovered that honest political judgments could be printed even in Vichy France, so long as they were presented in the guise of literary criticism" (xi). Superficially, "Chardonne 1940" critiques Chardonne's rhetoric and logic; below the surface lies an attack on his political positions. Rather than disagree with Chardonne's political statements, Gide dismisses his arguments as nebulous, paradoxical, and self-contradictory to the point of being meaningless (AQ 15). Of the historical events the French have just witnessed, Chardonne writes: "One finds them quite obscure and in general shocking. [. . .] Much later they will be explained; they will appear natural and almost always favorable."[80] However, Gide points out, Chardonne does not state—nor does he care—to whom these events are favorable. Equally meaningless is a rhetorical pirouette about the Riom trials, at which political and military figures of the Third Republic were blamed for the war and France's defeat. "The political figures tried before the court of Riom for the crime of irresponsibility are innocent," Chardonne states, immediately devaluing this assertion by adding: "like all criminals."[81] In these "tragic times," Gide affirms, Chardonne's own "innocence" (in the pejorative sense) and "lack of con-science" are nearly criminal (I.I. 151).[82] Chardonne's apparent failure to grasp the gravity of the situation, his rhetorical back-and-forth, and his tone of complacent acceptance alarm Gide, for the author sees something of himself in Chardonne: "with different voices arguing within me, as they do in him, I recognize in him a spirit akin to my own" (I.I. 153). That is why Chardonne's book serves as such an effective warning: "Seeing him reel and stagger, at once I stand erect." Chardonne's vagueness is salutary, Gide argues: "Thanks to his fluidity and inconsistency [. . .] we have a better sense of our own stead-fastness and, thanks to all these indistinct surrenders, of our own constancy" (I.I. 154).[83]

Chardonne responded to Gide's criticisms in the June 1941 issue of the *N.R.F.* Readers who objected to "L'Été à La Maurie," including "audacious writers, puritans of art, who were often sincere without the slightest scruple, former friends of this journal"[84]—an obvious allusion to Gide—were clinging to an outdated view of Germany, Chardonne declared in his essay "Voir la fig-ure." Such readers had no desire to know and understand contemporary Ger-many, he claimed.[85] In order to respond more fully to Gide's attack, Chardonne soon expanded "Voir la figure" into a book of the same title. Turning the accusations in "Chardonne 1940" back against their author, Chardonne declared: André Gide "is condemning himself, using me as a stand-in."[86] This assessment was seconded, in harsher terms, in an appendix by Maurice Martin du Gard (not to be confused with Gide's close friend Roger Martin du Gard).[87] Accusing Gide of the vagueness and changeability that he condemned in Chardonne, Maurice Martin du Gard outlines the "successive contradictions"[88] of Gide's political positions, especially regarding communism, and reminds readers that Gide found Hitler "admirable" in 1933. Chardonne, who had become increasingly firm in his pro-German opinions, rightly observed that it was not the "vagueness" of *Chronique privée de l'an 1940* but its clearly stated views on Franco-German relations with which Gide disagreed (*Voir* 100).

For the reading public, including Chardonne and his supporters, Gide had taken a decisive position: "Chardonne 1940" and his much-publicized withdrawal from the *N.R.F.* marked a clear separation between Gide and those who favored collaboration with Germany. Readers deluged Gide with letters congratulating him on "Chardonne 1940." Privately, however, Gide was tormented by acute uncertainty about his actions vis-à-vis the *N.R.F.* and about his fundamental views on the German Occupation.[89] A letter from Gaston Gallimard and a visit from Henri Thomas soon convinced Gide that he had acted unfairly toward Gallimard, the review, and its readers. Gide's showy withdrawal had dealt a mortal blow to the *N.R.F.*, Gallimard claimed, and appeared to justify accusations that the publisher had "compromised" a bit too much. For his part, Thomas insisted on the important role the *N.R.F.* played in the occupied zone: the press there had stooped so low that the *Nouvelle Revue Française* represented "the only intellectual nourishment possible for worthy people."[90] Feeling guilty that he had "betrayed" and "abandoned" Gallimard[91] and unjustly wronged the *Nouvelle Revue Française*, Gide envisaged resuming his connection with the review—even at the risk of appearing to swing this way and that like a weathervane (CAG 6: 238, 240).

Less than two weeks after the splashy "Chardonne 1940" incident, Gide made plans to resume writing for the *N.R.F.*: he would send them a planned article on Abel Bonnard, an Académie Française member known for his anti-Semitic and pro-German opinions,[92] to be accompanied by a letter to Drieu that Gide drafted during a sleepless night. Claiming that the press had made far more fuss than he intended about his decision to leave the *N.R.F.*, Gide's letter put the ball in Drieu's court: it would be up to the *N.R.F.* editor to prove to Gide that his concerns about the review were unfounded. Gide's friends cautioned him not to reverse his position hastily and without sufficient information: Drieu's prewar opinions were already fairly disturbing, Maria Van Rysselberghe pointed out, and he might well support German domination. Pierre Herbart worried that Gide's apparently incoherent series of reversals would make him lose all credibility: "you already have a couple of turnarounds [*volte-face*] to your credit,"[93] Herbart reminded his friend, but at least those reversals had solid grounding. At the very least, urged Maria Van Rysselberghe, Gide should make his next submission to the *N.R.F.* "subversive enough that its publication will be proof of [his] independence."[94] Swayed by his friends, Gide agreed to delay sending his letter to Drieu (NRF xxxi–xxxiii).

Herbart and Van Rysselberghe encouraged Gide to go to Paris to form his own opinions about intellectual life in the occupied zone. Nevertheless, Van Rysselberghe worried: "it is Gide himself who represents the biggest danger for Gide—a gaffe with the Germans would be irreparable. If only he didn't have to go to Paris alone!"[95] Gide concurred, hoping that Pierre Herbart, Henri Thomas, and his own daughter Catherine might accompany him. In the end, though, Gide abandoned plans for the trip. Self-imposed isolation seemed the prudent course for one as curious and easily swayed as himself, he wrote to Paul Valéry: "the demon of curiosity might well entice me into being regrettably imprudent. It is better that I stay far from temptations and conversations" (Gide and Valéry 323).[96] Paul Léautaud, the gossipmonger of the Parisian intelligentsia, put a suggestive twist on Gide's concern. According to Georges Duhamel, Léautaud provocatively reported, Gide had stated he might well return to the *N.R.F.* "if I were not afraid of meeting German soldiers whom I might in fact find likeable."[97]

From a political standpoint, Gide's comportment toward the *N.R.F.* seems indecisive, even incoherent. As Maria Van Rysselberghe aptly observed, it was his lack of political convictions that prompted Gide's "weathervane" antics. The amazing thing, Van Rysselberghe told Herbart, was that Gide was absolutely sincere in each of his contradictory actions. Herbart agreed, adding that Gide was sincere without conviction, and based most of his actions on "fellow-feeling."[98] Gide was perfectly aware of this dilemma: "It is through sympathy for friends that I hope for England's triumph, rather than through direct love for France, which will, I think, be able to benefit very little from the precarious liberty which that triumph promises her," he wrote in May 1941.[99] The writer lamented his loss of self-confidence: he listened to others rather than himself, but always came to regret it, wishing he could "erase every trace of [his] footsteps."[100] As he continued to waver, returning in June 1941 to the notion that "coming to terms with the Germans, in the main, seems wise," Gide was certain of only one thing: "There is not one line of everything I have written in the past six months that I do not regret having written."[101]

THE DEMISE OF THE *N.R.F.*

As established writers like Gide, Mauriac, and Valéry withdrew from the *N.R.F.*, the journal's political tone changed considerably. Many of the younger writers whose work now filled the journal's pages accepted or actively promoted collaboration with Germany. Indeed, of the French delegation to the 1941 Weimar conference promoting intellectual and cultural collaboration among European nations—Pierre Drieu La Rochelle, Robert Brasillach, Abel Bonnard, André Fraigneau, Jacques Chardonne, Ramon Fernandez, Marcel Jouhandeau—all but Brasillach were contributors to the wartime *N.R.F.* ("De jour" 3; Heller 68, 83; Hebey 429–34). With this new staff of writers under Drieu's leadership, the *N.R.F.*'s articles on Germany underwent a marked change: essays on literary and cultural life in Germany gave way to articles of a decidedly ideological nature. Whereas the early issues of the wartime *N.R.F.* primarily evinced an attitude of passive resignation toward the German Occupation and the Vichy government, later issues offered justifications and support for the new regimes (Richard 69, 84).

By Drieu's own admission, the *N.R.F.*'s new contributors were not up to the literary standard of the old guard, whose defections left the editor scrambling for decent copy (Drieu, *Journal* 272; CAG 6: 329). As the journal's quality declined and its pro-collaboration tone became evident, subscriptions dropped sharply: "shocked" by the journal's new tendencies, three thousand readers had canceled their subscriptions by May 1942 (NRF xxxix, xliii). Frustrated by what he perceived as the review's failure, Drieu began to speak of abandoning the *N.R.F.* in early 1942. On learning that Drieu wanted out, Gaston Gallimard panicked: without Drieu's protection, he believed, the publishing house would be seized. This could mean financial ruin for the publisher as well as the Éditions de la N.R.F.'s authors (G/P 255). Gallimard proposed reorganizing the N.R.F. as a purely literary periodical with no political content; while Drieu would remain director in name, the N.R.F.'s prewar editor Jean Paulhan would compose the issues with the assistance of secretary Maurice Blanchot (G/P 256, 261). In exchange for Paulhan's promise not to publish any overtly or covertly anti-German writings, Gerhard Heller of the Propaganda-Staffel agreed not to oppose texts by or about English, American, or Russian writers.[102] Heller stipulated, however, that contributions by Jewish authors would be out of the question, as "anti-Jewish actions" were about to be stepped up.[103]

The key to Gallimard's proposed reorganization of the N.R.F. was a two-tiered management composed of a team of younger editors and a board of directors made up of irreproachable figureheads. Drieu would join Marcel Arland, Marcel Jouhandeau, Jean Giono, Jean Paulhan, and Henry de Montherlant on the editorial committee. For the directorial committee "made up of old, incontestable assets," Drieu proposed André Gide, Paul Valéry, Paul Claudel, and Léon-Paul Fargue. To Jean Paulhan's mind, the first two were pivotal: "I can accept the task which Gaston [Gallimard] is offering me only if Gide and Valéry—whose estrangement brought about the failure of La N.R.F.—come back to us."[104] In the end, longtime friends Gide and Valéry both made their consent contingent on the other's acceptance (G/P 260–62, 266). By the time Gide tentatively agreed to come back on board, however, Valéry had decided that the proposed committee membership was unacceptable: it would be unthinkable to unite the old guard's names with those of the younger writers, many of whom were favorable to collaboration: "mixing one group with the other means ruining everyone," Valéry declared.[105] Ultimately, the antagonism between the politically irreconcilable editorial and directorial committees doomed the plan.[106] Writing bitterly of the failed negotiations, Drieu would claim that "the older generation—Gide, Valéry, Claudel—is sneaking away in its sneaky old way."[107]

Conversations and negotiations dragged on, and Gide wavered as he listened to the advice of first one friend then another. The decision was indeed a weighty one, for as Gide put it: "The N.R.F., in short, is my review."[108] Though he, Valéry, and Fargue might essentially be figureheads, they would be held responsible for whatever political direction the journal took. Normally scornful of public opinion, Gide nonetheless feared the consequences of public "interpretations" in wartime (NRF xl, lx–lxi; G/P 260). His friends seconded this viewpoint: noting Gide's "tendency to collaborate, to manifest the utmost goodwill," Maria Van Rysselberghe joined Roger Martin du Gard in pointing out that the reorganized N.R.F. would still be serving the Germans, if only as "proof of their generosity, their broadmindedness."[109] She thought it wisest for the N.R.F. to suspend publication as it had during World War I (NRF xxxix).

Ultimately, it was the journal's collaborationist editor Drieu La Rochelle whose 1943 resignation caused the *N.R.F.* to cease publication. Officially, Drieu cited declining subscriptions and a lack of high-quality manuscripts as the reasons for his departure; unofficially, he admitted that his own laziness and lack of motivation were equally to blame. By this time, Drieu no longer believed in the possibility of a German victory: "fascism is definitively doomed in France," he lamented. Musing on the journal's fate, Drieu half wished that the *N.R.F.* would be handed over to Paulhan and his crew: "I would greatly enjoy seeing those gentlemen finally 'collaborate' openly with the Germans."[110] With Drieu's withdrawal and the failure of Gallimard's proposed reorganization, the *Nouvelle Revue Française* ceased publication after its June 1943 issue. Its intellectual impact attenuated throughout the Occupation by France's division into two zones, the *N.R.F.* was easily supplanted by the flourishing resistance press, notably *Les Lettres Françaises*, and by staunchly collaborationist journals such as *La Révolution Nationale*, in which Drieu published most of his articles after leaving the *N.R.F.* (Richard 71; NRF xv).

Before giving up his position as director of the *Nouvelle Revue Française*, Drieu took stock of the review's two wartime years in the January 1943 "Bilan." He responded to criticisms of the journal's forays into political topics by pointing out, quite rightly, that he was continuing the tradition of the prewar *N.R.F.*, which had been a forum for political as well as literary writings. As for the journal's overwhelmingly collaborationist tone, Drieu claimed that he would have welcomed discreet expressions of oppositional thought (105). Gide, "moved by that famous and exasperating impartiality that still earns him enemies [. . . decades] after his death,"[111] found the essay most interesting, and considered many of Drieu's arguments well founded (J II: 967). Having agonized so long about whether and how to write for the wartime *N.R.F.*, moreover, he may well have felt a twinge of guilt about his failure to express his dissent in the review.

If Gide essentially agreed with Drieu's remarks on the *N.R.F.*'s editorial politics, one can only assume that his reaction to the "Bilan"'s political contentions was far more ambivalent. Without subscribing to Drieu's violently anti-immigrant stance, his belief that fascism was the only weapon against Europe's "decadence," or his assertion that "Hitlerism" represented Europe's only hope for freedom (105–06), Gide acknowledged that, at one time or another, he had flirted with similar beliefs. In the end, he wrote, "[m]y heart much more than my reason disapproves [Drieu's arguments] and I was not far from subscribing to them; but I think that I should have rapidly and bitterly reproached myself for having done so" (J 4: 222).[112] Despite his abiding ambivalence, Gide's heart and humanitarian leanings were already leading him away from his more reactionary views and his initial calm acceptance of the Occupation. Long before the *N.R.F.* shut down, he cautiously began to voice opposition to Germany's domination of Europe.

GIDE'S DAWNING OPPOSITION

Even as his "Feuillets" were appearing in Drieu's *N.R.F.*, Gide was publishing brief pieces that began to show glimmers of opposition. In the earliest cases, the circumstances of publication mattered more than the articles' content. "Sur une définition de la poésie," a literary essay devoid of political content, enhanced Gide's "image as a potential resistant," Michael Tilby explains, because it appeared in the journal *Poésie 41*, whose director Pierre Seghers had been a member of the intellectual resistance since the beginning of the Occupation (Tilby 109; Heller 54). "Auguste Bréal," a brief tribute to the recently deceased art and literature critic who had been Gide's classmate at the École Alsacienne, was similarly apolitical. In Gide's eyes, however, the homage gained importance "by the simple fact that it praises a Jew, so that it almost took a little courage to publish it and I am grateful to *Le Figaro* for doing so."[113]

Gide's first conscious step toward expressing dissent came in response to a letter from Greek intellectual Constantin Dimaras.[114] Following Greece's successful rebuff of the Italian invasion attempt in 1940, Dimaras wrote to those foreign intellectuals who seemed likely to take an interest in his nation's plight (292). His letter, which reached Gide in late December 1940, had been censored by the Germans, yet Gide was astonished that it had been delivered at all, so overt was the call for help (CAG 6: 215): "Say something on our behalf [, . . .] appeal to everyone's goodwill in our favor."[115] The Greek's plea found a willing listener in Gide: not only was the Frenchman moved by the Greeks' "heroic resistance" (CAG 11: 186), he was also eager to "compromise himself"[116]—to provoke a scandal that might counterbalance "the negative effect produced by [his] participation [*collaboration*] in the *N.R.F.*"[117] With any expression of support for Greece unpublishable in occupied France, Gide wrote his declaration for the Greek press, hoping that news of his paean—"Courageous Greek people! [. . .] You represent for us the triumph of valiant virtue"[118]—would reach France (J II: 745). Gide managed to convey his letter to the Greek Ambassador in Vichy, from whence it was smuggled to Athens, where it circulated clandestinely, repeatedly copied out by hand. Contrary to the author's hopes, however, no paper printed his statement; it was first published after his death in the April 1951 issue of *La Revue d'Athènes* (CAG 6: 220; Tatsopoulos-Polychronopoulos 218; Dimaras 292).

The homage to Greece was Gide's first hesitant attempt to express his wish for freedom. Following an old pattern—for, as Daniel Moutote shrewdly observes, "Gide never addresses domestic political issues: in fact, he sidesteps them by speaking of international politics"[119]—Gide expressed himself in a trio of love letters to places that had come to symbolize freedom—or the struggle for freedom—in newly significant ways. Greece, typically a model of sexual freedom in Gide's oeuvre, is refigured in his wartime writings, becoming instead a site of political resistance. North Africa undergoes a similar transformation in "Notre Afrique intérieure," an essay published in the Algiers resistance journal *Fontaine* in March 1941. Seeking hope and comfort across the Mediterranean, Gide restates his affinity for the region that once symbolized sexual liberation for him, but that now holds the promise of political freedom. Switzerland, anything but a land of sensuous freedoms in Gide's oeuvre, was also the subject of a wartime tribute, "Éloge de la Suisse," in the *Cahiers du Sud's* special 1943 issue on Switzerland. Just as the ill sought a cure in Switzerland's sanatoria during peacetime, Gide writes, so too did Europe's ravaged nations turn to neutral Switzerland to bandage their wounds in wartime (15–16). Essentially immobilized by the war, the writer once renowned for his travel journals turned to memory and imagination, cautiously evoking his hopes for resistance to the Reich through a clutch of tributes to politically inspirational nations.

The next decisive step in Gide's evolving opposition came in May 1941, when public threats from the Légion des Anciens Combattants established him as a persona non grata of the Vichy regime. At the urging of young writer Roger Stéphane, Gide had agreed to give a lecture at the luxurious Rühl hotel. Gide chose to offer his audience in Nice (and in Cannes, where the talk was to be repeated some days later) the diversion and comfort of a topic untouched by war: the works of young Belgian poet Henri Michaux. Roger Martin du Gard strongly disapproved of Gide's breaking his silence in this particular way: he found both the topic and the worldly venue "worthy neither of Gide nor of the circumstances."[120]

On 21 May, with his Michaux lecture scheduled for that evening, Gide received a letter in which the Vichy-affiliated Légion des Anciens Combattants threatened to prevent him from speaking. The letter's author, Noël de Tissot, expressed shock that Gide should dare to face the public despite "current events which condemn his oeuvre much better than could any critic." Dismissing Gide's political persona as too pale and indecisive to bother with, Tissot made it clear that it was his literary oeuvre that the Légion condemned. At a time when Marshal Pétain was striving to inculcate "the spirit of sacrifice," Tissot argued, there was no place for this champion of "the pleasure principle." If Gide did not understand this, the letter threatened, the Légion could force him to "understand."[121] Marc Allégret visited the Légion that afternoon and obtained their consent for Gide to deliver his speech after all. But Gide had no use for the endorsement of a group he despised: after a long consultation with Martin du Gard, Malraux, and others, he decided to cancel both the Nice and Cannes lectures.[122] That evening, Gide read a prepared statement to his listeners at the Rühl hotel: "[Let us have] no discord among Frenchmen; rather than provide a pretext for strife [. . .] *let us be silent*."[123] The overflowing crowd seemed well disposed to Gide's emotional announcement, and when a young man took the podium to read Tissot's letter, the audience loudly protested the Légion's threats. Prevented from reading his lecture, Gide promptly published it as *Découvrons Henri Michaux*, a slim volume devoid of reference to the incident in Nice (CAG 6: 246–49).[124]

Immediately following the lecture's cancellation, one hundred sixty Légion members resigned in protest (J II: 764). Maintaining that it was the insignificance of his lecture—not Tissot's threats—that had led him to cancel, Gide declared himself proud to have "embarrassed and even discredited the Légion."[125] To his chagrin, however, the press essentially hushed up the incident: *Le Petit Niçois* merely attributed the cancellation to circumstances beyond Gide's control, and articles clarifying the incident were apparently blocked by the censor (G/P 249; CAG 6: 247). To Gide's disgust, public opinion retained only the Légion's claim that Gide had acknowledged the error of his ways and acceded to their arguments (J II: 764; "Mise"). Further vituperations against Gide followed in the right-wing press. *L'Appel* declared that Vichy had taken "a positive public health measure" by preventing the lecture, which was to be delivered in "a 'chic' and undoubtedly Gaullist hotel in Nice" to "an audience of Jews, snobs, and repressed cretins."[126] Calling Gide "a veritable public enemy," *Le Rassemblement* applauded the Légion's action: "we merely regret that it did not take a more long-term decision."[127]

In the end, the Légion's attack on Gide—like the critiques in the press during the "querelle des mauvais maîtres"—may have had a salutary effect. Gide welcomed the conservatives' vilifications as confirmation of his own oppositional tendencies: "I like being a 'victim' of the Legion," he concluded: "I do not like the fact that it should be for so small a reason" (J 4: 69).[128] Moreover, as Pierre Hebey suggests, the animosity of Vichy ideologues and the right-wing leagues associated with the État Français may have protected Gide from himself by preventing him from collaborating actively with the wartime regime (48).[129] The Michaux incident clearly had a galvanizing effect on Gide, nudging him toward a more firmly oppositional stance. Within months of the confrontation in Nice, the writer would give Vichy further reasons to consider him an enemy: he would start voicing his opposition, discreetly but firmly, in the pages of *Le Figaro*.

THREE

Coded Messages

The "Interviews imaginaires"

SIX MONTHS AFTER announcing his break with the *N.R.F.* in the pages of
Le Figaro, Gide began writing a column entitled "Interviews imaginaires" for
that mainstream newspaper's literary supplement.[1] Running from November
1941 through June 1942, this series of conversations between Gide and a fictitious interlocutor ostensibly deals only with linguistic and literary issues.[2]
Beneath the surface, however, these essays convey a message of political opposition: "cutting the most mockingly habile arabesques on the thinnest of political ice," says George Painter, the "Interviews" "sustain a brilliantly ramified
and prolonged *double entendre* on the opposition between the French spirit and
the banal infamy of Pétainism" (126). Relying on a system of cross-references
like that of Diderot's *Encyclopédie*, Gide criticizes the occupier and Vichy government and offers tacit encouragement to resist. Arguing in favor of individualism, discipline, and prudence, and against the passive acceptance of totalitarianism, Gide seeks primarily to foster intellectual opposition. Nevertheless,
he leaves open the possibility of interpreting his essays as a call for more active
forms of resistance. With these quietly patriotic essays, Gide attempts to distance himself from his earlier expressions of ambivalence and continues the
political repositioning that began with his attack on Chardonne.

This chapter begins by examining Gide's strategies for outwitting Vichy
censors, then explores the political connotations with which Gide invested
his remarks on grammar, vocabulary, and literary genre. An analysis of the
essays' intertextual code focuses on Gide's use of literary quotes and allusions
to criticize Vichy and praise resistance efforts; it then examines the ways in
which these same literary allusions allowed Gide to revise his earlier positions
and distance himself from the *Journal* excerpts he had published in Drieu La
Rochelle's *Nouvelle Revue Française*.

WRITING BETWEEN THE LINES

Calling attention to the limitations on free expression in Vichy France, the foreword to *Attendu que . . .* , the 1943 compilation of "Interviews imaginaires" published in liberated Algiers, explains that the volume reinstates certain censored phrases, especially the names of Jewish thinkers Heinrich Heine and Albert Einstein (AQ 9).[3] While some overtly political passages were indeed stricken by the censor, the number of cuts is in fact surprisingly small. Gide's extensive self-censorship—often guided by the advice of friends like Roger Martin du Gard—accounts in part for the relative absence of censor's cuts. Gide also enjoyed the active support of *Le Figaro*'s editor Pierre Brisson, who went to considerable lengths to publish Gide's articles intact (CAG 6: 291).[4] Furthermore, though Vichy censorship was often more stringent than that in German-occupied Paris, the censors in Lyon, *Le Figaro*'s wartime headquarters, were perhaps less rigorous than those in other parts of the unoccupied zone; in fact, Gide may even have benefited from the complicity of sympathetic censors (Lottman, *Left* 154; Beauce; Patri 1).

At times, however, Gide expressed himself too bluntly for any censor—hostile or friendly—to pass his remarks. In January 1942, when *Le Figaro* began serializing Gide's introduction to the 1942 Pléiade volume of Goethe's dramatic works, Maria Van Rysselberghe reported that the censor had stricken two passages whose reference to current events was "highly transparent and unorthodox."[5] The censored passages concern Goethe's attitude toward the Napoleonic conquests; their evocation of the "unified Europe" that "Napoleon was creating [. . .] by force of arms" quietly invites comparison with Hitler's Europe (I.I. 99).[6] Had the text passed the censor unscathed, this parallel would have been explicit: Gide pictures an accomodationist Goethe *"accepting and celebrating a tyrannical power which left him full license to be a public figure and even enjoy certain prerogatives,"* satisfied so long as his "freedom of thought *and of expression of that thought*" remained intact. Such acceptance was possible, Gide adds, because "[n]ot once was Goethe touched, *as we are today, or at least as we were yesterday,* by the shadow of fear that the very soil from which he sprang and on which his genius rested might tremble and disappear beneath him" (adapted from I.I. 99, italicized passages deleted).[7]

Elsewhere in the "Interviews," Gide risked similarly overt allusions to wartime France; predictably, these comments also failed to pass the censor. In December 1941, the fictitious interviewer offers hope for the coming year, suggesting that reassuring gleams of light have begun to appear. Gide replies: *"Are you thinking of those of Vichy's National Revolution? . . .* In a tunnel artificial lighting serves as best it can" (adapted from I.I. 62, italicized passage deleted).[8] Ostensibly referring to France's new generation of poets, Gide again derides Vichy's "dim bulbs" in the penultimate "Interview": "One would be making a grave mistake, I believe, by judging France, by gauging her true, profound value simply by those parts of her which are most visible today. *In a vessel which has been roughly shaken, as we have just been, it is the lightest elements which first rise to the surface, not the finest ones*" (italicized passage deleted).[9] Despite the censor's cuts, the political implications are hard to miss. In fact, these two passages are, in their censored form, among those most frequently quoted in postwar discussions of the essays' subversive intent. It would seem, therefore, that Gide hedged his bets by embedding explicit political references in passages that make the same point in a metaphorical or elliptical manner. This doubling strategy guaranteed that at least an attenuated version of Gide's message would survive the censor's pencil.

For the most part, though, Gide was forced to renounce explicit political commentary and develop more sophisticated techniques for circumventing the censor. The dialogue form itself was one such strategy. Though the speakers are identified as "I" and "He," and though the interviewer character seems unreflectingly sympathetic to Vichy, Gide's meaning is clearly not restricted to the interviewee's pronouncements. Indeed, the conversants' voices sometimes blur, as when the interviewer claims to voice Gide's own unspoken thoughts, explaining the writer's influence in an amusing pastiche of Gidian style: "When talking with you, I try to be self-effacing; I regard myself as a mirror. I go so far as to imitate your fashion of speaking, your turns of phrase—oh! without meaning to do so" (adapted from I.I. 71).[10] In this manner, the self-described "creature of dialogue" (IID 234)[11] hints that readers should seek his message between the two voices of the "Interviews." Literally dividing a message between the two speakers was Gide's solution when the censor cut a quote from Renan (CAG 6: 289): the interviewee says that Renan wrote of "the great dangers incurred by morality and intelligence in a certain state of humanity"; later, the interviewer requests clarification about the dangers that would arise "as the result of a general reconciliation. Isn't such a reconciliation the goal we are hoping to reach?" (I.I. 53, 55).[12] A savvy ventriloquist, Gide has his interviewer complete the paraphrase, piously approving that "general reconciliation" that Gide, like Renan, found so pernicious.

When he is not throwing his voice, Gide sometimes withholds it. He dramatizes the silence of mourning when evoking the "monstrous cataclysms" of the invasion (I.I. 7)[13] and demonstrates the silence of dissent when the interviewer cries "Long live our National Revolution": after this outburst, "[t]here was a moment of silence" (I.I. 53).[14] Gide makes it clear, moreover, that silence is sometimes enforced. After reading the rather cautious "Interviews" with which the series began, Maria Van Rysselberghe urged the writer to state his opinions more boldly in future essays; Gide objected that it would do him no good to write passages that the censor would excise. In that case, Van Rysselberghe urged him, "at least do your best to show your interviewer that there are regions into which you cannot venture."[15] Following his friend's advice, Gide set his limits clearly: "'Please don't insist,' I said to him when he began plying me with questions about current [. . .] matters. 'There are many things it is better not to talk about today. Of one thing I am certain: literary subjects are all I can discuss with you'" (I.I. 51).[16] Gesturing to subjects that could not be broached, Gide offers a substitute: literary and linguistic issues would stand in for political considerations in the "Interviews imaginaires."

FATHERLAND, MOTHER TONGUE

Language anxiety was very much part of the zeitgeist during the Occupation: many of Gide's contemporaries addressed the issue through impassioned essays in which the mother tongue was a highly transparent stand-in for the fatherland.[17] Gide was among the first to link the nation's well-being to the preservation of its language: "A nation that stands by its language stands firm [*tient bon*]," he declared in a November 1941 "Interview" (I.I. 21).[18] What lifts this assertion above banality is its resonance: the phrase "stand by its language" [*tenir à sa langue*] evokes echoes of "La Dernière Classe," a story known to every French schoolchild. Alphonse Daudet's tale, set in German-occupied Alsace following the Franco-Prussian War, describes the final class conducted in French before German-speaking teachers took over the schools. The departing schoolteacher exhorts his pupils to master and preserve their mother tongue, for "when a nation has become enslaved, she holds the key which shall unlock her prison as long as she preserves her native tongue [*tient bien sa langue*]" (*Monday* 5–6).[19] As if following Daudet's advice, Gide probes current French usage in his "Interviews," seeking evidence of decay and opportunities to restore both linguistic and national integrity.

Like Gide's "Interviews," a *Figaro Littéraire* column called "Anti-Littré" (after Littré, the authoritative French lexicographer) "displace[d] [. . .] discussion of France's defeat and occupation on to the subject of grammar" (Lucey 101). By critiquing examples of bad usage in the works of contemporary writers, the column aimed to restore "the prestige of grammar, so gravely compromised, like so many other things in France."[20] Though Gide's goals resemble those of "Anti-Littré," his project is more overtly political: "Do you think it wise," he would like to ask the "Anti-Littré" columnist, "to make a fuss over trifles, at a time when so many glaring errors, which you are discreet enough not to mention, stand out from our almost official texts and startle us when we listen to the government radio?" (I.I. 19).[21] By pointing out the grammatical fallibility of these publications and broadcasts, Gide subtly undermines their authority.[22]

Worse than any mistakes were the manipulations of meaning that Gide observed all around him. In an October 1940 *Journal* entry, the author of *Les Faux-Monnayeurs* denounces German and Vichy pronouncements as so many "counterfeit coins":

> Hitler's great strength comes from the fact that he never tried to take in
> anyone but others with fine words. He knows what suits the French, alas,
> and that when they are told very forcefully and very often that their honor
> is intact, they eventually almost believe it. "Loyal collaboration," "neither
> victors nor vanquished"—so many checks without funds. (J 4: 52)[23]

The enforced circumspection of the published "Interviews" obliged Gide to
translate this critique into literary terms by paraphrasing a tale from the *Arabian Nights* in which a rich merchant invites a starving man to a banquet
where the names of the dishes take the place of actual food. "It is to such
feasts that literature too often invites us," Gide concludes. The writer's insistence that his critique is purely literary bespeaks more prudence than conviction, for his thrust is unquestionably political when he declares that "[t]oo
often, the word takes the thing's place, and the thing itself can disappear."[24]
Gide's target here is clearly collaborationist propaganda, for among the qualities replaced by hollow words he lists devotion, honor, faith, constancy, and
loyalty—terms often perverted by Vichy rhetoric (AQ 173).

While criticizing those who twist the meaning of words like "honor" and
"loyalty," Gide himself subjects words to strategic deformations, alternately
disavowing and manufacturing political connotations. Insisting all the while
on the purely literary nature of his essays, Gide accumulates terms like "épuration" (purification or purging), "collaboration," and, especially, "résistance"—a word with invariably positive connotations (Cowley xiv).[25] Elsewhere, Gide endows idiomatic expressions with political significance. When
the interviewer criticizes Gide for using the expression *par contre* ("by opposition"), the author responds:

> I realize that both Voltaire and Littré forbid us to use the expression, and
> that Littré advises *en revanche* [literally, "in revenge"] or *en compensation* ["as
> compensation"], but it hardly seems to me that these two phrases are [. . .]
> appropriate [. . . in any statement] to which one could add the word
> "alas!" [. . .] Would you think it proper for a woman to say: "Yes, my brother
> and my husband came back safe from the war, but *in revenge* I lost my two
> sons"? [. . .] I need "by opposition" [*par contre*] and, with all respect to Littré, I propose to keep it. (I.I. 66–67)[26]

With well-chosen examples, Gide calls attention to those losses for which
there can be no compensation or revenge and underscores the need for opposition. "Here and elsewhere," Malcolm Cowley argues, Gide's "real subject is
the grammar of resistance" (66).

Most of the grammatical reflections that pepper the "Interviews" concern the subjunctive mood. Referring to the 1916 essay "Crise du français,"
in which he had commented on the disappearance of the subjunctive from
both French and English—"from our language as from that of our allies"[27]—

Gide bemoans "the decay of the subjunctive, something I began to complain about during the other war" (I.I. 20).[28] Gide's 1916 essay attributes linguistic deterioration to the social upheavals of World War I—primarily the mobilization of proofreaders and the increased influence of women, whom Gide considers deplorably lax in correcting their children's grammatical errors (OC 9: 168–70). Insubordinate women are chiefly to blame for the "less faithful attention to relationships, dependencies, and subordinations"[29] to which Gide attributes the decline of the subjunctive. Though he is less concerned with concrete social phenomena in the World War II "Interviews," Gide continues to associate the subjunctive, a grammatical mood used primarily in dependent clauses, with more general notions of subordination and hierarchy: the subjunctive mood "indicates a certain type of connection between two statements, a dependence of one on the other, a subordination for which people have ceased to recognize the need." When the interviewer remarks that in England the subjunctive essentially disappeared long ago, Gide's reply is both pointed and wistful: "Precisely! Independence . . ." (adapted from I.I. 20).[30] Here Gide both reinforces the correspondence between grammatical and political subordination and points up the paradox inherent in this equation. If England, which has abandoned the mood of subordination, is an exemplar of independence, why doesn't Gide rejoice in the decay of the subjunctive in French? Because France is not England, and failure to acknowledge France's state of dependence amounts to self-deception. Working against the logic of the slogan "neither victors nor vanquished" (qtd. in J 4: 52),[31] Gide urges awareness of subordination and hierarchy.

Subordination can be stylistic as well as grammatical—a notion Gide develops in his 1943 essay "Du classicisme." The essay describes the ongoing struggle between prideful Romanticism—historically associated with Germany—and noble Classicism, which Gide characterizes as a quintessentially French mode of expression. True Classicism is never the result of external constraint, Gide argues; it is by no means restrictive or suppressive. From thinly veiled political allusions, Gide turns to explicit social commentary: "Classical perfection most definitely does not imply a suppression of the individual (I might almost say: on the contrary), but the submission of the individual, his subordination, and that of the word in the sentence, of the sentence on the page, of the page in the work. It is the *making evident of a hierarchy.*"[32] "Du classicisme" offers two important lessons for interpreting the "Interviews": it proposes a positive model of subordination within the nation, and underscores the capacity of French style—and French grammar—to make dependencies visible.[33]

These two concerns come together in the second "Interview imaginaire." As Michael Lucey has argued, "[d]ependent, or subjoined, clauses seem somehow to be linked not only to dependent populations (the French under the Germans), they seem also to be linked to what Gide viewed to be important social and political hierarchies within a country" (102). Lucey astutely associates a reference to France's social divisions with an atypical use of the subjunctive:

> Certainly the phrase "my country" [*Patrie*] is not understood in the same fashion by the plowman and the poet, by the poor and the rich. But still it is a rallying cry. And when we hear that our country is in danger, the next step is to rise as one man to defend it; even *if* what we defend *may be* [*si ce que nous défendons, ce soit*] specifically, for the peasant, our cultivated fields [*nos cultures*]; for the poet, our culture [*notre Culture*] in general; for the manufacturer and the workman, our industrial wealth; and even, for the stockholder, his own dividends. The phrase "my country" includes all these different elements; both the mind and the heart know what it means. (I.I. 11–12, emphasis added)[34]

"In the environs of this marked subjunctive," Lucey contends, "all the diverse levels of French society find their place and can suddenly put up a united front against the enemy" (102). The subjunctive mood's association with doubt works to enhance this message of unity. For the passage in question, Gide might have chosen either of two standard constructions: "it matters little that it be" [*peu importe que ce soit*] or "it matters little if it is" [*peu importe si c'est*]; instead, he combines the two, using the hypothetical *si* as well as the grammatical mood used to convey uncertainty. By stating that it matters little "*if* what we defend *may be*" different for each segment of society, the author seems to suggest that, deep down, all Frenchmen are defending the same values. Gide later defended this unorthodox use of the subjunctive after *si*, arguing that "the indicative would have given a false shade of meaning to what I was trying to say" (I.I. 21).[35] Perhaps he feared that the indicative would be read as an acknowledgment of the social divisions he wished to downplay. By using the subjunctive, he avoids the implication of social disunity within France; in so doing, he reverses his earlier position on what each segment of society values. "[T]ry to talk to the farmer of France's 'intellectual patrimony,' of which he will be very little inclined to recognize himself as an heir," Gide wrote in his diary on 13 July 1940: "Is there one among them who would not willingly accept Descartes's or Watteau's being a German, or never having existed, if that could make him sell his wheat for a few cents more?" (J 4: 31).[36] Although this specific passage remained unpublished at the time Gide wrote the "Interviews imaginaires," remarks of a similar nature had appeared in Drieu's *Nouvelle Revue Française*, leading some readers to label Gide defeatist, elitist, and unpatriotic. Attempting to distance himself from such unpopular statements, Gide exercised his rhetorical virtuosity in the "Interviews" to minimize the gap between those concerned with France's agriculture [*cultures*] and those who defend her Culture. Experimenting with the mood of doubt and dependence, he argues that the apparently disparate values of France's farmers, intellectuals, and industrialists are subordinated to the larger, unifying concept of *Patrie* (country).

Gide's self-conscious and unexpected use of the subjunctive takes a more subversive form in the third "Interview." After listing a number of passages in which Proust substitutes the subjunctive for the indicative and vice versa, Gide declares: "Stendhal wrote just as fast, just as impetuously, without rereading his manuscripts, and I hardly think [*je ne sache pas*] that one could find many such errors in his novels" (I.I. 25).[37] Denoting an attenuated affirmation, the locution *je ne sache pas* allows the writer to use the subjunctive—the mood of grammatical subordination that Gide explicitly associated with France—in a main clause. Perhaps Gide uses this turn of phrase to demonstrate that the French language—and by extension the French nation—has the resources to restore that which is subordinate to a position of independence. The essay's conclusion gestures toward Gide's own grammatical game: "I should doubt that there were many great writers who did not show an admirable mastery of the language; who were not able to utilize and profit from its resources while observing its rules, even if they sometimes manhandled them [*fût-ce en les bousculant un peu*]" (I.I. 25).[38] Gide's grammatical ingenuity is an act of insubordination, one that tacitly encourages the reader to bend the rules—grammatical or other—that govern dependence.

THE INTERTEXTUAL CODE

Though remarks on language occupy an important place in the "Interviews," literary criticism is the essays' primary vehicle for political critique. In its most direct form, Gide's commentary simply uses literature as a metaphor for political phenomena, as in a discussion of literary genre. Gide praises the novel, a genre that flourishes in societies that value individualism. Declaring that the masterpieces of the genre are Russian and, a fortiori, English novels, the author relates the rise of the novel to historical and political conditions. Dostoyevsky gave up his early ambition as a dramatist, Gide argues, because assembling large theatrical audiences was not possible in czarist Russia; knowing that he could reach only individual readers, he opted to write novels instead.[39] As for England, says Gide, "[t]he Theater flourished in those early days when people were still united. When the novel appeared [. . .], it was after the revolts and religious dissensions brought about by the Reformation, which was the mother of individualism. Cromwell closed the theaters, dispersed the spectators, sundered the mass into individuals (I.I. 65–66).[40] Having identified the Allied nations with independence and individualism, Gide describes the genre that Germany offers in opposition to these qualities: "*Par contre*, the form in which Germany excels and triumphs is the lyrical drama, a synthetic form [. . .] in which [. . .] the great social fusion of our time can recognize its most appropriate expression" (I.I. 64–65).[41] Such fusion is precisely what Gide's interviewer advocates when he calls for a poet who could rally French hearts and minds in unanimous enthusiasm. Gide disagrees: "real poetry, at least till the present time, has always been the expression of private personalities that addressed themselves, not to the public at large [*la masse*], but to individual readers," he declares,[42] going so far as to name resistance poet Louis Aragon—who argued for a literary "code" similar to Gide's in his June 1941 essay "La Leçon de Ribérac"—as an exemplar of France's poetic individualism (I.I. 43).[43] By associating literary genres with warring nations, Gide opposes German totalitarianism and affirms France's political alignment with Russia and England.

Here Gide is speaking of literature, but more often he lets literature speak *for him*: as Malcolm Cowley puts it, Gide's "best thrusts at Vichy and the collaborationists take the form of literary allusions that the censors had no time to track down" (xiv). Gide's *Journal* reveals the genesis of this project: during the phony war and early months of the Occupation, the writer focused on literature as an "untimely" alternative to current events; by early 1941, however, he was collecting literary quotations that might serve as commentary on France's political situation.[44] During the months preceding the debut of the "Interviews," Gide was rereading French Classical drama in order to give diction lessons to his daughter Catherine, who hoped to make a career as an actress. Racine's tragedy *Alexandre le grand*, which concerns the invasion of the Indian kingdoms of Porus and Taxile, struck Gide as particularly timely—so timely, in fact, that it would be impossible to stage in wartime France: "What allusions people would see in Porus' resistance and in the acquiescence of Taxile" (J 4: 75);[45] "people would inevitably see allusions to Laval or de Gaulle."[46] Though he identifies Racine's characters with specific players in France's drama of collaboration and resistance, Gide locates the primary relevance of *Alexandre* in the characters' discursive practices, rather than in their identities. What strikes Gide most is not Taxile's easy surrender, but his need to speak of honor "in order to cover up, even in his own eyes, his cowardice!

> Like you, my lord, I too hear honor's voice;
> But to save my empire is my proper choice."
> (J 4: 76)[47]

This indictment of Taxile's self-serving rhetoric echoes the *Journal*'s condemnation of Vichy slogans—especially the oxymoronic "[l]oyal collaboration" (J 4: 52).[48]

In the published "Interviews," of course, Gide could not comment so explicitly on a work's applicability to wartime France; indeed, certain texts were so patently relevant that he could not even quote them. Consequently, he developed various techniques for "writing between the lines."[49] Like the contributors to *Esprit*, which Michel Winock has called the most public clandestine review in occupied France (*Histoire* 226, 232), Gide expressed his criticisms of Germany and Vichy through irony, an allusive style, and, above all, choice quotations from literary works.[50] Gide's "Interviews imaginaires," which began to appear a few months after *Esprit* was shut down by Vichy authorities, are in some respects a continuation of this experiment in subversive intertextuality.

The "Interviews" are a literary treasure hunt, an exercise in erudition designed to mobilize the intellectual opposition of educated French readers. Gide turns France's literary heritage into a political tool by constructing a network of quotations and allusions that convey his heterodox messages. His first task is to warn readers that the essays contain such messages; naturally, he does so through literary references. It is Gide's fictitious interviewer who first suggests that classic works of literature may offer lessons for the present. Stating that he takes great comfort in a recent edition of Montesquieu's *Cahiers*, the interviewer quotes a passage in which Montesquieu rejoices that France has always recovered swiftly from calamity and is highly resourceful in overcoming "the internal vices of its different governments." The interviewer stops here, but resumes his reading at Gide's urging: "Perhaps this is to be explained by the very diversity of France, because of which no evil has ever been able to strike such deep roots that it could destroy entirely the fruit of her natural advantages." Gide replies with words of caution: "it is this diversity that is being attacked today. People would like to see it abolished" (I.I. 7).[51] In addition to conveying Gide's objection to the suppression of France's diversity, this conversation dramatizes the strategy of the partial citation. In this first "Interview," Gide walks his interlocutor and his readers through the process, urging them to complete the truncated quotation. In later essays, he will use more circuitous means to direct his readers toward daringly apposite literary passages.

Gide gives further hints about the "Interviews'" coded messages in his readings of hermetic poets Maurice Scève and Stéphane Mallarmé. A discussion of the Renaissance poet alerts readers to the potential for political allegory. "[W]hen Scève begins one of his *dizains* with the lines:

> Le Cerf volant[52] aux abois de l'Austruche,
> Hors de son giste esperdu s'envola.
>
> [The flying Stag, tracked down and flushed
> from his covert by the Ostrich, takes desperate flight]"

Gide affirms, he is indeed making a historical allusion, as he does in *dizain* fifty-five, "where he again refers to Charles V of Spain and Austria under the guise of the *Austruche*" (I.I. 116–17).[53] The fifty-fifth *dizain*, which Gide mentions but refrains from quoting, tells of the chiefly unsuccessful 1536 invasion of Provence by Holy Roman Emperor Charles V (Scève 386). In the first line of the poem, the emperor is portrayed as an eagle; by the final couplet, he is reduced to:

> *une Austruche errante,*
> *Qui vole bas, & fuit legerement.*
> (Scève 149)
>
> [A wandering Ostrich,
> That flies low and slowly flees.]
> (Hallett 83)

in a derisive allegory based on the resemblance between the words *autruche* (ostrich) and *Autriche* (Austria). Gide implicitly invites his readers to interpret the harassing then humiliated bird as a reference to Hitler, that twentieth-century "Austruche." By quoting a poet who lived four centuries before him, Gide could safely present this scathing allegory with little risk to himself.

"Saint Mallarmé l'ésotérique," an essay on the late nineteenth-century hermetic poet who mentored young Gide, hints at the reader's role in the "Interviews'" subversive manipulation of France's literary heritage. Gide illustrates Mallarmé's obscurity and taste for mystery with the following couplet:

> *Ma faim qui d'aucuns fruits ici ne se régale*
> *Trouve en leur docte manque une saveur égale.*
> (I.I. 114)
>
> [On no fruits here does my hunger feast,
> But finds in their learnèd lack the self-same taste.]
> (Mallarmé 84)

These lines are taken from "Mes bouquins refermés" ("My Old Books Closed"), a sonnet whose title evokes the lack of access to books that Gide repeatedly laments in his "Interviews"—as well, perhaps, as the notion that banned and censored books were effectively closed to wartime readers. Under such circumstances, a "learnèd lack" can become a tool in the production of meaning. I would argue that Gide mobilizes his readers through a savvy exploitation of literary lack, playing on their expectations and their memories. The code of the "Interviews" is built on well-orchestrated absences—the passage mentioned but not quoted, the first line of a couplet transcribed without the rhyming verse. This lack is a site for resistance, and an invitation to readers to exert themselves by remembering or researching the missing text. Gide hints at the reader's role by recalling his own early association with Mallarmé, who demanded a great deal from his readers. The poet articulated his expectations in a dedication to Gide:

> *Attendu qu'il y met du sien*[54]
> *Vous feuillets de papier frigide*
> *Exaltez-moi, musicien,*
> *Pour l'âme attentive de Gide.*
>
> [Because he also does his part,
> White paper in your frigid sheets
> Inspire the musician to new feats
> For André Gide's attentive heart.]
> (I.I. 114–15)

Like Mallarmé's listener, Gide's reader "also does his part."[55] Gide's essays, like Mallarmé's poems, are often recondite, but their obscurity serves a purpose beyond that of evading the censor: "To address oneself to the intellect is to invite it to protest," Gide asserts.[56] His "Interviews imaginaires" extend such an invitation to the politically receptive reader, who must collaborate in the production of clandestine meaning—and who may be spurred by that meaning toward other forms of protest.

Gide takes an autobiographical turn when he evokes his early days in Mallarmé's literary salon. Elsewhere, he reflects on his life more obliquely, through references to writers whose experiences in some way mirror his own. Four authors discussed in the "Interviews"—Goethe, Renan, Tacitus, and Hugo—merit particular attention because of Gide's implicit or explicit identification with these men and their historical predicaments. Gide alludes to political crises in the lives of all four writers: for Goethe, it is the Napoleonic conquests; for Renan, the Franco-Prussian War; for Tacitus, the tyranny of Emperor Domitian; and for Hugo, the coup d'état of Napoleon III. Gide's treatment of these earlier conflicts highlights their contemporary relevance. Moreover, the passages concerning these writers offer particularly fine illustrations of the coding strategies Gide employs to transmit his covert political messages.

In May 1941, eager to demonstrate his solidarity with the Gallimard publishing house despite his break with the *N.R.F.*'s new management, Gide agreed to write the introduction to the Pléiade's forthcoming edition of Goethe's complete dramatic works (CAG 6: 238–39).[57] For four weeks in early 1942, *Le Figaro Littéraire* serialized Gide's "Introduction au Théâtre de Goethe" in place of the "Interviews imaginaires." While Gide's "Introduction" devotes considerable attention to rehabilitating Goethe's image, it is hardly the "rallying"[58] text that Gaston Gallimard had hoped to offer the Germans (Assouline, *Gallimard* 297). In fact, as Gide contextualizes the criticisms leveled at Goethe, it becomes clear that he is essentially penning a work of self-defense by drawing parallels between the German writer and himself. Much of the condemnation directed at Goethe arose in a historical context uncannily like that which led to the "querelle des mauvais maîtres." When Dumas *fils* denounced Goethe as a "venerable goat" (I.I. 85)[59] Gide explains, he was stinging from France's 1870 defeat at the hands of the Prussian army:

> Those were the days when French writers were also being taken to task. In 1872 one magazine circulated a questionnaire dealing with "literary *corruption* in France," and many of the answers denounced the pernicious influence of Goethe on the French. [. . .] It is easy to see at a distance that such accusations were absurd. In those days, however, we lived in the shadow of defeat and were trying to regain our self-respect. (I.I. 86–87)[60]

In the 1940s as in the 1870s, literature was blamed for France's weakness and defeat, and Gide underscores this parallel through his choice of vocabulary. Himself reviled in post-Armistice debates linking literary and national recovery, Gide declares: "In the midst of the French effort toward national salvation [*redressement*], Goethe [. . .] was given the reprimand that suited his rank" (I.I. 87).[61] He further cements his identification with Goethe by applying characteristically Gidian terms—"fervor," "immorality," "serenity," "moving on" [*passer outre*]—to the German writer.[62] With its lexical echoes and its emphasis on political context, Gide's defense of Goethe doubles as a dismissal of his own attackers.

Through subtly crafted language, moreover, Gide molds Goethe's writings into a commentary on World War II France. His very free rendering of the Dactyls' chorus from Goethe's second *Faust* is a case in point:

> Who will free us?
> We smelt the iron
> From which they forge our chains.
> O deliverance
> Do not tarry!
> While we are waiting
> Let us be pliant.
> (I.I. 93)[63]

Jean Schlumberger took issue with this translation, criticizing the rendering of "*Uns loszureissen/ Ist noch nicht zeitig*" ("It is not yet time for us to break free") as "O deliverance/ Do not tarry!"[64] Gide has his fictional interlocutor echo this criticism in a subsequent "Interview":

> HE.—What you presented as an impatient desire was merely a statement of fact.

> I.—But the first line of the stanza: "Who will free us?" seemed to justify an impulse that came straight from my heart.

> HE.—In these days we must learn to repress many of our impulses. (I.I. 108)[65]

Gide further justifies his translation on the basis that he was attempting to preserve the rhythm of the original. This insistence on purely formal concerns is a typical subterfuge: indeed, the writer often accompanies his more provocative statements with excessive denials of any extraliterary intent.

The Franco-Prussian War, which prompted Dumas and others to vilify Goethe, provided a safe but specific cipher for the current Franco-German conflict in Gide's "Interviews." Ernest Renan's correspondence with German theologian David Friedrich Strauss offered an opportunity for particularly pointed commentary. When Jacques Chardonne tried to co-opt Renan's 1872 work *La Réforme intellectuelle et morale* to support his own collaborationist agenda (*Voir* 15, 43–45), Gide responded by revealing how selective Chardonne's reading was: Chardonne's position was comparable to Renan's "in his *first letter to Strauss*, shortly after our defeat in 1870," he explained (adapted from I.I. 52).[66]

In his letter of 1870, Renan takes a conciliatory tone, urging Germany to show generosity and pity toward France (189). But *La Réforme* reprints *two* letters to Strauss, Gide's interviewer helpfully points out, calling the reader's attention to the 1871 missive in which Renan heaps criticism on Germany. Renan's 1871 critique of German policy is, in many respects, equally applicable to the situation Gide encountered seventy years later. The nineteenth-century writer protests the annexation of Alsace, claiming that populations have a quasidivine right not to be transferred without their consent. Gide's contemporaries, having experienced a repetition of this annexation, might read this statement as an attack on the Third Reich's expansionist policies. In retrospect, though, it is Renan's critique of German ideology that has the greatest relevance for the Second World War. "Our politics is that of the right of nations," writes Renan; "yours is the politics of race: we believe that ours is better. The over-accentuated division of humanity into races [. . .] can lead only to wars of extermination. [. . .] Your ethnographic and archaeological politics [. . .] will be fatal to you."[67] Renan's argument is that Germany is creating an enemy in the Slavs, who may one day overpower Germany. He also hints that France, if crushed, might come to favor any cause or party that would threaten Germany (198–99, 208). Yet the nineteenth-century writer's remarks about "ethnographic politics" are uncannily applicable to the Third Reich's policy of racial genocide.

Because Renan's blistering philippic against the Germany of Bismarck was largely applicable to Hitler's Germany, it would have been dangerous or impossible for Gide to quote the text verbatim. Instead, he obligingly provides the date of the letter and the exact title of the book in which it can be found. He would exploit this technique elsewhere in the "Interviews," supplying a page number or translator's name to help readers track down a meaningful but unquotable literary passage.[68] In the eleventh "Interview," for example, Gide tells his interlocutor that he has just discovered a particularly heartening sentence in Tacitus's *Life of Agricola*: "Memoriam quoque ipsam cum voce perdidissemus, si tam in nostra potestate esset oblivisci quam tacere." For the benefit of those who do not read Latin, Gide conveniently offers André Cordier's translation: "We should have lost memory itself along with speech, if it had been as much in our power to forget as to be silent" (I.I. 108–09).[69] He then gestures toward other relevant passages in Tacitus's text: "In that whole section of the *Life of Agricola* there are reflections I should like to discuss with you, when we are again in a period of diastole"—that is, in a period of intellectual freedom (I.I. 109).[70] As Gide suggests, the surrounding passage is indeed revealing: the sentence he quotes concludes the chapter in which Tacitus describes censorship, book burning, and the exile of intellectuals under the despotic regime of Emperor Domitian. This second chapter of the *Agricola* bears citing at length:

> savage punishment was extended beyond [. . .] authors to their books. The police, under official instructions, made a bonfire in Comitium and Forum of those masterpieces of literary art. [. . .] In those fires doubtless the Government imagined that it could silence the voice of Rome and annihilate the freedom of the Senate and the moral consciousness of mankind; it even went on to banish the professors of philosophy and exile all honourable studies, so that nothing decent might be left to vex its eyes. We have indeed set up a record of subservience. Rome of old explored the limits of freedom; we have plumbed the depths of slavery, robbed even of the interchange of ideas by the secret police. We should have lost our memories as well as our tongues had it been as easy to forget as to be silent. (Tacitus 52)

This passage would have held particular significance for Gide, whose own works had been proscribed under the Nazi Occupation. Gide's protest against censorship is underscored by his insistence on the fact that he is not free to quote the passage in its entirety. This message is further reinforced by the very name of Tacitus, "the silenced one" (from *tacere*, to be silent). Yet in French this silence also evokes secret communication, for the name "Tacite" is identical with the adjective "tacit." The Latin author's name thus points to both enforced silence and resistance within that silence.

As he read the *Life of Agricola* during the winter of 1942, Gide savored the book's "bitter essence,"[71] no doubt remarking the many parallels between Agricola's triumphs and those of Germany (J 4: 100). The French, like the ancient Britons whom Agricola conquered, were weakened by internal dissensions: as Tacitus states, "nothing has helped us more in war with their strongest nations than their inability to cooperate" (62). Then, too, Tacitus's remarks on the easy defeat of the Britons would have read like an account of the 1940 Armistice and Occupation: when Agricola "had done enough to inspire fear, he turned to mercy and proffered the allurements of peace. As a result, many states which had till then maintained their independence abandoned their resentful mood and accepted the curb of garrisons and forts" (71).

Whereas the Britons' defeat has obvious parallels with that of the French in 1940, Tacitus's attitude toward that conquest—and, by extension, Gide's attitude toward his own nation's defeat—is more complex. The *Life of Agricola* is the biography of a prudent and illustrious man. It is, moreover, a work whose philosophy coincides in many respects with that of André Gide. Tacitus, like Gide, counseled moderation: "Let it be clear to those who insist on admiring insubordination that even under bad emperors men can be great, and that a decent regard for authority, if backed by ability and energy, can reach that peak of honour that many have stormed by precipitous paths, winning fame, without serving their country, by a melodramatic death" (94). By referring to Tacitus, Gide appears to be recommending moderate and circumspect resistance. This decoding of the allusion may, however, be a screen message that conceals another, more subversive idea. Early in his career, long before Domitian forced him into submission, Agricola conquered the peoples of Britain. Tacitus narrates this conquest, including the important battle of Mount Graupius. As he describes preparations for the battle, Tacitus embeds two discourses in his narrative: Agricola's speech to his Roman soldiers, and the stirring address that Caledonian general Calgacus makes to his troops. Thus, the *Life of Agricola*, a tale told from the Roman point of view, includes a fragment of discourse from the Caledonian "resistance." This speech is very convincing, especially when Calgacus criticizes the deceptive language with which the Romans cloak their violence: "Robbery, butchery, rapine, the liars call Empire; they create a desolation and call it peace" (80). Because these remarks on the deformation of language by the occupier are extraordinarily like those Gide makes elsewhere in the "Interviews," the reader is tempted to equate Gide's position with that of the Caledonian leader. In the "Interviews imaginaires," Gide's opinion is not always expressed by the character who says "I"; rather, it shifts between the two voices, or emerges from their confrontation. In the literary works cited—as in the "Interviews" themselves—the dominant voice is not always the one to follow. It is impossible to determine whether Gide favors Agricola's moderation or Calgacus's fervor—and this ambiguity is a central mechanism of Gide's tacit messages.

Tacitus teaches that memory persists even when voices are silenced. Gide builds on this lesson by enlisting his readers' literary memories, developing a strategy of elliptical citation that is among the essays' most successful mechanisms for conveying heterodox messages. Gide illustrates many of his comments on rhyme and meter with quotations from Victor Hugo. This choice was in itself a form of protest, for Hugo, "the poet who most clearly expressed the ideals of the French Revolution, was being abused by the critics who supported Vichy" (Cowley xv). Fearing that the Romantic poet's works might be unofficially proscribed, Gide deplores Hugo's disappearance from recent anthologies and schoolbooks (I.I. 28–29). He particularly objects to Thierry Maulnier's *Introduction à la poésie française*,[72] arguing that the anthology's fragmented quotations effectively silence Hugo: "we could smile at such vain devastation, if it weren't that the books under attack are on the way to being effectively suppressed from our bookshops" (I.I. 6).[73] Quoting single lines of verse is meaningless, Gide maintains, because "rhyme is what inspired the verbal genius of Hugo" (I.I. 126).[74] Gide's argument here is aesthetic, but it also sets up a coding strategy that exploits the convention of rhyme.

Gide develops this technique in the fourteenth "Interview" when he argues that rhyme, not emotion, generates the images in Hugo's poetry. The poet's desire to give his rhymes "a glorious fullness" inspired the lines

> *Et verrons-nous toujours les mêmes sentinelles*
> *Monter aux mêmes tours?*
>
> [And shall we forever see the same sentinels
> Climbing up the same towers?]

"to answer the call of the preceding verse":[75]

> *L'homme a-t-il sur son front des clartés éternelles?*
>
> [Does eternal brightness grace this brow of ours?]
> (I.I. 126–27)

This rhyme is surprising and evocative because it associates the lofty term "éternelles" with the military connotations of "sentinelles." Gide implies that the beauty and novelty of this image are produced by the two lines in tandem: neither verse alone could create such an impression. He analyzes this rhyme's effect on the reader more explicitly in the preface to his 1949 *Anthologie de la poésie française*:[76] "'Sentinelles' is [. . .] almost miraculously called forth by 'éternelles'; and immediately gives rise to a bold, surprising image, which evokes everything our individual imagination can endow it with: terror, doubt, and, according to our temperament, anguish or hope."[77] This dual message of anxiety about survival and hope for future change would be apparent to any reader familiar with the source of this quotation—a section of the *Contemplations* entitled "À la fenêtre pendant la nuit," in which the poet asks a series of questions about permanence and change. The poem moves from evocations of loss and destruction in the opening section to a promise of hope in the final stanza.[78] Hugo concludes by hinting that perhaps, even now, a tide of new constellations is welling up "from the depths of funereal night."[79] Just as important as the oblique message of hope are the demonstration of how rhymed verses work together and the suggestion that a single word or pair of words generates the image. Gide dissects the *éternelles/ sentinelles* rhyme as if he were breaking code—hunting for the secret words around which the text was elaborated. In this way, he models the interpretive strategies his own readers will need to use to decipher the "Interviews'" political messages.

Gide's comments remind us, moreover, that rhyme is a mnemonic convention. Gide exploits this convention, playing on his readers' expectation that a line of poetry has a rhyming mate. By citing verses in isolation, he turns Maulnier's habit of quoting single lines of poetry—a practice he condemns—into a coding strategy. Having accused Maulnier of sparing only "a few wing-beats" from the "soaring flight" of French Romantic poetry (I.I. 6),[80] Gide extends the bird metaphor to a discussion of Hugo's genius for rhyming: "One might say that the rhymes, those wild birds [. . .], gathered from the four corners of the horizon to seize the crumbs of intellectual nourishment that he held out to them" (I.I. 29).[81] Gide's strategy in the "Interviews" is similar: he offers a few "crumbs"—in this case, the first line of a couplet—and waits to see what will fly up to meet it. In the essay on Maulnier and Hugo, Gide quotes only the first line of a couplet from the poem "Ce que dit la bouche d'ombre":

> *Il descend, réveillé, l'autre côté du rêve*
> (I.I. 30).
>
> [Awakened, he descends the other slope of the dream.]
> (J 4: 167)

He leaves readers to look up or recall the rhyming line:

> *Son rire, au fond des bois, en hurlement s'achève*
>
> [Deep inside the forest, his laugh becomes a scream.]
> (Hugo, *Contemplations* 452)[82]

These lines come from a section of the *Contemplations* that tells how the spirits of the wicked are reincarnated as repulsive creatures; the couplet in question refers to a much-hated Roman politician who is transformed into a wolf. Though the "Interviews" give no indication that Gide equated the emperor with any specific individual, Gide's *Journal* suggests that the author did have someone in mind. In his diary entry of 4 February 1943, Gide discusses the German army's defeat at Stalingrad two days before. Of the "sacrificed" soldiers, he asks: "What could they have thought of Hitlerism and of Hitler during their agony? But what does Hitler think of himself?"[83] He then quotes Hugo: "Awakened, he descends the other slope of the dream" (J 4: 167) ["Il descend, réveillé, l'autre côté du rêve"] (J II: 896). In both the diary and the "Interviews," the first line becomes shorthand for the couplet, evoking the rhyming line and its portrayal of retribution.

Resemblance and repetition, the mainsprings of rhyme, are again at work when Gide praises Hugo's poem "L'Expiation" (I.I. 48). In this instance, however, the similarity and recurrence are historical in nature. "L'Expiation," a poem from the 1853 work *Les Châtiments*, consists of a litany of Napoleon's defeats. After each debacle, the poet asks whether this new humiliation is Napoleon's punishment for the coup d'état of the Eighteenth Brumaire. When the punishment finally comes, it is not Moscow, Waterloo, or the exile on Saint Helena. Rather, retribution takes the form of Bonaparte's nephew, who suppressed France's republican government in 1851, then had himself proclaimed Napoleon III. This derisive comparison between Napoleon Bonaparte and Louis Napoleon resembles the parallels outlined by Hugo's contemporary Karl Marx in his 1852 work *The Eighteenth Brumaire of Louis Bonaparte*: both Marx and Hugo see France's Second Empire as a parody of the first, Napoleon the Little as a contemptible imitator of Napoleon the Great.[84] Marx's *Eighteenth Brumaire* opens with the famous aphorism that history repeats itself, "the first time as tragedy, the second as farce" (15). Gide, too, implies that history is repeating itself: in this instance, Napoleon Bonaparte, who began his disastrous Russian campaign on 22 June 1812, is the historical model; Adolph Hitler, who started his Russian offensive on the same date in 1941, is the latter-day imitator. Like Napoleon's, Hitler's attempt to conquer Russia failed: Germany announced the suspension of its eastern campaign on 8 December 1941, attributing the halt to bad weather conditions (Snyder 174). The following week, *Le Figaro* published an "Interview" in which Gide refers to Hugo's "L'Expiation," a poem that opens with Napoleon's army retreating from Moscow across Russia's snowy plains:

> *Il neigeait. On était vaincu par sa conquête.*
> *Pour la première fois l'aigle baissait la tête.*
> (Hugo, *L'Œuvre* 409)

> [It snowed. A defeat was our conquest red!
> For once the eagle was hanging its head.]
> (Hugo, *Selected* 317)

Given the timing and the Reich's choice of an eagle as emblem, Hugo's depiction of a previous defeat might easily be construed as a comment on current events.[85]

Gide's extensive commentary on Hugo allows him to express a political position—one that is critical of the German dictatorship. It also allows him to revise an earlier literary position—one that was critical of Hugo. Having listened to Gide's praise for the Romantic poet, the interviewer asks him to explain why he once replied "Hugo, alas!" when asked to name the greatest French poet (I.I. 30).[86] Although he wishes for more rigor and authenticity in Hugo's lyrical works, Gide would make the same remark today; faced with the threat of Hugo's erasure, however, he defends the poet. Lest readers associate him with recent attacks on Hugo, Gide boldly mocks the poet's detractors: "should we not take them for what they are: the titans for titans, the dwarfs for dwarfs, and the pedants who attack Hugo for fools?" (I.I. 30).[87] While his aesthetic reservations have not altered, Gide now has political reasons to champion Hugo. The implications of this brief exchange extend far beyond public perceptions of a single poet. Indeed, this passage points to a theme that pervades the "Interviews imaginaires": Gide's changing political views and his regrets about earlier statements.

REVISIONS

In addition to staking out a position of cautious dissidence, the "Interviews imaginaires" tell the story of Gide's change of heart over the first two years of the war. With his customary honesty and a great deal of despair, Gide criticized his country and compatriots in the pages of his 1940 diary. He suggested, moreover, that France deserved—and should accept—her current lot. As the war progressed, the writer's opinions changed, and he came to regret the publication of early wartime *Journal* excerpts in Drieu La Rochelle's *Nouvelle Revue Française*. The "Interviews imaginaires" revisit Gide's thoughts from this early period, often taking a very different stance on the issues. One can trace the evolution of certain ideas through three distinct stages: the sometimes reactionary sincerity of the wartime diary, the pessimism and self-recriminations of the *N.R.F.* "Feuillets," and the cautious patriotism of the "Interviews imaginaires." Published as the tide of the war was turning, the "Interviews" seem designed to mitigate the negative impression left by the early wartime writings.[88]

Gide's comments on wartime rationing are among his most successful efforts to rewrite earlier infelicitous statements. In a July 1940 *Journal* entry, Gide observes: "To tell the truth, it is through the privations it involves, and only thereby, or almost, that the great majority will feel the defeat. Less sugar in one's coffee, and less coffee in one's cup—that is what they will feel" (J 4: 31).[89] Gide approaches the subject of restrictions in more moderate terms in his *N.R.F.* article of December 1940: "It is not given to so many Frenchmen to be constantly aware of the nation's great affliction. One is much more likely to experience individual sufferings; for most people, this means the inconvenience of the restrictions, the discomfort of exile, the fear of tomorrow's famine" (J 4: 30).[90] By the time he wrote the "Interviews" in 1941, Gide was using restrictions as a pretext for encouraging resistance. Explaining that he is suffering from tobacco rationing, Gide says he would like to stop smoking, but admits that he "yield[s] easily to temptations." "There is a new phrase today for yielding to temptations: people call it 'not saying no to life,'" the interviewer points out. But Gide refuses to fall for such sophistry: "To resist is a form of action," he replies firmly, "and [i]t isn't always by saying yes that we affirm our natures" (adapted from I.I. 10).[91] With deliberate ambiguity, Gide lets his meaning slip from his personal struggles with nicotine cravings to the more general concept of opposition. This transformation—from the 1940 accusation of petty selfishness to the 1941 exhortation to resist—constitutes one of Gide's more spectacular turnarounds.

Elsewhere, Gide uses literary shorthand in his attempts to rewrite unflattering observations about his fellow Frenchmen's patriotism. "The phrase 'my country' [*Patrie*] [. . .] is understood by both the mind and the heart," the writer declares: "I wish I could say as much for the word 'love'" (adapted from I.I. 12).[92] This assertion cleverly displaces the discussion of patriotism onto the notion of love. Gide's next move is to shift from the political to the literary register. Many French authors seem to be concerned only with love, he observes, lamenting: "if only [their characters] were exalted by love, as sometimes happens in life; if only it impelled men to heroism, women to virtue. [. . .] But for one *Princesse de Clèves*, there are a hundred *Manon Lescauts*" (adapted from I.I. 13–14).[93] The novels Gide cites present two very different conceptions of love: noble sacrifice and faithfulness in the face of temptation in one case, infidelity and crime in the other.[94] By declaring his preference for *La Princesse de Clèves*, Gide lets his literary judgment stand as an affirmation of patriotic loyalty—an affirmation meant to counterbalance his disparaging remarks on the inconstancy of love and patriotism in the diary and *N.R.F.* "Feuillets" (F 1: 84).

Gide further develops his rewriting of the "Feuillets" in his discussions of Tacitus, Goethe, and Renan. The passages on these authors attest to the cunning and inventiveness with which Gide transmitted his heterodox messages in an era of stringent censorship, for they exemplify the quotations, allusions, and fragments that make up the literary code of the "Interviews imaginaires." Yet allusions to these authors also illustrate the process of revision and reversal at work in the essays. In each case, it is the writer's life and historical circumstances, rather than his literary works, that hint at Gide's change of heart. The references to Tacitus and Renan, in particular, place the "Interviews" in the mode of retraction, revision, and regret.

Gide's discussion of Tacitus implicitly introduces the notion of remorse for past compliance. Prudence is a central theme of the *Life of Agricola*: throughout the work, Tacitus praises his father-in-law Agricola's political moderation. As Harold Mattingly argues, however, this defense of moderation may in fact be an apologia for Tacitus's own career as a senator:

Agricola had certainly never opposed the tyrannical Domitian. He was a great man as far as he was allowed to be, but he knew when he must submit. For Agricola the defence may be accepted as adequate; but the charge of subservience could equally well be levelled at Tacitus and his friends, and here the defence is less successful. They had suffered in silence, voting

> against their consciences for the condemnation of their friends.[95] They
> believed in the importance of their careers and felt no call to fruitless mar-
> tyrdom. But they were trying to make the best of both worlds—to survive
> under a bad emperor and to resume full rank as patriots under a good one.
> Tacitus's own conscience is obviously uneasy. (15)

Gide, like Tacitus, may have had a heavy conscience, regretting the accommodationist writings he had published early in the war. With an increasingly
organized resistance movement and the entry of the United States and Soviet
Union into the war, Gide, too, may have been preparing to take his role in a
postwar nation.

For a public figure, changing political circumstances may bring not only
a change of position but also concerns about the possible misuse of now-
rejected statements. Gide addresses this problem in the "Interviews" through
his discussion of the Strauss-Renan correspondence. Renan begins his 1871
letter to Strauss by situating his earlier missive within its historical context:
his first letter to the German scholar appeared in the *Journal des Débats* on
16 September 1870, just before the siege of Paris began (Renan 187–88;
Price 191).[96] He then declares that his views have changed in the intervening months: "In the past year I have experienced what always happens to
those who preach moderation in times of crisis. Events, as well as the opinions of the vast majority, have proven me wrong."[97] In addition to marking
his distance from the views he expressed a year before, Renan charges
Strauss with egregious misuse of his conciliatory 1870 letter, which Strauss
had translated and published in a brochure sold to benefit wounded German
veterans (190). Strauss's pamphlet led readers to believe that the French
writer supported this cause; moreover, it implied that Renan—whose accommodating letter in fact predated the siege of Paris—had condoned the attack
on the French capital. Portions of Gide's *Journal* were similarly misappropri-
ated during World War II. In his 1942 *Anthologie de la nouvelle Europe*, collaborationist writer Alfred Fabre-Luce reprinted pacifist excerpts from
Gide's interwar diary alongside writings by Drieu La Rochelle, Hitler, and
Mussolini. Gide's unauthorized "contribution," titled "Que serait-il advenu
si la France n'avait pas résisté à l'Allemagne?," consisted of two *Journal*
excerpts considering the benefits of nonresistance and quiet compliance
(266–67). By neglecting to date the entries accurately—they were from 19
September 1938 and 20 December 1915—Fabre-Luce seemed to imply that
Gide had welcomed the 1940 invasion.[98]

Establishing the historical and chronological context of earlier statements
is a primary concern for both Gide and Renan. In Gide's case, the question of
timing pertains not only to his interwar *Journal* but also to his post-Armistice
diary. As early as November 1940, Gide worried about the unclear chronology
of the *Journal* excerpts published in the *N.R.F.*: "I ought at least to have dated

(and left in chronological order) these *Feuillets* taken from my *Journal*, which I have just reread with displeasure in the issue of the resuscitated *N.R.F.* I am no longer in the same state of mind that made me write them" (adapted from J 4: 53–54).[99] In the "Interviews imaginaires," Gide deftly distances himself from his prior accommodationist stance by associating himself with Renan—another influential writer who experienced a change of heart.

Unlike the references to Renan and Tacitus—authors whose reversals and self-justifications simply invite readers to interpret the "Interviews" as a palinode—Gide's extended commentary on Goethe actually illustrates the author's efforts to touch up his public image. The "Introduction au Théâtre de Goethe" subtly alters the somewhat negative impression created by the numerous references to Goethe in the *N.R.F.* "Feuillets." Gide's stance in the "Introduction" is rather more critical, and the writer does not hesitate to express his discomfort with Goethe's conduct during the Napoleonic wars:

> We are a little embarrassed, or at least perplexed, by Goethe's attitude toward Napoleon, as well as by the opportunism [. . .] which caused him to display the Legion of Honor[100] on his breast, to the horror of his more patriotic fellow citizens, at a time when it would have seemed more fitting not to boast of his decoration and not to derive material advantages from something that wounded his country. But Goethe was still dazzled (as how could he fail to be?) by a dream that seemed on the point of being realized: the dream of a pacific and glorious unification of all Europe, one that might have cost most of the smaller states their autonomy and their reason for being, but that would have given at least to Weimar and at least to himself, Goethe, an even greater importance, while preserving all his liberty of thought—or so he believed. (I.I. 98)[101]

Having written of his bitter admiration for Hitler in his wartime diary, Gide probably anticipated negative comparisons between himself and Goethe.[102] On the one hand, this passage serves to distance Gide from the "opportunistic" German writer through its transparent critique of collaboration, for it is a small step from "Napoleon" to "Hitler," from "Weimar" to "France." On the other hand, the passage implicitly appeals for indulgence by presenting Goethe's reaction to the ideals of European unification as natural—"how could he fail to be [dazzled]?," asks Gide, whose own internationalist views left him open to charges of supporting Hitler's plan for Europe—and acknowledges the similarities between the two writers, each of whom believed he could retain his freedom of thought in a conquered nation (F 2: 348; I.I. 98).

Gide, like Goethe, initially believed that nothing could impinge on his freedom of thought. In his diary and *N.R.F.* "Feuillets," he argued that a politically restrictive atmosphere could benefit art and foster the life of the mind (F 2: 348). When Vichy authorities shut down two major periodicals, he went so far as to suggest that enforced silence could be beneficial:

> After *Temps nouveaux, Esprit* is reduced to silence.[103] (I propose as a motto for [*Esprit* editor Emmanuel] Mounier, both for his review and for the friends grouped around him: *Vires acquirit tacendo* ["He gains strength by keeping silent"[104]].) [. . .] I should almost say: This is proper. To begin with, we need order and discipline just as a seriously wounded man needs rest in order to get well. (J 4: 85–86)[105]

By the time his "Interviews" were published, however, Gide offered a very different take on this Latin motto. Developing an extended metaphor that associated poetry with opposition, he placed his hopes in the young "poets" who "are now holding their peace and allowing their thoughts and their qualities of heart to be fortified little by little in solitude and silence" (I.I. 39–40); "those upon whom we can count the most [. . .] are those who know how to wait, who mature as they wait. *Vires acquirit tacendo* is the best motto today."[106] Here Gide transforms the slogan he initially associated with submissive silence into a watchword for potential resisters.

By repeating the Latin motto in these vastly different contexts, Gide blurs the distinction between voluntary and enforced silence. His refusal—or inability—to make this distinction is one of the most confounding aspects of Gide's wartime writings. Throughout the Occupation, reports Pierre Herbart, Gide asserted that "*Art thrives on constraint and dies of freedom*—at a time when [. . .] we were facing harsh censorship." Herbart objected that Gide failed to differentiate between self-imposed stylistic constraints and the restrictions inflicted by Vichy censors. Gide, however, found both forces artistically productive: "the constraint I impose upon myself will lead me, if I have any talent, toward a certain perfection; that which others impose on me will compel me to invent the means to elude it. [. . .] Both forms of constraint will combine to form a scheme [*une combine*] allowing me to thumb my nose at that stupid, abject thing: power."[107] The "Interviews imaginaires" are an exemplary product of this dual constraint. Yet their very premise—the elaborate code that adapts to the constraints of censorship, even making an art of the necessary subterfuges—can be read as an attempt to rewrite the provocative remarks on oppression and artistic creation that Gide made at the outset of the war.

Gide's "Interviews imaginaires" are situated in an extremely rich textual network that functions at several levels. Beneath the literary criticism lies political critique; beneath the allusions to great authors, one finds Gide's efforts to retouch his own wartime writings. The change of heart first announced by Gide's break with the *N.R.F.* reaches its fullest expression in the "Interviews," in which the author overlays regrettable remarks from the early wartime diary with newer and more palatable commentary. This program of "spin control" prefigures the savvy editing that would characterize Gide's publications for the remainder of the Second World War.

FOUR

Battles on the Home Front

Domestic Allegory in the Tunis Journal

BY THE SPRING of 1942, food shortages and continued attacks in the press convinced Gide to leave the south of France for Tunisia. Tunis bookstore owner Marcel Tournier, whom Gide had befriended during his 1923 visit to North Africa, was instrumental in arranging the move. During a visit to Nice in March 1942, Tournier found the writer thin and anxious: "I no longer feel safe here. The press continues to unleash its fury at me; I am accused of having perverted French youth," Gide explained. Tournier persuaded his friend Admiral Esteva, the Resident General representing Vichy in the French protectorate, to facilitate Gide's passage to Tunis. "At least promise me that he will behave himself!"[1] Esteva joked. At first, Tournier thought that the admiral was referring to the possibility of subversive political activities on Gide's part; he soon realized, however, that Esteva had something very different in mind. Given Gide's advanced age, Tournier assured his friend, there was no cause to worry about sexual dalliances. Later, on reading Gide's account of his 1942–1943 stay in Tunis, Tournier would realize how much he had been mistaken (466–67).

Gide sailed from Marseille aboard the *Chanzy* on 4 May 1942, arriving in Tunis two days later (J II: 810, 814). He spent three weeks in the city, living at the Tunisia Palace hotel and working on his translation of *Hamlet* in the upstairs room of Marcel Tournier's bookstore La Rose de Sable (G/MG 245–46). Though he wrote enthusiastically of the abundance of food, Gide complained of the noise and heat in his letters to friends (CAG 11: 207; G/MG 251). Fortunately, he was soon able to leave his uncomfortable hotel for a pleasant villa in nearby Sidi-Bou-Saïd, where he was the guest of the Reymond de Gentile family: architect Théo Reymond and his ophthalmologist wife, their twenty-year-old daughter Suzy and fifteen-year-old son François. When Dr. Reymond de Gentile was diagnosed with a brain tumor in September 1942, her husband immediately accompanied her to Marseille for a life-saving operation. In November 1942, while she was convalescing, German forces invaded Tunisia and the formerly unoccupied south of France. Travel between France and North Africa became impossible, and the Reymonds were detained in France until December 1944 (DR 152). Gide would spend the six-month Tunisian occupation in the Reymonds' Tunis apartment with young François Reymond, his grandmother Chacha de Gentile, and the family servant Jeanne.

This chapter examines Gide's diary from the November 1942–May 1943 occupation of Tunis, focusing on the convergence of literature, politics, and sexuality in this portion of the *Journal*. After analyzing Gide's attempt to comprehend the war by means of a domestic allegory, discussion turns to François Reymond's subsequent bid to dislodge that explanation in *L'Envers du Journal de Gide: Tunis 1942–43*. The chapter then examines the events that forced Gide into hiding in the final months of the siege and concludes with the complex history of "La Délivrance de Tunis," Gide's account of the Allied liberation of the Tunisian capital.

GIDE'S TUNIS *JOURNAL*:
THE HISTORIC AND THE DOMESTIC

Gide's diary from the six-month occupation of Tunis differs from the rest of the wartime *Journal* in that the writer made entries on a nearly daily basis and attempted to chronicle the progress of the war. In May 1940, Gide had vowed not to discuss current events in his diary, though this choice meant that his entries were only sporadic (J II: 695). Three years later, as he looked back over his diary for the early months of 1943, Gide observed that his latest notebook "differ[ed] from the preceding ones, which I opened but intermittently and when the spirit moved. This last notebook became for me the buoy to which the shipwrecked man clings. There can be felt in it that daily effort to remain afloat" (J 4: 178).[2] Daily writing became one of the author's few means of sustaining his spirits.

Gide experienced the siege of Tunis with a mixture of anxiety and exhilaration. During most air raids, he scorned the relative safety of the cellar: "Three different times from the living-room window I watched at length the strange illuminations in the sky," he wrote on 14 December. Likening the tracer bullets to "glorious fireworks," Gide describes his "[s]avage, elementary state of excitement, as irrepressible as it is somehow shameful, [that] results from the havoc" (J 4: 139–40).[3] Excitement also mitigated his concerns about loved ones in Europe. With mail between France and Tunisia suspended, Gide worried about family and friends, but his distress was intermittent:

At times, but not always, I curse the beastly idea I had of coming here; then I think anxiously of those I left in France and shall perhaps not see again; I am worried by that increasing obscurity enveloping them, hiding them, stifling [us. . . .] But at times also I congratulate myself on being at a point where a perhaps decisive contest is taking place or is about to take place. (J 4: 177)[4]

Curious about the outcome of this crucial episode of the war, Gide twice declined offers of repatriation.[5]

Although Gide appreciated the historical importance of his situation, living in the occupied city meant that he had little access to meaningful news of the war. The lack of reliable information was a great source of anxiety for Gide: "I bend over the radio as often as six times a day with that childish illusion that my excessive attention is going somehow to hasten events" (J 4: 157).[6] He listened hungrily to radio bulletins in French, German, English, and Italian, except when frequent power cuts deprived him even of these biased reports (J II: 938, 870). Though he sought news obsessively, Gide found newspapers,[7] radio broadcasts, and official communiqués so full of propaganda that he complained of an "atmosphere of organized falsehood" (J 4: 139).[8] Nevertheless, he made a point of recording what information he could obtain, even if it was scanty or specious. As Justin O'Brien has observed, the Tunis episode is the most journalistic portion of Gide's diary, yet the writer says little of substance about the events of the war: his account is "a marginal history of events recorded by an eyewitness whose vision was necessarily limited" (Introduction vii).

Lacking substantive information about events, Gide filled his notebook with a running account of his daily interactions with young François Reymond, whom he calls "Victor" in the *Journal*. The hardships of the Axis occupation were bearable, Gide found, but sharing quarters with the teenager was almost intolerable: "Victor enjoys poisoning this life in common, which might be charming, despite the privations, if everyone showed a will." According to Gide, Victor is both egotistical—"his selfishness is manifest, resolute, cynical: he professes it"—and slovenly, "soil[ing] the toilet seat with his dung." Worst of all, he is insolent to his grandmother and to his elderly house guest: refusing to speak to Gide, Victor "seems to have no other concern than to show his scorn flagrantly" (J 4: 143, 153, 192, 167).[9] Gide's unsparing portrait clearly reflects the strain of sharing living quarters with near strangers under stressful wartime conditions. However, the portrait of Victor was never a wholly private matter: almost from the outset, it was charged with social symbolism.

Gide first sketched a portrait of François Reymond in a September 1942 letter to Roger Martin du Gard (G/MG 269–70). His friend responded enthusiastically: "the portrait of François[10] is very well done! And it goes *far beyond* an individual case. It is one of the models [. . .] of the 'youth' whom all the world leaders are trying to seduce, displaying all the Machiavellianisms of their propaganda."[11] Martin du Gard, who had previously urged Gide to devote more attention to his *Journal*, encouraged him to develop his portrait of the boy. This favorable response prompted Gide to resume writing in his diary: "your kind compliments have encouraged me and, spurred on by you, I have reopened my *Journal*," he informed his friend.[12]

Though this exchange took place in September and October 1942, Gide did not in fact write his first *Journal* entry on Victor until 7 December—that is, one week after recording the occupation of the city by German and Italian forces.[13] Appearing approximately once every three days from early December through the end of March, the twenty-five Victor entries are coextensive with the occupation of Tunis. This domestic chronicle is clearly a substitute for the military and political narrative to which Gide was denied access, for the writer made many of his Victor entries on days when power cuts, transparent propaganda, and conflicting reports left him with no war news to record.[14] Moreover, Gide's anxiety about the war's progress and the lack of contact with friends in Europe is displaced onto and reinforced by his distress at François Reymond's hostile silence. The convergence of these two concerns is confirmed by the final Victor entry Gide made before leaving the Reymond household: "Yesterday Victor deigned to break his silence for a moment to announce to us the occupation of Gabès" (J 4: 196).[15] As the boy sets aside some of his hostility to share news of an Allied victory, the domestic and historic conflicts intersect in a brief moment of détente. Thus, the *Journal*'s Victor episode is closed by a momentary truce—an atypical respite that fails to resolve either the domestic or the military conflict, but underscores their interdependence in Gide's diary.

GIDE VERSUS VICTOR: THE WAR *EN ABYME*

The fact that the *Journal*'s treatment of domestic conflict takes the place of a substantive historical account is an artifact of the war and of the information blackout it imposed. Yet Gide did not write about Victor *instead* of the war; rather, he wrote about the war *through* Victor. The semifictionalized portrait of François Reymond is Gide's attempt to comment on the causes of the war, albeit indirectly and on a small scale; it is also a reflection on the accounts of causality and influence propounded by Gide's attackers. Justin O'Brien addresses the symbolic dimension of this character sketch by describing Victor as "a portable microcosm of all that was distasteful in the world around [the author]" (Introduction vii). But Gide's portrait of Victor is far more than a social stereotype or a generalized symbol of what was wrong with the world: it is a harsh, precise allegory of pre-World War II France as the writer perceived it—an allegory in which the boy comes to represent "degenerate" interwar France.

The allegory begins with the pseudonym Gide chose for the boy. François Reymond is the only person in the Tunis diary whom Gide does not call by his real name or by the ubiquitous "X." Perhaps, as Martine Sagaert suggests, the name was inspired by the resemblances Gide perceived between the boy and Victor Strouvilhou, the leader of the counterfeiting band in his novel *Les Faux-Monnayeurs* (Introduction xxiii–xiv). This is not the only source of the name, however. I would like to propose an alternate derivation based on history and etymology. By changing the boy's name from François (Frenchman [*Français*]) to Victor (*vainqueur*), Gide comments on France's decadence following World War I. The French were victors in the First World War and, according to Gide, they abused this status. Remarks to this effect abound in Gide's *Journal* for the months after the fall of France: "We should not have won the other war. That false victory deceived us. We were not able to endure it. The relaxing that followed it brought us to our ruin"; "it would have been much better for [. . . France] had she been conquered in 1918 rather than to win that deceptive victory which put the finishing touches on her blindness and put her to sleep in decadence" (J 4: 23, 36).[16] Gide portrays François Reymond in a similar light: because the boy has never been punished, he behaves atrociously, dominating his parents and lording it over their elderly guest (J II: 884). When it comes to bad behavior, Gide depicts France and François in similar terms.

Like Victor, who was spoiled by his parents, the French people had been corrupted by excessive indulgence, in Gide's opinion. The connection between childrearing and the nation's welfare was surely present to his mind as he penned his first Victor entries, for in December 1942 he was reading *Émile*, Rousseau's blueprint for educating children to be citizens (J II: 858). Gide began pondering this link before meeting François Reymond: "I have always thought that we raise children badly in France," he declared in April 1942, after watching a group of children ransack a public park as their parents sat idly by. What is significant about this *Journal* entry is the political conclusion Gide draws from his observations: "Is this a question of the French temperament? Or merely, as I should prefer, of upbringing? Nation unworthy of the liberty they claim" (J 4: 104–05).[17] The writer proposed rigorous discipline for both the child and the nation.[18] Reflecting on his own attempts to correct Victor's behavior, Gide draws a political lesson from his reforming bent: "It is that constant [. . .] need [. . .] of correcting, of reforming [*redresser*], not only myself but others that often made me so unbearable [. . .] but that would make me, I think, so good a citizen of a real republic" (J 4: 195).[19] Thus, Gide uses his concerns about Victor's upbringing to promote the image of himself as a model citizen and educator—as the opposite, that is, of a *mauvais maître* (corrupting mentor).

The overindulgent parents were not solely to blame for Victor's behavior: according to the elderly Gide, the boy was also swayed by his classmate

Lévy. On 24 February 1943, when Victor had refused to speak to him for a week, Gide wrote: "His behavior toward me, I could swear, is prompted by his friend Lévy [*le camarade Lévy*], who wanders about the apartment daily, or almost, without speaking to anyone, who is inculcating in him the principles of Marxism, confirming him in his egoism and providing solid foundations for his spontaneous caddishness" (J 4: 179).[20] If Victor stands for decadent inter-war France, "Comrade Lévy" represents the "corrupting" influence of communists and Jews. Presenting Lévy as a deleterious influence brings Gide's domestic allegory very close to widespread right-wing explanations for France's decline and defeat. I do not mean to suggest that Gide subscribed wholeheartedly to such explanations; rather, I propose to compare this model with the views Gide expressed elsewhere in order to elucidate the purpose of the *Journal*'s domestic allegory.

Though he deserted communism in 1936, Gide did not vilify French communists, nor did he blame them for France's defeat in 1940. However, the writer's own communist sympathies were held against him by his post-Armistice attackers. Indeed, the most significant aspect of Gide's domestic scenario may be precisely that it reproduces the phobic reaction of his accusers—while placing the blame elsewhere. Accused of inspiring French youth with a taste for excessive freedom and individualism, the author of *Les Nourritures terrestres* presents himself as a model disciplinarian; taxed with weakening the nation through his support of communism, the "bourgeois would-be Bolshevik"[21] portrays himself as a victim shunned by hostile Marx-ists. In his role as communist propagandist, Lévy clearly serves the allegory's exteriorizing function. The picture is somewhat more complex, however, if we read Lévy as a symbol of Jewish influence.

In his Tunis diary, Gide does not blame his country's predicament on the Jews any more than on the communists—quite the reverse, in fact, for it was during his stay in Tunisia that Gide became aware of the brutal treatment to which Jews were being subjected. From Roger Martin du Gard, he learned of the mass arrests in the south of France: "you undoubtedly know about the pogroms which are terrifying the Riviera, the round-ups of foreign Jews, bru-tal and massive deportations, children separated from their parents, etc., before the eyes of an indignant but powerless and passive population."[22] Wit-nessing such abuses himself in occupied Tunisia, Gide repeatedly decried the sanctions inflicted on the Jewish population. He was particularly scandalized by notices informing Jewish residents that they would have to pay a fine of twenty million francs "as an aid to the victims of the Anglo-American bomb-ings, *for which they are responsible*, 'international Jewry' having, as it has long been well known, 'wanted and prepared for the war'" (J 4: 144).[23] Although Gide had always rejected such thinking outright, he had made his share of unambiguously anti-Semitic pronouncements over the years. His anti-Semi-tism most often related to literary issues: "there is today in France a Jewish literature that is not French literature," Gide asserted in a January 1914 *Journal* entry, developing his allegation that "the contribution of Jewish qualities to literature [. . .] is less likely to provide new elements [. . .] than it is to interrupt [*coupe[r] la parole à*] the slow explanation of a race [the French 'race'] and to falsify seriously, intolerably even, its meaning" (J 2: 4).[24] In the World War II diary, Victor's mentor Lévy embodies Gide's long-standing fear that Jewish influence might warp—and perhaps silence—France's "authentic" voice.[25] Despite Gide's empathy and outrage for the persecuted Jews, the *Journal's* domestic allegory betrays anxieties and animosities that the author could not fully repress.

The figure of Lévy makes the domestic scenario a site for reflecting on issues of literary and political influence—not just Lévy's influence, but Gide's own as well. Though couched in literary terms, Gide's anti-Semitism was nonetheless political, for his 1914 pronouncement on Jewish literature frames the issue in terms of race and portrays Jews as a threat to French culture. Gide was not blind to the political consequences of such statements: indeed, his 1938 review of *Bagatelles pour un massacre* reflects his uneasy awareness of the political ends that literary anti-Semitism could be made to serve ("Les Juifs" 634). His own writings proved to be no exception: the January 1914 diary entry "would regularly be trotted out by the French Right during the wave of anti-Semitism that greeted [Jewish statesman Léon] Blum and the Popular Front from 1936 through the Second World War" (Mehlman, *Legacies* 65). Vichy's most right-wing elements were using Gide's prewar anti-Semitism in ways he would never have condoned, while simultaneously excoriating him for the influence he had exerted through his defense of homosexuality—especially of man–boy relations. The question of pederasty, significantly absent from the diary's domestic vignette, would be reintroduced by François Reymond in his 1951 response to Gide's Tunis *Journal.*

COMPETING STORIES:
FRANÇOIS REYMOND'S RESPONSE

On publication of Gide's *Journal 1942–1949* in 1950, Maria Van Rysselberghe reported that "young V[ictor], whom Gide discusses so painfully in the latest volume of the *Journal* [. . .], is mad with rage and swears he will have his revenge."[26] François Reymond's revenge took the form of a book chronicling his side of the domestic battle. Using the pseudonym "François Derais,"[27] Reymond published *L'Envers du Journal de Gide: Tunis 1942–43* in December 1951, several months after Gide's death. In many respects, Reymond's unflattering portrayal of the elderly writer is a point-by-point response to Gide's depiction of him as a boy. Mutual accusations range from stinginess to bad table manners to monopolizing the affections of the family cat (J II: 881, 884, 904; DR 174, 123, 180–82). Many of the reciprocal criticisms relate to the privations of the war: each man accuses the other of hoarding food and help-ing himself to the best of the household's meager rations (J II: 881, 876, 877; DR 199, 203). Other criticisms convey the power struggle between Gide and Reymond: the man and the boy accuse each other of autocratic and incon-siderate behavior, and each says the other considers himself "the master here" (J 4: 160).[28] In this game of tit for tat, Reymond's harsh and sometimes child-ish criticisms of the well-known author serve to highlight the pettiness of Gide's own remarks about Victor in the *Journal*.

At the heart of Reymond's memoirs, however, lies an accusation that is anything but trivial: on 25 July 1942, Reymond claims, Gide sexually assaulted him. Young François, whom Gide describes as "terribly well-informed,"[29] was aware that Gide, like many men in his family's social circle, was homosexual. Though he had sometimes noticed "certain glances, certain innuendoes" which he "interpreted as discreet invitations" from family friends, those acquaintances "had always behaved toward me with perfect decency." Despite these previous advances and his knowledge of Gide's sex-ual orientation, Reymond initially considered the writer to be "a prestigious old man whose advanced age could only render him harmless in the field of carnal baseness." François realized he had been mistaken when he repeatedly witnessed Gide's behavior with the gardener's ten-year-old son Moktar. As the boy watered the flower beds, Reymond reminds his former house guest, "you stood behind him, [. . .] with your hand on his shoulder [. . .] your hand [. . .] moved back and forth, sometimes kneading, sometimes pulling the child toward you abruptly, sometimes, on the contrary, relaxing so as merely to graze his nipples."[30] The boy, afraid to move, kept watering the same spot; when his employer expressed his dissatisfaction with Moktar's work, the boy was relieved of his duties.

Deprived of access to Moktar, Gide turned his attentions elsewhere. With his "still childish, at times almost charming face" (J 4: 150),[31] fifteen-year-old François was "choice prey."[32] On a hot July day, Reymond recalls,

> [Y]ou found me reading, lying on the living room sofa, wearing only a short-sleeved shirt and very short shorts. [. . .] Under the totally phony pretext of taking an interest in what I was reading, do you remember what you did? We were almost alone then in the big house, and this time it involved more than just a shoulder. [. . .] I was restrained only by the fear that my mother might find out about it and question me, and that I would have to speak with her about what my immense modesty [. . .] commanded me to hush up. I finally managed to extricate myself without making a scene; barely in time, if I am to judge by your face and your extreme agitation! [. . .] That evening, I dared look no one in the eyes.[33]

A few days later, Gide made a second attempt, which François firmly rejected (DR 141).[34] His fear of further advances, Reymond explains, was at the root of his hostility toward Gide: "I assiduously avoided your company"; "I was terribly frightened that you would renew your advances."[35] Feeling increasingly vulnerable after his parents' departure for Marseille, François bolted his bedroom door at night, avoided being alone with Gide during the day, and made himself generally disagreeable so that the elderly visitor would keep his distance (DR 179, 202).

Though his *Journal* makes no mention of the assault described by Reymond, Gide did not deny the younger man's allegations. Reymond wrote his memoirs at the suggestion of Jean Amrouche, who had introduced Gide to the Reymond family, and to whom the young man had confided the reasons for his animosity toward Gide.[36] Amrouche subsequently showed Reymond's manuscript to Gide, who took exception to a few specific points but did not object to the substance of the text or to its publication (DR 145, 95, 260).[37] Gide and Reymond may not have disagreed on the events that transpired between them, but their interpretation of those events differed tremendously. Whereas Reymond experienced the older man's actions as abuse, Gide had a positive, even idealized conception of man–boy relations. The title character of his 1924 treatise *Corydon* asserts that the influence of a lover and mentor can be highly beneficial for a young boy: "the passionate attachment of an older man, or of a friend of the same age [. . .] can be the [child's] best incentive to courage, to exertion, to virtue." Moreover, *Corydon* portrays homosexuality as a civic virtue: "without going so far as to claim with Lycurgus [. . .] that a citizen cannot be honest and useful to the state unless he has a friend [lover], I do claim that uranism in and of itself is in no way harmful to law and order [*au bon ordre de la société, de l'État*]—quite the contrary" (*Corydon* [Eng.] 123–24, 119).[38] The ideals of *Corydon* resonate throughout the Tunis *Journal*,[39] in which Gide reflects on education and the state and describes his desire to mentor young Victor—who comes to represent a generation and, indeed, the French nation.

In contrast to Gide—who undoubtedly saw his advances as neutral or even beneficial—Reymond portrays the "unsuccessful fondling"[40] as a violation. His emphasis on aggression, sexual and otherwise (DR 189), leads us to the most significant feature of *L'Envers du Journal*—its reversal of Gide's political allegory. Scholars have, for the most part, ignored or dismissed Reymond's memoirs as inaccurate or gratuitous: Justin O'Brien implies that Reymond's claims are fallacious, and refers to *L'Envers du Journal* as a "painful and unnecessary little book" (*Portrait* 272); Armand Guibert gives credence to Reymond's narrative, but describes the book as "malicious gossip collected [. . .] between two covers."[41] More interesting than questions of truthfulness or taste, however, is the way in which *L'Envers du Journal* responds to the historical allegory in Gide's Tunis *Journal*, offering a rebuttal to Gide's narrative while underscoring the diary's capacity to produce political discourse.

The lexicon Reymond uses to describe his relationship with Gide is that of war: he refers to their interactions as "hostilities" and "combat," as a "struggle" and as "our battle"; he describes André Gide as "the adversary" and "the crafty enemy."[42] Through abundant and varied war imagery, Reymond constructs his struggle with Gide as a battle. In so doing, he proposes an allegory that challenges Gide's own symbolic presentation of the domestic conflict. Reymond's memoirs recast the domestic battle as an allegory not of the interwar years but of the Occupation itself—an allegory in which his adolescent self represents the resistance, his grandmother Chacha stands for the Vichy government, and Gide, the aggressive house guest, assumes the role of the occupier. Because his aims differ from Gide's, Reymond reverses the relation of the historic and the domestic in his allegory. In his *Journal*, Gide uses the personal to understand the political, making his treatment of the domestic quarrel serve as commentary on France's social and political situation. Reymond, on the other hand, uses the historical conflict to make claims about the domestic situation, refuting Gide's portrayal of the quarrel by emphasizing the older man's role as aggressor.[43]

In François Reymond's memoirs, Gide is portrayed not only as an attacker but also as an occupier, a constant and threatening presence. Gide is an unwelcome interloper—"throughout your stay on the avenue Roustan, I never for an instant ceased to consider you an intruder and a parasite"—and his friends are invaders: "your friends [. . .] had invaded us."[44] This invasion was not benign, for a brutal sacrifice followed the writer's arrival: the Reymonds had the gardener kill François's dog Tommy, whose barking prevented Gide from sleeping (DR 122).[45] Expansionism followed on the heels of assault, as Gide moved from the Reymonds' vacation home in Sidi-Bou-Saïd to their apartment on the avenue Roustan in Tunis, though he had not been invited to do so (DR 165). Accommodating this unwelcome long-term guest carried a financial burden like that of the Occupation: during his parents' absence, the household finances were precarious, Reymond says, and Gide contributed only "a paltry sum."[46] Though Gide claims to have shared household expenses with the boy's grandmother,[47] Reymond contends that Chacha was living "entirely at my parents' expense, and you were too!" If Gide represents the German occupier, François's grandmother personifies the Vichy government, an illegitimate authority that welcomed the intruder. Gide, who implies that he was Chacha's guest in Tunis, moved into the flat "knowing full well that Chacha had no right to make arrangements concerning the apartment." Without the old woman's cooperation, Gide might not have installed himself so firmly in the family's territory, Reymond implies, adding: "I had difficulty forgiving my grandmother for betraying the family a little."[48]

Gide, of course, presents the situation quite differently: he justifies his presence in the Reymond apartment by portraying himself as Chacha's protector. Having heard of Gide's plans to leave the Reymond apartment in February 1943, Chacha was "terrified at the idea of having to remain alone with her terrible grandson" and begged the writer to stay.[49] If Gide were to leave, Chacha threatened, both she and the family servant Jeanne would go as well, and the empty apartment would be occupied by the Germans (J 4: 176–77). Gide's decision to remain therefore appears altruistic and patriotic. Reymond counters that the penniless Chacha had nowhere else to go, and points out that neither Jeanne nor Chacha left when Gide went into hiding in April 1943.[50] He suggests, moreover, that Gide might better have repaid the family's hospitality by staying in Sidi-Bou-Saïd: the villa there, which remained empty, was pillaged during the Tunisian occupation (DR 167, 170–71).

Despite the men's opposing views on who was in the right, much of what Reymond suggests is implicit in Gide's diary. Gide's desire to discipline and improve Victor recalls the common notion that France would benefit from German discipline; his conception of himself as Chacha's protector also echoes prevalent justifications for the Occupation. Furthermore, Gide knew that François considered him an intruder and realized that Chacha's cooperation irritated the boy. He also suspected that young François's actions were designed to drive him out of the Reymond home (J II: 887)—but what Gide saw as adolescent spite was, in Reymond's eyes, a concerted program of "résistance" (DR 253).

Reymond's sexual rebuff was, in itself, a form of resistance. During and after the Occupation, sexual metaphors for collaboration abounded. The analogy takes its mildest form in Vercors's *Le Silence de la mer*, where the sympathetic German officer von Ebrennac hopes that the French Beauty will overcome her initial repugnance for the German Beast, thus transforming him into a handsome knight (41–42). In a similar vein but without the trappings of fairy-tale romance, Robert Brasillach, the only French writer sentenced to death during the postwar purge, declared: "All thinking Frenchmen, during those years, more or less slept with Germany."[51] Conveniently rejecting Brasillach's assertion that everybody had jumped into bed with the occupier, Jean-Paul Sartre effectively marginalized collaborators by branding them sexual deviants in his postwar essay "Qu'est-ce qu'un collaborateur?":

> Throughout Chateaubriant's, Drieu's, and Brazillach's (sic) articles one can notice queer metaphors which present Franco-German relations in the guise of a sexual union in which France plays the woman's part. And the feudal relationship between the collaborator and his master most certainly has a sexual aspect. Insofar as one can comprehend the collaborator's state of mind, one senses an atmosphere of femininity. [. . .] It seems to me that it contains a strange mixture of masochism and homosexuality. Moreover, the homosexual circles in Paris supplied numerous and brilliant recruits.[52]

In the postwar climate that condemned collaboration as "sleeping with the enemy" and explicitly related collaboration to homosexuality, François Reymond's rejection of Gide's sexual advances stands as a token of resistance.

The image of Reymond's conduct as resistance is supported by the teenager's actual involvement in subversive wartime activities. Reymond's friend Lévy—the classmate whose influence Gide so deplored—introduced him to the Jeunesses Communistes de Tunisie, which he joined in the spring of 1942 (DR 215). Joining the communist youth group represented a significant change in the boy's allegiances: "I belonged to the Vichy youth movement Les Compagnons de France, but I was persuaded to abandon those ideas and join the opposition to the regime then in power; a taste for danger, the appeal of the unknown, and also, whatever you may think, the noble ideas of social justice presented to me persuaded me to make this total about-face."[53] François's resistance activities consisted mainly of drawing graffiti featuring the communist hammer and sickle and the Gaullist croix de Lorraine as well as posting bills emblazoned with "incisive slogans about the occupiers and their henchmen."[54] François and his companions also distributed the clandestine newspaper *L'Avenir Social*,[55] and they tried to procure French identity cards for Jews and others forced to live underground. Reymond downplays the risk inherent in these activities, suggesting that he viewed the whole business as an exciting game. He admits that he confined most of his exploits to his own home, drawing graffiti only in the stairwell of his own building (DR 219) and stealing an identity card that family friends would willingly have given him.[56]

In Reymond's account, there is little difference between official resistance activities and his boyish program of domestic opposition. The most dramatic aspect of his home-front maneuvers was an extensive program of household espionage. After stating that his family was "separated into two camps" and that he used to "spy on the enemy," Reymond uses the lexicon of a military strategist to portray his forays into Gide's territory. He admits going into Gide's room in the writer's absence "in order to read [his] Journal in secret, and thus obtain some information about the enemy's morale."[57] Reymond makes it clear that his spying was of a specifically literary nature: denying the accusation that he broke the lock of Gide's trunk, he states that he was interested only in Gide's diary, which the writer left in plain sight on his desk (J II: 927; DR 186). Taking notes on the manuscript diary provided Reymond with ammunition he would later use to question the *Journal*'s veracity: "you modify your diary somewhat after the fact, as I was able to ascertain by comparing the published *Journal* with my memory of the passages I read furtively" during the war. Claiming that certain passages concerning himself were added, deleted, or altered in the published *Journal*—an allegation the diary manuscript tends to corroborate—Reymond maintains that the objectivity of the original diary was marred by Gide's desire to confirm his views on Victor's character.[58] I would argue, moreover, that Gide's alterations served the political project of the Tunis *Journal* by making the household conflict correspond more neatly to the political drama of interwar France.

With *L'Envers du Journal*, François Reymond attempts to beat Gide at his own game, constructing a political allegory that presents the author in a most unfavorable light. His efforts to redress the power imbalance between Gide and himself are not confined to the wartime *Journal*, however: in fact, Reymond mobilizes much of Gide's fictional and autobiographical oeuvre to comment on the writer's conduct and the fictionalizing project of the Tunis diary.

THE POWER OF LITERATURE:
GIDE'S OEUVRE AND THE DOMESTIC DRAMA

Gide's stature as a writer was a source of power, and his celebrity helped him gain access to young sexual partners: "I have no doubt that your fame and your advanced age have accustomed you to greater docility in the young subjects which chance delivers into your hands," writes François Reymond. In his own case, Reymond asserts, Gide abused his position of power: "you vilely deceived my parents, abused my trust in your prestige as an old man 'wreathed in glory.'"[59] There was always an inherent power imbalance between Gide and his young sexual partners: in addition to the difference in age, there were often differences of race, class, and nationality, as well as economic and educational discrepancies. Pierre Herbart attributes Gide's choice of partners to a fear of rejection: "his choice of little partners (children of the lower classes, those who do not speak his language, blacks) with whom only a physical exchange is possible reduces the potential for disappointment."[60] Another important reason for this choice was that Gide invariably had the last word in describing—or concealing—such encounters. Unlike the "children of the lower classes," however, François Reymond was able to talk back to Gide.

At age twenty-four, this highly literate son of a bourgeois family had the power and education to respond to Gide's sexual abuse and the harsh depiction of himself in the *Journal*. Ironically, one source of Reymond's ability to respond was Gide's own influence. In the afterword to *L'Envers du Journal*, Reymond acknowledges his intellectual debt to Gide: "throughout the process of writing these memoirs, I have been constantly aware of everything that my thoughts and reactions owe to you, as much to yourself as to your oeuvre. Why deny it? Those whom I respected in my youth, those to whom I owe some part of my present intellectual character, were your disciples."[61] Throughout *L'Envers du Journal*, power issues are played out around Gide's oeuvre. In fact, Reymond's memoirs, Gide's Tunis *Journal*—and, to a certain extent, the quarrel that those texts recount—are interwoven with Gide's fictional and autobiographical writings.

On learning that Gide would be staying with his family, says Reymond, "my first step was to carry into my room two or three of your books, [. . .] which I began to read or reread, in order (I originally hoped) to take full advantage of your presence." One lesson the boy had clearly learned from his reading concerned Gide's predilection for young boys; indeed, he interpreted a family friend's allusions to Gide's writings as a come-on: "Eugène K. [. . .] had asked me, with a curious insistence in his voice and his eyes, if I had read Gide's books, what I thought of them, etc."[62] François's knowledge gave him a degree of power over Gide. After reading *Si le grain ne meurt*—the autobiographical text that describes Gide's first pederastic experiences during his travels in North Africa some fifty years before—the boy stayed up late to confront the author. Baited by the smirking adolescent, Gide acknowledges—then swiftly dismisses—his attraction: "any desire to fondle him quickly gave way to a desire to box his ears once I heard his insolent remarks."[63]

In his memoirs, as in his interactions with the author, Reymond uses Gide's writings against him. Because *L'Envers du Journal* is explicitly intended as a rebuttal to Gide's diary, Reymond includes numerous quotes and footnotes referencing the *Journal 1942–1949*, but he also makes potent use of quotations from Gide's fictional oeuvre. Reymond first uses his own words to describe his reaction to Gide's assault: "Ah, you never knew how I rushed into the bathroom, soaped up, scrubbed myself with a scrub brush so hard that I bled, washing so feverishly that I repeatedly banged into the faucet and the bathtub walls." He follows this explanation with a hauntingly similar quotation from Gide's *récit La Porte étroite*, in which the young Jérôme reacts violently to his aunt's unwanted caresses:

> "she drew my face down to hers, passed her bare arm around my neck, put her hand into my shirt, asked me laughingly if I was ticklish—went on—further. [. . .] I rushed away to the other end of the kitchen-garden, and there I dipped my handkerchief into a little tank, put it to my forehead—washed, scrubbed—my cheeks, my neck, every part of me the woman had touched." (Gide, *Strait* 19–20)
>
> One couldn't put it better, Jérôme . . . except that you were not a pretty young aunt.[64]

Here Reymond appropriates some of the writer's power and authority by reading Gide's actions through his oeuvre.

Gide's power as a writer was indeed considerable. As Martine Sagaert has argued, the author-protagonist of the Tunis *Journal* resembles the novelist Édouard in *Les Faux-Monnayeurs*, transforming himself and those around him into literary characters. Sagaert supports this assertion by demonstrating the similarities between Gide's portrait of Victor and the piggish Gnathon in La Bruyère's *Caractères*: like Gnathon, Victor occupies more than his share of space at table, serves himself first, eats with his fingers, and picks his teeth (Introduction xxii–xxiii; J II: 884; La Bruyère 329). The Tunis *Journal*'s most important intertexts, however, are drawn from Gide's own oeuvre. Afraid of the frequent bombings, François's grandmother Chacha spends every night in a tiny cloakroom. Gide compares her to Blanche Monnier, whose case he had chronicled in *La Séquestrée de Poitiers*. Like Monnier, who begged to return to the room where her family had kept her hidden for twenty-five years, Chacha "speaks of her little storeroom where she takes refuge as the sequestered girl in Poitiers used to speak of her 'dear big black Malampia'" (J 4: 155).[65] Though the comparison with the sequestered madwoman is hardly flattering, Gide is merely pointing out similarities between Chacha and another real-life woman he described in a nonfictional text. Chacha's grandson, on the other hand, becomes fodder for Gide's fictionalizing enterprise. In an October 1942 letter to Roger Martin du Gard, Gide acknowledges that a more fully developed portrait of François would be, in part, a work of fiction: "nothing is more banal or easier to invent than the characteristics of selfish cynicism."[66] Referring to this cynical selfishness in the *Journal*, Gide explicitly considers the boy as a potential source of fictional material: "Had I known him earlier, I should have enriched with his features the Strouvilhou of my *Faux-Monnayeurs*" (J 4: 153).[67] What Gide does not acknowledge is the extent to which Strouvilhou's traits and those of other fictional characters color his portrait of Victor, and the extent to which his literary and political agenda informs his depiction of the boy.

In *L'Envers du Journal*, François Reymond exposes Gide's fictionalizing project and rewrites the Tunis episode from his own perspective: "For the first time perhaps, one of your characters, part real and part invented, has spoken up in response and told his story himself."[68] One of the elements Reymond attempts to debunk is Gide's lyrical description of a brief liaison with fifteen-year-old "F.": "This past June in Tunis, I experienced two nights of pleasure such as I thought never to encounter again at my age," Gide wrote in August 1942. Gide stresses the boy's gratitude—"[h]is entire being sang out: 'thank you'"—and declares that the age difference was no impediment: "He seemed to care so little about my age that I came to forget it myself."[69] "Ah, I know of another boy who did care about [your age]," Reymond retorts in *L'Envers du Journal*.[70] He contends that the adventure with "F." is a fabrication and suggests that the episode is a displaced version of Gide's unsuccessful attempts to seduce him:[71] "By an unfortunate coincidence, his initial is also the initial of my first name; but is that even a coincidence?"[72] François's initial comes to designate a willing young lover, and François himself is rebaptized "Victor"— a name that links him to a despicable fictional character and makes him a symbol of a corrupt and tainted nation.

Gide's fictionalization of Victor is a bid for control and an attempt to deny the real reasons for the boy's animosity. Throughout the Tunis *Journal*, Gide tries to explain away the boy's hostility: "For my obnoxious attitude, for the fact that I was insolent, selfish, and deceptive toward you, you give a variety of rather fanciful explanations," writes Reymond.[73] Most of these explanations are deterministic in nature. Rather than admit that the boy's rebuffs might be a form of protest, Gide dismisses his surliness as an inborn trait: "I convince myself that this is merely a result of his natural caddishness" (J 4: 167). He even suggests that the boy's behavior is hereditary: when a neighbor mentions that he has never received a smile or greeting from Théo Reymond, Gide muses, "How can Victor, who so closely resembles his father, endure being to such a degree the prisoner of his heredity? In his stubborn silence toward me there is perhaps less resolve than surrender to his natural inclination" (J 4: 199).[74] Contemplating the boy's physical development as well as his character, Gide repeatedly states that the boy is prepubescent.[75] Though the *Journal* does not mention Gide's sexual advances or François's rejection, Reymond's memoirs make the connection explicit: "If I don't want to have sex with you, it's not, of course, because the idea doesn't appeal to me, but because I am prepubescent!"[76] Unwilling to face the true source of the boy's animosity, Gide generates alternative explanations; moreover, he deflects attention by making the household quarrel symbolize France's political troubles.

Ultimately, Gide's domestic allegory is motivated by two parallel concerns: to explain François's hostility in ways that do not implicate himself, and to propose a model for France's downfall in which his own literary influence plays no part. By making the home-front battle represent the historic conflict, Gide attempts to parry both domestic aggravations and political accusations.

HIDING AND DELIVERANCE

The domestic battle between Gide and François Reymond ended abruptly in April 1943 when the writer left the Reymond home under dramatic circumstances. In early March, Gide's friend Gérard Boutelleau was arrested on charges of espionage.[77] During the raid on the Boutelleau home, Gide's diary manuscript—which he had entrusted to Gérard's wife Hope for typing—was seized by the Italian police and promptly handed over to the German authorities (J II: 915, 918–19).[78] Boutelleau's arrest and the seizure of his own manuscript *Journal* led Gide to worry not about his personal safety but about certain manuscripts left in his Paris apartment. He was particularly concerned about "the manuscript relating to Em."—the account of his marriage with Madeleine Rondeaux, which would later be published under the title *Et nunc manet in te*—and "the confidential notebooks of Luxor"[79]—the *Carnets d'É-gypte*, which recount Gide's sexual adventures with young boys during his 1939 journey through Egypt and Greece (J 4: 184). These manuscripts were sensitive not because of any political content but because they dealt with intimate aspects of Gide's private life. The wartime *Journal* was another matter entirely, and certain blatantly anti-German entries aroused the displeasure of the authorities (J II: 919). With the Allied armies rapidly approaching Tunis, Gide feared arrest—if not as a suspect, then at least as "a witness likely to talk and whom they prefer not leaving to the English." The prospect of being used as a mouthpiece precipitated Gide's decision to go underground: "Even though I find it hard to convince myself that [. . .] my person or my voice could be of any importance, it was better not to run the risk of a forced voyage and sojourn in Germany or Italy" (J 4: 204).[80]

On 13 April 1943, Gide took refuge in the apartment of an acquaintance, Odette Duché, who was already concealing a couple named Bigiaoui (Sagaert, Notes [J II] 1462). Sought by the Germans, Gide's "companions in captivity" had been in hiding for nearly six months.[81] In a symbolic gesture, Gide decided to let his beard grow for the duration of his confinement: "I am waiting for the liberation before shaving again." Living conditions were difficult: "We are living here without electricity and consequently without any news from the radio; often without water, almost without alcohol or gas or oil, on our almost exhausted remaining supplies, barely kept alive by meals that become less adequate every day" (J 4: 206, 205).[82] Odette Duché's clandestine guests had strict orders to remain indoors and stay away from the balcony and windows for fear of detection. Gide did not always take her warnings seriously, however: disguised as a Sicilian fisherman, he went for a walk through the neighborhood on 1 May 1943 (J II: 949; Sagaert, Notes [J II] 1462). He did not enjoy his stroll, however, and returned to his hiding place after half an hour: "No pleasure; pleased to return to my grotto" (J 4: 208).[83] Hirsute, undernourished, and preferring confinement, Gide himself resembles the sequestered woman of Poitiers by the end of the Tunis siege; indeed, he implicitly compares his month-long ordeal to Blanche Monnier's quarter century of confinement.[84]

On 8 May 1943, the day after Allied troops entered Tunis, Gide and his companions came out of their hiding place into "the wildly rejoicing city" (J 4: 210).[85] Shortly thereafter, the Beirut newspaper *La Syrie et l'Orient* published Gide's *Journal* entries chronicling the city's first week of freedom under the title "La Délivrance de Tunis." This jubilant article was one of the earliest World War II victory narratives by a major French writer.

"La Délivrance de Tunis" marks the convergence of history and personal experience: as Martine Sagaert has observed, the closed world of Gide's domestic drama "opens onto a scene of deliverance, when the private and the public celebrate the same liberation."[86] After six months in the dark, Gide was finally witness to a narratable moment: at last he could piece together the story of the North African campaign and relate his experience of the siege to the progress of the war as a whole.[87] "La Délivrance" begins with a bang as the retreating Germans blow up their munitions depots. By the next day, however, a feeling of anticlimax takes over: "While I was writing these lines yesterday, the Allies were already entering the city. [. . .] You can hardly believe that what you have been so long waiting for has taken place, that *they* are here; you don't yet dare believe it" (J 4: 209–10).[88] Once again, the witness to history misses the immediate experience of events; as during the siege, uncertainty colors his narrative. Nevertheless, information that was unavailable throughout the Tunisian occupation pours in, and Gide records it all avidly. After resolving a few of the mysteries that had plagued him and other Tunis residents, however, Gide declares: "I have no need to note here what belongs to history" (J 4: 211).[89] Indeed, the week following the liberation of Tunis is the final journalistic portion of Gide's wartime diary. Thereafter, the *Journal* resumes its customary "scorn [. . .] with regard to History."[90]

Despite his refusal to write history, Gide used "La Délivrance" as an opportunity to take a political stand, articulating strongly pro-Allied opinions and praising the Anglo-American forces that freed the Tunisian capital. Throughout the siege of Tunis, Gide had bitterly criticized the Allies' delay in liberating the city: "The Allies are apparently not at all in a hurry to win and, whereas their crushing numerical superiority would have given them victory long ago, they prefer to wait," he wrote in March 1943 (J 4: 193). Should the American army's delay be interpreted as "a skillful strategy or a blunder, wise patience or timorous incompetence?," he wondered (J 4: 159). Gide finally answered this question in the *Journal* entry that would conclude "La Délivrance de Tunis":

> From all sides it is reported to us that the American troops, just as much as the English or French forces, fought admirably. The delays with which one could justifiably reproach them at the outset were but measures of prudence so long as they were insufficiently equipped. It was essential not to begin the combat until having full assurance of being able to carry it through to victory. The event dissipated whatever doubts might remain and proved the wisdom of that procrastination, whereas precipitation might have compromised everything. (J 4: 214)[91]

In addition to praising the Allies, "La Délivrance" constitutes Gide's first and strongest public condemnation of Hitler and the Axis. Having described the general euphoria and ringing cries of "Vive la France!" (J II: 952), Gide goes on to predict the successful conclusion of the war: "all the conquered peoples now under the German yoke will derive from this great setback to the oppressor an extraordinary encouragement to resistance. It is possible to hear in it the announcement of a general collapse" (J 4: 213).[92]

"La Délivrance de Tunis" marks an important moment in the evolution of Gide's perceptions of the war. Its publication history is also of significant interest. After Gide authorized its publication in *La Syrie et l'Orient*, "La Délivrance" became a popular set piece, appearing six more times between 1943 and 1944. Gide was acutely aware of the irony of this success: "I have written nothing flatter; and no text of mine has ever encountered such a reception; all that remains is to serve it up in the high school anthologies!" Following its publication in

Beirut, Gide's "anthology piece" was translated into English and published in America "with a great deal of absurd praise."[93] The essay was then translated back into French and published without the author's knowledge or permission in the Buenos Aires weekly *La France Nouvelle* and the Algiers paper *Combat*, where it bore the title "La Libération de Tunis."[94] This twice-translated article contained "atrocious mistranslations"[95]—including one error that was beneficial to Gide's image as a survivor of wartime hardships. Whereas Gide's text briefly evokes time spent in hiding, the doubly translated version leads readers to believe that his ordeal had lasted a full six months, rather than a few weeks: "Quickly, before leaving my retreat, I shave the *four weeks'* beard and go down with the companions of my captivity into the street, where *they* have not dared appear for exactly six months," Gide's *Journal* entry reads (J 4: 210, emphasis added); "I hastily shave my shaggy beard and then, with the companions of my captivity, I go down into the street, where *we* have not ventured for exactly six months," states the *Combat* article (emphasis added).[96] Shortly after the liberation of Paris, the original French text of "La Délivrance" appeared in a volume published by the formerly clandestine Éditions de Minuit,[97] and was reprinted in November 1944—again without Gide's knowledge or permission—on the front page of *Les Lettres Françaises*, the newspaper of the largely communist Comité National des Écrivains. Having seen his work reproduced against his will in the collaborationist *Anthologie de la poésie allemande* and *Anthologie de la nouvelle Europe* at the height of the Occupation, Gide now found his writings "borrowed" to serve the aims of the Gaullist and communist resistance.

THE END OF GIDE'S WAR STORY

The 1943 liberation of Tunis marks the end of the war as far as Gide's *Journal* was concerned.[98] As Martine Sagaert has observed, the one-year Tunis interval is a cohesive unit, framed by the arrival and departure of the diarist (Introduction xxiv). Furthermore, the six-month occupation of the city allowed the writer to document the war in miniature. When France fell to the Germans in 1940, Gide had resolved to avoid all mention of the war in his diary (J II: 695). Observations on the war crept into the *Journal*, however, and by the end of 1940 some of those reflections had appeared in Drieu La Rochelle's *Nouvelle Revue Française*. By the time he arrived in Tunisia in 1942, Gide had revised his early opinions, and undoubtedly wished to begin anew. When the occupation of Tunis thrust him into the center of a decisive conflict, Gide seized the chance to tell his war story from the beginning—a chance he had missed in 1940.

This enterprise was hindered, however, by a lack of hard facts to record. Consequently, Gide presented the historical conflict symbolically, through the domestic allegory he constructed around François Reymond. This blending of the domestic and the historic, which arose from necessity, was also a way for the author to rethink the divisions between private and public, between the personal and the political. Indeed, much of Gide's trouble during World War II and its aftermath arose when he—or his critics—blurred or transgressed those boundaries. Post-Armistice attackers attributed political consequences to Gide's sexuality and his literary oeuvre. Postwar critics focused on published excerpts from the wartime *Journal*—passages characterized by the sincerity of a personal diary but eliciting the political consequences of any text published in a time of national emergency. In his writings concerning the 1942–1943 Tunis interlude, Gide creatively unsettles the boundaries between what is inherently private and what can legitimately enter the political realm, shuffling these categories to his advantage.

Gide's year in Tunis was a time of enforced passivity. Cut off from metropolitan France, physically confined during the final month of the siege, Gide had few outlets for political involvement. He therefore used his private life as a vehicle for political commentary, constructing a domestic allegory to illustrate France's problems as he understood them. This narrative is full of gaps and silences, however: it is informed by the historical conflict Gide was unable to narrate, and by the sexual violence he refused to represent. In many respects, Gide's construction is a work of self-defense. Because it displaces the domestic conflict onto a historical struggle, the Victor allegory excuses Gide from acknowledging the source of François Reymond's hostility. Because it constructs an alternative explanation for France's downfall, this scenario is an indirect response to those who blamed Gide for the nation's defeat.

Going public with this highly personal account of the Tunisian occupation became a source of conflict in Gide's circle. Maria Van Rysselberghe deemed publication of the Tunis *Journal* imprudent: "in a time still tortured with misery and catastrophe, this personal diary runs the risk of exasperating the reader."[99] Roger Martin du Gard had a similar reaction to the 1944 publication of "La Délivrance de Tunis." He was struck by the discrepancy between Gide's wartime experience and that of other Frenchmen: "It is so awkward, at a time when all the 'heroes' are recounting their odysseys, and when so many of Gide's colleagues and readers have 'heroic' recollections, to publish this text on current events, this 'war diary' which can only serve to highlight the difference between Gide's wartime sufferings and those of the majority of the French people!"[100] Martin du Gard's view contrasts sharply with that of Gide's friend Jean Amrouche, who cited Gide's private hardships in the writer's defense. Amrouche stressed the similarities between Gide's experience and that of his fellow citizens in occupied France: "He submitted to the harsh discipline experienced by everyone in occupied Europe who lived outside of German laws."[101] Though Gide himself avoided such sensational language, he did emphasize the difficult conditions he experienced while in hiding in a December 1944 letter to Roger Martin du Gard, Jean Schlumberger, and Dorothy Bussy. Defending his decision to publish "La

Délivrance," Gide explained that he assembled the *Journal* entries "for lack of anything better, and unable to write anything new 'ad hoc,'" adding that he was "extremely depressed by a month of confinement with barely sufficient food [. . .] forbidden not only to go out, but even to look out the window because of the people in the house opposite." In addition to describing the hardships he had endured, Gide took this opportunity to point out that he survived the final month of the occupation thanks to "the extreme devotion of communist friends who housed me and brought me my daily rations."[102] At a moment when he was under attack by the communist zealots of the post-war purge, stressing this affiliation seemed crucial.[103] Thus, Gide used an account of domestic adversity to respond to political attacks.

For André Gide, the personal and the political, the sexual and the literary intersected in particularly explosive ways during the Second World War. Reflecting on this convergence and parrying his critics, Gide offers his own fusion of these elements in the Tunis *Journal*, where he blends the historic and the domestic to figure the war *en abyme*.[104]

FIVE

Repositionings

Pages de Journal *and* Thésée

THREE WEEKS AFTER the deliverance of Tunis, Gide left for Algiers, which had been liberated in November 1942. He would spend the remainder of the war there, except for brief trips to Morocco and the Sudan, finally returning to Paris in May 1945. A guest of the Heurgon family,[1] Gide soon found himself at the heart of a literary and intellectual circle made up of the many French writers who had flocked to the city since its liberation by the Allies the previous fall. The new arrivals included novelist André Maurois, pilot and author Antoine de Saint-Exupéry, and Jean Amrouche, a young journalist who had followed Gide from Tunis to Algiers and encouraged the older writer in his newfound Gaullist fervor (Fouchet 126–27; Heurgon-Desjardins 6). Longtime Algiers residents in Gide's circle included Max-Pol Fouchet, founder of the literary resistance magazine *Fontaine*, and Edmond Charlot, whose Éditions Charlot would publish Gide's *Attendu que . . .* and *Pages de Journal* during the writer's stay in Algiers.

Algiers was more than a vital center for literary and cultural life: the coming of Charles de Gaulle—within days of Gide, coincidentally—and the founding of the Comité Français de Libération Nationale made it the new capital of Free France (J II: 962; Sagaert, Notes [J II] 1469). Just weeks after the writer and the general arrived in Algiers, friends arranged for them to meet at a dinner party. Their conversation was awkward at times, and Gide worried that his persistent defense of novelist André Maurois—who continued to support Pétain—had lessened the general's opinion of him (J II: 965; Mauriac, *Conversations* [Fr.] 266). The reverse was true for Gide's view of the general: having recently read and admired some of de Gaulle's writings, Gide came away from their interview highly impressed (J II: 964). "He is certainly called upon to play an important role and he seems 'up to it,'" Gide wrote in his diary the following day: "I shall not find it hard to hang my hopes on him" (J 4: 221).[2]

This chapter examines the first year of Gide's Algerian stay, a period in which the author reexamined his early wartime views and positioned himself to take his place in postwar France. I look first at the serialization of Gide's 1940–1943 *Journal* in *L'Arche*, the Gaullist literary monthly that Gide cofounded in 1944. These diary excerpts aroused fierce condemnations from members of the communist resistance. Gide responded by editing future versions of his *Journal* so as to give a picture of swift, uncomplicated evolution from defeatism to support for the resistance. The chapter concludes with a reading of *Thésée*—a reworking of the Theseus legend that Gide composed in Algiers in the spring of 1944—as an allegory of Vichy's defeat and an attempt on Gide's part to ally himself with the Gaullist resistance.

REEMERGENCE ON THE LITERARY SCENE

From the moment the press reported that Gide was safe in liberated Tunis, there was a renewed interest in the writer as a potential spokesman for the Allied and resistance causes.[3] Because Gide frequented the English literary and political elite in Algiers and was a friend of Pierre Viénot, a prominent member of de Gaulle's London staff, the British pursued him at least as energetically as did the French. Novelist E. M. Forster's 1943 "Homage to André Gide," commissioned by the British Council, enhanced the British perception of Gide as a significant voice of opposition to the Vichy regime. Forster portrayed the French writer as a major opposition figure, citing Gide's denunciation of abuses in the Soviet Union and the Congo as evidence of his intellectual independence and "indifferen[ce] to authority": "How natural, that, to-day, such a mind should be with the Free French!" Forster exclaims. His paean concludes in lofty but somewhat exaggerated terms: thanks to his intellectual fervor, says Forster, Gide "has stood out like a light house amidst the storms of war and the fogs of collaboration, and has become a beacon to his colleagues overseas" (1–2). British Foreign Office staffer Stewart echoed Forster's view: in a May 1943 memo, he informed a colleague that Gide "showed considerable moral courage in the articles he wrote in the 'Figaro' [. . .] since the French collapse." This memo reinforced the perception of Gide as a resistance writer by pointing out that he was commonly thought to be the author of *Le Silence de la mer*, Vercors's novella "depicting internal French moral resistance to 'cultural collaboration' with Germany" (Stewart). As Michael Tilby[4] explains, "[t]he Gidean attribution was doubtless encouraged by the introductory note that accompanied the serialization of *Le Silence de la mer* in the then London-published *Marseillaise*. Not only was it attributed to 'un grand écrivain' [a great writer], tribute was paid to 'la claire pureté de cette langue, la noble et logique ordonnance du récit' [the clear purity of the language, the noble and logical structure of the tale]" (109).

Throughout the summer of 1943, British officials in Algiers and London considered the possibility of bringing Gide to the United Kingdom. Raymond Mortimer, literary editor of *The New Statesman and Nation*, declared that "[de Gaulle's] B.B.C. French" were "particularly anxious" to have Gide in London. Mortimer's own goal was to have Gide "write for English papers about French resistance and culture. We have no first-rate French writer in this country, and we need one" (Mortimer). Gide was enthusiastic about the plan, and sent Simon Bussy a Red Cross card stating: "Hope to join your in-laws soon."[5] In the elliptical language of wartime postcards, this message signified a trip to England, for Bussy's in-laws were the Strachey family, whom Forster and Mortimer knew through their association with the Bloomsbury group.

Plans for Gide's proposed journey soon became mired in political and practical concerns, however. Were Gide's age, health, outspokenness about homosexuality, and "strong Gaullist sympathies" likely to cause problems? Would the invitation "be resented by the Soviets"? Should Gide come under the auspices of the Ministry of Information, with the understanding that he would engage in propaganda work, or should his visit be construed as primarily cultural and therefore be sponsored by the British Council (Peake; Macmillan 6 July 1943; "Auspices"; Macmillan 15 July)? The Foreign Office staff deferred to French Section Head Enid McLeod, who knew Gide personally. McLeod was of the opinion that neither the Political Warfare Executive (P.W.E.) nor the Ministry of Information should sponsor the trip: since Gide had "never in all his life had to do anything he did not want" and was "by nature the sort of person who immediately wants to do the opposite from anything which is suggested to him," she was convinced that "it would be utterly impossible ever to get him to sit down and write a pamphlet for P.W.E. or to give a lecture for the Ministry." Nevertheless, McLeod believed that inviting Gide to England would have a positive effect on the French, especially the intelligentsia. Gide would certainly agree to broadcast to France from the B.B.C., and articles he might write for periodicals like *The New Statesman* could be sent into France and around the world. Finally, though McLeod was unsure how strong Gide's Gaullist leanings were, she was certain that "the [Free] French at Carlton Gardens" would find ways to use the writer's talents (1–2). While the British debated, Gide grew "very fretful and sulky at receiving no news about his proposed trip to England," according to Algiers Resident Minister Harold Macmillan, who in mid-August pressed the Foreign Office for a speedy decision ("André Gide's Proposed Visit"). In the end, nothing came of the plan: Max-Pol Fouchet, founder of the Algiers resistance magazine *Fontaine*, was invited to England instead, and Gide remained in North Africa (Tilby 110).

Although the British initiative came to naught, Gide quickly associated himself with the literary resistance in Algiers. At the June 1943 party where Gide and de Gaulle first met, the two men chatted privately about "the advisability of creating a new review to group together the intellectual and moral forces of free France or those fighting to free her" (J 4: 220).[6] February 1944 saw the debut of Gide's new journal, *L'Arche (The Ark)*. The name was appropriate, Maria Van Rysselberghe remarked, since "so many things need to be saved!"[7] Gide's "Appel" in the inaugural issue states the journal's mission unambiguously: "The role of *L'Arche* [. . .] is to rally and group the Resisters [. . .] who are scattered today across America, England, North Africa, and the colonies, until the day when we will also be able to rally those in France."[8] Contributors to the first issue had impressive literary credentials as well as irreproachable resistance leanings: the issue featured Saint-Exupéry's "Lettre à un otage," Pierre Mendès-France's "Récit d'une évasion," plus writings by Jacques Maritain, Joseph Kessel, and a number of resistance poets.

Nearly identical in format to the prewar *Nouvelle Revue Française*, *L'Arche* seemed designed to replace the "tainted" review usurped by Drieu La Rochelle. Like the *N.R.F.*, it was closely associated with André Gide—especially because the first issue's unsigned "Manifeste" had an unmistakably Gidian tone.[9] While many applauded the appearance of *L'Arche*, many others— on both the left and the right, in North Africa as well as occupied France—found cause to attack the manifesto, the journal, and its patron André Gide. With the war far from over, the manifesto's declaration that "France glories in having 'gone beyond war'"[10] struck some readers as inappropriately soft (Mégret 3). Henri Hell, an editor at the rival journal *Fontaine*, objected to the text "on the grounds that it paraded a definition of France to which no-one could object, not even [right-wing leader Charles] Maurras" (Tilby 114).[11] Given the manifesto's abstract language, Hell's assessment had some merit, but competition between the two magazines may have been an additional motivation for the *Fontaine* editor's criticisms. By 1944, Algiers had three resistance-oriented literary journals: *L'Arche*, its offshoot *La Nef*, and the more established *Fontaine*. The three reviews were in competition for a limited supply of quality copy by French writers, and material from occupied France, which had to be smuggled out to North Africa, was especially at a premium (Fouchet 130, 132).

Like the rival magazine, the communist resistance faction was quick to attack Gide's new journal. Ilya Ehrenburg, the Soviet correspondent to the Algiers paper *La Marseillaise*, condemned *L'Arche* for its allegedly anti-Soviet statements (Tilby 113; "Criticism" 112).[12] At the same time, ironically, *Le Cri du peuple* in occupied France was denouncing the journal as a Soviet propaganda organ (M. C., "L'Arche"). A July 1944 broadcast on German-controlled Radio-Paris attempted to undermine the "dissident" journal by claiming that Gide had authored an article entitled "Les Émigrés ont toujours tort." The broadcast—subsequently published in the right-wing paper *Le Petit Niçois*—quoted Gide's alleged assertion that "history always reveals that emigrants are in the wrong and those who remain on their country's soil are in the right"[13]—turning this fabricated statement against Gide himself, the foreign dissident press, and, by implication, de Gaulle's rival government in Algiers.

As Gide resumed his role as a public intellectual, attempts to discredit him gained strength in occupied France. By May 1944, all of Gide's writings were banned (CAG 6: 317). Hostile and fallacious rumors about his activities abounded during the final years of the war.[14] Citing Gide's prewar writings, journalists argued that Gide's newly declared resistance allegiance was either paradoxical or insignificant. *L'Union Française* prefaced anti-Semitic passages from Gide's prewar *Journal* with the ironic observation that: "The Jew-lovers in Algiers can rejoice at André Gide's arrival."[15] Fernand-Demeure was scandalized that Gide—who had not hesitated to praise German culture during World War I, and who leaned toward "Europeanism"—was now among "Europe's adversaries."[16] Jacques Dyssord declared outright that Gide should have turned to Nazism rather than to communism: "What greater grounds for exaltation [. . .] André Gide might have found in the National-Socialist ideal for which his knowledge of Nietzsche had prepared him! How much better this communitarian spirit, so respectful of indispensable hierarchies, might have satisfied his mind than the base demagogy of communism."[17] Taking a more even-handed approach, Lucien Rebatet retraced Gide's political wanderings of the previous half-century, concluding dismissively that "Gide's 'Gaullism' is really nothing more than a rather negligible episode among his infinite variations." Though Gide's Gaullism might be transitory, Rebatet regretted the prestige Gide's name brought to the opposition: while questioning de Gaulle's claim that "nearly one hundred percent of French intellectuals" were on his side, he nevertheless admitted that the general had accumulated an impressive roster of writers who supported his cause.[18]

PAGES DE JOURNAL: AN "INTELLECTUAL ITINERARY"

Whereas Rebatet dismissed Gide's Gaullist fervor as a transitory phase, Gide himself posited a clear teleology, placing the evolution of his wartime thought under the sign of conversion. By far the most substantive and elaborate conversion narrative Gide published during the war is *Pages de Journal*, serialized in *L'Arche* between March and July 1944, then published in book form in both New York and Algiers. The book's complete title—*Pages de Journal (1939–1942)*—hints at political position-taking through its resemblance to *Pages de Journal (1929–1932)*, the book in which Gide publicly declared his sympathy for communism and the Soviet Union.[19] Like the earlier *Pages de*

Journal, the 1944 volume had its own political agenda: declaring the author's scorn for collaboration and the Vichy regime.

Gide's most overtly political books—*Voyage au Congo*, *Le Retour du Tchad*, *Retour de l'U.R.S.S.* and *Retouches à mon retour de l'U.R.S.S.*—also serve as precedents for the *Pages de Journal*'s political project, albeit in a less obvious way. These works all present a political awakening in the context of a travel narrative: Gide's 1925–1926 journey through French Equatorial Africa made him aware of the French concessionary companies' abuses; his 1936 travels in the U.S.S.R. showed him the totalitarian tendencies of the Soviet regime. After returning from his African and Soviet journeys, Gide felt motivated to take a public stand, educating his readers about the abuses he had witnessed. The link to these earlier voyages can be found in the September 1943 foreword to the *Pages de Journal*, in which Gide presents his early wartime experiences as a metaphorical journey: "I should like these pages, and especially those of the beginning, to be granted but a relative value: if altogether they contain a lesson, let it be in the manner of an intellectual itinerary by marking the stages of a slow progress out of darkness into light" (J 4: 307).[20]

The trope of the voyage is underscored by the literal journey that closes the *Pages de Journal*. The book opens shortly after the declaration of war and ends with the author's imminent arrival in North Africa—his "escape" to a place of freedom. Having experienced a sensual awakening in Tunisia as a young man, Gide had always associated the region with liberation; by the 1940s, however, North Africa represented political rather than sexual freedom. In his essay "Notre Afrique intérieure," published in *Fontaine* in March 1941, Gide evoked his early contact with North Africa and his frequent desire to return: "This is [. . .] why, toward the end of my life and throughout this tragic year, I have been so particularly touched by everything that comes from that other France, and why I smile so joyfully at this glorious awakening, all across our North Africa, of young people who are so fervent, so intact, and on whom we base so many hopes."[21] By the time *Pages de Journal* was published in 1944, Gide's political hopes for North Africa had been fulfilled, with Algiers established as the home of de Gaulle's provisional Free French government. The Mediterranean crossing that concludes *Pages de Journal* can therefore symbolize Gide's journey away from Vichy and toward the "other France"—that of the resistance.

The Algiers editions of *Pages de Journal* (both the book and the serialization in *L'Arche*) begin with Gide's first journal entry after the declaration of war in September 1939 and conclude with his arrival in Tunis in May 1942. The entries from 1940 revisit the principal landmarks of Gide's "journey": his initial depression after France's defeat, his favorable then unfavorable reactions to speeches by Pétain, his criticisms of France and the French, his belief in coming to terms with one's former enemy, and his glorification of "constrained" thought. The turn of the year brings a decisive change of heart in the narrative proposed by the *Pages de Journal*: as of January 1941, the majority of the entries are resolutely opposed to Franco-German collaboration. With less frequent entries than in 1940, the diary's early diffuseness falls away, and the pace of the narrative accelerates. Entries from January condemn Germany's proposal for collaboration as duplicitous and hint that Hitler's persecutions may end up strengthening that which the dictator hoped to suppress (PJ [A] 81–83). March brings an account of Gide's break with Drieu's *N.R.F.* From this point on, Gide's contempt for Vichy is clear: he annotates the entry from 5 July 1941—"Alas, for months, for years now, France has hardly given us any reasons to be proud"—with a footnote specifying that his remark refers to *Vichy* France (J 4: 73). Gide further marks his distance by contrasting France's recovery (*redressement*) with the "personal recovery" (*redressement intime*) illustrated by his diary: his own recovery, he declares, "does not always follow the direction proposed by Vichy's commands" (J 4: 79). On New Year's Day 1942, Gide writes derisively of "this farce of a 'national revolution'" (J 4: 96).[22] In an entry dated 13 April 1942, he obliquely criticizes Vichy's principal "actors," describes collaboration with Germany as a shameful abdication, and announces his plan to leave France for North Africa. The following entry is made aboard the *Chanzy* en route to Tunisia, and the book concludes with the ship's imminent arrival in Tunis (PJ [A] 105–07, 112).

Gide intended his *Pages de Journal* to be an enlightening and honest depiction of one man's political evolution during the early years of the war, and hoped readers would find "surveying the distance covered both instructive and comforting."[23] In order to highlight the distance traveled, he maintained the early accommodationist statements that had, by 1944, become politically unpopular. Roger Martin du Gard strongly disapproved of his friend's decision to publish the *Pages de Journal*, for Gide's political commentary was sure to invite criticism (J II: 1037). His prediction was accurate, and the attack began even before *L'Arche* had finished serializing Gide's diary excerpts.

A FORETASTE OF THE PURGE

Algiers was not only the home of the provisional government that would rule France after the Liberation: it was also the site where the postwar purge began. The first official purge defendant to face trial was Pierre Pucheu, the former Vichy Minister of the Interior.[24] Pucheu clearly held some fascination for Gide: at a luncheon with de Gaulle and British diplomat Harold Nicolson, the writer provocatively announced that he was working on a biography of the much-hated Vichy minister (Stéphane 111–12). Gide attended three sessions of the Pucheu trial, which filled him with "indescribable uneasiness."

He was especially horrified by prosecutor Bernhard Weiss's definition of Pucheu's "main crime: he believed in the German victory."[25]

Four months later, Gide found himself accused of a similar "crime." The communist paper *La Liberté* launched the attack on 6 July 1944. Paraphrasing passages from the "Pages de Journal" recently printed in *L'Arche*, an anonymous journalist condemned Gide's disparaging comments on French patriotism and issued a barely veiled threat of retribution ("Le Patriotisme"). The following day, communist delegate Arthur Giovoni attacked Gide in the Assemblée Consultative (the legislative body of the provisional Free French government). "Is it possible to print in Algiers remarks such as these," the outraged *député* asked, quoting at length from the diary entries for 13 and 14 July 1940: "Today literature is a weapon. That is why I demand prison for André Gide and public prosecution of the managing editor of *L'Arche*."[26] Like the anonymous attacker in *La Liberté*, Giovoni urged that the paper allotted to *L'Arche* be redistributed to "the few patriotic newspapers and reviews of Algiers" (qtd. in J 4: 308–09).[27]

Gide responded to Giovoni's accusations in a short text entitled "Rester unis." Though the essay never appeared under Gide's name, much of its content was reproduced by means of quotations and paraphrase in Guy Mémoire's article "Offensive contre Gide."[28] "Rester unis" begins by comparing Giovoni to the Légion des Anciens Combattants, whose threats had prevented Gide from delivering his 1941 lecture on Michaux.[29] Having used the Michaux anecdote to establish his bona fides as an enemy of Vichy, Gide quotes from the resistance paper *Combat* to demonstrate that he was not the only one to experience despair after the fall of France, "when our country seemed definitively crushed, when it was abandoned to itself, in dreadful solitude, and any hope seemed like madness."[30] Fully aware that his own diary entries expressing such sentiments would cause a negative reaction, Gide published them nonetheless in order to show the scope of his—and the nation's—turnaround.[31] Gide concludes "Rester unis" with a dramatic flourish. "You are calling for my death," he tells Giovoni, "[b]ut I know of no more admirable destiny than to die for freedom of thought; and by that I also mean: for France. I am entirely at your disposal." He adds to this gesture of martyrdom by stating that he would nevertheless prefer that the "cup of hemlock" be proffered by "our mutual enemies, against whom [. . .] all the forces of the Resistance should remain united."[32] Through his allusion to hemlock, Gide implicitly compares himself to Socrates, with whom he indeed had much in common: both men stood by the motto "know thyself"; both fought censorship; both were accused of corrupting youth and were condemned by their nations' officials.

Unprepared to follow the example of Socrates's self-sacrifice, Gide opted to make concessions in the publication of his wartime diary. In the spirit of his exhortation to "remain united," he made alterations to the third installment of the "Pages de Journal"—the portion published after Giovoni's attack—and to the Algiers edition of *Pages de Journal*. Protesting his reluctance to furnish any "pretext for division among Frenchmen," Gide claimed to have deleted the controversial passages "not out of fear [. . .] but out of a sense of decency."[33] This concern for French unity is certainly in line with the ideals Gide expressed in "Rester unis," the *Journal*,[34] and the "Appel" in *L'Arche*: "let us not protest about division among Frenchmen. The only division we need take into account today is the discord between those who *consent* and those who *resist*."[35] However, these appeals for solidarity within the resistance represent a complete about-face from the outset of the Occupation, when concern for national unity led Gide to favor submission to the new regime: "There is nothing to do but submit and accept, alas! the inevitable, against which any revolt can succeed only in dividing the French among themselves," he wrote in June 1940.[36] This is not the only argument in "Rester unis" to be based on a half-concealed version of Gide's wartime writings: calling particular attention to the 24 June 1940 diary entry criticizing Pétain and expressing support for de Gaulle[37] and to the 25 November 1940 assertion that patriotic feeling "assures and affirms itself in resistance" (J 4: 54),[38] Gide adduces textual evidence from his wartime diary to substantiate his change of heart ("Rester" 1–2). What Gide does not reveal is that he soon withdrew his 24 June condemnation of Pétain and that he removed references to "oppression" and "resistance" from the *N.R.F.* version of his 25 November entry (J 4: 54; J II: 705; F 2: 351). Responding to attacks from the powerful communist resistance faction, Gide exercises selective memory to present himself as an early supporter of the resistance. Moreover, he fails to acknowledge the ways in which his deliberate editing of diary entries for publication in the *N.R.F.* may have served the review's collaborationist mission. The selective truth-telling of "Rester unis" is typical of the rewriting Gide undertook once the success of the resistance—and the potential violence of the postwar purge it would orchestrate—became apparent.

EDITING THE *PAGES DE JOURNAL*

It was always Gide's practice to edit his diary before publication.[39] Chronological and thematic concerns often dictated the organization of diary selections published in advance of the "complete" *Journal* text (Sagaert, Notice 1111). *Pages de Journal* follows this pattern: structured around a physical and intellectual journey, the text is governed by both temporal and thematic logic. Other groupings and omissions were motivated by a concern for privacy: the passages touching on Gide's marriage to Madeleine Rondeaux, for example, were published as *Et nunc manet in te* only after the writer's death. But Gide's claim that "apart from the notes on Madeleine, *I have never omitted anything* from my *Journal*"[40] is patently false. "Excessively studied [. . .] corrected," "faked [. . .] expurgated," "touched up"[41]—such are the judgments of the wartime *Journal*'s more attentive critics. To put such charges in perspective, however, one must acknowledge that Gide's editorial choices exemplify the reticence and manipulations typical of many French wartime narratives.

Nowhere is Gide's rewriting more apparent than in the Algiers *Pages de Journal*. At 112 pages, the volume is considerably slimmer than the 147-page edition published in New York some weeks before Giovoni's attack. Comparing the "thin, abridged little volume"[42] to the New York edition—as well as to subsequent, more complete editions of the *Journal*—allows us to take the full measure of Gide's self-censorship.[43]

In his preface to the *Pages*, Gide defends his defeatist statements of 1940 with a claim of sincerity: "In these pages from the journal that I kept [. . .] during the somber months following our defeat, I do not recognize that I have any right to change anything" (J 4: 307). In the original version alone—the "Avant-propos" published with the first "Pages de Journal" installment in *L'Arche*—the sentence continues: "not even the right to choose only the least somber pages, to exclude those which portray a state of extreme discouragement which I no longer recognize today."[44] By the time the diary appeared in book form, Giovoni had made his showy stand in the Assemblée Consultative, and Gide was consciously suppressing statements that might invite further attacks. In the Algiers volume and all subsequent editions, therefore, Gide attenuates his claims of authenticity by deleting the assurance that he had made no changes whatsoever.

The changes Gide did make in his Algiers *Pages de Journal* fall into three main categories: modifications, omissions, and reordering of material from the original diary. Modifications might be as simple as the addition of a single word, as when Gide attenuates a controversial remark about German domination by emphasizing his criticism of Vichy: "I even go so far as to think subjection to Germany preferable for a time, with its painful humiliations, less harmful for us, less degrading, than the *stupid* discipline that Vichy offers us today" (adapted from J 4: 66, emphasis added).[45] The adjective "stupide," included in the Algiers *Pages de Journal*, appears in no other published version of Gide's diary. The entry for 12 September 1941 has a similarly suspect variant. In this passage, where Gide comments on the forced closings of the periodicals *Temps Nouveaux* and *Esprit* and proposes the slogan "Vires acquirit tacendo," all editions not published in Algiers conclude on a note of acceptance: "I leave it to others to be astonished. I am so little inclined, intellectually, toward insubordination, toward refractoriness . . . that I should almost say: This is proper" (J 4: 85–86).[46] In the *L'Arche* and Charlot versions, however, Gide follows the Latin saying with a very different message: "This should be able to serve as a motto for all those who are silenced. At least I hope that it is true for many people."[47]

These small but significant changes appear to be a concession to the political climate in liberated Algiers.

Omissions from the original diary serve primarily to sharpen the *Pages de Journal*'s focus on the political and mold the book's political message into an acceptable narrative of evolution. Gide shies away from the diary's frequent remarks on how little he personally suffered from the war, giving an overall impression of greater involvement.[48] He also omits quantities of purely literary reflections and emphasizes the political—rather than the literary—reasons for his withdrawal from the *N.R.F.* All published versions of the 25 November 1940 diary entry express Gide's "displeasure" on reading the first installment of his "Feuillets" (J 4: 53). The New York volume alone makes it clear that Gide was not displeased with the issue's overall contents or with the journal's new management and political aims. Rather, he was dissatisfied with the poor showing his "Feuillets" made when compared with other writers' contributions: "In comparison with the vigorous pages which surround it, those by Drieu or Petitjean, they read like an old man's ramblings."[49] In addition to revealing the somewhat selfish stylistic concerns at the root of Gide's dissatisfaction with the wartime *N.R.F.*, this remark might be construed as approval for two writers who had since emerged as major contributors to collaborationist publications (Assouline, *L'Épuration* 161–62).

It would be inaccurate to suggest that Gide deleted all politically sensitive remarks from the *Pages de Journal*, for he included several passages that appeared shamefully accommodationist by the standards of 1944. Nevertheless, he managed to minimize the impact of such statements through strategic deletions. Arguably the most damning diary passages are those in which Gide deems France unready for—and unworthy of—the freedom she desires. The Algiers *Pages* contain a few reflections on the benefits of dictatorship, but the New York *Pages* and subsequent editions add an accumulation of similar material. Likewise, a single reference to Gide's horrified fascination with Hitler is amplified in the more complete editions of the *Journal*, which reveal the recurring nature of this line of thinking (PJ [A] 16–17, 40). Selective omissions in the Algiers *Pages de Journal* made objectionable opinions seem like occasional passing thoughts, presenting them as ephemeral rather than enduring.[50] These revisions also served to preserve the flow of the narrative, its illusion of straightforward linear progress.

Reordering of diary entries is one of Gide's subtlest and most effective strategies for transforming the raw material of his diary into the tale of an unwavering journey from "darkness into light." Chronological accuracy was a major concern for Gide, whose second installment of *N.R.F.* "Feuillets" concluded with the regretful declaration that "I ought at least to have dated (and left in chronological order) these *Feuillets* taken from my *Journal*" (adapted from J 4: 53).[51] The "Feuillets'" undated diary excerpts failed to show the evolution of Gide's views over the months in which he penned those entries.

Moreover, the "Feuillets" were sometimes misleading, for a number of passages actually predated the Occupation. For example, the pre-invasion observation that "[t]here is a certain . . . romanticism in grieving that things are not otherwise than what they are" (J 4: 16) immediately precedes a passage whose references to the debate about literature's supposedly deleterious influence seem to place it squarely within the period of the Occupation.[52] Restored to its chronological context, this fatalistic-sounding pronouncement clearly does not indicate acceptance of the Occupation.

Reestablishing chronology also meant restoring the historical and political context of the "Feuillets." The *N.R.F.* excerpts are disembodied and introspective; their references to current events are infrequent and oblique. *Pages de Journal* reveals the intensity of Gide's political opinions and demonstrates the extent to which his "untimely meditations" are grounded in specific political concerns. In places, the volume restores criticisms of Vichy and Germany that were unpublishable in occupied France;[53] elsewhere, it reinstates excessively accommodationist statements that Gide had undoubtedly deleted to avoid the appearance of too closely following Drieu's collaborationist agenda.[54] Whether admirable or objectionable to Gide's Liberation-era readership, these reinstated passages did much to erase the impression of unconcern and incoherence created by the detached and disordered "Feuillets."

With the *Pages de Journal*, in fact, one could argue that Gide went too far in the interest of political and chronological coherence. Just before the book's concluding sequence of entries made during Gide's crossing to Tunis, the Algiers *Pages de Journal* has an entry dated 13 April 1942. The date is fictitious, and the passage is cobbled together from three diary entries in which Gide criticizes Vichy leaders and condemns supporters of Franco-German collaboration.[55] These anti-Vichy statements—the final political remarks in the Algiers *Pages*—were in fact written in late May and June 1942, after Gide's arrival in North Africa. This chronological manipulation allows Gide to conclude his *Pages de Journal* with a sharp critique of collaborationist politics while maintaining the geographical voyage structure that subtends the book's "intellectual itinerary." In a similar fashion, Gide attempts to preserve the timeline he has constructed in the *Pages* by suppressing a 6 May 1941 diary entry in which he envisaged collaboration as an acceptable alternative (J II: 760). The Algiers edition contains only anticollaboration remarks from January 1941 onward, thereby implying that any doubts, hesitations, and reversals were confined to the early months of the Occupation. This chronological fiction is underscored by the foreword's emphasis on March 1941— when Gide read Chardonne's *Chronique privée de l'an 1940* and consequently broke with the *N.R.F.*—as a decisive turning point (PJ [A] 9). The May 1941 entry, which postdates the Drieu-Chardonne crisis, reveals that the trajectory of Gide's "intellectual itinerary" was not so simple as the Algiers *Pages* would have it.

Gide's most misleading alterations involve both omission and reordering of diary entries. The first installment of "Pages de Journal" in *L'Arche* concludes with an entry dated 26 June 1940, which is in fact a modified version of an entry originally dated 30 August 1940 (J II: 726–27; Sagaert, Notes [J II] 1403). The altered passage (quoted here in its modified version) concerns Gide's political uncertainty and the fact that he is easily influenced by the opinions of others:

> Is there anyone left with whom I take real pleasure in talking? I can no longer assert anything without my affirmation's seeming at once to force my thought somewhat. None of my convictions is now sufficiently solid for the slightest objection not to upset it immediately. [. . .] More and more I fear that an idea may seem to me right merely because it is well expressed. (adapted from J 4: 26)[56]

Given the *Pages de Journal*'s insistence on progress, it was to Gide's advantage to imply that his moods of profound doubt and disarray occurred quite early in the war. He therefore changed the placement of this entry to make it coincide with the Armistice. More important, though, the 30 August entry supplants the long-suppressed 26 June entry in which Gide retracted his 24 June condemnation of Pétain (J II: 705). This transposition of entries allows Gide to replace a passage that *reveals* his political vacillations with one that merely *describes* them. This substitution is a typically Gidian compromise. Given the author's insistence on the developmental flow of the *Pages de Journal*'s narrative and his repeated references to the anti-Pétain entry of 24 June, however, the transposition bespeaks a certain degree of bad faith. In defending his wartime diary, Gide claimed that entries like that of 24 June "explain and [. . .] correct"[57] the tone of acceptance in earlier entries cited by his attackers. The sincerity of this claim is dubious, however, for Gide straightens out the path of his wartime "itinerary," omitting an entry that spoils the tidy course of his narrative from momentary approval to firm condemnation of Pétain.

Despite Gide's sometimes deceptive editing practices, the broad sweep of *Pages de Journal* makes room for a degree of political ambivalence. Not so the three collections of diary excerpts published by the resistance and mainstream press in 1944. Prepared without the author's direct participation,[58] these selections eschew defeatist comments from the early months of the war, retaining only those passages that condemn Germany and Vichy and support the resistance. The earliest group of entries, dating from November 1940 through January 1941, appeared in *Les Lettres Françaises*, a French literary magazine published in Buenos Aires; these "Nouvelles pages de journal" feature criticisms of Hitler and repeated assurances that Gide's frame of mind has changed since he wrote the *N.R.F.* "Feuillets." The next chronological swath, from January through September 1941, appeared as "Pages de Journal" in *Le Figaro* shortly after the Liberation;[59] with few exceptions, the excerpted entries are overtly or covertly critical of the collaborationist regime. Selected entries from January 1942 through May 1943 appeared under the title "Fragments d'un journal" in the clandestine Minuit press's July 1944 *Chroniques interdites II*; predictably, this resistance volume highlights Gide's contempt for the "National Revolution," his condemnation of German propaganda, and his faith in the Soviet army (26–28, 30).[60]

By selecting diary excerpts that showed Gide as a voice of opposition, the editors of *Les Lettres Françaises*, *Le Figaro*, and the Éditions de Minuit used Gide's literary reputation to serve their own causes—incidentally improving Gide's political image at the same time. In so doing, they were no more and no less biased than Giovoni and the hostile journalists who used fragments of the wartime diary to condemn the author. The diversity of opinion expressed in Gide's World War II *Journal* lends itself to a multiplicity of narratives and a variety of political agendas. Ultimately, reactions to Gide's wartime *Journal* depended not only on the individual reader's political orientation but also on the extent to which he or she accepted the narrative of progress and redemption that Gide proposed. In a December 1944 review in the Algiers journal *Combat*, F. Després wholeheartedly adopted the journey structure in Gide's defense: "What is the use of writing an account of one's journey if nothing happens between the departure and the arrival, if the outcome is a foregone conclusion. [. . .] Gide's *Journal* is all about progress."[61] Others rejected this model, seeing Gide's wandering wartime trajectory as "all over the map."[62] The omissions, alterations, and transpositions in the Algiers *Pages de Journal* all contributed to Gide's high-stakes effort to straighten out the path of his wartime diary and convince readers of his straightforward march from understandable despair to admirable resistance.

FASHIONING LEGENDS: GIDE, DE GAULLE, AND *THÉSÉE*

With *Pages de Journal*, Gide presents the labyrinthine trajectory of his wartime thought as a tidy journey. *Thésée*, his reworking of the Theseus legend, also uses strategic modifications to craft an unambiguous narrative of progress with a view to preparing the writer's place in the postwar nation.

Gide had long planned to write a life of Theseus, but the project finally took shape as World War II approached. In the fall of 1938, he shared an outline of his *Thésée* with Dorothy Bussy, but at that point the projected *récit* lacked political content. Daniel Durosay attributes this to "the paralyzing effect of world events"[63]—namely, the 1938 Munich crisis—and to Gide's withdrawal from political engagement following his 1936 rejection of communism ("Thésée" 204–05). By 1944, however, Gide had a political agenda that the Theseus legend could help him fulfill: he needed to straighten out the twisting political course of his earlier wartime writings and align himself with the forces that would soon be victorious. Living in Algiers, surrounded by preparations for Allied victory and France's postwar democracy, Gide composed his *Thésée* during May and June 1944, "in a state of joyful ardor that I had not known for a long time and thought I should never know again. [. . .] Furthermore, exalted by events and the recovery of France" (J 4: 240).[64] The writer's joy, fueled by the positive political situation, brings a resurgence of the creative powers whose loss he had mourned in his 1940 diary and *N.R.F.* "Feuillets": "I never wrote anything good save in joy; and at moments I wonder if my heart still contains a single spark of it" (J 4: 13).[65]

Knowing that the Gaullist resistance would soon come to power, Gide used his adaptation of the Theseus legend to reposition himself politically, allying himself with de Gaulle through the character of Theseus. Two key episodes in *Thésée*—the adventure in Crete and the founding of Athens— symbolize France's imminent victory and the subsequent task of rebuilding the nation. Gide implicitly compares Thésée's exploits as a hero and statesman to the military and political achievements of Charles de Gaulle. Certain parallels are obvious: both men purged the world of "a host of tyrants, bandits, and monsters" (TL 64)[66] and both established new democracies. In his *Journal*, moreover, Gide underscores the two heroes' similarities by applying Thésée's motto, "passer outre" (R 1418, 1419, 1437)—a phrase one might translate as "to move on, disregarding obstacles"—to de Gaulle's heroic disobedience: "I asked him how and when, in his opinion, an officer could and should take it upon himself to disregard a command [*passer outre*]. He replied most appropriately that this could only be at the time of great events and when the feeling of duty entered into opposition with a command received" (J 4: 220).[67]

If Thésée represents de Gaulle in Gide's *récit*, then the hero's successful exploit in Crete can stand for victory over France's collaborationist regime. Similarities between the emblems of King Minos and those of Vichy France substantiate this interpretation. Gide's highly detailed and exceptionally accurate description of Cretan customs and decorative motifs is drawn largely from works by Gustave Glotz: the *Histoire grecque* and, especially, *La Civilisation égéenne* (Pollard 291). One emblem Gide adopted for his *récit* is the double axe, which figures prominently in the illustrations and descriptions of *La Civilisation égéenne*. Gide surrounds King Minos with the symbols described by Glotz: "The double-headed ax hung above his throne, and with his right hand he held a golden scepter. [. . .] In the other hand was a trilobed flower" (adapted from TL 69).[68] Glotz tells us that the king "had as insignia the scepter and the double axe, the *labrys*."[69] Though it was worshipped throughout Crete, Glotz says, the double axe was particularly significant in the palace-sanctuary of Knossos, where it gave its name to the *labyrinthos*, or labyrinth (*Aegean* 149, 387). Indeed, in Gide's *récit*, the double axe decorates the entrance to the labyrinth as well as Minos's throne (R 1438).

The double axe was a token of both political and religious power: it was an emblem of royal authority, and it conferred a divine right on the priest-king who served the Minotaur. "Two thousand years before it became the symbol of authority in Rome, the axe already held that position in the palace of the Labyrinth,"[70] Glotz explains (*Aegean* 234, 149), referring to the *fasces*—a bundle of rods often surrounding an axe carried by the lictors of ancient Rome to symbolize the authority of the magistrates. At the time of Gide's writing, of course, this symbol did not belong merely to antiquity, for it had been adopted as the emblem of Mussolini's fascist party. Vichy France had its own symbol taken from antiquity: the *francisque*, which is essentially identical to the Minoan *labrys*. The *francisque* was a two-bladed battle-axe used by the Franks, the "ancient tribe from which the 'good' Frenchmen of the Vichy regime were supposed to have descended."[71] Vichy iconography sometimes associated the *francisque* with farming imagery consistent with the government's call for a "return to the soil," thereby reproducing the ancient association of the double axe with trees, flowers, fruits, and animals (Ferro 41; Glotz, *La Civilisation* 270).

In addition to the *labrys*, Gide places a second symbol of royal power, the trilobed flower, in Minos's left hand (R 1420). This, too, is consistent with ancient sources: Glotz informs us that, in addition to the axe, the kings of Knossos may have had another emblem, the fleur-de-lys. This stylized trilobed flower is, of course, the heraldic emblem of French royalty— "[s]trange coincidence,"[72] Glotz remarks as he describes this symbol of the kings of Knossos (*Aegean* 149). In Gide's description of Minos on the throne, the simultaneous presence of the *labrys* and the fleur-de-lys is overdetermined, not coincidental: Gide's use of ancient symbols and wartime iconography makes Crete look a great deal like Vichy France. Thésée's victory represents that of democracy over totalitarianism and, more specifically, triumph over the Vichy regime.

After victory comes the time to rebuild. It is in the nation-building phase that Thésée's similarities with de Gaulle are most apparent. Both men suppressed local rivalries to unite their peoples: Thésée, the "valiant gatherer of cities," consolidated the Athenian government, abolishing the "little courts of local justice" and the "regional council chambers" (TL 92, 105);[73] de Gaulle fused his London-based Free French with the Algiers-based government of General Giraud to form the Comité Français de Libération Nationale in June 1943. Both leaders established egalitarian democracies: Thésée founded a "government of the people" in which "each citizen of the state [. . . had] an equal right to sit on the council" (TL 105);[74] in September 1943, de Gaulle created the Assemblée Consultative, composed of representatives from all resistance movements and parties, which would become the provisional government of postwar France. Both the Greek and the Frenchman enlarged their nations: in order to increase Athens's size and power, Thésée welcomed newcomers, promising them "the same rights as were enjoyed by those who were natives of Athens or who had settled there earlier" (TL 106);[75] at the January 1944 Brazzaville conference, de Gaulle laid the foundations for granting French citizenship to the inhabitants of all French overseas territories—though unlike Thésée's new Athenians they would not have precisely the same status as inhabitants of metropolitan France.

Thésée's government, which closely parallels that established by de Gaulle, also embodies the political and social ideals of André Gide: in Pierre Renauld's words, this government is a "curious mixture of aristocratic individualism and socialism."[76] Likewise, the hero's character and values correspond to the qualities Gide prized. Needless to say, these traits were not universally endearing, and some of Gide's contemporaries reacted negatively to his interpretation of the Greek hero. In a 1946 essay comparing the original New York edition of *Thésée* with the standard Gallimard edition,[77] René Étiemble described the earlier *Thésée* as a "fascist" (45).[78] Dorothy Bussy compared Gide's protagonist not to de Gaulle but to Hitler (CAG 11: 418). Gide's Thésée does bear a certain resemblance to the German dictator as the writer conceived him during the Second World War. Writing of his anguished admiration for Hitler in an August 1940 *Journal* entry, Gide uses the phrase that would become Thésée's motto: "I cannot help feeling for Hitler an admiration full of anguish, fear, and stupor; a dazed admiration. [. . .] Horror and terror cannot counteract it; my admiration grows anyway [*passe outre*] and, like Hitler himself, completely disregards those feelings."[79] Thésée, a sometimes ruthless but nevertheless admirable character, may represent an attempt to work through these early feelings of grudging admiration and redirect them toward the more "heroic" de Gaulle. Then, too, the authoritarian side of Thésée may represent de Gaulle as Gide would have liked him to be, for when Max-Pol Fouchet expressed concern about de Gaulle's increasing authoritarianism, Gide replied: "What would worry *me* would be if he were not authoritarian enough."[80] Whatever his motivations, Gide endows his Thésée with characteristics common to himself and to the Free French general. Projecting his own values onto Thésée and the government he establishes is one of the ways in which Gide links himself to the ancient hero and his twentieth-century counterpart, de Gaulle.

Gide presents himself as the literary equivalent of the modern-day "gatherer of cities" (TL 92); what de Gaulle would accomplish in the political realm, Gide would attempt in the literary domain by founding *L'Arche*. As Gide tells it, he took personal risks in order to launch the journal. In his diary and correspondence, Gide acknowledges that it was "imprudent" to publish his *Pages de Journal* in 1944, given the political climate in Algiers and metropolitan France. "'My hand was forced' by *L'Arche*, to which I had nothing else to contribute,"[81] Gide explains, implying that he exposed himself to virulent attacks in order to serve a greater good—supporting the resistance journal he had founded with de Gaulle's blessing.

The Theseus legend gave Gide an opportunity to revisit and rework the controversial views published in *L'Arche*, placing them in the context of his entire literary oeuvre. In the *récit*, Thésée looks back on his life as an adventurer and statesman, and André Gide retraces his literary career. *Thésée* is a stylistic and thematic recapitulation of Gide's literary oeuvre: descriptions of Thésée's youthful hedonism recall the lyrical excesses of *Les Nourritures terrestres*, while his recognition of the need for discipline is couched in the more sober, classical style of Gide's later writings. Considered in the historical context of the Second World War, this apparently retrospective narrative proves to have a forward-looking purpose—dealing with the unfinished business of the war to prepare the author's place in a postwar world.

It is through the historical and political allegory of *Thésée* that André Gide reviews his most recent past. If the hero's triumph in Crete symbolizes victory over France's collaborationist regime, the attitudes of those on the island represent the mentality that many Frenchmen—not the least of them André Gide—had to overcome. King Minos embodies the fatalism Gide himself experienced at the beginning of the Occupation: as Ariane tells Thésée, "Minos [. . .] puts up with everything. He thinks it's wisest to allow what cannot be prevented" (TL 81).[82] The king's attitude is strikingly like Gide's own position in the early months of the war, when he praised the wisdom of accepting the inevitable and described himself as "in no wise inclined toward revolt" (J 4: 47).[83] A similar disinclination to rebel descends on Thésée's companions when they enter the labyrinth, where narcotic vapors and satisfactions for all appetites abound. Thésée finds his men "so incapacitated by drink as to be incapable of resistance." "I insisted, saying that I had come to deliver them. 'Deliver us from what?' they shouted" (adapted from TL 96).[84] Thésée's companions are like those who accepted the État Français as legitimate—perhaps deriving certain advantages from the regime—and who did not see this new France as a prison from which to be delivered. To Gide's mind, this initial acceptance and torpor were nearly inevitable, but could eventually give way to a galvanized resolve not to give in. This view is captured eloquently by Dédale's description of the labyrinth. "Nothing is easier than to get into the labyrinth," Dédale tells Thésée, "nothing less easy than to get out. Nobody finds his way in there without first he lose it" (TL 92).[85] Emerging from the labyrinth after succumbing briefly to its confusion, the Greek adventurers echo Gide's presentation of his own wartime itinerary as a journey "out of darkness into light."

Gide's personal experience of the war is inscribed in the *récit*'s silences as well as in its treatment of the legend. Summarizing the differences between Gide's *récit* and Plutarch's *Life of Theseus*, on which it is largely based, Daniel Durosay observes that Gide shapes the hero's life into "a virtuous and uninterrupted ascent toward triumph. [. . .] Instead of an ambiguous existence, [. . .] Gide gives us unequivocal victory, stabilized in the wisdom of old age."[86] One major change is the omission of the hero's exile: as Helen Watson-Williams points out, "Gide suppresses the legendary exile of Theseus in order to allow his hero to await his death quietly in his own city" (128). This deletion is a significant departure from Plutarch's version of the legend and from Gide's own wartime experience. Though he longed to return to metropolitan France, attacks from the communist resistance forced the writer to remain in North Africa until long after the liberation of Paris. In the *récit*, however, exile is eliminated, and the hero's life is free of blame and ambiguity. The only mention of exile is displaced from text to paratext, and refers to the author's experience, not that of the Greek hero: in *Thésée*'s dedication, Gide thanks the Heurgons, Amrouche, and others for their friendship and encouragement "during a long period of exile" (TL 60).[87]

Gide's *Thésée* does more than depart from Plutarch's familiar version of the legend: it also reflects on stories that diverge from the events they portray, and on the ways in which legends develop. Gide's fictional hero readily admits his own contributions to the legend surrounding him: "Certain imaginary incidents have enriched the mythology of my person. [. . .] I took care never to deny these rumors, for they all enhanced my prestige. I even improved upon some of them" (TL 103).[88] Perhaps this statement reflects Gide's ironic awareness of the ways in which the public figures around him strove to reinvent themselves during the war and in its aftermath. Perhaps it discreetly gestures to the author's own efforts—and the efforts others made on his behalf—to rehabilitate his image. Like the hero who tinkers with his legend, Gide displayed a mixture of bad faith and political savvy in editing his wartime diary to fit changing sensibilities. His efforts were at least partly successful: in an October 1943 speech to the Alliance Française of Algiers, Charles de Gaulle listed Gide alongside Aragon, Kessel, Romains, and other writers he associated with resistance thought (de Gaulle 333). Like Thésée's legend, which was enhanced by the gossip surrounding his exploits, Gide's own World War II "myth" benefited from interpretations like de Gaulle's.

In the end, *Thésée* is about how one relates to the past, as well as how one presents it. The *récit*, which investigates an individual's connection to his past, presents some interesting points of comparison with the "Appel" and "Manifeste" from *L'Arche*—texts that consider the nation's negotiations between past and future. For the hero of Gide's *récit*, the future is predicated on the past. As he equips the adventurer with the thread that will help him escape the labyrinth, Dédale tells Thésée: "This thread will be your link with the past. Go back to it. Go back to yourself. For nothing can begin from nothing, and it is from your past, and from what you are at this moment, that what you are going to be must spring" (TL 86–87).[89] Gide's "Appel," which appeared in *L'Arche* just months before he began *Thésée*, uses nearly identical terms but expresses a message diametrically opposed to Dédale's: "Links to the past carry little weight with me. I like and admire what France was, the part she has been able to play in History. But I am falling in love with her *future*."[90] Between the February 1944 "Appel" and the publication of *Thésée* two years later, Gide had learned that certain vocal compatriots would not easily disregard the "errors" of his own recent past. *Thésée*'s turn to the past offered two ways to mitigate this situation. First, the work's recapitulation of Gide's oeuvre served to refocus attention on his literary works and reaffirm the writer's accomplishments, stature, and influence. Second, the *récit*'s political allegory—like the *Pages de Journal*—proclaimed unambiguous triumph over the defeatism and confusion that the writer's enemies so frequently decried. With both *Thésée* and the *Pages de Journal*, Gide was tending his legend, revisiting the past in order to *passer outre*—to move on.

SIX

Coming Home

The Purge and the Aftermath

FOR A BRIEF TIME in 1944, André Gide's return to the intellectual power circles of metropolitan France looked to be both imminent and triumphant. Plans were under way to fill the Académie Française—whose rather undistinguished wartime membership included many active or passive supporters of Vichy and Germany (Novick 129)—with first-rate writers not associated with collaboration, and rumors in post-Liberation Paris held that Gide would be a willing candidate. Apprised of his friend's potential candidacy in October 1944, Jean Schlumberger wrote to Gide in Algiers, encouraging him to return to Paris for a few weeks in order to renew his contacts and assess the political climate before taking any official steps. Gide, however, immediately denied any desire to join the "venerable institution": "As for the Académie Française . . . *quae te dementia cepit?* ['What madness has seized you?'']," he asked, quoting Virgil's *Eclogues*; "They could shove the chair under my backside and I'd still refuse to sit on it."[1] Gide himself had learned of his supposed candidacy from an article in a Parisian newspaper, and hoped his friends would soon dispel the rumor that he intended to return to Paris as an *Immortel* (G/Sch 956, 958–59). Within weeks, however, he faced an abrupt reversal of fortune: following Louis Aragon's November 1944 allegation that he had abetted France's enemies, Gide had to defend himself not against unwanted nominations to the nation's most illustrious intellectual body but against a full-fledged trial in the press. For months to come, personal attacks and the vindictive climate of the postwar purge would make Gide's return to metropolitan France out of the question.

This chapter examines attacks on Gide during the postwar purge, showing how old animosities about his rejection of communism resurface after

127

the Liberation, and how the *épuration* informs Gide's writings for the remaining years of his life. Opening with the communist-inspired salvos in the post-Liberation press, the chapter examines Gide's evolving response to the purge and to his friends and associates—a representative spectrum ranging from collaborators facing postwar justice to resistance members returning from Nazi concentration camps. Of particular interest are the aging writer's thoughts on the changing intellectual and aesthetic landscape and his reaction—by turns hopeful and elegiac—to the rise of the younger generations. The chapter concludes by reading Gide's final work, *Ainsi soit-il*, as a reassessment of the author's wartime experiences and an ultimate assertion of resistance sympathies.

HISTORY REPEATS: A SECOND TRIAL IN THE PRESS

The chief body effecting the purge of intellectuals and journalists in postwar France was the Comité National des Écrivains (C.N.E.), a formerly clandestine group whose members included the nation's most influential writers.[2] Like the Occupation, the purge began with a blacklist (Assouline, *L'Épuration* 106): the C.N.E. met in September 1944 to draw up an initial list of twelve "undesirable writers" whose works must no longer be published. The following month, the committee announced a definitive list of 165 writers "whose attitude or writings during the Occupation morally or materially abetted the oppressor"[3] and with whom C.N.E. members refused to have any professional contact (Aron 240). Gide's name was not among the 165. On the contrary, Gide joined the C.N.E. on learning that his friends François Mauriac, Jean Schlumberger, and—he was falsely led to believe—Roger Martin du Gard were among the committee's leadership (G/MG 290). He signed on in the fall of 1944, assuming that the C.N.E.'s newspaper *Les Lettres Françaises*, would simply announce his membership with a brief note (CAG 11: 602). Instead, the news that Gide had joined the *Comité* was splashed across the front page of *Les Lettres Françaises*, accompanied by an unauthorized reprint of "La Délivrance de Tunis."

The following week, the front page of *Les Lettres Françaises* featured a virulent attack on Gide by C.N.E. Secretary General Louis Aragon, whose role as the "official poet of the resistance" granted him unsurpassed influence during the purge (Assouline, *L'Épuration* 114). "Le Retour d'André Gide," an open letter to the paper's editor Claude Morgan, expresses Aragon's outrage at seeing Gide's article and portrait on the front page of *Les Lettres* in the honored place usually reserved for writers who had demonstrated "calm French courage" before the enemy. Though he did not oppose Gide's joining the C.N.E., Aragon was scandalized that the paper founded by former *N.R.F.* editor Jean Paulhan and the martyred Jacques Decour should help effect Gide's "triumphant" return to public intellectual life. Unlike Deputy Giovoni in

Algiers, Aragon did not call for Gide's death; instead, he attempted to silence his old adversary by instituting a shadow blacklist: "I am not asking for M. Gide's execution; I ask that he not be published [. . .] in *Les Lettres Françaises*."[4]

The source of Aragon's animosity was no secret: his grudge dated back to Gide's 1936 retraction of support for the U.S.S.R., which in retrospect seemed tantamount to paving the way for German expansionism. Calling Gide the "anti-Bolshevik predecessor" of collaborationist opinion-makers, Aragon labels him "a major weapon in the hands of enemy propaganda."[5] (This argument would be trotted out again the following summer in *Ce Soir*, a communist paper then headed by Aragon: while sifting through the rubble of Hitler's chancellery, Berlin correspondent Georges Soria claims, he found an anticommunist brochure featuring Gide's portrait and a selection of unfavorable remarks made after his voyage to the Soviet Union [Soria].) As further evidence of Gide's "betrayal," Aragon adduces a tendentious but damning selection of quotations taken—out of context—from the Algiers *Pages de Journal*. Wherever possible, he connects Gide's prewar and wartime statements, as when he links the writer's horrified admiration for Hitler with his abandonment of communism. He also expresses shock at "M. Gide's sudden attention to the study of the German language beginning at the end of June 1940, as revealed in this *Journal*."[6] Though these examples may seem flimsy, other quotations—including Gide's now-infamous remarks on flagging French patriotism and his own unlimited powers of acceptance—were guaranteed to infuriate post-Liberation readers.

What is most significant about Aragon's choice of quotations is that they are nearly identical to those cited by other communist writers and politicians who sought to condemn Gide. Michael Tilby has argued convincingly that Aragon's article and the July 1944 attacks in Algiers were "Moscow-inspired [. . .] more specifically, they were the result of the influence of Gide's former associate Ilya Ehrenburg." Ehrenburg's June 1944 article denouncing Gide and *L'Arche* in the Algiers paper *La Marseillaise* may indeed have provoked the attacks in the Assemblée Consultative and the communist press. That the Soviet journalist influenced Aragon is even more certain: his article "A Chain of Evil," published in *Pravda* in October 1944, preceded Aragon's "Retour" by only weeks and referred to precisely the same "Pages de Journal" passages (Tilby 113, 115).[7] When "Le Retour" is read against contemporaneous attacks by Ehrenburg, Giovoni, and Soria, the articles' striking similarities reveal a well-orchestrated effort on the part of the communists to discredit the former fellow traveler.

Echoes of the Aragon attack persisted in the communist-influenced press for many months. One week after "Le Retour," *Les Lettres Françaises* printed an anonymous letter purporting to defend Gide—a supposed "defense" that, by playing on Gide's reputation as an anti-Semite, actually constituted another attack ("Le Cas" 2; CAG 6: 320). Later that month, Julien Benda took up Aragon's charges, this time linking Gide's prewar oeuvre to the philosophy of wartime Germany. His front-page article in *Les Lettres Françaises* denounced the made-in-Germany cult of "dynamism," which reached its fullest expression in the Third Reich's imperialist pretensions: "The principle of leading one's life in defiance of all moral considerations that might limit it has been preached to the individual; in Germany, by Nietzsche with his will to power; in France, by Gide with *L'Immoraliste* and the 'gratuitous act.'"[8] In his 1945 book *La France byzantine ou le triomphe de la littérature pure*, Benda also held Gide responsible for the weakness that led to France's defeat. Complaining that the leading writers of interwar France included "a notorious invert who theorized his own case" (Gide) and a man who spent his life "surrounded by narcotics in a shuttered room" (Proust), Benda wonders whether "this deficiency of moral ideals among the literary leaders [. . .] was not in some part responsible for France's recent misfortunes."[9] Such allegations point to an ironic aspect of Gide's second trial in the press—the fact that post-Liberation debate frequently echoed post-Armistice discussions of Gide's deleterious influence on youth and the nation.[10]

Gide's friends had anticipated hostilities and were relieved that Aragon's attack had, for the most part, failed to turn opinion against Gide (G/MG 289; CAG 11: 312). The whole business seemed so dishonest that Jean Schlumberger and Roger Martin du Gard half suspected that the announcement of Gide's C.N.E. membership and the concurrent publication of "La Délivrance de Tunis" were a setup designed to give Aragon a pretext for his offensive (G/Sch 964–65; G/MG 295). While cautioning him not to respond to Aragon and Benda's attacks, Gide's colleagues attempted to devise strategies for rehabilitating his image. Because the volume *Pages de Journal* was unavailable in France, most readers had to rely on Aragon's quotations to form an opinion of Gide's wartime diary (CAG 11: 298–99). Schlumberger thought of publishing an alternative selection of excerpts, as editor Pierre Brisson had done in *Le Figaro* two months before. Aragon's attack had complicated matters, however, and the choice of diary passages was now "very tricky, for if it is tendentious, the summary of what is omitted may arouse unfavorable remarks."[11] Reviews, rather than reprints, would turn out to be the primary forum for debating Gide's wartime conduct over the ensuing months.

Postwar reviews of Gide's *Journal* followed the pattern of the press debate surrounding Giovoni's attack in the Assemblée Consultative: Gide's detractors quoted objectionable passages from the diary, while his defenders praised his sincerity and emphasized the evolution of the writer's thought over the course of the war. Almost alone in his lucidity, Charles Eubé pointed out that both camps "excessively simplif[ied] the issue."[12] A central point of contention in reviews of the *Journal* was the tension between literary and political concerns—a dispute best illustrated by reactions to Gide's September 1940 exclamation "Hurrah for thought held in check!" (J 4: 49).[13] Beginning

with Aragon's article, where Gide's paean to constrained thought was followed by a litany of deportees' names, critics condemned Gide's failure to dis-
tinguish between intellectual constraint and other forms of oppression
("Retour" 5). While acknowledging that "in September 1940 we had only a
very slight idea of what Nazism might bring about in the occupied countries,"
Gabriel Marcel accused Gide of envisioning oppression "in the truly benign
guise of censorship."[14] Maurice Nadeau leveled a similar charge in *Combat*: "It
was necessary for him to superficially compare social constraint to the constraints writing imposes on the man of letters in order to persuade himself
that oppression does not debase truly free men."[15] At best, Gide's detractors
deemed him hopelessly out of touch with his compatriots' wartime experiences; at worst, they judged him guilty of conflating stylistic and political
constraint to minimize the latter.

Reviews of the "Interviews imaginaires"—reprinted in the 1943 volumes
Interviews imaginaires and *Attendu que . . .*—were, on balance, more positive.[16]
While some reviewers condemned the "Interviews'" apparent focus on literary matters to the exclusion of political concerns (Lévy 4; Hoog 5), many
more commended the courage of Gide's allusive "Interviews" (de Magne;
Noulet). Émile Henriot's front-page article in *Le Monde* praised Gide for his
"parenthetical dissidence" and the spirit of opposition infused throughout his
"audacious" essays. But the muted message of opposition, so thrilling to
wartime readers, was evidently not enough for the zealots of the purge, Henriot lamented: "now Monsieur Gide is being attacked by former friends, who
threaten to blacklist him. This is not the first time people have tried to prevent him from speaking. I seem to recall that that happened to him before,
in Nice or Cannes, under the Vichy regime."[17]

Several articles on the Aragon–Gide controversy stressed the similarity
between post-Armistice and post-Liberation attempts to silence the writer,[18]
and Gide himself sensed the parallels acutely. His writings from this period of
exile—and indeed for the remaining years of his life—turn repeatedly to the
topic of France's postwar "totalitarianism."[19] He compares the purge to three
historical instances of oppression, beginning with the post-Revolutionary Terror. When he describes Justice as "wearing a red bonnet,"[20] he is adopting a
common trope: the purge is to the Liberation as the Terror was to the French
Revolution—the degeneration into violence and injustice of an initially salutary rebellion. The second model Gide cites is, not surprisingly, the Soviet
Union: "oppression of thought [. . .] is beginning to be exercised, in imitation
of the U.S.S.R., in France. Any thought that does not conform becomes suspect and is at once denounced" (J 4: 251–52).[21] Gide's final and most frequent
point of comparison is also his most provocative: "Freedom of thought is in
even greater peril than in the era of Vichy and the German Occupation."[22]
Whereas the underground press had at least provided a forum for dissident
opinion under the German Occupation, the formerly clandestine newspapers

had now become the establishment and had imposed a strict party line (J II: 999). France's post-Liberation leaders had implemented their own brand of "anti-Nazi totalitarianism" (J 4: 252), Gide felt, and he grieved because "in this manner, Nazism carries off one of its most indirect and perfidious victories."[23]

GIDE ON JUSTICE

In this new totalitarian era, the threats to André Gide were very real. Claude Mauriac, son of novelist François Mauriac and personal secretary to General de Gaulle, advised Gide to delay his return to metropolitan France: "in spite of the great desire I have of seeing you again, I do not advise your immediate return: passions are at their height," he wrote in January 1945 (*Conversations* [Eng.] 220).[24] Even before Aragon's attack, Gide had doubted the wisdom of an immediate return. With the discretion and double entendre characteristic of censored wartime correspondence, he explained his hesitations in a letter to Jean Denoël: "Various reasons, including my lack of resistance . . . to the cold, induced me to delay my return."[25] Roger Martin du Gard took up the politico-medical pun as he pleaded with Gide to remain in North Africa. Aware that Gide's chronic skin troubles would be exacerbated by cold weather and inadequate nourishment, Martin du Gard wrote: "I think, no pun intended, that it would quite simply be *risking your hide* [*risquer votre peau*] to face the kind of life the French are presently made to lead before good weather is firmly established in France."[26] Heeding his friends' counsel, Gide put off his return for nearly six months as he waited "until the climate in France, materially as well as emotionally, becomes a little more clement" (Mauriac, *Conversations* [Eng.] 219).[27]

During the waiting winter of 1944–1945, the self-exiled writer issued strongly worded pronouncements on major political issues of the day. This was a period of reaction for Gide, a phase during which he seemed to stifle many of his natural political and literary inclinations. As we trace Gide's evolution from the post-Liberation crisis through the more secure years preceding his death, however, we see a return to those views most commonly associated with the author: an initially punitive attitude toward Germany gives way to a uniquely conciliatory stance; condemnation of accused collaborators transforms itself into a proud claiming of blame; sympathy for Jews' suffering fades as familiar anti-Semitic opinions resurface; artistic silence ends, and long-cherished aesthetic values reassert themselves. It is, I will argue, this notion of return—particularly the return to his well-worn role as mentor to the young—that serves as the basis for the "resistance myth" Gide would craft in his final years.

Gide began paving the way for his homecoming immediately after the July 1944 attacks in the Assemblée Consultative and the Algiers press. His "Réponse à une enquête," originally intended as a response to a London *Sunday Times* survey on France's political and cultural future, appeared in *L'Arche* some months later. When the "evidence" cited by the Algiers communists resurfaced almost verbatim in Louis Aragon's November 1944 screed, Gide immediately arranged to have his rebuttal reprinted in the Parisian press. Jean Schlumberger had misgivings, for Gide was hopelessly out of touch with metropolitan France and had no idea how capriciously the political winds could shift. In post-Liberation Paris, "Réponse à une enquête" might seem dated and naïve, so Schlumberger felt obliged to make major cuts before the article's publication as "D'une France nouvelle" in the 23 December 1944 issue of *Combat* (G/Sch 969, 968). What is most noteworthy about Schlumberger's aggressive editing is the forcefully political tone—*not* the banality—of the passages he chose to omit. As Schlumberger's reaction reveals, Gide's friends and colleagues did more than present him in the best light during the confusing and dangerous months of the purge: they actively prevented him from pandering too much to the then-dominant communists, staying the excesses of his own panicky "spin control."

Gide's "Réponse" begins with a panegyric to de Gaulle and the martyrs of the resistance, a resoundingly patriotic introduction that Schlumberger apparently found too commonplace to retain. A paean to French peasants' patriotic fervor[28] was cut because it seemed designed to "erase" the July 1940 diary entry disparaging farmers' lack of patriotic feeling—a passage that Aragon had quoted in "Le Retour d'André Gide" (G/Sch 968; J II: 712). However, Schlumberger retained Gide's assertion that France would play an "important role in tomorrow's Europe, alongside prodigious and glorious Russia"[29]—despite his strong misgivings about this "unfortunate sentence [. . .] that seems designed to make readers forget his *Retour de l'U.R.S.S.*"[30] Gide's tribute to France's eastern ally is followed by harsh condemnation of her enemy: "It matters not only that [. . . Germany] be defeated, but that it *feel* its defeat; and that we not repeat that grave mistake of the First World War, of not pursuing victory right to the heart of the country, all the way to Berlin."[31] This hawkish assertion is uncharacteristic of Gide, who had repeatedly criticized the harsh terms of the Versailles Treaty and declared that the treaty's humiliating conditions made Hitler's rise to power inevitable.

In the immediate post-Liberation phase, Gide gave the impression of calling for severe justice not only for Germany but also for those accused of collaboration. The editorial decisions of others were largely responsible for creating this image. *Combat* editor Albert Camus drew Gide into his skirmish with François Mauriac—Camus favored "swift and thorough justice" while Mauriac "warn[ed] of the dangers of slipshod justice"—by publishing Gide's review of Julien Benda's latest book under the title "La Justice avant la charité" (Lottman, *Purge* 142–43; J II: 1010). Camus's title betrays the sense of Gide's essay, however, for the review of *La Grande Épreuve des démocraties* is in fact a warning against the passionate excesses of the purge. Defending Benda, who was often criticized for refusing to let passion or sentiment cloud his reasoning,

Gide argues that rational thinking would be indispensable for rebuilding the nation. Reason alone would never have given rise to the resistance, Gide concedes: fierce love of country and hatred of the enemy were the passions that restored France's liberty. "But when French soil is finally reconquered, passion must yield, not to edulcorated sentiments—and here Benda is quite right to recall Malebranche's saying: 'One must always dispense justice before practicing charity'—but it is precisely to reason that justice must appeal; the new State will have to be founded on, and rest upon, reason."[32] When the title imposed by Camus thrust him against his will into the debate on judgment and clemency, Gide felt compelled to elucidate his opinions in a second article, "Justice ou charité?" In this February 1945 essay, Gide contrasts the human ideal of justice—which he associates with Jewish values—with the superhuman Christian ideal of charity. Under the present circumstances, he argues, France cannot afford to turn the other cheek, since such charity might mean the loss of "the homeland, and [. . .] all that attaches us to it." Nevertheless, Christian consciences are sorely tried by the current need for sanctions, purges, and placing "the entirely human and approximate idea of justice over the one, so clearly superior, but ruinous, of charity" (AL 244).[33]

"Justice ou charité?" provoked both "violent protests" and "enthusiastic approbation"[34] and earned Gide a new reputation: "in the eyes of those zealots of just charity, or of charitable justice, I now come across as a ferocious and impious proponent of the purge."[35] Gide, who deplored postwar excesses, was anything but a zealot of the purge. Nevertheless, the articles he contributed to the Parisian press during the winter of 1944–1945 take a harsher stance toward France's enemies and wartime collaborators than any of his other writings. The tone of these essays is manifestly a reaction to the purge-era attacks Gide himself endured. As he prepared to return to the capital, Gide felt obliged to adopt—if only briefly—some of the patriotic rhetoric those in power demanded of "good Frenchmen."

Gide's evolving reactions toward blacklisted intellectuals—especially those brought to trial during the winter of 1944–1945—help elucidate his opinions on justice and provide a way to gauge his own reintegration into the intellectual life of postwar France. The essay "Justice ou charité?" exposes the lineaments of Gide's tripartite standard of guilt for the postwar accused: those who poisoned public opinion deserve punishment, whereas those who were misled merit clemency; above all, only those who benefited from their actions are truly guilty.[36] As these criteria suggest, Gide tended to reserve his praise, hopes, and indulgence for the young, his criticisms for the mature generation. The only accused collaborator Gide actively defended was his former secretary Lucien Combelle, who had served as editor-in-chief of the weekly *La Révolution Nationale* and contributed to other collaborationist periodicals. Thanks to the letters from Gide and other influential supporters, thirty-one-year-old Combelle avoided the death penalty and was sentenced instead to fifteen years' hard labor at his December 1944 trial (Assouline, *L'Épuration* 42). Despite the disturbing details he later gleaned about Combelle's wartime conduct, Gide continued to believe the younger man misguided rather than self-serving (Combelle 107; CAG 11: 321).[37]

Despite his sympathy for "errors" like Combelle's, Gide did not make a practice of intervening on behalf of accused intellectuals. The most notorious collaboration trial in which he was asked to intervene was that of Robert Brasillach, a former Action Française member and editor-in-chief of *Je Suis Partout*. After Brasillach was condemned to death in January 1945, his mother—no doubt aware of Gide's successful intervention on behalf of Combelle—begged the writer to sign a petition for clemency addressed to General de Gaulle (Rousso 44; CAG 11: 321).[38] Although his friends François Mauriac, Jean Paulhan, Jean Schlumberger, and Paul Valéry were among the petition's fifty-nine signers, Gide declined to support the appeal (Assouline, *L'Épuration* 159). Whereas Lucien Combelle and Marcel Jouhandeau[39] might be excused as misguided, Brasillach had long exerted a harmful influence on public opinion: "I only know Brasillach from his articles, which in the past moved me to indignation. To pardon such poisoners is to harbour a public danger" (Gide and Bussy 236).[40]

In this and similar instances, Gide may have been thinking about more than the public good. To a certain extent, the purge vindicated Gide, for a number of his former attackers—Béraud, Maurras, Mauclair, Maurice Martin du Gard—found themselves accused in the aftermath of the Liberation.[41] Brasillach was a prime example: in 1930, he had dismissed Gide as a has-been in a mock "Oraison funèbre pour André Gide" (Brasillach 100); the following year, he published a series of interviews with conservative writers whose criticisms of Gide prefigured those of the post-Armistice "querelle des mauvais maîtres" (Kaplan, *Collaborator* 10). Unable to pardon the damage to himself and others, Gide refused to follow the example of his friend François Mauriac,[42] who intervened on behalf of Charles Maurras, leader of the extreme nationalist Action Française group, and journalist Henri Béraud, who had attacked Gide in a series of articles in the 1920s (G/Sch 975; CAG 11: 321; Sagaert, Notes [J II] 1167). For Gide— as for Louis Aragon—the postwar purge brought a settling of scores. Without taking an active role like Aragon, Gide nevertheless refused to act on behalf of many purge victims, especially his former enemies.

It may seem paradoxical that Gide, himself a victim of the purge, should assume a more severely judgmental stance than his colleagues, especially those who, like Jean Paulhan, had actively resisted the occupier. Yet his own shaky status was precisely what prompted Gide to take a hard line against accused collaborators lest he face further accusations himself (G/P 302). As late as March 1947, Gide sought to withdraw an essay promised to Paulhan's new *Cahiers de la Pléiade* because it was to appear with articles by blacklisted writers Jean Giono and Marcel Jouhandeau. The latter's fall from grace appeared to be over, Paulhan informed his friend: Malraux and Camus were willing to be published alongside Jouhandeau, and Sartre had recently invited him to contribute to *Les Temps Modernes*. Gide, however, felt that his own position was insufficiently secure to allow him such a gesture. He eventually yielded to Paulhan's exhortation not to "hand Aragon such a triumph,"[43] and the *Cahier* in question elicited no hostile reactions (G/P 302–03, 307).

Precisely one year later, Gide publicly took a very different position toward those blacklisted during the purge. Several events had occurred in the intervening year to make the author feel more secure about his position. Shortly after his March 1947 exchange with Gide, Jean Paulhan had protested the blacklisting of writers like Giono, Jouhandeau, and Montherlant in an interview with *Le Figaro*'s Jean Duché (Duché 2). He resigned from the C.N.E.—as did Duhamel, Schlumberger, and others—and this mass defection helped limit the purge committee's power and influence. Above all, the year 1947 had brought major international honors to Gide: in June he received an honorary doctorate from Oxford; in November he was awarded the Nobel Prize for Literature (Starkie 55; CAG 7: 78). It was perhaps this international recognition that gave Gide the confidence to name himself among those who had been "mistaken" during the war. In his April 1948 essay "Courage," Gide explains that he knew his wartime *Pages de Journal* would provoke severe criticism: "It certainly required no courage to write them; it did, perhaps, to publish them at a time when they could do me the most harm." Furthermore, Gide claims, the publication of his wartime diary was intended to elicit compassionate reactions toward other accused intellectuals: "I had the right to hope that those pages would temper the fury of the accusations made against the Gionos, Jouhandeaux, the Montherlants, against those who were deceived. That mistake of judgment was mine, too. I could be reproached as they were. [. . .] If you condemn them, condemn me in the same way" (adapted from AL 249).[44] Securely "Nobélisé" ("Nobelized"), the Gide of 1948 presents himself as a defender of all unjustly accused intellectuals—as a retrospectively willing martyr of the purge.[45]

As the war receded in the collective memory and Gide's own position became more secure, less noble sentiments also came to the surface, most notably on the topic of anti-Semitism. In his writings from the immediate postwar period, Gide took particular care to emphasize his enmity toward anti-Semitic writers like Maurice Barrès and Charles Maurras. Yet the uncomfortable question of Gide's similarity to these influential anti-Semites persisted. Like Maurras, whose vicious attacks on Prime Minister Léon Blum "won him a sentence for incitement to murder" in the 1930s (Marrus and Paxton 250), Gide had published diary passages in which personal criticisms of Blum served as the basis for more general anti-Semitic reflections (J I: 763); reprinted in Lucien Rebatet's 1941 book *Les Tribus du cinéma et du théâtre* (123–24), Gide's statements helped fuel anti-Semitism during World

War II. After the war, Gide continued to articulate his reflections on "the Jewish question" around the person of Léon Blum, his former classmate and only surviving friend of his generation. The war years had been dramatic and difficult for Blum: arrested in 1940, he was among the defendants at the Riom trials, where political and military figures of the Third Republic were blamed for the war and France's defeat. After his courageous testimony obliged the Vichy government to suspend the trials in April 1942, Blum was deported to Buchenwald, where he remained until 1945 (Sagaert, Notes [J II] 1502). From December 1946 to January 1947, Blum headed the caretaker government that laid the foundations for France's Fourth Republic. Following Blum's return to power, Gide affirmed that his admiration for his old friend had steadily increased, especially since "the sinister—and for him glorious— Riom trial" had showcased his valor. His admiration and sympathy did not prevent Gide from standing by his earlier remarks, however: "I am very grateful to him for not holding against me the rather harsh passages of my *Journal* about the Jews and about him (which, by the way, I cannot disown, for I continue to think them utterly correct)" (J 4: 285, 286).[46]

The occasion for Gide's 1948 musings was Jean-Paul Sartre's recent book *Réflexions sur la question juive*. Unconvinced by Sartre's famously provocative assertion that "it is the anti-Semite who creates the Jew" (*Anti-Semite* 143),[47] Gide maintained that there was "none the less a 'Jewish question,' painful and obsessive, and far from being settled" (J 4: 286).[48] Sartre did not sufficiently illuminate the psychological and historical reasons underlying anti-Semitism, Gide argued—reasons such as jealousy of Jews' achievements. Gide had reflected on this issue in wartime Tunis, where Jewish high school students stayed at the top of their classes despite the persecution they faced. "If persecution were to cease, they are the ones who rightfully would fill the highest positions; and the anti-Semites would have an easy time of it, new occasions to protest, to exclaim: You see that we were right to exclude them," he wrote in 1942. In his January 1948 diary, Gide revisited his wartime observation about the clever Jewish pupils at the Tunis *lycée*, this time adding: "[I] am very wary of precocity" (J 4: 141, 286).[49] To a certain extent, Gide was going back on the philo-Semitic observations prompted by wartime persecution of the Jews. Now that the danger had passed, his deep-seated anti-Semitism began to resurface. The fact that he couched his argument as a rebuttal of Sartre is also significant, for it shows Gide chafing against the new intellectual power generation that dominated postwar Paris—a generation of which Sartre was the undisputed leader.

THE CHANGING LITERARY LANDSCAPE

Having resigned himself to a temporary exile from metropolitan France, Gide immediately began pressing friends to visit him in Italy or North Africa.

When Maria Van Rysselberghe agreed to his proposal, Gide mobilized his connections to facilitate her trip, and she joined Gide in the Heurgons' Algiers home in February 1945. The two friends had much to discuss, including the recent birth of Isabelle, Gide's granddaughter and Van Rysselberghe's great-granddaughter (CAG 6: 321–24). They spent much of March and April touring in Algeria. In early May, Gide received the necessary paperwork for his return to France, and the pair arrived in Paris on 6 May 1945. Because the family had not received the telegram announcing the elderly travelers' arrival, no one met Gide and Van Rysselberghe at Le Bourget airfield. Arriving at rush hour, "burdened like donkeys [. . .], we must have looked like two old provincials arriving in Paris who hadn't taken the metro since the war began," Van Rysselberghe remarks humorously. Two days after returning to their adjoining apartments at 1 *bis*, rue Vaneau, Gide and Van Rysselberghe heard de Gaulle's proclamation of victory on the radio. For Van Rysselberghe, it was a "momentous and staggering moment";[50] Gide, on the other hand, said nothing of the historic event in his *Journal*. He did, however, inform his Algiers hostess Anne Heurgon that he had returned just in time for VE Day: "the news is spreading, racing by word of mouth, and all night long peaceable aircraft flew over the city, dropping stars; flares shot into the sky, from the Sacré-Cœur and the Trocadéro, in preparation for this evening's fireworks."[51] This brief passage—the peacetime equivalent of the diary entries in which Gide confessed his enjoyment of the air raid "fireworks" in the skies over Tunis (J II: 855)—constitutes Gide's only written acknowledgment of the war's end.

The Paris to which Gide returned in 1945 was characterized by intellectual renewal—though not always in ways he found pleasing. As the purge silenced one writer after another, a new generation of intellectual leaders came to the forefront. The increasing influence of communist writers and the rising existentialist movement created a demand for political engagement from public intellectuals, but Gide's lack of decisive opposition to the German Occupation and Vichy regime left him little authority in the postwar political sphere. On the other hand, writing about timeless literary topics would be "unseemly" at this juncture, and might reinforce the public's impression of Gide as a "wealthy dilettante."[52] This left Gide in a double bind.[53] In many respects, arranging his literary *rentrée* would be as tricky as making his way home geographically.

As the first furor of the purge died down, Gide was much sought after as an emblem of continuity and a guarantor of literary quality whose name could help relaunch postwar intellectual life. With France's premier intellectual institution, the Académie Française, in upheaval—Academicians Bonnard, Hermant, Maurras, and Pétain had been sentenced to national degradation and excluded from the Académie following the Liberation—Charles de Gaulle himself mooted André Gide's name for a postwar Académie designed to improve France's prestige abroad.[54] Gide, who had reacted negatively to the idea of Académie membership just a year before, had a change of heart after the 1945 death of his longtime friend Paul Valéry: if he could occupy Valéry's seat, he might let himself be tempted by de Gaulle's proposal.[55] He also planned a somewhat subversive entrance into the august institution: he would devote his reception speech to *Corydon* (CAG 7: 19), and his first act as an *Immortel* would be to publish a new preface "declaring that I consider this book to be the most important and *serviceable* [. . .] of my works."[56] In the end, de Gaulle's proposal to streamline the cumbersome nomination process failed, and plans for Gide's candidacy went no further (Assouline, *L'Épuration* 84).

Like the Académie, the French press was transformed in the months following the Liberation. Many periodicals, including Gide's own *Nouvelle Revue Française*, were barred from publication, and many were supplanted by new periodicals growing out of the resistance press. Pierre Herbart founded a new paper, *Terre des Hommes*, that Gide helped launch with an "Avant-propos" calling for solidarity in the fight against "all the forces of fascism and falsehood."[57] Following the liquidation of the *Nouvelle Revue Française*, former N.R.F. editor Jean Paulhan created the *Cahiers de la Pléiade*, which he hoped to open with some "particularly precious" contribution of Gide's. Gide, who had been saving *Thésée* for the resumption of the N.R.F., ultimately offered his "*Coup de dés*"—his swan song—to Paulhan,[58] unofficially confirming the *Cahiers* as the N.R.F.'s successor. Among the many periodicals that sprang up in the wake of the Liberation, the most influential by far was Jean-Paul Sartre's *Les Temps Modernes*, which Paulhan described as the N.R.F.'s Hegelian antithesis (G/P 274). With its declaration that literature should serve society, Sartre's manifesto in the inaugural issue greatly troubled Gide, who saw the new existentialist school as a threat to his most cherished values—both aesthetic and political: "I fear that [. . .] barbarity [. . .] may invade your ranks [. . .] camouflaged as freedom," he cautioned.[59]

From Gide's vantage point, "freedom" was often a hollow word during the postwar purge, and those who posed the greatest threat to freedom of thought were often "those who talk only of 'Freedom.'"[60] Having denounced Vichy's linguistic deformations in his "Interviews imaginaires" (AQ 172–73), Gide was chagrined to find France's postwar leaders guilty of similar abuses: "Everywhere could be seen cheating, exploitation, corrupt practices; and words themselves had lost the authentic meaning around which one might have liked to rally" (SBI 150).[61] "Défense de la langue française," a series of five articles published in *Le Figaro* between December 1946 and March 1947, underscores Gide's perception that the threat to freedom persisted in post-Liberation France. The subtle presence of political concerns in these essays recalls the wartime "Interviews imaginaires," which appeared in the same paper.[62] Like the "Interviews," in which Gide asserts that "[a] nation that stands by its language stands firm" (I.I. 21),[63] the "Défense" essays relate the state of the French language to the state of the nation. Here, too, the examples of usage that Gide critiques are quite suggestive. As an illustration of his compatriots' failure to pronounce the aspirated "h" carefully, Gide asks: "was there any better occasion to pronounce the aspirated h than in the name *Hitler* itself?"[64] Claiming that he alone used the correct form *"du hitlérisme"* before and during the war, Gide regrets that copy editors routinely substituted *"l'hitlérisme."* Gide's insistence on maintaining the aspirated "h," a marker of foreignness, can be interpreted as resistance to the assimilation represented by the elided form *"l'hitlérisme"*—not only the semantic and syntactic assimilation of the word, but also the assimilation of the political and moral values it represents.[65]

Believing that his cherished values were disappearing, and seeing his own generation eclipsed by a new cohort of intellectuals and leaders, Gide reacted by turning to the very young. In a series of four lectures delivered in 1946 and 1947, Gide spoke over the heads of the then dominant generation—that of Sartre, Camus, and Malraux—and placed his hopes in those yet to come. At a time when most of the world was holding Germany at arm's length, Gide accepted an invitation to speak at a 1947 youth conference in Munich. Though he refused to play an official role in Franco-German rapprochement, declining an invitation to meet with representatives of the University of Tübingen, his appearance at the Munich conference made Gide one of the first internationally recognized figures to reach out to the German people (Foucart, *Gadouille* 145, 156, 176).[66] Applying his lifelong pedagogical preoccupation to the sociopolitical realm, Gide had argued in 1944 that the youth of postwar Germany must be "brought up more soundly" than the generation raised on Hitler's teachings; hope for Germany's future would depend on a "painstaking process of re-education."[67] Putting his principles into practice, Gide delivered a warmly encouraging address in which he expressed tolerance toward France's former enemy, recognized wartime dissidence within the German population,[68] and warned against totalitarianism of any political stripe ("Nicht" 34).

Gide feared that the younger generation's wartime sufferings might lead them to seek the comfort of unthinking adherence to doctrine. A young reader, Bernard Enginger, wrote that Gide's writings had helped him survive in the German concentration camp to which he had been deported as a member of the resistance. Now that he was free, the young man could find no "new mentors,"[69] and wondered what purpose his liberty served. Gide responded with a warning against unquestioning devotion to any teacher, philosophy, or cause. He was more heartened by the letter from a young student in Baghdad who believed that Gide's lesson of "perpetual and invigorating restlessness"[70] offered the only means for the younger generation to maintain its integrity (AL 212). Gide was willing to be a mentor, but only one who dispensed a message of individualism and insubordination: "The world will be saved, if it can be, only by the *unsubmissive*," he declared (J 4: 264).[71]

While reasserting himself as an adviser to the young, Gide was also thinking back to the lessons of his own youth. In "Souvenirs littéraires et problèmes actuels," a lecture delivered in Beirut in April 1946 and repeated two months later in Brussels, Gide commented on current events via memories of his own literary mentor Stéphane Mallarmé. The poet's teaching was moral as well as intellectual, Gide states: he imparted an intransigent need for integrity and justice, and upheld a belief in absolute truths.[72] This belief was the polar opposite of the opportunistic truths then in fashion "under the form of *engaged literature*" (adapted from AL 196).[73] The "engaged" writer of his own youth was ultraconservative Maurice Barrès, Gide claims (FA 90), yet "to-day it is in the camp of the adversary, it is among the communists, that the ravages of the relativist doctrines are now making themselves felt, that of 'the end justifies the means'" (AL 202).[74] Pessimism and a sense of absurdity were an additional link between the dominant philosophies of Gide's youth and old age. Concurring with young Enginger's complaint that "[t]he terrifying absurdity of the Sartres and the Camuses [. . .] merely opens horizons of suicide" (J 4: 262),[75] Gide drew a parallel between existentialist tenets and the beliefs of Maurice Barrès, who declared that "the universe and our existence are senseless confusion" (qtd. in AL 211).[76] A philosophy that deemed the world absurd, he implied, could have no use for enduring ethical values.

In the aesthetic realm as well, the upheavals of war and the ensuing pessimism of the younger generation had brought about a revolution. Postwar art and literature were characterized by a disregard for permanence that reflected a more global phenomenon: lack of faith in the future. It is in the preface to his 1949 *Anthologie de la poésie française* that Gide most poignantly reflects on this aesthetic crisis. Ironically, the monumental and retrospective *Anthologie*, which features poets from the Middle Ages through the early twentieth century, is prefaced by the declaration that there may be no future for the literary past enshrined within. The *Anthologie*, Gide concludes, may be the "obsolete breviary of a vanishing generation"[77] because the war has brought about an irrevocable crisis in poetics. In an age of destruction and impermanence, traditional poetic structures based on memory are outmoded:

> There is no longer any talk of permanence.[78] Lack of confidence in the future has caused literary newcomers to develop an excessive predilection for the present, for immediacy. [. . .] The old poetic system that held sway until quite recently, a system so intelligently constructed [. . .] to allow memory to retain the eloquent turns of phrase in which emotion and beauty are inscribed; with its regular meter, repetition and alternation of rhymes, accented syllables marking caesuras, all of those rules, in short, that were so deeply inculcated in us that they seemed inevitable, natural, and indispensable; all that no longer has any reason to exist, from the moment that the moment alone matters and there is no longer any *future*.[79]

This rupture threatened Gide's own moral and aesthetic projects: "Before the war, I wrote: 'I will win my case on appeal,' or: 'I write to be *reread*'—and that no longer means anything, now that appeals are not an option and there is no longer any question of *rereading*." More important, if ties to both past and future are truly severed, "that will be the end of our culture and the tradition we fought so hard to preserve."[80] At moments like this, it seemed to Gide that the fears for the future of culture he had expressed at the outset of the war— "all that might well disappear, that cultural effort which seemed to us wonderful" (J 4: 3)[81]—had indeed been fulfilled.

Despite these pessimistic musings, the anthology preface concludes on a relatively hopeful note, with a quotation from Saint-John Perse's 1945 work *Vents*. This gesture is significant, for Saint-John Perse, the only living poet included in the *Anthologie*, exemplifies the break with traditional prosody (Gide, "Don" 23). Citing a stanza that evokes both resignation and rebirth, Gide appears to be stepping aside to make way for new voices:

> When violence had remade the bed of men on the earth,
>   A very old tree, barren of leaves, resumed the thread
> of its maxims . . .
>   And another tree of high degree was already rising from
> the great subterranean Indies,
>   With its magnetic leaf and its burden of new fruits.
> (Saint-John Perse 185)[82]

RESISTANCE BY ASSOCIATION

As fitting as it may be, this stanza from *Vents* cannot stand as the final word on André Gide's relation to the Second World War and its aftermath. Though his life was nearing its end and his era of intellectual predominance was, admittedly, over, Gide—like the "old tree" in Saint-John Perse's poem—"resumed the thread of [his] maxims." In his life's final writings—the *Journal* and *Ainsi soit-il*—Gide returned inexorably to thoughts of the war. He often used the wartime experiences of friends and acquaintances to rethink or re-present his position on significant issues. This process began just days after Aragon's vituperative attack in *Les Lettres Françaises*, when Gide congratulated himself on his friends' wartime conduct: "Will they be able to name a single one of my friends [. . .] who did not behave very well during these tragic years; many of my younger friends, especially, conducted themselves admirably. [. . .] Those who declared themselves against me, on the other hand, can be found in the other camp."[83] Emphasizing his connection to those in the opposition, Gide begins to promote the notion of innocence—even resistance—by association.

Gide began publicly associating himself with de Gaulle's comrades and supporters with the August 1944 tribute "Un Serviteur de la France nouvelle:

Pierre Viénot," published in the London-based Gaullist magazine *La France Libre*. Viénot, the son-in-law of Gide's friend Loup Mayrisch, had been under-secretary of state for foreign affairs during the Popular Front government and was among the representatives who left France for Morocco aboard the *Massilia* in July 1940. Brought back to France and condemned for desertion, Viénot joined the resistance, was arrested, escaped, and joined de Gaulle in London in April 1943. He died of a heart attack in July 1944, one month after returning to France with de Gaulle (CAG 6: 181, 384–85). Viénot was a paragon of courage and judgment, Gide writes, and with his passing de Gaulle has lost "one of his most faithful devotees." Pointing out that he had shared living quarters with Viénot for several months during the war, Gide underscores his own early resistance sympathies by asserting that he and Viénot "saw eye to eye on everything."[84]

The death of Antoine de Saint-Exupéry afforded a further opportunity for Gide to declare his allegiance to de Gaulle. Before the pilot's disappearance during a reconnaissance flight over Corsica on 31 July 1944, Saint-Exupéry and Gide had seen a great deal of each other in Algiers. Gide, who "believed himself—or claimed to be—a Gaullist,"[85] was exasperated by the younger writer's witty criticisms of de Gaulle. In his February 1945 tribute in *Le Figaro*, Gide praises Saint-Exupéry enthusiastically and declares that the two writers had only one point of discord: their assessments of the Free French general. Saint-Exupéry's aversion to de Gaulle was well known, but Gide had a scoop to report: shortly before his fatal mission, Saint-Exupéry had heard de Gaulle speak at a session of the Assemblée Consultative; immediately afterward, he expressed his admiration for the general to a mutual friend ("Saint-Exupéry" 1).[86] "So many of de Gaulle's former adversaries—whether or not they agreed with Vichy's disastrous politics (and Saint-Exupéry was at no point and in no way a Vichy supporter)—are forced to acknowledge today [. . .] that de Gaulle is saving France," Gide concludes.[87] In the midst of the post-Liberation purge, Gide used his tribute to Saint-Exupéry to attest to his friend's supposed Gaullist conversion while pointing out that his own resistance allegiance preceded that of the downed pilot.

As Gide claimed, many of his friends and associates engaged in military and intellectual resistance activities during the war. Dutchman Jef Last lived underground for three years, hiding from the Gestapo and publishing an illegal monthly, *De Vonk* (G/Las 108). Jacques Copeau's son Pascal played a major role in the French resistance, working with Jean Moulin and helping to organize the Conseil National de la Résistance and the Mouvement de Libération Nationale (CAG 13: 506). Some of Gide's friends suffered atrociously for their resistance endeavors. Former *N.R.F.* editor Jean Paulhan was placed in solitary confinement at the Santé prison after German authorities learned about the mimeograph machine in his apartment—a machine on which the first clandestine paper, *Résistance*, was duplicated.[88] Louis Martin-Chauffier, the editor of Gide's *Œuvres complètes*, joined the resistance in 1941, becoming the editor-in-chief of the underground paper *Libération*. Arrested in 1944, he was deported to the Neuengamme and Bergen-Belsen concentration camps (Martin-Chauffier, *L'Homme* 7, 81, 209).[89]

Gide had even closer contact with *résistant* Pierre Herbart (Maria Van Rysselberghe's son-in-law), though he remained largely unaware of his illicit activities until after the war. Herbart began his clandestine activities by helping young men cross the Pyrénées into Spain to avoid the Service du Travail Obligatoire; by June 1944, he had become head of the Mouvement de Libération Nationale in Brittany (Herbart, *La Ligne* 141–42).[90] After returning from Brittany, Herbart installed his headquarters at 1 *bis*, rue Vaneau. Having narrowly escaped capture by the Gestapo in the Corrèze region, André Malraux joined the household in March 1944. Expertly casing the exits and exuding an air of mystery, he made a dramatic entrance: "If he were acting in the film *Malraux* he couldn't play the part any better," Van Rysselberghe joked.[91] Three months later, the rue Vaneau resistance contingent expanded when Albert Camus, director of the clandestine paper *Combat*, came to live in Marc Allégret's old studio (CAG 6: 317). Though not in the same resistance group, Malraux and Herbart's efforts often overlapped, and "the Vaneau" became the site of "secret meetings, consultations, comings and goings, all extremely secretive as befits conspirators." Maria Van Rysselberghe's one regret was that Gide was missing the action: "Ah! if only Gide were here! How all this would excite him, and how his presence would add to the pathos of the situation."[92]

Gide, who returned to Paris in May 1945, encountered only the vestiges of this resistance activity. Behind rows of rarely consulted works in his bookshelves, he was astonished to find "an extraordinary supply of papers [. . .] and of rubber stamps—enough to supply a whole army with false identities, and enough to justify shooting those who had taken on the rash mission of distributing them" (SBI 149).[93] The narrative of this discovery vividly captures Gide's reaction to the find—a touch of pride, a degree of amusement, a definite *frisson*, and a certain wistfulness at having missed the fun. Then, too, life seemed to be imitating art, for the production of false identity papers recalls the pervasive usurpation and creation of identities throughout Gide's novel *Les Faux-Monnayeurs*.[94] The discovery of a clandestine resistance network in his own apartment mirrors the unearthing, in the novel, of an underground criminal gang that produces and circulates counterfeit coins. The abstract and theory-driven novel planned by the writer-protagonist Édouard pales in comparison with the discovery of an actual counterfeit coin and its shadowy makers. Undoubtedly as deflated as his novelist character, Gide reacts in a manner consistent with his conception of the novel—that is, with the novelist's view of himself as an arranger of plots. If he missed out on plotting—in the sense of intrigue—during the war, Gide could write himself into the resistance, mastering narrative plots that would put him more squarely at the heart of the action.

This effort is particularly striking in Gide's final memoir, *Ainsi soit-il (So Be It)*. Despite the volume's subtitle, *Les jeux sont faits (The Chips Are Down)*, Gide is clearly still playing the game, adjusting the perception of his wartime positions even in the final weeks of his life. With *Ainsi soit-il*, Gide attempts to rewrite his own war story, minimizing early ambivalence and underscoring evidence of his opposition to Germany and Vichy. Recalling his enemies' bitter criticisms of certain entries written at the beginning of the Occupation, Gide acknowledges that at one point he thought all was lost, and reminds readers that he chose not to conceal any of his "weaker moments." He goes on to elucidate the reasons for his early pessimism: living in isolation in the south of France and receiving little news from Paris, Gide explains, "nothing justified me in supposing that there was even a ghost of resistance. And an organization of resistance seemed to me even more fanciful" (SBI 146–47).[95] The first news to the contrary came from an unnamed visitor who spoke with Gide in Nice early in the first winter of the war (SV 1061).[96] Gide's hopelessness dissipated more fully on a stormy night in February 1941, when the Russian-born scholar Boris Vildé[97] came to visit him in Cabris. The young man brought news of the developing resistance network in Paris: various cells were forming in the occupied zone and several clandestine papers were beginning to circulate (CAG 6: 227). Was Vildé's aim to recruit Gide for the resistance? Possibly—he made direct overtures to André Malraux, whom he visited around the same time, but was turned down because Malraux did not take his efforts seriously (Blumenson 142; Lottman, *Left* 138; CAG 6: 229). Although Vildé made no explicit attempt to include Gide in his endeavors, the elderly writer deemed the interview pivotal. Until Vildé brought news of the developing resistance network, Gide had thought opposition impossible; from that time forward, the writer claims, he counted himself squarely on the side of the resistance.

The account of Vildé's visit takes on special significance because of the active role the writer attributes to himself.[98] Gide emphasizes his central position in a social network that would later become a political one: when the young linguist-ethnologist needed a job, Gide explains, "I had warmly recommended him to Paul Rivet, who was then the head of the Musée de l'Homme at the Trocadéro" (SBI 147–48).[99] Through his work at the museum, Vildé met Rivet, Anatole Lévitzky, and the other colleagues with whom he would organize the Réseau du Musée de l'Homme in July 1940 (Blumenson xiv; Le Témoin des martyrs 19). The Réseau, one of the earliest resistance networks, published occupied France's first clandestine newspaper, *Résistance*, throughout the winter of 1940–1941 (Blumenson 117, 163–64). The group also helped people escape to London where they could join de Gaulle's Free French (Aveline 1). Having stressed his role in bringing members of the Réseau du

Musée de l'Homme together, Gide describes how he introduced Vildé to another prominent resistance figure: on hearing Vildé's news that rainy night in Cabris, "I did not hesitate to put him in contact with Pierre Viénot, who was sleeping [. . .] in the room next to mine." The young leader of the Réseau du Musée de l'Homme and the future member of de Gaulle's Free French government in London clearly had a great deal to discuss, for "[t]heir conversation lasted until morning" (SBI 148).[100] As he narrates his decisive meeting with Vildé, Gide seems to be establishing minor resistance credentials for himself: though too old and ill to join the fighting, Gide implies, he did his part as the go-between who brought major resistance figures together.

Perhaps the deepest significance of this passage lies in its resonance with an earlier meeting narrated in *Si le grain ne meurt*. Unlike Louis Aragon and Claude Aveline, who consistently spell the Russian's surname "Vildé," Gide insists on writing "Wilde"[101]—as in Oscar (J II: 995). I would argue that this is more than a simple orthographic choice, for there are striking parallels between Gide's 1941 meeting with Vildé in Cabris and an earlier encounter with Wilde in Algiers. One night in early 1895, Oscar Wilde took Gide to a Moorish café. Seeing the Frenchman gaze admiringly at a young flute player, Wilde asked: "*Dear, would you like the little musician?*" (IID 286).[102] Gide choked out "*oui*," and Wilde arranged a rendezvous for later that evening. The tone of Gide's narration forges a link between the Wilde and Vildé encounters. The Algiers incident is characterized by suspense and adventure: Gide describes the assignation as "clandestine" and evokes his own terror as he and Wilde tried to avoid the policemen who appeared moments before the rendezvous (SBI 287; SV 308–09). The episode reads like a spy story—the sort of adventure Gide would have enjoyed had he been actively engaged in the resistance during World War II. Moreover, Wilde's function as go-between may be a model for the role Gide gives himself when he recounts the Vildé meeting in 1941: in that passage, Gide is the mentor who orchestrates important encounters.

Deep similarities of character and action unite Oscar Wilde and Boris Vildé. Each man took risks for the sake of principle, and each was punished for his daring. As Gide tells it, both meetings took place at dramatic junctures—just before each of his heroic friends went off to face his fate. Shortly after the "memorable evening"[103] in Algiers, Oscar Wilde was called back to England to deal with the accusations leveled by the Marquess of Queensberry, father of his young lover Lord Alfred Douglas (SBI 292). As a result of his bold libel suit against the marquess, who had called him a sodomite, Wilde was condemned to two years' hard labor in Reading Gaol. As for the young resistance leader, "[j]ust a few days after that meeting at Cabris, Wilde, surrounded, was shot at Saint-Etienne" (SBI 148).[104]

More important, Wilde and Vildé both initiated Gide into the possibility of liberation, paving the way for him to follow his natural inclinations.

The young Arab flute player was not Gide's first male sexual partner, but the evening engineered by the Irish writer was an epiphany—largely because of the frank conversation with Wilde that preceded Gide's assignation with Mohammed: "Ah! what a hell I had been through! And without a friend I could speak to, without a word of advice; because I had believed that coming to terms was impossible, and because I had begun by refusing to surrender, I came near sinking to perdition" (adapted from IID 288).[105] Similarly, after months of isolation from anyone who could tell him of France's embryonic resistance movement, Gide experienced a revelation during Vildé's visit, "and my whole sky was lighted up by it" (SBI 147).[106] By echoing the adventure in Algiers, the Vildé passage implies that resistance to Vichy and the Germans was Gide's natural bent—all he needed was the news that protest was feasible: "from the first instant when resistance seems possible, becomes possible, it goes without saying that I am part of it [*j'en suis*]."[107] Gide's use of the expression *en être*, which in colloquial French means to be gay, underscores the parallels between the two encounters. In both 1895 and 1941—in both sex and politics—Gide's brief, catalyzing contact with a courageous and experienced friend made him realize that he was "one of them."

Homosexuality was central to Gide's personal identity and public persona; it was an area in which he became a leader and a role model. His 1924 treatise *Corydon* was more than a scholarly defense of homosexuality: it was designed to help young men like himself accept and act on their desires. Boris Vildé's visit had a similar effect on Gide. The evolution of Gide's wartime thought and writings hardly follows the single, upward curve he evokes in *Ainsi soit-il*. Nevertheless, the meeting was a turning point: the month after the Russian's visit, Gide broke with Drieu's *Nouvelle Revue Française*; shortly thereafter, he began writing his discreetly defiant "Interviews imaginaires." Like *Corydon*, these essays served to let readers know that there were like-minded people around them. Toward the end of his life, Gide sketched similar claims with respect to resistance thought. Incriminated at the outset of the war for an oeuvre that encouraged an "attitude of insubordination, of revolt; or even initially and simply an attitude of inquiry," Gide declared in his postwar diary: "That turn of mind (that vicious turn of mind) that people used to blame in me was what saved France" (J 4: 256).[108] By stressing the marginalized, critical nature of his thought—its "queerness," in today's terms—Gide portrays himself *as resistance thinker*—as a spiritual mentor to those who won France's liberation.

What Happened to André Gide

"WHATEVER HAPPENED to André Gide?" The provocative query is Paul de Man's, the title of a 1965 essay on the waning of Gide's intellectual influence. Insofar as that essay affirms Gide's fading rather than explaining it, I would argue that de Man has merely posed a rhetorical question of the type he so brilliantly dissected in "Semiology and Rhetoric."[1] My aim here is to examine what *did* happen to André Gide, both during the war and in the postwar years, through comparisons with other prominent intellectuals of the period. Working from the hypothesis that Gide's slide into relative oblivion was in part an aftereffect of the war, I examine how his fall from prominence was hastened by the figureheads of two successive intellectual generations—the existentialists, as represented by Jean-Paul Sartre and Simone de Beauvoir, and the deconstructionists in the person of Paul de Man. After examining these thinkers' intentional or inadvertent efforts to eclipse André Gide, I explore the ironic and often uncanny similarities between their wartime experiences and those of Gide himself, arguing that these writers' assessments of Gide—in works that both analyzed and affected Gide's influence—are symptomatic of their authors' relationships to the war. In conclusion, I challenge the validity of the past half-century's marginalization of Gide and call for a reshaping of the way we read his oeuvre today.

BURYING GIDE

The postwar purge hastened the marginalization of many writers through official or unofficial blacklisting and through a shift in literary values. Of the writers not associated with collaboration, those who died during or shortly after the war were, of course, the most irrevocably relegated to "minor" or "outdated" status. Gide, who was seventy-five when the war ended, and who had less than six years left to live, joined the likes of Mauriac, Giraudoux,

Rolland, and Martin du Gard—writers deemed important but obsolete—in the minds of the postwar generation. Some younger writers who did not survive the war were eclipsed without even token acknowledgment of their intellectual contributions. Gide's friend Antoine de Saint-Exupéry, who opposed the Occupation and Vichy but openly criticized Charles de Gaulle, was cheated of recognition for works like *Pilote de guerre*, an autobiographical account of a dangerous aerial reconnaissance mission during the 1940 invasion, for purely political reasons. In October 1943, on the occasion of the sixtieth anniversary of the Alliance Française, General de Gaulle delivered a speech in Algiers praising the "leading French writers who had helped save the spirit of France by preferring exile to the ignominy of Vichy." As drafted by one of de Gaulle's aides, the address included the names of André Maurois, Saint-John Perse, and Antoine de Saint-Exupéry. As delivered by the general, however, the speech omitted any reference to these three openly anti-Gaullist writers, though it did name André Gide, who had recently declared his allegiance to de Gaulle, as well as a number of rather minor writers who happened to support the general (Cate 507; de Gaulle 333). Whereas Maurois and Saint-John Perse lived to be recognized as major writers, Saint-Exupéry disappeared during a reconnaissance flight over the Mediterranean in July 1944. The combination of a premature death and a very public snubbing contributed to his subsequent reputation as a somewhat minor novelist, one who would be "ostracized" by France's secondary and postsecondary teaching establishments. Another motive for Saint-Exupéry's demotion lies in the guilty consciences of less actively committed intellectuals, argues François Gerber: embarrassed by the aviator-novelist's record of matching his actions to his philosophy, the Gaullist and communist intelligentsia of the postwar era essentially erased Saint-Exupéry from the official history of the war (Gerber 273, 12).

Gide's fate was gentler than Saint-Exupéry's. Though he was castigated at the war's end by communist intellectuals like Louis Aragon, he benefited from Charles de Gaulle's stamp of approval. After the initial postwar quarrels died down, Gide was still recognized as a major French thinker. Unfortunately, he was labeled irrelevant and out of date by the chief postwar opinion-maker, Jean-Paul Sartre. In "New Writing in France," an essay recapitulating one of the themes of his 1945 U.S. lecture tour, Sartre declared that Gide had lost all influence on French youth. Gide's philosophy, better suited to an earlier, happier era, was of no use in a tormented postwar world. Sartre went further, asserting that the over-sixty generation was only partially affected by the events of the war: "They could *give* their time, their money, their deeds, to the Resistance; they could only *lend* their spirit. Immediately after liberation, they returned to their accustomed habits of thought." In contrast, the younger generation—Leiris, Cassou, and especially Camus—learned, through their risky involvement with clandestine resistance publications, that "writing is an act" that implicates both author and reader. Consequently, the "literature of involvement" flourished at the center of postwar French intellectual debates, and the old guard no longer seemed relevant (84). By promoting this cohort of writers and linking existentialism's ethos of commitment with the risky business of underground publishing, Sartre enhanced his own prestige—and the impression of his own importance as a resistance writer[2]—while hastening the decline of the older generation.

Despite his dismissive pronouncements in the war's immediate aftermath, Sartre had gained a new appreciation for Gide's contributions to French intellectual life by the time of Gide's death in 1951. "We thought him sacred and embalmed: he dies and we discover how much he remained alive," Sartre observed in "Gide vivant," a homage published in his opinion-making newspaper *Les Temps Modernes*. The nastiness and resentment apparent in so-called tributes to the departed author proved the continuing influence of the man who had "managed to unite both right- and left-wing [intellectuals] against him." Gide remained a crucial landmark in the landscape of French thought, Sartre asserted, and "every intellectual effort was a step either toward or away from [him]."[3] Although Sartre meant to praise Gide, Paul de Man wrote some fifteen years later, his portrayal of Gide as a "constant irritant" against whom contemporary thought defined itself went "a long way toward explaining the relative neglect in which [Gide had] fallen." Ironically, de Man repeated Sartre's unintentional nudge into oblivion in his 1965 essay "Whatever Happened to André Gide?": while making a sound case for Gide's continued significance, de Man's opening line—"It has almost become a commonplace of today's criticism to state that André Gide's work had begun to fade away even before the author's death in 1951"—became a refrain that made a renascence of Gide's influence seem improbable (*Critical* 131, 130).

In fact, de Man was making a case for Gide's ongoing relevance in the postwar age. Even before Gide's turn to political causes in the 1920s and 1930s, de Man argued, the portrayal of domestic dramas—replete with "sociological details" about the financial and class disparities underlying the power dynamics within a family or a couple—made his fictions inherently political. The politics of sexuality also fueled those works, in which the heroes' ambiguity often "stem[med] from a hidden confusion, in Gide's mind, between the other human being considered as a conscious, moral person and as an object for erotic gratification." In works like *Les Nourritures terrestres*, de Man saw an omnipresent but inward-turning sexuality that made use of "the outside world—including others—to explore and refine the awareness Gide ha[d] of his own selfhood" (*Critical* 133–35). While I would not contest the selfishness of much of Gide's sexual conduct, I disagree with de Man's interpretation of his sexuality as entirely solipsistic. As I have argued in my reading of the Tunis *Journal*, sexual interactions can offer opportunities for political commentary. It was perhaps de Man's own emphasis on textual (and, in this case, sexual) self-referentiality that caused him to ignore the real-world implications of sexuality in Gide's narratives.

The pertinence of Gide's self-exploration did not escape him, however. In de Man's eyes, Gide's life writings offered particularly salutary lessons: "The constant self-analysis that underlies the autobiographical works, the *Journal*, and most of the novels, is always aimed at dispelling false constructs of the self that would allow him to strike seductive but artificial poses. It is perhaps not a very good sign for our own time that he now receives so little attention" (*Critical* 131). The great irony is that these are the words of a man known for his reticence, for his lack of confession and self-analysis (Kaplan, "Paul de Man" 279). The story de Man failed to confess and examine was, of course, that of his World War II experiences—and he was not alone in his reticence.

WARTIME ACTIONS, POSTWAR STORIES: SARTRE, BEAUVOIR, AND DE MAN

"Looking back on the Occupation, writers often indulged in minor distortions of the truth to place their conduct in a favourable light," says historian Julian Jackson (303). The chief example Jackson cites is that of Jean-Paul Sartre and his companion Simone de Beauvoir. Unlike Gide, who had the relative good fortune to live in the unoccupied zone, Sartre and Beauvoir came into daily contact with the German occupiers in Paris, where even the most innocent interactions could lead to accusations and denials. Because heating fuel was severely rationed during the Occupation, for example, Beauvoir sought the warmth of a café in which to write: "Most evenings I spent in the Flore, where no member of the occupation forces ever set foot," she affirmed in a 1960 autobiography (*Prime* 377).[4] In point of fact, the Café de Flore was "the favored hangout of the German propaganda staff in Paris," and Beauvoir would spend the rest of her life denying the rumor that she "had not been averse to their company," or indeed that she and Sartre had "allow[ed] themselves to be enticed into a quiet but very real sort of intellectual collaboration" (Bair 242). In later years, Beauvoir would defend her wartime actions with the claim that she had merely done what was necessary to survive. Like all teachers in occupied France who wished to retain their employment, Beauvoir was forced to sign a statement declaring that she was "neither Jewish nor a Freemason." Clearly ashamed of her acquiescence, Beauvoir later declared: "I signed it because I had to. My only income came from my teaching; my ration cards depended on it, my identity papers—everything" (qtd. in Bair 242).[5]

If truth be told, however, Beauvoir and Sartre went well beyond what was strictly required to survive, pursuing the advancement of their literary careers even though it meant publishing in the German-controlled media. It is in the matter of her intellectual activities—as well as those of Sartre and like-minded peers—that Beauvoir is most starkly disingenuous: "the first rule on which all the intellectuals of the Resistance were agreed was: 'No writing for Occupied Zone papers,'" she alleges.[6] Beauvoir admits that Sartre briefly contributed to *Comoedia*, the arts weekly that became a vehicle for German propaganda during the Occupation, but hastens to add that he promptly quit on realizing that the paper was not as independent as he had hoped (*Prime* 384–85). Beauvoir oversimplifies, however: the paper's editor René Delange "remained [Sartre and Beauvoir's] 'benefactor'" and, says Pierre Assouline, "it was in *Comoedia* that [their] writings," including Beauvoir's first novel, *L'Invitée*, "found their best reception and the promptest review" (Bair 282).[7] Sidestepping the issue of the career benefits she and Sartre derived from such reviews, Beauvoir frames the issue in terms of where one's own work appeared: "The writers on our side of the zonal border had tacitly formulated certain rules and stuck to them. No one was to write for any journal or magazine in the Occupied Zone, nor to broadcast from Radio Paris" (*Prime* 408).[8] Sartre's brief involvement with *Comoedia* aside, this sweeping claim is a study in self-contradiction, for the German-controlled Radio-Paris station was Beauvoir's employer for much of the Occupation.

Beauvoir's switch from academia to the media, a sector heavily implicated in collaboration, was the result of a sex scandal—one with curiously Gidian echoes insofar as it involved a teenager. The scandal arose in 1943 after Beauvoir's pupil Nathalie Sorokine and her Jewish boyfriend moved into the hotel where Beauvoir resided. The girl's fiercely anti-Semitic mother urged Beauvoir to use her influence with Nathalie, pressuring the girl to end her "unfortunate liaison" and resume a relationship with a wealthier, more "suitable" boy (Bair 277–78). When Beauvoir refused, the girl's mother accused her of "corrupting a minor." "Before the war the affair would have gone no further," Beauvoir explained (*Prime* 427–28),[9] but with collaborationist Abel Bonnard at the helm of the Ministry of Education, there was a very real danger, especially "since Madame Sorokine's complaint held allegations of unnatural sex acts, a serious charge that led to prison and sometimes deportation." Beauvoir protested her innocence, but to no avail: after twelve years of teaching, she was summarily expelled from the profession. Her companion Jean-Paul Sartre, by that time involved with intellectual resistance, urged her to forego an appeal process that might "arouse German or collaborationist interest in her and, by extension, him" (Bair 278, 260). Perhaps to shield Sartre, Beauvoir quietly left the academy and sought work in another field.

"I can't remember how I managed to wangle a job as a features producer on the national radio network," Beauvoir wrote in 1960 (*Prime* 428).[10] This claim is also patently disingenuous: it was *Comoedia* editor René Delange who, at Sartre's request, used his considerable "influence in the German-dominated media" to secure Beauvoir a position at the Radiodiffusion

Nationale. The state-run station, also known as Radio-Paris, was notorious for broadcasting collaborationist propaganda: "Radio-Paris lies! Radio-Paris is German!"[11] was the slogan chanted over the B.B.C. airwaves and scrawled on the walls of the station's Parisian premises.[12] Although Beauvoir unquestionably knew of the station's reputation (Bair 279–80), she justified her employment at Radio-Paris on the basis of the nature of her work: "our unwritten code allowed us to work for this organization: it all depended on what you did there. I suggested a neutral, colorless program: reconstructions of traditional festivals, from the Middle Ages to modern times, complete with speech, music, and background effects" (*Prime* 428).[13] Over the years, Beauvoir would defend her work on various grounds: she needed money and was happy to take the Germans'; she worked behind the scenes, and did not actually speak over the airwaves; above all, her research was historical and had nothing to do with current events (Bair 280).

Beauvoir's insistence on the politically uninvolved nature of her work at Radio-Paris is difficult to reconcile with the existentialists' emphasis on socially committed literature, and raises questions about the uncomfortable memories lurking behind the postwar ethos of *littérature engagée*. Moreover, her rationalization calls into question the very possibility of apolitical writing, and resonates with similar assertions in Gide's early wartime *Journal*. Having decided to remain silent on current events, Gide declared that: "It is only in its timeless elements that thought can remain valid," and decided to "store up" his "unseasonable thoughts, until better times" in his diary notebook (J 4: 47, 5).[14] Yet Gide did not keep his "untimely thoughts" private: it was from these diary entries that he compiled the two installments of "Feuillets" that appeared in the early issues of Drieu La Rochelle's *Nouvelle Revue Française*. As I have argued in my analysis of Gide's contributions to the wartime *N.R.F.*, the "timeless" nature of these observations actually served the Germans' aims by contributing to the impression that the *N.R.F.*, the French literary world—and, by extension, the nation itself—were in no way changed by the German Occupation. Once he understood the cause his works were serving, the author of the "Feuillets" made a showy public break with the *N.R.F.* André Gide, a world-famous writer, could afford such a gesture; Simone de Beauvoir—young, little-known, and financially dependent—could not. Though she justified her work as apolitical, Beauvoir would forever remain "uneasy" about her stint at Radio-Paris (Bair 280), aware perhaps that even "timeless" programs served the agenda of the collaborationist media.

Although "no formal or official accusation was made about either Sartre or Beauvoir" during the postwar purge, the couple were "haunted" throughout their lives "by allegations that [. . .] their careers profited and their literary reputations flourished while others took the more honorable path of not writing for German-controlled media" (Bair 260, 295–96).[15] Like many ambitious young intellectuals of their generation, Sartre and Beauvoir yielded at times to the temptations of career advancement. Their compromises were of a fairly common and ambiguous nature, but postwar existentialism's rather self-righteous convictions made little room for such ambiguity. Scrutiny of dubious experiences was banished on both the personal and the public front: Beauvoir persistently resisted questioning about her work at Radio-Paris and "glossed over it in her memoirs" (Bair 296, 280); for his part, Sartre declared that postwar France was concerned only with the "literature of involvement," effectively banishing the sometimes uncomfortable introspection of works by Gide and his ilk ("New" 84).

While Simone de Beauvoir and Jean-Paul Sartre were negotiating the political and ethical challenges of intellectual life in occupied Paris, an even younger writer was facing similar decisions in German-occupied Brussels. Twenty-one-year-old Paul de Man had attempted to flee through France to Spain at the time of the invasion, but had been turned back at the Spanish border and returned to Belgium. When the Free University of Brussels where he was enrolled "closed its doors because it would not cooperate with the German occupying forces," the young scholar's uncle Hendrik de Man used his connections to get him a job writing for *Le Soir*, "the leading French-language daily in Belgium." He would cover cultural rather than current events, writing a literary column and reviewing books, "concerts, recitals, [and] artistic exhibitions" (Waters ix–x). Like *Comoedia* and the *Nouvelle Revue Française* in Paris, *Le Soir* had been taken over by a pro-German management that "followed the Nazi line" (Kaplan, "Paul de Man" 266; Waters x). Yet de Man's career at *Le Soir* was markedly different from Sartre's brief stint at *Comoedia* or Gide's association with the wartime *N.R.F.* Unlike the *Comoedia* contributors whose neutral cultural articles merely served to legitimize the paper's pro-German "Page européenne" or the old-guard authors who lent authority and prestige to Drieu's collaborationist-leaning *N.R.F.*, de Man actually espoused the philosophies of the "occupied" press. According to Lindsay Waters, "[t]he young Paul de Man was a cultural nationalist. In some of his writings for *Le Soir* and [the Flemish-language journal] *Het Vlaamsche Land* he espoused a form of national aestheticism that was complicit with National Socialism" (xv).

The most disturbing example of de Man's "complicit" wartime writing is unquestionably the essay "Les Juifs dans la littérature actuelle," which appeared as part of a March 1941 spread on Jewish influence in contemporary culture. Positioning himself in opposition to "vulgar anti-Semitism," de Man refutes the notion that post-World War I literature and culture are "degenerate and decadent, because they are under Jewish influence." Unlike those who would deem all contemporary literature "polluted and harmful" because a few Jewish writers have been discovered "under Latinized pseudonyms,"[16] de Man minimizes the extent of Jewish influence by dismissing all Jewish writers of French expression as mediocre.[17] He lists André Maurois,

Tristan Bernard, and Julien Benda among the writers he considers second-rate,[18] but significantly fails to mention one of the foremost French novelists of Jewish—or any—extraction: Marcel Proust (de Man, *Wartime* 45; Mehlman, "Perspectives" 326). De Man goes on to argue that "resistance" to Jewish influence confirms European culture's vitality: "By preserving, despite the Semitic intrusion into all aspects of European life, an originality and a character that have remained intact, our civilization has shown that it is healthy in its deep nature" (qtd. in Waters xxv).[19] Though his conclusion is the direct opposite of Gide's in the 1914 diary—Gide feared that Jewish influence was in fact corrupting French literature—de Man frames his assertion in terms stunningly similar to those used by Gide: "the contribution of Jewish qualities to literature [. . .] is less likely to provide new elements [. . .] than it is to interrupt the slow explanation of a race and to falsify seriously, intolerably even, its meaning" (J 2: 4).[20] Whereas Gide would exclude Jews from French literature—finding it far preferable for their works to "[come] to us [only] in translation" (J 2: 5)[21]—de Man goes considerably further, arguing for geographical rather than linguistic separation:

> we can anticipate that a solution of the Jewish problem that would envisage the creation of a Jewish colony isolated from Europe, would not result, for the literary life of the West, in regrettable consequences. The latter would lose, all in all, some people of mediocre value, and would continue as in the past to develop according to its own great laws of evolution. (qtd. in Waters xxv)[22]

Although de Man could have had no knowledge of Hitler's plans for a "Final Solution to the Jewish Problem" at the time he wrote this essay—those plans would be formulated several months later at the January 1942 Wannsee Conference (Waters xxv)—his attitude is clear: literary criteria override other concerns, and the segregation of an entire people is morally acceptable.

Was it the very visible implementation of the Final Solution in Belgium, the disasters at Stalingrad and El-Alamein that spelled defeat for Germany, or—as de Man himself claimed—a desire "to protest German control of what was being published in the newspaper" that prompted the young Belgian to resign his position at *Le Soir* in November 1942 (Atlas 68; Kaplan, "Paul de Man" 277; Waters x)? Was de Man fired, or did he leave for more lucrative employment? Theories abound, and it is unclear whether the young journalist broke with *Le Soir* out of "conscience or expediency" (Atlas 67). It was probably lucky for de Man that he left when he did: while his association with the paper was enough to warrant his appearance before a postwar tribunal charged with judging Belgians suspected of collaboration, he avoided the prison sentence meted out to many other *Le Soir* contributors. With all charges against him dismissed, de Man emigrated to the United States in 1947[17] and embarked on a brilliant academic career at Harvard and Yale (Waters x). In America, he successfully concealed his pro-Nazi journalism.

The only dangerous moment came in 1953, when he was anonymously denounced as a wartime collaborator to the Harvard Society of Fellows, of which he was a member. De Man denied the charge, even claiming that "he had in fact been a member of the Belgian resistance" (Wiener 22). It was not until 1987, some years after de Man's death, that Belgian scholar Ortwin de Graef unearthed de Man's wartime writings for *Le Soir* ("Yale" B1). The discovery sparked a lively media debate reminiscent of Gide's post-Liberation ordeal in the French press.

When de Man's wartime writings came to light, scholars and journalists hastened to expose covert autobiographical references in his scholarly oeuvre. They found a troubled relation to the past in de Man's reading of Nietzsche (Wiener 23)—especially in his attention to the *Untimely Meditations* in which Nietzsche claims that we must sometimes forget the past in order to live and act,[23] and that "we try to give ourselves a new past from which we should have liked to descend instead of the past from which we actually descended" (qtd. in de Man, *Blindness* 149–50). In his analysis of Rousseau, critics discerned an unwillingness to claim responsibility: quoting the passage of the *Confessions* in which Rousseau admits blaming a servant girl for the theft of a ribbon he himself had taken, de Man asserts that "it is always possible to face up to any experience (to excuse any guilt), because the experience always exists simultaneously as fictional discourse and as empirical event and it is never possible to decide which one of the two possibilities is the right one" (Norris 179; de Man, *Allegories* 293). Given deconstruction's insistence on textual indeterminacy—not to mention de Man's assertion that texts "masquerade" as historical events[24]—some critics denounced the entire deconstructionist enterprise as a reprehensible denial of historical realities.[25]

These readings of de Man's postwar oeuvre suggest that the Belgian scholar told his war story only in spite of himself: in an ironic confirmation of deconstructionist tenets, that story surfaced in de Man's impersonal, theoretical writings despite—or because of—his efforts to suppress it. However, if he eschewed public confession himself, de Man devoted considerable attention to the confessional writings of Rousseau, Gide, and Sartre; and while he may have "mocked" Sartre "for airing his personal laundry in public" in his 1964 autobiography *Les Mots*, he also praised the work as "a moving document about human inconstancy and the search for self-knowledge" (Kaplan, "Paul de Man" 279; *Critical* 117). De Man's quarrel was not so much with self-examination—for Nietzsche (and perhaps for himself), he had argued, "the rejection of the past is not so much an act of forgetting as an act of critical judgment directed against himself" (*Blindness* 149–50)—as with *engagement*. In this sense, his tribute to the confessional Sartre, whom he deemed "Gide's successor" in the tradition of French autobiographical writing, can be read as a rejection of the political Sartre (*Critical* 117). Here again, de Man's discomfort with his own past comes into play as he unconsciously reverses a shift he made during World War II. In the early years of the war, de Man had published very positive articles about Gide's writings (*Wartime* 11–12, 52). By 1943, however, he was tempering his praise for the generation of "Gide, Valéry, Claudel, Roger Martin du Gard, [and] Mauriac," declaring that the old guard had already been outdistanced by the succeeding generation. His assertion foreshadowed Sartre's postwar assessment, but the successor generation he praised—Drieu La Rochelle, Chardonne, Montherlant, Arland, Jouhandeau (*Wartime* 51, 158, 378–79)—was the antithesis of the resistance-oriented cohort Sartre would extol in "New Writing in France." Although de Man devoted some wartime columns to writers like Aragon and Saint-Exupéry, the preponderance of his writings on contemporary French literature focused on decidedly collaborationist authors.[26] The memory of these critical proclivities—and of his own complicit journalism—helps explain de Man's postwar hostility toward "the engaged intellectual who put mind and pen in service of state or party": as Lindsay Waters astutely argues, "[t]he man he attacks when he disparages Malraux, Hemingway, Jünger, and Sartre [. . .] is just as much the kind of intellectual that he himself had been" (xv).

Just as the politically engaged existentialist generation had turned against the introspective, artistic works of Gide and his peers, so too did the deconstructionists reject the previous generation's ethos of political commitment. This gesture of burying the past was repeated with the discovery of de Man's wartime journalism, which some scholars used as grounds for dismissing the deconstructionist school so closely identified with the Belgian theorist. Each of these intellectual "revolutions" brought a forgetting or devaluation of earlier thinkers. Insofar as these shifts were motivated by an uneasy relationship to the past—specifically, to the still-controversial past of World War II—the voices of those they would silence warrant reexamination.

REREADING GIDE

The story of Gide's war—and the stories Gide told about it—offer valuable perspectives on the intellectuals whose theories dominated the postwar decades. Before Beauvoir's, there were Gide's rationalizations and evasions; before Sartre's, there were his exaggerated claims of involvement and influence; before de Man's, there were Gide's denials and silences. In his writings from and about World War II, Gide deploys as full a range of strategies and stances as any of these writers: indeed, the most revealing characteristic of his wartime oeuvre may lie in its dialectic of involvement and withdrawal, of claiming and denying.

To the existentialists and deconstructionists, Gide was something of a navel-gazer, a profoundly insightful has-been whose allegiance to aesthetic values made him hopelessly irrelevant. I offer this reading of Gide's war as a corrective not only to the Sartrean and de Manian views, but also to the Gidian, for I contest not only Gide's blanket insistence on "sincerity" but also his deceptive claim of "antihistoricity" (J 4: 50).[27] I would argue that we have too readily taken Gide on his own terms, reading him as ahistorical and apolitical—at least as far as World War II is concerned. The man who experienced and chronicled that war was not detached from politics and history, as Sartre (and often Gide himself) would have it. Rather, he was an introspective man whose mental, sexual, and domestic life—as well as the readings of literature that colored his every thought—proved to be profoundly political and historical. It is therefore by reading against Gide's self-characterization that we unearth some of the most significant lessons of his wartime writings.

Gide's experience of World War II, while specific to the writer's temperament, values, and political understanding, has universal implications, for the intellectual's reaction to profound political crisis raises issues that transcend time and place. As we reread Gide, we see Gide engaged in the process of rereading: reassessing information that has proven erroneous or propagandistic, revising his views accordingly, and reshaping the story of his own political and moral evolution. This process is doubly instructive: it confirms the value of Gidian *disponibilité* (openness)—of openness to reorienting ourselves, to rethinking our views; at the same time, it puts us on guard, alerting us to the pervasiveness of "spin control" and the need for ever-critical attention to political crises and the stories told about them. Watching present-day crises unfold, we recognize Gide's writings on the Second World War as both paradigmatic and premonitory.

Notes

INTRODUCTION

1. While Gide himself initiated much of this vast program of "spin control," friends like the astute and cautious Roger Martin du Gard also encouraged judicious editing and placement of the wartime writings.

2. "[U]n itinéraire intellectuel [. . .] marquant, au sortir d'une ombre épaisse, les étapes d'un lent acheminement vers la lumière" (J II: 1104).

3. To be sure, Gide was not the only Frenchman to alter his political views with the changing events of the war, nor was he the only writer to publish in periodicals with varying political tendencies. Sartre, for example, contributed to both the collaborationist arts weekly *Comoedia* and the clandestine newspaper *Combat* during the course of the Occupation. Yet Gide makes a particularly illuminating object of study because his wartime publications cover a very wide political range—in terms of both content and organ of publication—and because he made a methodical effort to reinvent himself during the course of the war.

4. "Je souhaite la victoire de l'Allemagne" (qtd. in Ferro 187).

5. Jeannine Verdès-Leroux has demonstrated the extent to which Gide's wartime opinions made him "an 'ordinary' citizen" ("un citoyen 'ordinaire'") (273). The only divergence from the mainstream of public opinion comes in the early glimmers of dissidence that Gide showed by late 1941—somewhat ahead of the curve. But then, Gide was probably better informed than the average Frenchman: his admirers and well-connected friends provided him with all sorts of contraband, from rationed tobacco to clandestine newspapers (J II: 1427; CAG 6: 281).

6. Gide's father Paul Gide was a professor of law and his uncle Charles was a noted economist.

7. Maria Van Rysselberghe, known affectionately as "la petite dame," occupied the apartment adjoining Gide's at 1 *bis*, rue Vaneau in Paris and chronicled Gide's activities in great detail from 1918 until his death in 1951.

8. See Maaike Koffeman, "André Gide et l'évolution de la première NRF, ou la stratégie des satellites."

9. Gay writers of Gide's acquaintance included his *N.R.F.* associates Henri Ghéon and Jean Schlumberger, Jean Cocteau (his rival for the affections of teenaged Marc Allégret), Marcel Jouhandeau, Henry de Montherlant, and the two writers now recognized as the gay icons of the period, Oscar Wilde and Marcel Proust.

10. It was Montherlant who initiated the gender-switching code in his correspondence with diplomat and writer Roger Peyrefitte, who shared his taste for prepubescent boys (Krauss 153).

11. "[T]ransposer 'à l'ombre des jeunes filles' tout ce que ses souvenirs homosexuels lui proposaient de gracieux, de tendre et de charmant, de sorte qu'il ne lui reste plus pour *Sodome* que du grotesque et de l'abject" (J II: 1126).

12. "[L]es homosexuels normaux" (Gide, *Corydon* [Fr.] 123).

13. "Quant aux invertis [. . .] il m'a toujours paru qu'eux seuls méritaient ce reproche de déformation morale ou intellectuelle et tombaient sous le coup de certaines des accusations que l'on adresse communément à tous les homosexuels" (J I: 1092).

14. Gide thought that a young boy would benefit more from a man's love than from a woman's (*Corydon* [Fr.] 127). In privileging homosexual over heterosexual relationships, he differed from his contemporary and fellow pederast Henry de Montherlant, who rationalized that pederasty was not really homosexuality: "pederasty [. . .] is sensual love for children and adolescents (until they have their first beard [. . .]), that is to say, love of the femininity that is in them, that is to say that [pederasty] is heterosexuality with a very slight difference" ("La pédérastie [. . .] est l'amour sensuel pour les enfants et adolescents (jusqu'à leur première barbe [. . .]), c'est-à-dire l'amour de la féminité qu'il y a en eux, c'est-à-dire qu'elle est l'hétérosexualité à la petite différence près") (qtd. in Sipriot 19).

15. Segal explains that Gide's theory of pederasty was not identical to the classical norm: "*Corydon* is dedicated to trying to create a new norm by means of the old genre of the Socratic dialogue" (22).

16. "[L]'interprète-procureur"; "choisie et sacrifiée"; "la prétendue impudeur des Noirs, [. . .] le cynisme des Blancs"; "l'avantage des goûts homosexuels qui du moins n'entraînent jamais ces détresses et ces involontaires cruautés" (SV 1253).

17. *Voyage au Congo* retains the narrative of Marc Allégret's sexual tourism but omits any reference to Gide's own sexual exploits, which would have detracted from his authority as a witness to colonial abuses in French Equatorial Africa (Durosay, "Notice" 1203).

18. Léon Werth assessed matters more tartly, deriding Gide as "a conformist nonconformist, a perturbed jerk-off" ("un anti-conformiste conformiste, un branleur ébranlé") (564).

19. "Comment lutter de sincérité avec André Gide? Nous n'en [. . .] avons qu'une et il en a douze. [. . .] Hypocrite? du tout. Sincère à chaque instant, pour un instant" (Prévost 100–01).

20. During World War II, however, this self-imposed silence would be short-lived.

21. "L'on s'apprête à entrer dans un long tunnel plein de sang et d'ombre" (J I: 821).

22. "Je transcris ces lignes avec une émotion bien vive, mais d'autant plus volontiers que je m'y associe de tout mon cœur" (J I: 969).

23. Portions of Gide's letter to Maurras were also published as a footnote to a 1916 diary entry in a 1935 volume of Gide's *Œuvres complètes* (OC 9: 426).

24. "[J]e suis toujours resté, malgré vous et malgré les vôtres, très près de votre pensée" (J I: 970).

25. "[C]ette vague de socialisme qu'il sent monter et qu'il pressent devoir submerger notre vieux monde après qu'on croira la guerre finie"; "l'organisation de résistance"; "*c'est le seul*" (J I: 1060).

26. "Je me lève avec un horrible dégoût de tout et de moi-même"; "Il y a tout à revoir, tout à reprendre, tout à rééduquer en moi. Ce contre quoi j'ai le plus de mal à lutter, c'est la curiosité sensuelle"; "Dans ma charité, constamment, trop de sensualité s'insinue" (J I: 920, 916, 929).

27. "[C]ette *Liberté* que nous prétendons représenter et défendre, n'est le plus souvent que le droit d'en faire à notre tête, à notre guise, et serait mieux nommée: insubordination. Autour de nous je ne vois que désordre, désorganisation, négligence et gaspillage des vertus les plus radieuses—que mensonge, que politique, qu'absurdité" (J I: 1068).

28. In his 1918 "Feuillets," Gide mused: "if I get to the point of wishing France a king, even if he were a despot, this is because everything proves to me, alas, that of all the peoples I know, the Frenchman is the one who most lacks a feeling of the public weal and of that solidarity without which a republic results in the greatest prejudice to all" (J 2: 243) ("si j'en viens à souhaiter pour la France un roi, fût-ce un despote, c'est bien que tout me prouve, hélas, que le Français est de tous les peuples que je connais celui chez qui fasse le plus défaut le sentiment de la chose publique et de cette solidarité sans laquelle une république tourne au plus grand dam de chacun") (J I: 1089).

29. "Ne sais-tu pas que ce que tu as pris pour la haine et le dégoût de toi-même n'était que de l'impuissance à renouveler ta joie et ton bonheur?" (G/Ali 168).

30. The shared journey caused an irreparable rift in Gide's marriage: Madeleine Gide destroyed all the letters her husband had written to her since childhood when she learned that Marc was to be André's traveling companion.

31. "Je ne nie point, certes, le grand mérite de quelques œuvres juives. [. . .] Mais combien les admirerais-je de cœur plus léger si elles ne venaient à nous que traduites! Car que m'importe que la littérature de mon pays s'enrichisse si c'est au détriment de sa signification" (J I: 764). Later, in a 1931 diary entry, Gide offered a blanket condemnation of Jewish novelists and playwrights, claiming that "they all have this in common, that from their work all idea of nobility is excluded. It is a debasing literature" (J 3: 152) ("tous ont ceci de commun que, dans leur œuvre, toute idée de noblesse est exclue. C'est de la littérature avilissante") (J II: 260).

32. "Quand un Juif parle en allemand, il ment!" (qtd. in Poliakov 4: 329).

33. "[J]e n'aime pas plus les Juifs [. . .]; et au contraire ne les ai jamais crus plus dangereux" (J I: 1441).

34. Zola's famous manifesto "J'accuse" had appeared in the newspaper *L'Aurore* (Sheridan 150–51).

35. "Je sais nettement que l'art Gidien, après l'art Wildien, après l'art Proustien, font partie de l'implacable continuité du programme juif. Amener tous les goyes à bien s'enculer. Pourrir soigneusement leur élite, leur bourgeoisie par l'apologie de toutes les inversions" (Céline 214–15).

36. "[I]l n'est d'aucune portée quant à la question juive"; "Nombreuses considérations sur la question juive. Gide n'est pas loin de penser qu'elle est la plus importante de toutes" (CAG 6: 76).

37. Céline "fait de son mieux pour qu'on ne le prenne pas au sérieux" (Gide, "Les Juifs" 631).

38. "[U]n jeu littéraire qui risque, la bêtise aidant, de tirer à conséquence tragique." "If it were necessary to see in *Bagatelles pour un Massacre* anything other than a game," Gide continues, "Céline, despite all his genius, would be inexcusable for stirring up banal passions with such cynicism and casual thoughtlessness" ("S'il fallait voir dans *Bagatelles pour un Massacre* autre chose qu'un jeu, Céline, en dépit de tout son génie, serait sans excuse de remuer les passions banales avec ce cynisme et cette désinvolte légèreté") ("Les Juifs" 634).

Interestingly, Gide's review may have inspired Hannah Arendt's famous observation on the banality of evil. Reminding us that "banality is an important truth about fascist discourse," Alice Kaplan surmises that Arendt may have read the 1938 letter to Max Horkheimer in which Walter Benjamin calls attention to Gide's use of the term "banal" in the review of *Bagatelles* (*Reproductions* 49, 48): "The word *banal* speaks for itself. As you will recall, I was also struck by Céline's lack of seriousness. Gide, being the moralist he is, otherwise pays heed only to the book's intent and not to its consequences" (Benjamin 558). Ironically, Walter Benjamin was among those who experienced the consequences of anti-Semitism most tragically: shortly after his failed attempt to flee from Nazi-occupied France into Spain and then to America, he committed suicide, convinced that he was about to be deported to a concentration camp in Germany or occupied France.

39. Gide's friend Dorothy Bussy was among the many readers who disapproved of his apparent defense of Céline: "A joke? Perhaps. But when people are actually being tortured, it's not the most appropriate moment to mock them" ("Une plaisanterie? Peut-être. Mais quand des gens sont effectivement soumis à la torture, le moment n'est pas très délicatement choisi pour se moquer d'eux") (CAG 11: 75).

40. "[I]l y a, dans l'Europe d'aujourd'hui, ceux qui veulent l'extermination des Juifs [. . .] et qui, sous l'appareil stupide du scientisme raciste ou des documents forgés, dissimulent [. . .] l'espoir fou d'un massacre général de la race de Moïse et de Jésus" (Maritain, *Les Juifs* 46). Maritain is referring to the well-known hoax *Protocols of the Sages of Zion*.

41. "[C]et élément hétérogène"; "des éléments gênants" (Gide, "Les Juifs" 635–36). By suggesting that Maritain saw Jews as a troublesome element to be toler-

ated, Gide was seriously misinterpreting Maritain's argument. The philosopher later rebutted Gide's misreading of *Les Juifs parmi les nations* in his "Réponse à André Gide" (1021).

42. "[C]ette gêne peut devenir salutaire, d'autant plus utile et prémonitoire que la tendance à l'uniformisation se fait plus outrancière" (Gide, "Les Juifs" 636).

43. "[D]u moins puis-je déclarer mon indignation profonde devant un crime collectif qui dépasse en férocité, en perfidie et en lâcheté ce que l'on pouvait craindre d'un régime d'oppression"; "la médiocrité des réactions, en France, devant de tels abus de pouvoir." Citing Gide's cautious tone and rhetorical hesitancy—"I am not qualified to speak about the Jewish question in such a way as to throw new light on this distressing problem" ("Je n'ai pas qualité pour parler de la question juive de manière à jeter quelques clartés nouvelles sur cet angoissant problème") (Gide, "Déclaration" [*La Revue Juive*] 105)—Martyn Cornick has expressed reservations about the seriousness of Gide's "Déclaration": "In his reply, Gide seemed to be more concerned about the style and presentation of his opinion than about making any bold pro-Jewish or anti-Hitlerian statement" (175).

44. "Gide est plutôt d'opinion, d'esprit antisémite. [. . .] N'empêche que *La Revue de Hongrie* étant venue récemment l'entretenir des Juifs en Allemagne sous la dictature de Hitler, il a donné pour cette revue une sorte de protestation, signée par lui, contre les malheurs infligés à ces pauvres gens" (Léautaud 12: 246).

45. The interview Léautaud mentions does not appear to have been published in the *Nouvelle Revue de Hongrie* (successor to *La Revue de Hongrie*) or indeed in any of the major Hungarian or Jewish periodicals of the day.

46. "En cette période d'antisémitisme européen, Gide laisse parler son cœur. Et il déclare que sa sympathie va à tous ces malheureux. [. . .] Ah! oui, le cœur! Il devrait cependant se méfier. [. . .] C'est le cœur qui l'a conduit [. . .] à Moscou" (Combelle 98–99).

47. "[L]e meilleur de la pensée allemande s'élève contre la Prusse qui mène l'Allemagne au combat" (Gide, "Réflexions" 36).

48. "[C]omment ne comprenez-vous pas, vous qui voulez rejeter tout de l'Allemagne, qu'en rejetant tout de l'Allemagne vous travaillez à son unité?" (Gide, "Réflexions" 36).

49. France refused to accept revisions of the Versailles Treaty proposed at the Lausanne Conference in 1932 (LE 14–15).

50. "Si le hitlérisme ne s'était jamais fait connaître autrement, il serait mieux que simplement acceptable. Reste à savoir où cesse le vrai visage, où commence la grimace" (J II: 412).

51. One could argue that dissenters were also being silenced in the Soviet Union, he conceded, but in that case "certain painful abuses of force" ("certains pénibles abus de force") were undoubtedly necessary for the creation of a new society that would give a voice to those formerly consigned to silence (LE 20–22, 24).

52. In the wake of the First World War, Gide was among the first intellectuals to recognize the threat of another massive European conflict (Moutote 157). As early as

1932, he was convinced that "the passions, interests, and ideas that are pushing us toward war threaten to become overwhelming and draw the entire world into an abominable conflict, then into horrible ruin" ("les passions, les intérêts et les idées qui poussent à la guerre menacent de devenir les plus forts et d'entraîner le monde entier dans un abominable conflit, puis dans une ruine affreuse.") Unable to attend the 1932 Grand Congrès Mondial contre la Guerre in Amsterdam and unconvinced that such conferences would yield any tangible results, Gide settled for signing pacifist leader Félicien Challaye's 1932 petition opposing war at any cost (LE 15–16).

53. Herbert Lottman has cogently summarized the role of Soviet agents behind the scenes of the left-leaning Parisian intellectual establishment in the 1930s (*Left* 54–58).

54. "La littérature n'a pas à se mettre au service de la Révolution"; "Une littérature asservie est une littérature avilie, si noble et légitime que soit la cause qu'elle sert" (LE 52, 58).

55. "[C]'est en étant le plus particulier que chaque être sert le mieux la communauté" (LE 85).

56. "Je crois que mon concours [. . .] peut être de plus réel profit à votre (à notre) cause si je l'apporte librement et si l'on me sait *non* enrôlé" (LE 18).

57. Throughout the 1930s, the Soviets wooed numerous Western writers and intellectuals with royalties and junkets to the U.S.S.R. Malraux, Duhamel, and Céline were among those who traveled to the Soviet Union to collect and spend the royalties on Russian translations of their works (Lottman, *Left* 61–63).

58. Maria Van Rysselberghe, who saw her friend off on 16 June 1936, reports: "Yves and Marc photograph Gide, several times, taking care that he not be framed against the large swastika that is on the airplane's tail" ("Yves et Marc photographient Gide, plusieurs fois, en prenant soin qu'il ne se détache pas sur la grande croix gammée qui est sur la queue de l'appareil") (CAG 5: 548).

59. "[J]e doute qu'en aucun pays aujourd'hui, fût-ce dans l'Allemagne de Hitler, l'esprit soit moins libre, plus courbé, plus craintif (terrorisé), plus vassalisé" (SV 774).

60. "[B]y relying [. . .] on the worst practices of fascism [. . .] Stalin seems to justify Hitler" ("en faisant appel [. . .] aux pires procédés du fascisme [. . .] Staline semble justifier Hitler") (J II: 590). After the German-Soviet Non-Aggression Pact was signed in 1939, Gide recalled the similarities he had noted shortly after his Soviet journey: "When I said, more than two years ago, that we would see Hitler and Stalin form a partnership, everyone exclaimed that [my claim] was paradoxical" ("Lorsque je disais, il y a plus de deux ans, que nous verrions s'associer Hitler et Staline, on criait au paradoxe") (J II: 683).

61. Gide signed a December 1936 declaration protesting France's neutrality and declared his support for the "admirable Spanish people" ("l'admirable peuple espagnol") in the newspaper *Vendredi* (LE 151, 153).

62. "[D]u même côté de la barricade" (CAG 5: 576).

63. "The help that the Soviet Union is giving to Spain shows us what fine capabilities of recovery it still possesses. The Soviet Union has not yet finished instruct-

ing and astonishing us" (Gide, *Return* 72) ("L'aide que l'U.R.S.S. apporte à l'Espagne nous montre de quels heureux rétablissements elle demeure capable. L'U.R.S.S. n'a pas fini de nous instruire et de nous étonner") (SV 785).

64. "[L]a 'protestation' du nouvel allié des Marocains et des Chemises Noires, du méchant vieillard, du pleureur de Moscou" (qtd. in LE 197).

CHAPTER ONE. FROM MUNICH TO MONTOIRE: NATIONAL CRISIS AND THE MAN OF LETTERS

1. Gide would later express his relief that his wife was spared the anxiety of wartime: "Madeleine would not have been able to bear the anguish into which we have been plunged" ("Madeleine n'aurait pu supporter cette angoisse où nous voici plongés"), he wrote to Marcel Copeau shortly after the declaration of war (CAG 13: 477).

2. The phrase is British Prime Minister Neville Chamberlain's.

3. "La démocratie s'est suicidée" (G/Las 59–60).

4. "[La guerre] que Hitler a prédite et désirée dans son livre *Ma lutte*: la guerre sainte de l'Allemagne pour l'annihilation de la France" (G/Las 60–61).

5. "[L]a 'chose publique'" (J II: 624–25).

6. Other intellectuals, most notably novelist Jean Giono, took a more critical stance. When the discovery of antiwar tracts including excerpts from his *Refus d'obéissance* led to Giono's arrest shortly after the declaration of war (Grenier 205), Gide joined the protest campaign, writing to Premier Daladier to urge the novelist's prompt release. Privately, though, Gide shared Jean Paulhan's fear that release from prison would amount to compromising Giono's honor and principles. Neither Gide nor Paulhan could predict that within a year Giono would become an apologist of "peace at all cost" ("[l]a paix à tout prix") and the ideal of a peasant utopia promoted by Vichy (G/P 224, 228, 244).

7. In a letter to Gide, Valéry claimed that he had been coerced into speaking on the radio, and applauded those who criticized his broadcast "Message" (G/V 518).

8. "It makes one want to vomit. It makes one wonder whether we really deserve victory" ("C'est à vomir. C'est à se demander si nous méritons vraiment la victoire"), Gide wrote to Martin du Gard (G/MG 205).

9. "[Q]uelques cinglés"; "calmer les flots" (CAG 13: 476).

10. Pierre Herbart traveled to the capital in Gide's stead to inquire whether the Ministry of the Interior had any other service Gide might perform (CAG 11: 157).

11. "[M]y thought [. . .], if pressed into service, would lose all value" ("ma pensée [. . .] perdrait, à s'enrôler, toute valeur") (J II: 680).

12. "[J]e ne veux pas avoir à rougir demain de ce que j'écrirais aujourd'hui" (J II: 680).

13. "[L]es petits garçons noirauds et rieurs qui, devant le camp, jouent à la pelote" (Mauriac, *Conversations* [Fr.] 169–70). Mauriac's observation echoes Gide's own worries, during World War I, that too much sensuality was slipping into his charitable acts (J I: 929).

14. "[L]a misère des camps" (Mauriac, "La Décade").

15. The diary notebook Gide began in October 1939 bears poignant testimony to his concern and involvement: following his habit of jotting memos to himself in the pages of his *Journal* notebooks, Gide recorded pages of names and addresses, notes on immigrants whose papers had been revoked, and the text of a December 1939 letter ordering an unnamed person to appear at a "Centre de Rassemblement" with warm clothing, blankets, and food for two days (ms. γ1638: 35).

16. "[D]es preuves suffisantes d'attachement à la France" (G/P 225). Gide, Martin du Gard, and Simon and Dorothy Bussy collaborated to obtain the release of their friend Thea Sternheim (G/Ster lxxiii; CAG 11: 174) as well as that of Gide's German translator Ferdinand Hardekopf and his companion Sita Staub (CAG 6: 186, 188; G/MG 214–15).

17. "[T]einté de rouge" (G/Sch 896).

18. "Be wary of *my* recommendation" ("Méfiez-vous de *ma* recommandation"), Gide wrote to Thea Sternheim, who hoped he could help arrange her release from the Gurs camp, where she was interned in the summer of 1940: "I *fear* that I am more disreputable than 'in favor'; but it goes without saying that I am prepared to do everything that is in my power" ("Je *crains* d'être plutôt compromettant que 'bien en cour'; mais il va sans dire que je suis prêt à faire tout ce qui est en mon pouvoir") (G/Ster 46–47). To Roger Martin du Gard, he remarked: "My name is held in such poor regard and is so suspect that I am afraid any intervention on my part would be ineffective and even compromising" ("Mon nom est si mal vu, si suspect, que je crains que toute intervention de ma part soit inefficace et même compromettante") (G/MG 221).

19. After the fall of France, the internment program was stepped up. This acceleration was facilitated by the presence of ready-made camps: the infamous detention camp at Gurs in the Pyrénées, for example, opened in the spring of 1939 to accommodate Spanish Republican refugees; it was later used for refugees from Germany and Austria. After the Armistice, the camp came under Vichy's control, and was used to house dissidents and Jews, many of whom had been expelled from Belgium and Germany. Many internees would later be transported to Nazi death camps via the Drancy transit camp in the suburbs of Paris.

20. Maria Van Rysselberghe noted in August 1940 that Gide acknowledged "the legitimacy of the concentration camps" ("le bien-fondé des camps de concentration") (CAG 6: 185).

21. "Quand il s'agissait de Blum, vous disiez: un juif ne peut pas être un vrai patriote parce qu'il n'a pas de réelle patrie. Et maintenant [. . .] vous dites: tout juif allemand est Allemand avant d'être juif, reste Allemand en dépit des persécutions, des massacres. [. . .] Ceci dit, j'ajoute en hâte que j'applaudis de tout cœur à la décision prise d'interner indistinctement tous les Allemands [. . .] et quand il n'y aurait parmi eux qu'un traître sur cent ou sur mille, on a raison d'agir ainsi: le péril est trop grand" (J II: 697).

22. "Je ne veux pas partir, je veux rester avec vous tous, sur le même radeau" (CAG 6: 195).

23. Although he refused to leave France, Gide accepted a passport in case he should change his mind and promised to contact the Emergency Rescue Committee should he have difficulties with the French or German authorities (CAG 6: 195; Fry 141).

Gide also contemplated but ultimately rejected a private invitation for his teenaged daughter Catherine to wait out the war in the United States. In November 1940, Élisabeth Van Rysselberghe's friend Tania Bennet Tombs invited Catherine to spend the rest of the war at her home in Atlanta. Tombs, a friend of Eleanor Roosevelt, used her connections to cut through the bureaucratic obstacles quickly, and Loup Mayrisch agreed to pay for Catherine's journey. For four months the family and their friends worked on obtaining authorization for Catherine to travel. In the end, Catherine herself decided to abandon the plan: given the current state of affairs, the war and her absence might last several years. Her father and grandmother were ultimately relieved, since the separation would have been painful (CAG 6: 205–06, 230–31).

24. "I was dealing with [. . .] an elite group," Gide later wrote: "I offered the gang-plank that was at my disposal to people who deserved to be saved" (SBI 142) ("[C]'est à une élite que j'avais affaire; la passerelle que j'étais à même d'offrir, je la tendais à des gens qui méritaient d'être sauvés") (SV 1058).

25. After two years of efforts, including telegrams from Gide to Venezuelan diplomats, Malaquais and his companion Galina Yurkevitch finally made their way to Mexico via Venezuela. Safely aboard a ship across the Atlantic, Malaquais wrote on 8 October 1942: "If not for André Gide, Galy and I would be on our way toward fertilizing the fields of the Third Reich with our ashes" ("N'était André Gide, Galy et moi serions en route pour fertiliser de nos cendres les sillons du Troisième Reich") (G/Mal 137, 164–66; Malaquais 333).

26. "P.V. (Valéry) fait dire à l'oncle G. (Gide) que s'il veut revenir à Paris l'Académie n'attend que cela pour l'élire" (qtd. in CAG 6: 249).

27. It is uncertain whether Gide received this message: he does not mention any of Romains's speeches in his diary or correspondence, nor does Maria Van Rysselberghe comment on the broadcasts (CJR 1: 132).

28. "[L]'état des esprits dans cette autre France" (G/MG 237).

29. "[I]l se dit [. . .] commis voyageur en idées, et ce sont les plus subversives, voire les plus dangereuses" (CAG 6: 272).

30. "[L]'attentisme passif" (Cohen-Solal 314).

31. "[G]irouette" (CAG 6: 240); "caméléon" (Heurgon-Desjardins 9).

32. Gide's circle was international in character: during the early part of the war he spent a great deal of time with Belgian national Maria Van Rysselberghe and Aline "Loup" Mayrisch from Luxembourg, and corresponded with Englishwoman Dorothy Strachey Bussy and Dutchman Jef Last. The political views of Gide's friends and colleagues ranged from Last's radical communism to the more conservative stance of

Roger Martin du Gard, one of Gide's most trusted advisors. Friends' political engagement ran the gamut as well: Lucien Combelle and Yvonne Davet, Gide's prewar and postwar secretaries, chose the collaborationist course, whereas Pierre Herbart, Pierre Viénot, Boris Vildé, and André Malraux were involved with the resistance, though Gide would not discover the extent and nature of their activities until after the war.

33. "Je suis un être de dialogue" (SV 267).

34. "Ce n'est pas impunément que, toute une vie durant, mon esprit s'est exercé à comprendre *l'autre*" (J II: 746).

35. When he made this comment in January 1941, Gide was rereading Jean Schlumberger's 1913 essay "En lisant Thucydide." Gide identified with the Athenian Thucydides, who listened to enemy Sparta's arguments because he wanted to know "the concerns of both sides" (*"les affaires des deux partis"*) and felt curiosity and sympathy toward the enemy (qtd. in CAG 6: 219–20).

36. "Ce manque de rigueur intellectuelle donne la mesure de son désarroi" (Herbart, *Recherche* 22).

37. "In the present state of France she was no longer in a position to hope for victory. *I am almost inclined to say* that she did not deserve it" (J 4: 36) ("Dans l'état actuel de la France, elle n'était plus en mesure d'espérer la victoire. *Pour un peu, je dirais* qu'elle ne la méritait pas") (J II: 718), Gide wrote in July 1940. In September 1941, he noted that several periodicals had been shut down by the authorities, adding: "*I should almost say*: This is proper" (J 4: 86) (*"pour un peu je dirais*: c'est bien fait") (J II: 783). Elsewhere, Gide analyzes his efforts to come to terms with his nation's downfall: "I go about persuading myself, or *trying to persuade myself* that what constitutes my reason for living cannot be touched by the defeat. I am not entirely convinced of it . . ." (J 4: 40) ("je vais me persuadant, ou *tâchant de me persuader*, que ce qui fait ma raison de vie reste inatteignable par la défaite. Je n'en suis pas bien convaincu . . .") (J II: 723) (all emphases added). Gide's insertion of "I try to persuade myself" ("je tâche de me persuader") into the 25 July/ 28 September 1940 diary entry published in Drieu La Rochelle's *Nouvelle Revue Française* is equally significant (see chapter two).

38. "Oui, tout cela pourrait bien disparaître, cet effort de culture qui nous paraissait admirable (et je ne parle pas seulement de la française)" (J II: 677).

39. The family consisted of Maria Van Rysselberghe, Gide's close companion and chronicler, Van Rysselberghe's daughter Élisabeth and her husband Pierre Herbart, and Catherine, the teenaged daughter of Élisabeth Van Rysselberghe and André Gide.

40. "[É]vénements monstrueux"; "six mois de félicité calme auprès d'amis parfaits [. . .] à l'abri de la tourmente" (J II: 690).

41. "Époque passionnante bien qu'odieuse" (Mauriac, *Conversations* [Fr.] 136).

42. "[L]es 'événements' m'intéressent, et puissamment, je l'avoue; mais comme ferait un spectacle" (G/V 525).

43. "[N]'affectent en rien ma pensée" (J II: 736).

44. "Mes pensées intempestives, en attendant des jours meilleurs, je les veux engranger dans ce carnet" (J II: 680–81).

45. "[C]ette anti-historicité de mon esprit" (J II: 736).

46. "Par pudeur je ne m'occupe, dans ce carnet, que de ce qui n'a pas trait à la guerre; et c'est pourquoi, durant tant de jours, je reste sans y rien écrire. Ce sont les jours où je n'ai pu me délivrer de l'angoisse, pu penser à rien qu'à *cela*" (J II: 695).

47. "Je continuerai à couvrir les pages de ce carnet *comme si de rien n'était*" (J II: 725).

48. "[L]es consternantes nouvelles" (J II: 692).

49. "Comment, malgré la hideuse horreur de la guerre, ne pas se sentir joyeux ce matin?" (J II: 693).

50. The "exodus," which began in Belgium, soon spread to northeastern France, then to Paris and beyond as the German army advanced (Jackson 119). Gide and his companions also faced the masses displaced by the 4 June evacuation of Menton, which would be occupied by Italy within weeks (J II: 699).

51. Gide divided his time between Cabris and Nice until May 1942, then traveled to North Africa, where he would remain until 1945.

52. "[T]out simplement admirable" (J II: 702).

53. "Depuis la victoire, l'esprit de jouissance l'a emporté sur l'esprit de sacrifice. On a revendiqué plus qu'on n'a servi. On a voulu épargner l'effort; on rencontre aujourd'hui le malheur" (Pétain, *Actes* 450).

54. "On ne peut mieux dire, et ces paroles nous consolent de tous les *flatus vocis* de la radio" (J II: 702).

55. "[D]ans l'indépendance et dans la dignité. [. . .] Nous savons que la patrie demeure intacte tant que subsiste l'amour de ses enfants pour elle" (Pétain, *Actes* 451). Churchill's speech and Pétain's reply were published in the newspaper *Le Temps* on 25 June 1940 (Sagaert, Notes [J II] 1395, 1396).

56. There is no indication in Gide's *Journal* or in Maria Van Rysselberghe's memoirs that Gide heard Charles de Gaulle's now famous "Appel" from London on 18 June 1940. In fact, a relatively small number of people residing in France heard the speech when it was initially broadcast.

57. "Hier soir nous avons entendu avec stupeur à la radio la nouvelle allocution de Pétain. Se peut-il? Pétain lui-même l'a-t-il prononcée? Librement? On soupçonne quelque ruse infâme. Comment parler de France 'intacte' après la livraison à l'ennemi de plus de la moitié du pays? Comment accorder ces paroles avec celles, si nobles, qu'il prononçait il y a trois jours? Comment n'approuver point Churchill? Ne pas donner de tout son cœur son adhésion à la déclaration du général de Gaulle? Ne suffit-il pas à la France d'être vaincue? Faut-il en plus qu'elle se déshonore?" (J II: 702–03).

58. "Notre défaite est venue de nos relâchements. L'esprit de jouissance détruit ce que l'esprit de sacrifice a édifié. C'est à un redressement intellectuel et moral que, d'abord, je vous convie" (Pétain, *Actes* 454).

59. "Les explications de Pétain sont nettes, raisonnables et les seules que l'on était en droit d'attendre. Je me rends à ses raisons, et ne puis maintenir mon esprit dans son état de protestation d'avant-hier. Il n'est que de se soumettre, d'accepter,

hélas! l'inévitable, et contre quoi toute révolte ne peut réussir qu'à diviser entre eux les Français" (J II: 705).

60. "Si Pétain n'était pas, au fond, le plus 'gaulliste' de nous tous" (J II: 837).

61. "[J]e vais jusqu'à me demander si Laval lui-même n'est pas beaucoup plus habile qu'il paraît [. . .], si son rôle, ingrat entre tous, n'est pas indispensable, et s'il ne le joue pas comme il faut" (J II: 837).

62. "[U]ne admiration pleine d'angoisse, de crainte et de stupeur" (J II: 723). This rather provocative statement was deleted from published editions of the *Journal* until 1997. It is, however, consistent with Gide's ongoing fascination with the German dictator, a fascination indicated by his musing to his secretary in 1939, "Who is the Shakespeare who will write the tragedy of Hitler?" ("Quel est le Shakespeare qui écrira la tragédie de Hitler?") (qtd. in Combelle 97).

63. After French planes bombed English ships in retaliation for the Mers el-Kébir assault, Gide observed indignantly that France was expected to be grateful to Germany for allowing it to attack the "common enemy" ("l'ennemi commun") (J II: 708–09).

64. "[P]eut-être est-ce Hitler qui est destiné à rétablir ce monde nouveau?"; "Qui sait, peut-être faisons-nous tort à Hitler en pensant que son rêve final n'est pas l'harmonie du monde?" (CAG 6: 179, 204).

65. "[L]a voix de l'enfer" (J II: 747).

66. "Ne dis pas, Hitler, que je ne parviens pas à te comprendre. Je ne te comprends que trop bien; mais pour t'approuver il faudrait que je ne comprenne que toi" (J II: 748). The apostrophe to Hitler is crossed out in the manuscript (Sagaert, Notes [J II] 1409), and was omitted from all French editions of the *Journal* until 1997.

67. "[G]rand jardinier de l'Europe" (J II: 748).

68. "Hitler en somme est une manière de symbole de toutes les réformes qui permettraient une vie nouvelle, sur d'autres bases" (CAG 6: 221).

69. "Les persécutions mêmes agissent alors à la manière de la taille qui précipite toute la sève sur les quelques bourgeons épargnés, alors qu'elle ne suffisait plus à alimenter tout l'arbuste." Gide further developed the botanical allusions in his diary entry of 1 September 1940, in which he argued that Hitler's strength lay in his "inculture." Disagreeing with those who blamed France's artistic flowering for the "decadence" that supposedly led to her 1940 defeat, Gide asserted that the German "plant" was robust because it did not flower (J II: 750, 728).

70. "[L]e déracinement peut être une école de vertu" (Gide, *Prétextes* 48).

71. "[C]ertaine justice opportune" (J II: 465).

72. "Pour l'instant je ne sens en moi que de l'attente; et de l'espoir . . . mais je ne sais encore de quoi" (J II: 705).

73. "Composer avec l'ennemi d'hier, ce n'est pas lâcheté, c'est sagesse; et d'accepter l'inévitable. [. . .] À quoi bon se meurtrir contre les barreaux de sa cage? Pour souffrir moins de l'étroitesse de la geôle, il n'est que de se tenir bien au milieu" (J II: 729).

74. "[J]e ne suis nullement enclin à la révolte"; "Sans doute est-il bon, est-il sage, de se résigner lorsqu'on ne peut faire autrement"; "il est mauvais de ne pas y voir clair" (J II: 732).

75. "All the accounts one hears lead one to doubt whether much remains to be saved in France" ("Tous les récits que l'on entend laissent douter s'il reste encore grand-chose à sauver de la France"), Gide wrote to Martin du Gard on 23 July 1940: "[Our] disorder, carelessness, incapacity, stupidity, and slackness, which have left us where we are, go beyond anything I could imagine. Given France's condition before the war, we had no right to hope for victory, and it was pure delusion to launch into the dreadful enterprise that has left us prostrated today" ("Le désordre, l'incurie, l'impéritie, la bêtise, la veulerie, qui nous ont menés où nous en sommes, dépassent ce que je pouvais imaginer. Dans l'état où nous étions, une victoire était inespérable, et nous ne pouvions sans aveuglement nous lancer dans l'atroce aventure qui nous laisse aujourd'hui prostrés") (G/MG 212).

76. "[D]e penser et d'aimer librement" (J II: 711).

77. "I think we are dying of freedom and one more false step would knock us to the ground and leave us at Germany's mercy. I believe that only a dictatorship (or its equivalent) can get us out of this mess, and all we can hope for is that it will be a left-wing dictatorship that will not play into Hitler's or Stalin's hand—nor imitate either of those [dictators]" ("Je crois que nous crevons de liberté et qu'un faux-pas de plus nous mettrait à terre, à la merci de l'Allemagne. Je crois que seule une dictature (ou l'équivalent) peut nous tirer du pétrin, et que tout ce que nous pouvons souhaiter c'est que cette dictature soit de gauche et ne fasse ni le jeu de Hitler, ni celui de Staline—ni non plus n'imite l'un ou l'autre"), Gide wrote to Jef Last in November 1938 (G/Las 72). He echoed this thought in a diary entry of February 1940: "One must expect that after the war, and even though victors, we shall plunge into such a mess that nothing but a determined dictatorship will be able to get us out of it. One can see the soundest minds gradually progressing in that direction" (J 4: 10) ("Il faut s'attendre à ce que, après la guerre, encore que vainqueurs, nous plongions dans une telle gadouille que seule une dictature bien résolue nous en puisse tirer. L'on voit les esprits les plus sains s'y acheminer peu à peu") (J II: 685).

78. Observing the many Belgian soldiers in the south of France in July 1940, Gide remarked on their "charming faces not yet marked by life" (J 4: 27) ("charmants visages non encore marqués par la vie")—youthful faces that seemed much more open and joyful than those of French soldiers (J II: 707). While this observation holds echoes of the cult of youth and joy promoted in Hitler's Germany, the key point for Gide is the Belgian soldiers' more childlike qualities.

79. "[P]essimistes, défaitistes, immoralistes et corydons"; "[le] mauvais maître a exercé une influence [. . .] redoutable" (Billy 2).

80. Camille Mauclair, writing in *La Gerbe*, denounced Valéry, Gide, Proust, Mauriac, Blum, Apollinaire, Lautréamont, and the surrealists; Claudel, on the other hand, won his praise (7). Jean de Fabrègues evaluated interwar writers along similar lines in the Jesuit paper *Demain*, condemning the surrealists and dadaists but praising Péguy, Claudel, and Bernanos (6).

81. "On ne peut nier l'influence exercée sur la littérature contemporaine et sur l'esprit de la jeunesse par les ouvrages d'André Gide. C'est contre cette influence considérable, mais néfaste, qu'il faut aujourd'hui réagir. L'auteur séduisant de l'*Immoraliste* et du *Traité de Narcisse* (sic) a fait une fâcheuse école. Il a formé une génération orgueilleuse et déliquescente; il l'a élevée, sous prétexte de sincérité, dans la perversion du sens moral" ("La Jeunesse" 1).

82. Arnold Naville encouraged Gide to dispute the article in *Le Temps*, but Gide thought it would be useless to protest "that old accusation of *corrumpere juventutem*" (J 4: 34) ("cette vieille accusation de *corrumpere juventutem*"). Rather, he believed, it would be up to French youth to defend him (J II: 715).

83. "[L]'intoxication de la jeunesse par le doute" (Mauclair 7).

84. "Rien de mieux contre le 'nazisme'" (J II: 716).

85. "[U]n jeune homme de grande espérance, avait été perverti, dégradé, et finalement amené au suicide par l'influence d'André Gide" (Gillouin 3).

86. In his diary, Gide riposted: "Shall I cite in return the testimony of those I have saved from despair, of those already close to suicide?" (J 4: 103) ("Citerai-je, en revanche, le témoignage de ceux que j'ai tirés du désespoir, de ceux déjà près du suicide [. . .]?") (J II: 804).

87. "Cette histoire est, d'un bout à l'autre, de pure (ou impure) invention: ce que l'Anglais appelle *a forgery*" (J II: 804). Gide points out that the preface by a certain "Mgr de Beaumont, fortunately deceased" (J 4: 102) ("Mgr de Beaumont, heureusement décédé")—author of a 1772 text condemning Rousseau's educational treatise *Émile*—should alert readers to the apocryphal nature of Privaz's anecdote (J II: 804).

88. "[Le] souffle pestilentiel de ses livres obscènes" (qtd. in Privaz 25).

89. Writing in the pages of the right-wing *Le Cri du Peuple* in November 1940, A. Janvier rejoiced at the banning of more than a thousand books that had "poisoned" public opinion in France. Janvier denounced the "subversive philosophies" and "debilitating theories" ("les philosophies [. . .] subversives et les théories [. . .] débilitantes") that had informed French thought, and particularly condemned André Gide's prestige and influence. Lamenting "the extraordinary efflorescence of debauched novels in which filth was mixed with talent" ("l'extraordinaire floraison du roman de 'mauvaises' mœurs où s'alliaient l'ordure et le talent"), Janvier calls for "health" ("santé") and "truth" ("vérité") in the literature of a "reborn France" ("la France rénovée") (Janvier).

90. "Un romancier de l'immoralité, qui, nous l'espérons bien, n'aura plus de lecteurs, en leur apprenant que 'tout plaisir est bon à prendre', les mettait sur la voie des défaites" (qtd. in Halls 163).

91. "[L']intelligentzia folâtre et décadente" (Mounier 202).

92. "Un certain climat gidien, un certain détachement valéryen, un certain pathos bergsonien, un certain conformisme politique à polarités opposées, une certaine littérature de luxe ont collaboré à la décomposition de l'âme française" (Mounier 201).

93. "Byzantine, éludant croyance et vertu, une partie au moins de la littérature depuis 1918 n'a pas été digne de la victoire éphémère. [. . . Elle a] contribué à un désastre qui ne fut pas un coup imprévu du sort, mais l'inévitable conséquence d'abandons généralisés. Tandis qu'outre-Rhin une jeunesse fanatisée abdiquait les séductions et les désordres de l'individualisme, et les immolait à un idéal collectif, nos ténors littéraires détruisaient à plaisir la cohésion nationale" (Mauclair 7).

94. "Cette production [littéraire] plus ou moins habile et putréfiante fut présentée à l'étranger comme l'expression suprême du goût et des aspirations des Français d'après guerre" (Mauclair 7).

95. When *Le Figaro*'s editor Pierre Brisson urged Gide to reply to the survey, "his first reaction was to refuse to respond; however, having explained why in a letter to Brisson, he discovered that he had responded [to the survey]" ("[s]on premier mouvement est de refuser de répondre; seulement, en expliquant dans une lettre à Brisson pourquoi, il se trouve avoir répondu"). After several rewrites, Gide mailed his essay to Brisson for publication (CAG 6: 196).

96. "Notre littérature faisait-elle fausse route avant la tourmente?" (AQ 25).

97. "Il me paraît aussi absurde d'incriminer notre littérature au sujet de notre défaite, qu'il l'eût été de la féliciter en 1918, lorsque nous avions la victoire" (AQ 25). With the "Interviews imaginaires," which began appearing in *Le Figaro* the following year, Gide implicitly responded to the charge that literature had contributed to France's downfall. The very project of using literary references to communicate patriotic messages can be read as an attempt to counteract this perception and restore some of literature's prestige.

98. "[C]omme le grain de l'Évangile, de mourir elle-même d'abord et se renoncer. C'est de l'autre côté du tombeau que, 'le troisième jour', elle resurgira rajeunie" (AQ 26).

99. In the 1941–1942 "Interviews imaginaires," Gide develops this notion further, giving it a more explicitly political resonance: France's future lies in the hands of her poets, Gide maintains, repeatedly associating poetry with the term "résistance" (AQ 148, 159, 162). He reinforces this link through repeated references in the "Interviews" to poets like Paul Éluard and Louis Aragon, who were associated with the resistance. (Gide frequently praises Aragon in the "Interviews," and concludes his sixth essay with an extensive quotation from Aragon's 1940 poem "Zone libre.") In a post-Liberation review of the "Interviews imaginaires," a sympathetic critic asked: "Why does he speak so often of Paul Éluard or Aragon, if not for the pleasure, knowing of their roles in the resistance, of paying homage to them in the face of those they were combating?" ("Pourquoi parle-t-il si souvent de Paul Éluard ou d'Aragon, sinon pour le plaisir, connaissant leur rôle dans la résistance, de leur rendre hommage à la barbe de ceux qu'ils combattent?") (Larnac).

100. "[S]a qualité maîtresse: la critique. Je parle de la critique non point comme d'un 'genre' mais comme d'une qualité très rare, la plus indispensable pour toute réelle culture, où la France se montre incomparable. [. . . C'est] la critique, de nos jours, qui se trouve le plus en danger et, partant, c'est à nos qualités et vertus critiques qu'il importe de s'attacher" (AQ 26–27).

CHAPTER TWO. ACCOMMODATION
AND REACTION: THE WARTIME *N.R.F.*

1. "Il y a trois puissances en France: la banque, le parti communiste et *La N.R.F.* [. . .] Commençons par *La N.R.F.*" (qtd. in Hebey 13). Several variations on this anecdote circulated in wartime Paris, with the Catholic Church and the Freemasons substituting for the banking establishment and the Communist Party. Pointing out the anecdote's apocryphal ring, Pierre Hebey suggests that *N.R.F.* editor Jean Paulhan may have invented Abetz's alleged remark himself (14).

2. "[U]ne nouvelle catastrophe européenne" (Cornick 119).

3. "Une équipe de malfaiteurs"; "patrimoine intellectuel" (Riche).

4. "[E]njuivée et belliciste" (Heller 41).

5. "*La N.R.F.* [. . .] va ramper à mes pieds. Cet amas de Juifs, de pédérastes, de surréalistes timides, de pions francs-maçons, va se convulser misérablement" (Drieu, *Journal* 246).

6. "[Le] détournement possible de grandes œuvres à des fins antifrançaises" (Assouline, *Gallimard* 270–71).

7. "[U]n précieux outil de propagande" (CAG 6: 199).

8. The *Convention de censure* states: "An impartial examination of the *Liste Otto* reveals the large number of foreign authors who had found asylum on our French soil and whose works had come to encumber our literary domain. French thought has risen to such a height in the history of the world that we need have no fear. Rid of these foreign elements, it will attain its full potential and continue to exert its influence" ("Un examen impartial de la liste Otto dénote le nombre important d'auteurs étrangers qui avaient trouvé asile sur notre terre de France et dont les œuvres étaient venues encombrer notre domaine. La pensée française s'est élevée à une telle hauteur dans l'histoire du monde que nous ne devons avoir aucune crainte. Ainsi débarrassée, elle s'exprimera dans toute sa plénitude et poursuivra son rayonnement") (qtd. in Assouline, *Gallimard* 276).

9. "[C]larifier la situation en matière de propriété, [. . .] épurer la direction [. . . et] nettoyer sa production conformément aux intérêts du Reich allemand" (qtd. in Fouché I: 63–64).

10. Directors Louis-Daniel Hirsch and Robert Aron were Jewish, as were editor Jacques Schiffrin and many of the *N.R.F.* authors (Fouché I: 67).

11. Frequent miscommunications among the various German authorities in Paris—the military, the embassy, the Institut Allemand, and the Propaganda-Staffel—were most likely to blame for this administrative blunder (Heller 45).

12. Gallimard sought to convince Gide that the *N.R.F.* would be allowed to resume publication because he had resisted the Germans, not because he had made any compromises with them (CAG 6: 212). Swayed by these assertions, Gide came to believe that his publisher friend had won the first round of negotiations with the Germans (CAG 11: 182).

13. "'[L]a production spirituelle et politique' de la maison" (Assouline, *Gallimard* 281).

14. "[À] la nouvelle idée de coordination politique de l'Europe [. . .] et à la collaboration entre l'Allemagne et la France" (qtd. in Fouché I: 73).

15. The journal's Jewish directors, including Robert Aron and commercial director Louis-Daniel Hirsch, were forced out by the Jewish Statute (Assouline, *Gallimard* 284). As policies toward Jewish ownership evolved, the company took the necessary steps toward "Aryanization": in January 1942, the firm offered to buy back the shares held by its Jewish directors; in December of that year, Gaston Gallimard and Jean Schlumberger formally declared, on behalf of themselves and fellow directors André Gide and Emmanuel Couvreux, that they were "Aryan, independent of the former stockholders," and that the firm's capital came from Aryan investors ("[ils] déclarent [. . .] être: aryens, indépendants vis-à-vis des anciens titulaires des actions et les fonds d'origine aryenne") (Fouché I: 151–52).

16. "[F]aire passer le poisson douteux (les articles de la 'pensée collaborante') grâce à la sauce littéraire des plus grands écrivains français" (Winock, *Siècle* 365).

17. Gide's name was so closely associated with the *N.R.F.* that the journal planned a special issue in honor of his seventieth birthday in November 1939. Once war was declared in September, Gide deemed the publication of such an issue "gravely indecent" ("d'une grave indécence"), though editor Jean Paulhan thought it would be a "sign of strength and confidence" ("[un] signe de force et de confiance") (G/P 209, 213, 215, 220). Plans for the *N.R.F.*'s "Hommage à Gide" were soon abandoned.

Throughout the phony war, *N.R.F.* editor Jean Paulhan repeatedly urged Gide to contribute to the review. Anything, even a purely literary essay, would be welcome, but Paulhan especially wished Gide to make some pronouncement about the war (G/P 220, 226, 233). The author declined, and nearly withdrew his "Lettres du Cameroun," for which he had merely written the introduction. Gide undoubtedly worried that readers would deride these sometimes naïve letters from France's colonial subjects—a "deplorable" prospect at a time when colonial troops were being mobilized. The letters, accompanied by a note from Gide designed to preclude any such interpretation, eventually appeared in the June 1940 issue—the final *N.R.F.* issue published before the German Occupation (G/P 240–41).

18. During a December 1940 meeting, Gallimard also conveyed a request for Gide to authorize a film based on *La Symphonie pastorale*. The director and actors would be French, but under closer questioning Gallimard revealed that the Germans, who had taken control of all film studios in the occupied zone, would finance the film. On learning this, Gide refused to authorize the production (NRF xxiv–xxv).

19. "[L]a vraie résistance" (NRF xxiv).

20. "[U]ne tendance spontanée à la collaboration, à la non-résistance" (NRF xx).

21. "[C]ollaborer loyalement avec l'Allemagne"; "duperie" (NRF xx).

22. "[Q]uoi que fasse *La N.R.F.*, si votre nom est mêlé à cette reprise, c'est vous qu'on tiendra pour responsable" (CAG 6: 198).

23. Gide was loath to join a committee that would effectively supplant his friend Jean Paulhan, the journal's prewar editor (G/P 247).

24. "[À] suivre" (CAG 6: 200); "Si la censure allemande blanchit et dénature mon texte" (J II: 744).

25. "[L]a portée que son acte pouvait avoir en zone occupée" (NRF xix).

26. "[J]'entre aujourd'hui dans la voie de la collaboration" (Pétain, *Actes* 550).

27. "[D]epuis que j'ai accepté de collaborer à la nouvelle *N.R.F.*, le mot *collaboration* a pris un sens général, absolu, qu'il n'avait pas" (NRF xx).

28. "[P]éniblement extraits" (G/P 247).

29. "C'est seulement dans ce qu'elle a d'inactuel que la pensée peut demeurer valable" (F 1: 96).

30. "[S]ouffle[r] dans le sens du vent" (J II: 681).

31. "[M]ais les instituteurs avaient d'autres programmes et s'intéressaient eux-mêmes bien davantage à la 'lutte des classes', d'un rendement qui paraissait égoïstement plus immédiat" (F 1: 84).

32. "[U]ne école de division, de lutte sociale, de destruction nationale" (Pétain, *Actes* 489–90). Pétain informed British and American emissaries that France had lost the war because its reserve officers had been educated by socialist schoolteachers: "schoolteachers and politicians, rather than generals, brought France to her knees" ("les instituteurs et les politiciens, plutôt que les généraux, ont mis la France à genoux") (qtd. in Handourtzel 54). Despite some similarities of opinion, Gide—a fervent advocate of individualism—surely dissented from the marshal's attack on prewar France's "school of individualism" ("école d'individualisme") (Pétain, *Actes* 486).

33. "Il nous faudra payer toutes les absurdités de l'intangible traité de Versailles, les humiliations, les vexations inutiles [. . .] et le peu digne abus de la victoire. C'est à présent leur tour d'abuser" (F 2: 343–44); "Sans doute eût-il été chimérique de compter sur de la 'reconnaissance', mais le meilleur moyen d'empêcher Hitler, c'était de ne pas lui donner raison d'être" (J II: 704).

34. "[L]e retour à la terre"; "recul et résignation" (F 1: 85).

35. "[N]otre production agricole vassalisée" (J II: 732).

36. Ironically, as Gide would later observe, the German occupying authorities appeared to be more liberal than Vichy, for the *N.R.F.* passage on the "return to the soil" would never have been tolerated in a "free zone" publication (CAG 11: 190).

37. "Le sentiment patriotique n'est [. . .] pas plus constant que nos autres amours—qui, certains jours, si l'on était parfaitement sincère, se réduisent à bien peu de chose" (J II: 713; F 1: 84).

38. "[L]es défaillances et intermittences du sentiment patriotique"; "Rien de tel que *l'oppression* pour redonner à ce sentiment de la vigueur. Je le sens de toutes parts qui se réveille en France, et surtout dans la France occupée. Il s'assure et s'affirme dans *la résistance*, comme tout amour combattu" (J II: 741, emphasis added); "Rien de tel que *l'adversité* pour [. . .] redonner cohésion et vigueur [au sentiment patriotique]. Comme tous les amours combattus, celui de la patrie se fortifie dans *la gêne* et le martèlement le durcit" (F 2: 351, emphasis added).

Incorrectly assuming that the *N.R.F.* "Feuillets" give the original text of this entry, Henri Guillemin condemns Gide for adding the word "résistance" in the 1946 edition of his *Journal 1939–1942*: "Artfully, everything is changed and the word that counts, furtively slipped in, suddenly gives a 'resisting' air to an article that, in the 'German' *N.R.F.* of 1941 to which André Gide contributed [*collaborait*], had neither such an appearance nor indeed such an intention" ("Habilement, tout est changé et le mot qui compte, glissé là avec un soin furtif, vous donne tout à coup un air 'résistant' à ce qui n'avait, dans la N.R.F. 'allemande' de 1941 à laquelle collaborait André Gide, ni cette allure, certes, ni cette intention") (213). In fact, the references to "oppression" and "résistance" appear in the *Journal* manuscript (ms. γ1639: 62).

39. These omissions were made partly in response to Jean Schlumberger's advice to eliminate "a certain excessively resigned passage" ("certain passage par trop résigné") (NRF xxvi).

40. The "Feuillets," like the early wartime diary, are dominated by references to German literature, for Gide was rereading Goethe during the summer and fall of 1940 (CAG 6: 214). The majority of Gide's quotations are from Goethe, whose works bear no resemblance to Nazi ideology; indeed, Gide considered Goethe to be "the least German of Germans" ("le moins allemand des Allemands") (Gide, "Réflexions" 46). The "Feuillets" also refer to exiled novelist Thomas Mann, who was no friend of the Reich. Nevertheless, Pierre Herbart cautioned Gide to minimize the German quotations "if he doesn't want to appear to have a [pro-German] bias" ("si on ne veut pas que cela ait l'air d'un parti pris") (CAG 6: 214).

41. "To investigate what is and not what pleases" (J 4: 45).

42. "'Untersuchen was ist, und nicht was behagt', dit *sagement* Goethe. *Si* je sens en moi d'illimitées possibilités d'acceptation, c'est qu'elles n'engagent nullement l'être même" (F 1: 85, emphasis added).

43. "Composer avec l'ennemi d'hier, ce n'est pas lâcheté, c'est sagesse; et d'accepter l'inévitable"; "À quoi bon se meurtrir contre les barreaux de sa cage? Pour souffrir moins de l'étroitesse de la geôle, il n'est que de se tenir bien au milieu" (J II: 729).

44. In the diary, Gide states: "I feel limitless possibilities of acceptance in me; they in no wise commit my innermost self" (J 4: 45) ("Je sens en moi d'illimitées possibilités d'acceptation; elles n'engagent nullement l'être même") (J II: 729). The "Feuillets" have the hypothetical "*[i]f* I feel limitless possibilities of acceptance," (adapted from J 4: 45, emphasis added) ("*[s]i* je sens en moi d'illimitées possibilités d'acceptation") (F 1: 85, emphasis added).

45. "Si demain, comme il est à craindre, *la* liberté de penser, ou du moins d'expression de cette pensée, nous est refusée, je tâcherai de me persuader que l'art, que la pensée même, y perdront moins que dans une liberté excessive. [. . .]*Je tâche de me persuader* que c'est aux époques non libérales que l'esprit libre atteint à la plus hautaine vertu" (F 2: 348, emphasis added).

46. "[J]e tâche de me persuader"; "*toute* liberté de pensée"; "Vive la pensée comprimée!" (J II: 734, emphasis added). The original version of this entry, dated 28 September 1940, is the only such passage in the diary manuscript (ms. γ1639: 60–61). The Pléiade edition of the *Journal* includes both the "Feuillets" adaptation, fictitiously dated 25 July 1940 (J II: 720), and the original entry of 28 September 1940:

If tomorrow, as I fear, all freedom of thought or at least of expression of that thought is denied us, I shall try to convince myself that art, that thought itself, will lose less thereby than through excessive freedom. Oppression cannot debase the best; and as for the others, it matters little. Hurrah for thought held in check! The world can be saved solely by a few. It is in non-liberal epochs that the free mind achieves the highest virtue. (J 4: 49)

[Si demain, comme je le crains, toute liberté de pensée ou du moins d'expression de cette pensée, nous est refusée, je tâcherai de me persuader que l'art, que la pensée même, y perdront moins que dans une liberté excessive. L'oppression ne peut avilir les meilleurs; et quant aux autres, peu importe. Vive la pensée comprimée! Le monde ne peut être sauvé que par quelques-uns. C'est aux époques non libérales que l'esprit libre atteint à la plus haute vertu]. (J II: 734)

47. "[S]ous l'inspiration de l'occupant" (G/MG 230).

48. "On y sent une résistance sourde" (NRF xxv).

49. "[D]égonflé" (NRF xxv). By the time the inaugural issue appeared, Gide had considerable misgivings about his contribution's content, for the first installment of "Feuillets" reflected an attitude of resigned acceptance he no longer felt (CAG 11: 189).

50. "[E]t vous ne ressentirez plus le mépris que vous inspirait notre Europe balkanisée" (Fabre-Luce, "Lettre" 72).

51. Like Gide, the press in occupied Paris received the issue rather favorably. Clandestine French papers and the London Gaullist press reacted unfavorably, however (Hebey 146–47).

52. "[F]ort tourmenté" (J II: 743).

53. "Vous ne savez pas quel apport vous donnez ainsi à la propagande ennemie, votre collaboration sera présentée par eux, comme la preuve de leur libéralisme" (CAG 6: 217).

54. "[Ma] collaboration à *La N.R.F.* [. . .] paraît acquiescer à un ordre de choses que de tout mon cœur je réprouve. [. . . L]a politique ennemie saura faire arme de l'apparence, fût-ce contre la réalité" (J II: 745).

55. "[P]our moi aussi, la solution la plus aisée serait de vivre en spectateur, de me gargariser de la résistance, du courage des autres [. . . mais o]n ne peut à la fois se refuser d'être solidaire, et accepter les avantages matériels d'une activité qu'on réprouve" (qtd. in J II: 744). Gallimard made his case in a letter to Roger Martin du Gard, which the latter shared with Gide—no doubt as the publisher intended.

56. Accustomed to a steady royalty income that exceeded his living expenses, Gide had made no investments and spent considerable sums helping others. By the fall of 1940, the writer claimed to have no financial reserves whatsoever. He and Martin du Gard had been petitioning the publisher for five months' back royalties, but, as Gide pointed out, the monies due were from before the invasion and had nothing to do with profits from wartime publications (CAG 6: 187; G/Sch 910; G/MG 212, 219). As a matter of principle, Gide declared himself willing to forego payment: "it would

hardly seem decent to me if we writers were more or less the only people not to suffer from the Germans' domination" ("il me paraîtrait peu décent que nous littérateurs soyons à peu près les seuls à n'avoir point à souffrir de la domination allemande") (G/MG 225).

57. "À mes propres yeux, je ne me paraîtrais suspect de complaisance que du jour où je retirerais quelque avantage que ce soit de mon geste" (CAG 11: 188).

58. Martin du Gard analyzed his friend's protracted wavering in an unpublished text entitled "Dialogue avec Gide." Identifying Gide's lack of firm, personal political convictions as the main problem, he wrote: "You have no opinions; for the moment. You have only . . . friendships. *The worst luck of all* is that you live in the center of a little chapel in which one is sheltered from everything, in which one feels vague remorse, and in which, to compensate, one indulges in the luxury of armchair heroics and Platonic ideology" ("Vous n'avez pas d'opinion; pour l'instant. Vous n'avez . . . que des amitiés. *Pour comble de malchance*, vous vivez au centre d'une petite chapelle, où l'on est à l'abri de tout, où l'on en éprouve un vague remords, et, où, pour se dédommager, l'on se donne le luxe de faire de l'héroïsme en chambre et de l'idéologie platonique"). According to Martin du Gard, Gide's desire to withdraw from the *N.R.F.* was motivated not by personal principles but by his friends' criticisms: "the whole little chapel has fallen upon you" ("toute la petite chapelle vous est tombée dessus") (G/MG 228–29).

This characterization of Gide's circle as composed entirely of armchair resisters would prove unfair, for the writer's entourage at this time included Pierre Viénot, a future leader in de Gaulle's London-based Free French, and Pierre Herbart, who would take a decisive role in the liberation of Brittany. Martin du Gard's analysis of Gide's easy yielding to influence was right on target, though, as Gide himself acknowledged: "For a mind configured like mine, ah! how troublesome it is to have to take a position! and to have to stick by that position! [. . .] One cannot with impunity train oneself throughout one's lifetime to understand others, as any good novelist must. [. . . A]s you say, in this wavering state of mind it is, in the end, fellow-feeling that wins out" ("Pour un esprit de la forme du mien, ah! que cela est donc gênant de devoir prendre position! et de devoir s'y tenir! [. . .] Ce n'est pas impunément que, toute une vie durant, en parfait romancier, on s'exerce à comprendre l'autre. [. . . C]omme vous le dites, dans cet état de flottement, c'est en fin de compte, la sympathie qui décide") (G/MG 231).

59. Gide's hesitations and compunctions meant that the installment missed the deadline for the second issue of Drieu's *N.R.F.* The "Feuillets" appeared instead in the third issue, published in February 1941. Gide and Gallimard agreed that the difficulties in communicating between the occupied and free zones could easily explain the delay (NRF xxvii).

60. "[J]e ne sais vraiment plus si je dois tant déplorer d'avoir collaboré à *La N.R.F.*, cela peut même me donner plus d'élan pour la résistance à venir" (CAG 6: 223).

61. "Venez à Paris, c'est indispensable"; "'l'homme du Voyage en Russie se doit ce nouveau voyage' (Comprendre, évidemment: de renier publiquement ses préjugés)" (qtd. in NRF xxvii, xxviii). The pressure on Gide was exacerbated by the fact that Drieu's letter was published in the newspaper *Je Suis Partout* (Lottman, *Left* 131).

62. "De la part des siens on accepte tout" (Chardonne, "L'Été" 7).

63. Chardonne's story is so similar to Vercors's wartime classic *Le Silence de la mer* that Gérard Loiseaux has read the latter work as a parody of "L'Été à La Maurie" (Kidd 40). The similarities outlined by William Kidd are indeed striking. Chardonne describes the Charente region, where Jean Bruller (pseudonym: Vercors) also spent part of the summer of 1940, and where *Le Silence de la mer* is implicitly set. Both stories feature a German officer with impeccable manners and excellent French—a reference to the colonel's "excellent French" ("excellent français") in the *N.R.F.* version of Chardonne's text (Chardonne, "L'Été" 11) is omitted in *Chronique privée de l'an 1940*—who is billeted with a French family. Moreover, both deal with "the theme of reconciliation and dialogue between victors and vanquished," though with opposite political aims (Kidd 38–40).

64. "J'aimerais mieux vous avoir invités. Mais je ne peux rien changer à ce qui est. Appréciez mon cognac; je vous l'offre de bon cœur" (Chardonne, "L'Été" 11–12).

65. Though Gide was to claim that "Chardonne's text seemed to me, when I became aware of it, decidedly regrettable" ("le texte de Chardonne m'a paru, lorsque j'en ai pris connaissance, nettement regrettable") (J II: 744), he made no public or private objection at the time of its publication.

66. "[D]e simples manques de tact"; "l'expression d'une position pro-allemande nettement déclarée" (Heller 86; NRF xxviii).

67. "Certains régimes que nous regardions comme oppressants pour la personne humaine" (Chardonne, *Chronique* 114–15).

68. "[L]'esprit libéral"; "cette aisance de l'être que nous appelons civilisation, ni rien de ce qui constitue pour nous la valeur humaine"; "plus d'un peuple aujourd'hui attend de notre force guerrière sa résurrection, ou la défense de sa liberté" (qtd. in AQ 21, 20).

69. "La défaite suffit-elle pour changer à ce point la direction des idées?" (CAG 6: 234).

70. "On annonce que cette société ne sera pas libérale. Cela vaut mieux, car elle ne l'était plus du tout. Le libéralisme n'est pas possible en toute saison. Il y a beaucoup de choses qu'il faut enterrer pour qu'elles refleurissent" (Chardonne, *Chronique* 132). This passage, taken from the *Chronique privée* version of "L'Été à La Maurie," does not appear in the original *N.R.F.* essay.

71. "[M]ourir elle-même d'abord et se renoncer. C'est de l'autre côté du tombeau que, 'le troisième jour', elle resurgira rajeunie" (AQ 26). Gide made this statement in his October 1940 "Réponse à une enquête" in *Le Figaro*.

72. "La censure ne me gênera pas. Elle ne peut m'interdire que des futilités. Si pourtant je suis jugé subversif, je me tairai. Le meilleur d'un écrivain lui est venu de son étouffement" (Chardonne, *Chronique* 93).

73. "Vive la pensée comprimée!" (J II: 734).

74. "[S]tupeur et consternation" (J II: 754).

75. "Il agit sur moi, ce livre, par réaction; car je sens nettement, en le lisant, que cette position est à l'opposé de celle que je dois et veux prendre; et il m'importe de le

déclarer aussitôt. Mon esprit n'est que trop enclin, par nature, à l'acceptation; mais dès que l'acceptation se fait avantageuse et profitable, j'entre en garde; un instinct m'avertit: je ne puis accepter d'être avec eux du 'bon côté'; je suis de l'autre" (J II: 755). Gide repeated this image in the preface to his *Pages de Journal, 1939–1942*, declaring that Chardonne's book "acted on my mind like a reagent" (J 4: 307) ("agit sur mon esprit à la manière d'un réactif") (J II: 1103–04). In one of his "Interviews imaginaires," Gide claimed to have exerted a reciprocal effect on Chardonne. Referring to Gide's scathing article "Chardonne 1940," the fictional interviewer says: "Apparently your article acted on him like one of those chemical agents that form what is called a *precipitate*" ("Il semble que votre article ait agi sur lui à la manière de certains réactifs chimiques, amenant ce que l'on appelle un *précipité*"), causing Chardonne to adopt even stronger collaborationist views (AQ 76).

76. André Rousseaux describes René Lasne and Georg Rabuse's *Anthologie de la poésie allemande* as "right in line with the Hitlerian enterprise that seeks to make Germany Europe's leader" ("dans le droit-fil de l'entreprise hitlérienne qui prétend mettre l'Allemagne à la tête de l'Europe") (qtd. in Hebey 296).

77. "SENSIBLE À VOTRE CORDIALE LETTRE ET DÉSOLÉ, APRÈS LECTURE DES DERNIÈRES PAGES DU LIVRE DE CHARDONNE ÉCLAIRANT VOS POSITIONS, DEVOIR VOUS PRIER ENLEVER MON NOM DE COUVERTURE ET ANNONCES VOTRE REVUE" (J II: 754).

78. Gide had not originally intended to announce his withdrawal publicly, but when editor Pierre Brisson telegraphed requesting permission to print the news, Gide agreed (CAG 6: 236). Consequently, a 12 April 1941 column in *Le Figaro* reporting the whereabouts and activities of various writers began with the announcement that "M. André Gide has informed M. Drieu La Rochelle, who has *become* the director of the *N.R.F.*, that he requests that his name be removed from the list of the journal's contributors [*collaborateurs*]" ("M. André Gide a fait savoir à M. Drieu la Rochelle, *devenu* directeur de la N.R.F., qu'il le priait de ne plus faire figurer son nom parmi les *collaborateurs* de la revue") ("Aux quatre" 3, emphasis added). The language here is discreet but revealing: Drieu has "become" the director of the *N.R.F.*, and the magazine's contributors are referred to by the now-ambiguous term *collaborateurs*.

79. "La place, et pas seulement la place, me manque" (AQ 18). Gide does quote extensively from Chardonne's prewar and wartime *Chroniques* in his diary entry of 6 April 1941 (J II: 755) and in the 1943 reprint of "Chardonne 1940" in the volume *Attendu que. . . .*

80. "[O]n les trouve très obscurs et en général affreux. [. . .] Beaucoup plus tard ils seront expliqués, ils paraîtront naturels et presque toujours favorables" (qtd. in AQ 16).

81. "Les hommes politiques poursuivis devant la cour de Riom pour crime de légèreté sont innocents [. . .] comme tous les criminels" (qtd. in AQ 16–17). The actual text reads "des innocents" (Sagaert, Notes [J II] 1411; Chardonne, *Chronique* 102).

82. "[C]onjonctures tragiques"; "innocence"; "inconscience" (AQ 17).

83. "[É]coutant se combattre en moi, comme en lui, des conseils divers, je me reconnais l'esprit parent du sien"; "Je le vois devant moi qui titube, qui chancelle; aus-

sitôt cela me redresse"; "Devant sa fluidité, son inconsistance [. . .] nous sentons mieux notre solidité, et, devant tant d'acquiescements indistincts, notre constance" (AQ 19).

84. "[D]es écrivains hardis, puritains de l'art, et qui furent souvent sincères sans aucun scrupule, anciens amis de cette revue" (qtd. in CAG 6: 387).

85. Gide, ever open to opposing points of view, confessed himself touched by Chardonne's article (CAG 6: 252).

86. "[André Gide] se condamn[e] lui-même dans ma personne" (Chardonne, *Voir* 100).

87. Maurice Martin du Gard's article "La Méprise de M. Gide" originally appeared in *La Dépêche de Toulouse* on 29 April 1941.

88. "[C]ontradictions successives" (M. Martin du Gard 118–19).

89. Gide's doubts were reinforced by the very accolades he received. He felt like an orator who wonders, while listening to thunderous applause: "Did I say something foolish?" ("Aurais-je dit une bêtise?") (CAG 6: 238).

90. "[L]a seule nourriture intellectuelle possible pour les êtres dignes" (CAG 6: 239).

91. "[U]ne trahison envers Gallimard, un inamical abandon" (J II: 759). In a conversation with Gallimard, Gide assured the publisher that he had broken only with Drieu's management, not with the Gallimard publishing house (CAG 6: 238–39).

92. Gide's article on Bonnard, which was primarily literary in nature, was never published (CAG 6: 387).

93. "Vous avez déjà quelques volte-face à votre actif" (NRF xxxii).

94. "[S]uffisamment subversif pour que sa publication soit une preuve d'indépendance" (CAG 6: 240).

95. "[C]'est de Gide que j'ai le plus peur pour Gide—une gaffe avec les Allemands serait irréparable. S'il pouvait ne pas aller seul à Paris!" (CAG 6: 240–41).

96. "[L]e démon de la curiosité pourrait bien m'inviter à de très regrettables imprudences. Mieux vaut me tenir loin des tentations, des conversations" (G/V 522).

97. "[S]i je ne craignais d'y rencontrer des soldats allemands que je pourrais, en effet, trouver sympathiques" (Léautaud 12: 340–41). Léautaud repeats this anecdote on 19 June 1941 and again on 7 September 1942, this time simply saying that Gide was afraid he would meet likeable Germans, not necessarily German soldiers (13: 355–56, 14: 334).

98. "[D]es raisons de sympathie" (NRF xxxiii).

99. "C'est par sympathie pour des amis que je souhaite un triomphe de l'Angleterre, plutôt que par direct amour pour la France, qui ne pourra, me semble-t-il, profiter que bien mal de la précaire liberté que ce triomphe lui promet" (J II: 759).

100. "Et je voudrais alors effacer toutes les traces de mes pas" (J II: 759).

101. "[C]omposer avec les Allemands, au fond, [me] paraît sage"; "Il n'y a pas une ligne de tout ce que j'ai écrit depuis six mois que je ne regrette d'avoir écrite" (CAG 6: 252).

102. Paulhan acknowledged that Heller's superiors at the Propaganda-Staffel and Institut Allemand might well override his decisions about the *N.R.F.*'s publishing policies (G/P 259).

103. "[L]'action antijuive va être encore renforcée" (qtd. in G/P 259).

104. "[C]omposé de valeurs anciennes et incontestables"; "Je ne puis accepter la tâche que me propose Gaston que si Gide et Valéry—dont la désaffection a fait l'échec de *La N.R.F.*—reviennent à nous" (G/P 256).

105. "[M]êler ceux-ci et ceux-là, c'est noyer tout le monde" (G/V 527).

106. Gide objected to the presence of Jouhandeau and Giono, Paulhan deemed Montherlant unacceptable, and Valéry opposed both Jouhandeau and Montherlant (G/P 260, 262, 256). Moreover, nearly all the major writers—Valéry, Mauriac, Duhamel, and Malraux—objected to Drieu's continued presence at the *N.R.F.* (Because his daughter's mother was Jewish, Malraux explicitly refused to have any dealings with an avowed anti-Semite like Drieu.) Gide, who claimed to bear Drieu no ill will, was the only one who did not object to his participation (NRF xxxvi; G/P 257, 261).

107. "La vieille génération—Gide, Valéry, Claudel—se dérobe avec ses vieux procédés de dérobade" (Drieu, *Journal* 295).

108. "*La N.R.F.*, en somme, est ma revue" (NRF xl).

109. "[C]ette tendance à collaborer, à montrer un maximum de bonne volonté"; "preuve de leur libéralité, de leur largeur d'esprit" (NRF lx–lxi, xxxviii).

110. "Le fascisme est définitivement condamné en France"; "je m'amuserais bien de voir ces Messieurs 'collaborer' enfin ouvertement avec les Allemands" (Drieu, *Journal* 339).

111. "[A]nimé de la célèbre et horripilante impartialité qui lui fait encore des ennemis quarante ans après sa mort" (Deschodt 305).

112. "[C]'est mon cœur bien plus que ma raison qui les désapprouve, et peu s'en fallut que je n'y souscrivisse; mais je crois que je me le serais vite et amèrement reproché" (J II: 967).

113. "[P]ar le seul fait qu'elle loue un Juif, de sorte qu'il y avait presque un peu de courage à la publier et j'en sais gré au *Figaro*" (CAG 11: 190–91).

114. During their 1939 journey through Greece, Gide's traveling companion Robert Levesque had introduced him to a number of Greek intellectuals. Many of Gide's Greek acquaintances disapproved of his attitude after the fall of France, especially condemning his contributions to Drieu's *N.R.F.* (Tatsopoulos-Polychronopoulos 235, 218).

115. "[D]ites quelque chose pour nous [, . . .] faites appel à toutes les bonnes volontés en notre faveur" (qtd. in CAG 11: 185–86).

116. "I was intent [. . .] on compromising myself" ("Il me tenait à cœur [. . .] de me compromettre"), Gide later wrote of his letter to Dimaras. He subsequently crossed out this remark, substituting the assertion that he was eager to express his enthusiasm for the Greeks' resistance to the Italian aggression ("Texte" 293).

117. "[L]e mauvais effet produit par ma collaboration à la N.R.F." (CAG 11: 188).

118. "Valeureux peuple grec! [. . .] Vous représentez pour nous le triomphe de la vertu vaillante" (CAG 11: 601). After Greece succumbed to Germany in the spring of 1941, Gide expressed his "ardent sympathy" ("ardente sympathie") for Greece—"for its admirable success at first, and then, alas! for its cruel martyrdom" ("pour son admirable succès d'abord, puis, hélas! pour son atroce martyre")—in a 1943 letter to the Greek poet George Seferis, then living in Cairo and working for the press services of the Greek government in exile ("Letter" 296). Another wartime text, "Reconnaissance à la Grèce," outlines France's debt to Greece. In the past, Gide explains, France's gratitude was directed primarily toward the ancient Hellenic culture that gave birth to Western—and especially French—civilization. In 1940, however, the world witnessed a revival of Greece's "semi-legendary heroes" ("héros semi-légendaires"). Gide took great comfort in the new flowering of Greek literature that accompanied the nation's patriotic resistance to the German war machine (303–04).

119. "Gide n'aborde jamais les questions de politique intérieure: en fait il les tourne par la politique extérieure" (Moutote 169).

120. "[N]i à l'échelle de Gide, ni à l'échelle des circonstances" (CAG 6: 245).

121. "[U]ne actualité qui condamne son œuvre beaucoup mieux que n'importe quelle critique"; "l'esprit de sacrifice"; "l'esprit de jouissance"; "On peut aussi 'obliger' les gens à comprendre" ("Mise").

122. According to Malraux, Gide came close to sending the Légion a letter saying how well he understood their point of view, abandoning his plan only when Malraux objected (Grenier 261).

123. "[P]as de discorde entre les Français: plutôt que de fournir prétexte à des dissentions (sic) [. . .] taisons-nous" (Gide, Déclaration [Nice]).

124. In *Découvrons Henri Michaux*, Gide simply states that his text was meant to be heard, not read, and that he would not have published his lecture had he been able to deliver it as planned on 21 May 1941 (7).

125. "[D]écontenancé et même discrédité ceux de la Légion" (CAG 6: 247).

126. "[U]ne bonne mesure d'hygiène publique"; "un hôtel 'chic' et sans doute gaulliste de Nice"; "un public de Juifs, de snobs et de crétins refoulés" ("Le Gide").

127. "[U]n véritable ennemi public"; "regrettons simplement qu'elle n'ait pas pris une décision à plus longue portée" (Bobin).

128. "Il me plaît d'être 'victime' de la Légion. Il me déplaît que ce soit pour si peu de chose" (J II: 764).

129. Jean-Jacques Thierry goes even further, suggesting that Gide's wartime status as persona non grata sufficed to let the writer pass for a *résistant* after the Liberation (170).

CHAPTER THREE. CODED MESSAGES:
THE "INTERVIEWS IMAGINAIRES"

1. Pierre Lepape argues that the publication of Gide's "Interviews" in *Le Figaro* "makes even more visible his break with the *N.R.F.*, where these brilliant essays

should have been published" ("ren[d] plus visible sa rupture avec la *NRF* où ces bril-lantes chroniques auraient dû trouver place") (433).

2. Wartime issues of *Le Figaro* suggest that, in an age of stringent censorship, lit-erary criticism was an acceptable middle ground between news coverage and silence. A growing emphasis on literature went hand in hand with increasing silence on polit-ical issues and current events in the 1940–1942 issues of *Le Figaro*, which had relo-cated to Lyon after the fall of France. When German troops invaded the unoccupied zone in November 1942, the newspaper briefly reinvented itself as a purely literary publication before shutting down entirely (*Le Figaro* 1). Publication of *Le Figaro* would resume only after the Liberation.

3. The name of the German-Jewish poet who expressed ambiguous opinions about Germany was indeed stricken from the sixth "Interview" (Gide, "Peuple"), but the physicist's name was not deleted when the "Introduction au Théâtre de Goethe" appeared in *Le Figaro* (Gide, "Introduction [suite et fin]").

4. Following Pétain's February 1941 decision to aid the Parisian papers that had relocated to the southern zone, *Le Figaro*—like many other newspapers—received financial assistance from the Vichy government. Because it enjoyed considerable readership and support in Pétain's circle, *Le Figaro* was granted relative freedom of expression, particularly in its literary pages (Aron 174, 82).

5. "[F]ort transparente et peu orthodoxe" (CAG 6: 291).

6. "[C]ette Europe une que Napoléon forgeait par les armes" (AQ 124).

7. "*[A]dmettant et félicitant une puissance dominatrice qui lui laissait toute licence de se manifester, de se produire, et même avec quelques prérogatives*"; "liberté de pensée *et d'expression de sa pensée*"; "]amais Goethe ne fut effleuré *comme nous le sommes aujour-d'hui, ou du moins comme nous le fûmes hier*, par la crainte de voir le sol même où son esprit prenait et tenait ses assises chanceler et se dérober sous lui" (Gide, Introduction xxi; AQ 124; "Théâtre," italicized passages deleted).

8. "*Vous songez à celles de la Révolution Nationale?* . . . Dans un tunnel l'é-clairage artificiel fait de son mieux" (AQ 85, italicized passage deleted). This overt reference to the National Revolution figures in the volume *Attendu que* . . . but does not in fact appear in the "Interviews" manuscript (ms. γ890, dossier T, f. 122). It is not clear whether the remark was stricken from an earlier draft (either by the cen-sor or by the author himself) or whether, despite Gide's assurances that *Attendu que* . . . makes no substantive changes to the "Interviews," the phrase was added after the fact.

9. "On commettrait une grave erreur, ce me semble, en jugeant la France, en jaugeant sa valeur réelle et profonde, simplement par ce qui se manifeste d'elle aujour-d'hui. *Dans un vase très secoué, ainsi que nous venons de l'être, ce sont les éléments les plus légers qui d'abord viennent à la surface; non les meilleurs*" (Gide, *Interviews imaginaires*, ms. γ890, dossier X, f. 135; AQ 163, italicized passage deleted).

10. "Devant vous, je m'efface de mon mieux; je me fais reflet. Je vais jusqu'à imiter votre façon de parler, vos tournures; oh! malgré moi" (AQ 93).

11. "Je suis un être de dialogue" (SV 267).

12. "[Les] grands dangers que la moralité et l'intelligence courraient dans un certain état de l'humanité"; "par suite d'une pacification générale . . . que pourtant nous souhaitons, n'est-ce pas?" (AQ 76, 79). The manuscript gives the entire quote: "The day when humanity should become a great pacified Roman Empire would be the day when morality and intelligence would run the greatest risks" ("Le jour où l'humanité deviendrait un grand empire romain pacifié serait le jour où la moralité et l'intelligence courraient les plus grands dangers") (qtd. in ms. γ890, dossier MM, f. 215).

13. "[C]ataclysmes monstrueux" (AQ 34).

14. "Vive notre Révolution Nationale"; "Il y eut une minute de silence" (AQ 76–77).

15. "Du moins, arrangez-vous pour montrer à votre interviewer qu'il y a des terrains sur lesquels vous ne pouvez vous aventurer" (CAG 6: 286).

16. "N'insistez pas, lui dis-je, comme il me pressait de questions sur des sujets actuels. [. . .] Il est quantité de choses dont il vaut mieux, aujourd'hui, ne point parler. J'y suis bien résolu: les sujets littéraires sont les seuls qui m'occuperont avec vous" (AQ 75).

17. "Nothing remained of this country except its language" ("Il ne restait de ce pays que son langage"), declared Louis Aragon (*Diane* 7); "my Homeland is the French language" ("ma Patrie, c'est la langue française"), wrote Louis Martin-Chauffier ("Ma patrie" 64). Jean Schlumberger asserted that every writer becomes responsible for his language, "which is the form of national honor entrusted to him" ("qui est la forme, à lui confiée, de l'honneur national") (114).

18. "Un peuple qui tient à sa langue tient bon" (AQ 47).

19. "[Q]uand un peuple tombe esclave, tant qu'il tient bien sa langue, c'est comme s'il tenait la clef de sa prison" (Daudet, *Contes* 7). Because "tenir sa langue" also means "to hold one's tongue," Daudet's story also acknowledges the possibility that a people may be obliged to defend its language while remaining silent.

20. "[L]e prestige de la grammaire, si gravement compromis, comme tant d'autres choses en France" ("Anti-Littré" 3).

21. "Sied-il [. . .] de vous achopper à des vétilles [. . .] alors que tant de fautes grossières, que vous laissez passer et pour cause, émaillent des textes presque officiels et nous font sursauter lorsque nous écoutons la radio d'État?" (AQ 46).

22. The gist of a July 1941 *Journal* entry is similar: Gide argues that proofreading exercises would imbue children with a healthy skepticism about "the authority of the printed word, which too often inspires awe" (J 4: 73) ("l'autorité de l'imprimé qui trop souvent en impose") (J II: 768).

23. "La grande force de Hitler vient de ce qu'il n'a jamais payé de mots que les autres. Il sait ce qui convient aux Français, hélas! Et que lorsqu'on leur a dit bien fort et bien souvent: l'honneur est sauf, ils finissent presque par le croire. 'Collaboration loyale'; 'ni vainqueurs ni vaincus'; autant de chèques sans couverture" (J II: 739).
William Kidd reminds us that reflections on "the bankruptcy of words and concepts, prostituted by politicians of left and right for their own purposes" were common to the discourse of both collaboration and resistance (47). German apologist Jacques

Chardonne declared that England and the French Third Republic had "discredited the words law, justice, peace [. . .] by associating them with force or with the feeble remnants of force, ultimately using them to conceal their weakness" ("discrédité les mots droit, justice, paix [. . .] en les associant à la force ou aux débris de la force, pour les employer enfin à cacher la débilité") (*Chronique* 106). Resistance writer Jacques Debû-Bridel argued a similar point, asking: "Of what use [. . .] would speech be in a country where the most essential words had lost their meaning [. . .]? Where each term, and especially the most noble ones, betrayed the values they were supposed to represent, where the word 'love' signified 'hate,' or 'fidelity,' 'betrayal?'" ("De quelle utilité [. . .] serait la parole dans une contrée où les mots les plus essentiels auraient perdu [. . .] leur signification? Où chaque terme, et surtout les plus nobles, trahiraient la valeur qu'ils sont censés représenter, où le mot 'amour' signifierait 'haine', ou bien 'fidélité' 'trahison'?") (94).

24. "C'est à de semblables festins que nous invite trop souvent la littérature"; "Trop souvent, le mot tient lieu de la chose et la chose peut s'en aller" (AQ 174, 172).

25. On *épuration*: Having recounted a Congolese fable in which public outcry causes "compromising" passengers to disembark from a sinking ferryboat, Gide remarks: "People are beginning to talk about *purifying* and *purging*. Naturally I am speaking only of literature. It is being accused of many crimes, including that of having enervated, discouraged, and devitalized the nation" (I.I. 5, emphasis added) ("c'est bien d'*épuration* qu'il s'agit. Naturellement nous ne parlons ici que de littérature. On accuse celle-ci de bien des méfaits; et d'avoir énervé, découragé, dévirilisé la France") (AQ 33, emphasis added). Though the term *épuration* has come to be associated with the postwar purge, official Vichy documents used the verb *épurer* in reference to "cleaning up" public and private administrations (Assouline, *L'Épuration* 8).

On *collaboration*: Goethe "represent[s] man's striving toward culture. He does not abandon his effort toward an always more luminous perfection except to plunge deeper into his subject and participate in the harmony of an ordered universe. As soon as he ceases to *oppose*, he *collaborates*" (I.I. 82, emphasis added) ("incarne l'effort de l'homme vers la culture; il ne relâche sa tension vers une perfection toujours mieux éclairée, que pour entrer plus avant dans le jeu et participer à la ronde d'un univers harmonieusement ordonné. Dès qu'il ne *s'oppose* plus, il *collabore*") (AQ 106–07, emphasis added).

On *résistance*: The term occurs most often in discussions of poetry, especially when Gide argues that the laws of prosody constitute a productive obstacle: "the magic of poetry depends on laws observed and *resistance* overcome" (I.I. 123, emphasis added) ("le ravissement poétique naît d'une astreinte, d'une *résistance* vaincue") (AQ 147–48, emphasis added).

26. "Je sais bien que Voltaire et Littré proscrivent cette locution; mais 'en revanche' et 'en compensation', formules de remplacement que Littré propose, ne me paraissent [. . .] convenables [. . .] dans aucun cas où l'on pourrait ajouter 'hélas!'. Trouveriez-vous décent qu'une femme vous dise: 'Oui, mon frère et mon mari sont revenus saufs de la guerre; en *revanche* j'y ai perdu mes deux fils'? [. . .] 'Par contre' m'est nécessaire et, me pardonne Littré, je m'y tiens" (AQ 89–90).

27. "[D]e notre langue comme de celle de nos alliés" (OC 9: 161–62).

28. "[L]a défaillance du subjonctif que déjà je déplorais du temps de l'autre guerre" (AQ 46).

29. "[U]n souci moins constant des relations, des dépendances et des subordinations" (OC 9: 171).

30. "[Le subjonctif] marque, entre deux propositions et de l'une à l'autre, une dépendance, une subordination dont les esprits ne reconnaissent donc plus le besoin"; "Précisément! L'indépendance . . ." (AQ 46–47).

31. "[N]i vainqueurs ni vaincus" (qtd. in J II: 739).

32. "La perfection classique implique, non point certes une suppression de l'individu (peu s'en faut que je ne dise: au contraire), mais la soumission de l'individu, sa subordination, et celle du mot dans la phrase, de la phrase dans la page, de la page dans l'œuvre. C'est la *mise en évidence d'une hiérarchie*" (Gide, "Classicisme" 257).

33. The resistance message of "Du classicisme" was underscored by the articles surrounding it in *Domaine Français*, the 1943 issue of the dissident journal *Messages* in which it appeared. Nearly all of France's literary pantheon was represented: Aragon, Bataille, Camus, Claudel, Éluard, Leiris, Sartre, Valéry—only those writers who were openly committed to collaboration or to fascist ideology were excluded. Certain contributions seem to have been included only as a pretext for mentioning their authors' martyrdom: Saint-Pol-Roux's 1885 text allowed the editor to state: "Saint-Pol-Roux was assassinated in 1940" ("Saint-Pol-Roux est mort assassiné en 1940"); Jacques Decour's was followed by a terse biographical sketch: "Born in 1910.—Executed on 30 May 1942" ("Né en 1910.—Fusillé le 30 mai 1942") (*Domaine* 446, 304).

34. "Certainement le mot *Patrie* [. . .] n'est pas compris de même par le cultivateur et par l'intellectuel; par le pauvre et par le riche. Mais c'est un mot de ralliement. Et lorsque nous entendons que 'la Patrie est en danger', l'important c'est que nous nous levions et unissions pour la défendre. Peu importe *si* ce que nous défendons, *ce soit* particulièrement, pour le paysan, nos cultures; pour l'intellectuel, notre Culture; pour l'industriel et l'ouvrier notre industrie, et même, pour le rentier, ses revenus. Le mot Patrie comprend à la fois tout cela; il est compris fort bien à la fois et par l'esprit et par le cœur" (AQ 39–40, emphasis added).

35. "[L]'indicatif eût un peu faussé ma pensée" (AQ 47).

36. "[A]llez donc parler au cultivateur du 'patrimoine intellectuel' de la France; dont il ne se sentira que fort peu, lui-même, l'héritier. Lequel d'entre eux n'accepterait pas volontiers que Descartes ou Watteau fussent allemands, ou n'aient jamais été, si cela pouvait lui faire vendre son blé quelques sous plus cher?" (J II: 712).

37. "Stendhal écrivait aussi vite, aussi impétueusement, sans se relire, et je ne sache pas qu'on puisse relever chez lui de semblables erreurs" (AQ 51).

38. "[J]e doute que l'on trouve beaucoup d'exemples de grands écrivains qui ne possèdent admirablement leur langue, qui ne sachent profiter et jouer de ses ressources, tout en tenant compte de ses règles, fût-ce en les bousculant un peu" (AQ 51).

39. The interviewer later adds that the reverse process is at work in Soviet Russia: "the Russian novel has evolved since then, either by inner compulsion or, more likely, as a result of social upheavals; it has become, so to speak, disindividualized. [. . .] Robinson Crusoe is never alone; he is a group of pioneers" (adapted from I.I. 65)

("sous l'inspiration, ou plutôt: sous la contrainte des bouleversements sociaux, le roman russe évolue et, pour ainsi dire, se désindividualise. [. . .] Robinson, chez eux, n'est jamais seul; c'est un groupe de pionniers") (AQ 88).

40. "[L]e théâtre ne fut florissant qu'au temps d'un peuple unanimiste. Le roman n'a commencé de naître [. . .] qu'après les révoltes et les dissensions religieuses, favorisé par la Réforme, mère de l'individualisme. Cromwell a vidé le théâtre, a dispersé les spectateurs, rompu les masses au profit des particuliers" (AQ 88).

Gide's reflections on the unity that allows the theater to flourish may have been inspired in part by his friend Jacques Copeau's 1941 book *Le Théâtre populaire*. Copeau considered a certain "unity of hearts and minds [. . .] indispensable for the creation of a new type of audience and for the rebirth of the theater" ("unité d'âme ou d'esprit [. . .] indispensable pour créer un vrai public et un renouveau du théâtre"). Suspecting a degree of opportunism behind Copeau's declaration, Maria Van Rysselberghe wondered whether the director perceived this kind of unity "in the Marshal's politics" ("dans la politique du Maréchal") (CAG 6: 275).

41. "*Par contre*, le genre spécifiquement allemand c'est le drame lyrique, genre synthétique où l'Allemagne excelle et triomphe [. . .] où la grande fusion sociale actuelle peut reconnaître, il me semble, son expression la plus parfaite" (AQ 87, emphasis added). This ironic assertion recalls Thierry Maulnier's claim—quoted in the "Interviews"—that German poetry is "diffused through the German soul and mingled with German daily life, to such a point that it inspires the composers, directs and gives a cadence to marching youth, and shapes the political movements" (qtd. in I.I. 44) ("diffuse dans les âmes allemandes, mêlée à l'existence quotidienne allemande, au point d'inspirer les musiciens, de guider et de rythmer la marche de la jeunesse, de modeler les mouvements politiques") (qtd. in AQ 69).

42. "[L]a vraie poésie a toujours, du moins jusqu'aujourd'hui, été l'expression d'individualités particulières et s'adressant non à la masse, mais à des êtres particuliers" (AQ 68).

43. In "La Leçon de Ribérac," Aragon "invoked the *clus trouver* (sic) (the closed art), of the Troubadours which allowed them 'to sing to their ladies in the presence of their Lords'. He argued that contemporary poetry could exploit similar stratagems" (Jackson 305) ("Le 'clus trover' permettait aux poètes de chanter leurs Dames en présence même de leur Seigneur") (qtd. in Sadoul 76).

44. Gide transcribes a passage from *L'Année terrible*, Victor Hugo's 1872 poem on the Franco-Prussian War in a January 1941 *Journal* entry, observing that Hugo's words are "so gaily caustic and so painfully applicable to our policy of surrendering our principles" (J 4: 58) ("d'une causticité si allègre et si péniblement applicables à notre politique de compromissions") (J II: 749).

45. "Quelles allusions ne verrait-on pas dans la résistance de Porus, dans l'acquiescement de Taxile" (J II: 771).

46. "[O]n n'y verrait qu'allusions à Laval ou à de Gaulle" (CAG 6: 258).

47. "[A]fin de couvrir, fût-ce à ses propres yeux, sa lâcheté! 'J'écoute comme vous ce que l'honneur m'inspire,/ Seigneur; mais il m'engage à sauver mon empire'" (J II: 772).

48. "[C]ollaboration loyale" (qtd. in J II: 739). Corneille's *Polyeucte* inspires a similar political interpretation. Rereading the tragedy in August 1941, Gide rebels against the notion that the heroine Pauline should accept the hated husband forced on her by her father: "What is this duty which is indistinguishable from idiotic obedience?," Gide asks (J 4: 80) ("Qu'est-ce que ce *devoir*, qui se confond avec une obéissance idiote?") (J II: 777). This diary entry was among those reprinted as "Pages de Journal" in a 1943 issue of the Algiers resistance journal *Fontaine* (12).

49. Ambiguous expressions, brief indications, and a savvy arrangement of quotations—techniques Leo Strauss enumerates in *Persecution and the Art of Writing*—are among the tactics Gide adopts in the "Interviews" (Strauss 24–35, passim).

50. The example of *Esprit* is a vexed one. Robert Paxton asserts that *Esprit's* "doctrinal position [. . .] overlapped with Vichy pretensions of ending the class struggle and finding a more organic replacement for political democracy" (272). Michel Winock, himself a contributor to the postwar *Esprit* and an admitted apologist for the journal, does not deny these similarities. In fact, he enumerates themes common to *Esprit* and the writings of Vichy: "condemnation of the previous regime; hostility toward individualism and its corollary, the theme of community; criticism of capitalism; criticism of communism" ("la condamnation du régime précédent; l'hostilité à l'individualisme et son corollaire, le thème de la communauté; la critique du capitalisme; la critique du communisme"). However, Winock claims, editor Emmanuel Mounier's intent was to challenge Vichy's "perversion" of *Esprit's* personalist notions. Winock's case for heterodox messages in the wartime issues of *Esprit* is supported by Vichy treatment of the magazine and its editor: in August 1941, *Esprit* was ordered to suspend operations "because of the general tendencies it manifests" ("pour les tendances générales qu'il manifeste"); Emmanuel Mounier was arrested and imprisoned in January 1942 (*Histoire* 216–17, 223, 235).

51. "[L]es vices intérieurs de ses divers gouvernements"; "Peut-être en doit-elle la cause à cette diversité même, qui a fait que nul mal n'a jamais pu prendre assez de racine pour lui ôter entièrement le fruit de ses avantages naturels"; "c'est à cette diversité qu'on s'en prend. On la voudrait aujourd'hui réduire" (AQ 35).

52. The "cerf volant" represents the *Connétable* or supreme commander of the French army: as I. D. McFarlane explains, the flying stag is "a feature of the Connétable's arms" (Scève 375).

53. "[L]orsque Scève commence un de ses dizains par [. . .]"; "dans le dizain LV où il est également question de Charles-Quint sous figure de 'l'Austruche'" (AQ 141).

54. Mallarmé's poem may have influenced Gide's choice of the title *Attendu que . . .* for the 1943 volume containing his "Interviews imaginaires" and other wartime essays. The title also connotes judgment, the expression "attendu que" (considering that) being used in legal judgments.

55. "Mallarmé is the musician," glosses Malcolm Cowley: "it is Gide as the listener who 'also does his part' [y met du sien]" (I.I. 115).

56. "S'adresser à l'esprit, c'est l'inviter à protester" (AQ 141).

57. Although Gide agreed to write the introduction to the Pléiade volume of Goethe's dramatic works, he avoided projects like René Lasne and Georg Rabuse's

1943 *Anthologie de la poésie allemande des origines à nos jours*, which Pierre Assouline describes as a "clever attempt to recuperate Goethe for the benefit of the thousand-year Reich" ("habile entreprise de récupération de Goethe au profit du Reich millénaire") (*Gallimard* 325). This bilingual anthology had an unmistakably collaborationist mission: Karl Epting, director of the Institut Allemand, prefaced the volume by expressing his hope that the dissemination of German poetry would help foster peaceful relations between the French and German peoples (ix). The anthology's title page lists some two dozen contributors (Lasne and Rabuse v)—including André Gide, whose "contribution" consists of a 1932 translation of Goethe's "Faust et Chiron" reprinted from the *N.R.F.* (Goethe 155). It is unlikely that Gide, who had been living in North Africa for a year at the time of the anthology's publication, authorized the use of his Goethe translation for this politically loaded project. The volume's publisher, Stock, had sought Gide's participation in an anthology of German poetry before the war. Since 1941, however, Gide had been at odds with the company's director, Jacques Chardonne (Dhérin et al. 370).

58. "[U]ne sorte de ralliement" (NRF xxxv).

59. "[P]olisson vénérable" (AQ 111).

60. "Alors aussi l'on incrimina notre littérature. Une enquête parut, en 72, à propos *de la corruption* littéraire en France', où la pernicieuse influence de Goethe sur les Français était dénoncée. [. . .] À distance, l'absurdité de pareilles accusations ressort mieux. Mais en ce temps, mal ressuyés de la défaite, nous cherchions à nous ressaisir" (AQ 111).

61. "Dans cet effort de redressement français, Goethe en prit pour son grade" (AQ 111). Marshal Pétain brought the term "redressement" to the forefront in his 25 June 1940 broadcast justifying the Armistice, urging his fellow Frenchmen to work toward "intellectual and moral reform" ("un redressement intellectuel et moral") (*Actes* 454). *Le Figaro*'s survey on the future of literature—the springboard for Gide's "Réponse à une enquête"—took up this terminology, asking: "Was our literature on the wrong track before the turmoil? [. . .] If so, do you think a 'reform' is necessary?" ("Notre littérature faisait-elle fausse route avant la tourmente? [. . .] Un 'redressement' dans ce cas, vous paraît-il nécessaire?") (AQ 25).

62. "[F]erveur" (AQ 122–23); "immoralité" (AQ 111); "sérénité" (AQ 109, 115, 120); "passer outre" (AQ 110, 119).

63. "Qui nous libérera?/ Nous extrayons le fer./ Ils en forgent nos chaînes./ O délivrance,/ Ne tarde pas!/ En t'attendant,/ Demeurons souples" (AQ 118).

64. Gide defends his translation in a February 1942 letter to Schlumberger: the lines in question mean that "we must continue to wait; but it is only a short step from there to 'as little as possible!' [. . .] an idea that is implied in the German" ("il faut attendre encore; mais, de là à 'le moins possible!' il n'y a qu'un pas, [. . . qui] est sous-entendu dans l'allemand") (G/Sch 937–38).

65. "Vous tourniez en impatient souhait ce qui n'est qu'une constatation"; "Le premier vers du couplet permettait, me semblait-il, cet élan de mon cœur"; "Il faut aujourd'hui savoir réprimer maints élans" (AQ 133).

66. "[L]ors de sa *première lettre à Strauss*, sitôt après notre défaite de 70" (AQ 76).

67. "Notre politique, c'est la politique du droit des nations; la vôtre, c'est la politique des races: nous croyons que la nôtre vaut mieux. La division trop accusée de l'humanité en races [. . .] ne peut mener qu'à des guerres d'extermination. [. . . Votre] politique ethnographique et archéologique [. . .] vous sera fatale" (Renan 199).

68. In places, Gide indicates relevant passages in a rather dramatic fashion. When the interviewer, at Gide's invitation, picks up Thierry Maulnier's *Introduction à la poésie française*, "[t]he book opened of its own accord to page 39" (I.I. 44) ("[l]e livre s'ouvrit de lui-même à la page 39") (AQ 69).

69. "Nous aurions perdu la mémoire même avec la parole, s'il nous était aussi possible d'oublier que de nous taire" (qtd. in AQ 133).

70. "Il y a, dans la *Vie d'Agricola*, tout autour de cette phrase, quelques réflexions dont je vous ferais part, en temps de diastole." Gide is developing a metaphor whereby "diastole" symbolizes periods of intellectual freedom and "systole" represents periods of constraint (AQ 133–34, 132).

71. "[S]uc amer" (J II: 801).

72. Right-wing intellectual Jacques Talagrand, alias Thierry Maulnier, had criticized Gide's support for communism in his 1936 book *Mythes socialistes* (Sérant 211). In some respects, Gide was taking up an ongoing quarrel when he denounced Maulnier's "lamentable zeal" ("zèle atroce") and "partisan ferocity" ("férocités de partisan") and claimed that political concerns dictated Maulnier's praise and condemnation of various poets in the *Introduction à la poésie française* (I.I. 27; AQ 53). After Gide obliquely linked him to book-banning, Maulnier responded with an article entitled "Controverse à propos des anthologies," in which he denied Gide's allegations that he wished to blacklist certain poets (3). Gide's ninth "Interview" includes a lengthy but fairly conciliatory discussion of Maulnier's reply (AQ 90).

73. "[I]l n'y aurait qu'à sourire de ces vaines dévastations, si les livres incriminés n'étaient en passe d'être effectivement supprimés de nos librairies" (AQ 34).

74. "[C]'est sur la rime que s'exalte le génie verbal de Hugo" (AQ 150).

75. "[U]ne glorieuse plénitude"; "pour répondre à l'appel du vers précédent" (AQ 150).

76. The first half of Gide's *Anthologie* preface is roughly contemporaneous with the "Interviews imaginaires" and reproduces many of the poetic examples and interpretations found in the *Figaro* essays.

77. "'Sentinelles' est, ici, comme miraculeusement appelé par 'éternelles'; et surgit aussitôt une image hardie, surprenante, évocatrice de tout ce que notre imagination personnelle peut y verser d'effroi, de doute et, suivant notre tempérament, d'angoisse ou d'espoir" (AP 38).

78. Terms like "ruin" ("ruine"), "collapse" ("écroulement"), and "everything is disappearing" ("tout s'en va") abound in the poem's opening stanzas (Hugo, *Contemplations* 377).

79. "[D]u fond des nuits funèbres" (Hugo, *Contemplations* 380).

80. "[Q]uelques coups d'aile"; "l'admirable essor" (AQ 34).

81. "On dirait que les rimes, ces oiseaux farouches [. . .] accourent du fond de l'horizon s'emparer du peu de substance qu'il leur tend" (AQ 55).

82. In his *Anthologie* preface, Gide cites this couplet and the one from "À la fenêtre" as examples of the surprising and suggestive juxtapositions he terms "distant rime" ("la rime lointaine") (38).

83. "Qu'ont-ils pu penser de l'hitlérisme et de Hitler, durant leur agonie? Mais qu'est-ce qu'en pense Hitler lui-même?" (J II: 896).

84. Richard Terdiman points out the prevalence of this intellectual trope: "Marx satirized the nephew's coup d'état as a base, derivative forgery of the uncle's epochal seizure of power. This theme of an ignoble imitation of a prestigious original dominates numerous accounts of the event and of the régime it inaugurated" (718).

85. Understandably, Gide does not quote the dangerously relevant lines in his "Interview."

86. "Hugo, hélas" (AQ 56). Students taking the *baccalauréat* examination at Pau in 1942 were asked to comment on Gide's well-known slur ("De jour" 3). At a time when the poet's works were disappearing from schoolbooks, this topic may have been an attempt to co-opt Gide for the anti-Hugo campaign.

87. "[N]e saurions-nous [. . .] prendre les gens pour ce qu'ils sont: les colosses pour des colosses, les nains pour des nains et les détracteurs de Hugo pour des sots?" (AQ 56).

88. At times, Gide is clearly writing for himself, as when he revisits unpublished diary entries or passages published in a highly attenuated form. Yet Gide's diary was never wholly private: the *Journal* through the year 1939 had been published shortly before the war, and there was no question that the diary for subsequent years would eventually appear in print.

89. "À vrai dire, c'est à travers les restrictions qu'elle entraîne, et par cela seulement, ou presque, que le grand nombre sera touché par la défaite. Moins de sucre dans le café, et moins de café dans les tasses; c'est à cela qu'ils seront sensibles" (J II: 712).

90. "La grande désolation du pays, il n'est pas donné à tant de Français, ni constamment, de la sentir. Ce que l'on éprouve bien plutôt, c'est la gêne des restrictions, l'inconfort de l'exil encore, et la crainte de la disette de demain" (F 1: 83).

91. "Je suis [. . .] facile aux tentations"; "Y céder, c'est ce que l'on appelle aujourd'hui: ne pas dire *Non* à la vie"; "C'est agir que de résister et ce n'est pas toujours dans le *oui* que l'être s'affirme" (AQ 38).

92. "Le mot Patrie [. . .] est compris fort bien à la fois et par l'esprit et par le cœur"; "J'en voudrais pouvoir dire autant du mot: *amour*" (AQ 39–40).

93. "Encore si cet amour exaltait, comme il advient parfois; s'il poussait l'homme à l'héroïsme, la femme à la vertu. [. . .] Mais pour une *Princesse de Clèves*, ce sont des *Manon Lescaut* sans nombre" (AQ 41).

94. Madame de Lafayette's 1678 novel *La Princesse de Clèves* recounts a young noblewoman's struggle to remain faithful to her husband though she is in love with another man. She admits her feelings to her husband, who dies of a broken heart.

After her husband's death, the princess is free, but refuses to marry the Duc de Nemours, for remarriage would, in her mind, constitute infidelity toward her late husband. Abbé Prévost's 1731 novel *Manon Lescaut* concerns the affair between Manon Lescaut, an unfaithful woman who may be a prostitute, and her lover des Grieux, who resorts to theft and dishonesty to please her.

95. Under pressure from the emperor, Tacitus and his fellow senators had condemned several of their friends to death or imprisonment (Tacitus 97).

96. Renan and Strauss carried out their correspondence by means of open letters published in the *Augsburg Gazette* and the *Journal des Débats* (Renan 167–68). Their letters were both public and private: they were available for all to read, but also contained remarks intended specifically for the addressee. This public-yet-private communication resembles Gide's "Interviews imaginaires" in *Le Figaro Littéraire*: though the essays were accessible to the reading public, they contained esoteric messages meant only for literate French readers sympathetic to his cause.

97. "Il m'est arrivé depuis un an ce qui arrive toujours à ceux qui prêchent la modération en temps de crise. Les événements ainsi que l'immense majorité de l'opinion m'ont donné tort" (Renan 191). In an early draft of the "Interviews," Gide compares Renan's stance in the 1870 letter to that of collaborationist Jacques Chardonne, as well as to his own pacifist views from the interwar period (ms. γ890, dossier MM, f. 213). By emphasizing the message in Renan's second letter, Gide suggests that he, like the nineteenth-century writer before him, can no longer afford to take a conciliatory stance toward Germany.

98. Citing slow communication between the occupied and unoccupied zones, anthology editor Alfred Fabre-Luce acknowledges that Gide's *Journal* excerpts were reprinted without the author's permission (Gide, "Que" 267). Gide may, however, have been aware of Fabre-Luce's plan. A February 1942 letter to Martin du Gard, in which Gide expresses his inability to prevent a reprint and his concern that his writings be properly contextualized, most likely refers to Fabre-Luce's anthology project: "How could I respond, other than to accept? But I asked [. . .] that the sources be clearly indicated [. . . and] that the two texts, which are artificially joined, be separated by quotation marks and by the phrase 'and, elsewhere' [. . .] and that ellipses indicate that the text is interrupted" ("Que pouvais-je répondre, sinon accepter. Mais j'ai demandé [. . .] que les références soient bien indiquées [. . . et] que les deux textes, artificieusement réunis, soient disjoints par des guillemets et par un 'et, ailleurs' [. . .] et que des points de suspension indiquent que le texte est interrompu") (G/MG 243).

99. "J'aurais dû pour le moins dater (et laisser dans leur ordre chronologique) ces *Feuillets*, extraits de mon *Journal*, que je viens de relire dans le dernier numéro de la *N.R.F.* Déjà je ne suis plus dans la disposition d'esprit qui me les fit écrire" (F 2: 350–51; J II: 741).

100. Although he avoided such ostentatious displays, Gide, too, had been honored by the nation that now occupied his country. He personally sought no advantage from his 1932 Goethe Prize, but young Henri Thomas, who occupied Gide's Paris apartment while the writer remained in the south, prominently displayed the Goethe medal as a "talisman" against an eventual visit by the German authorities (Lambert 62–63).

101. "L'attitude de Goethe en face de Napoléon nous laisse un peu gênés, du moins perplexes; et cet opportunisme [. . .] qui le faisait, au scandale de ses meilleurs concitoyens patriotes, arborer sa décoration de la Légion d'honneur au moment où il semblait décent de ne pas s'en targuer, de ne point tirer avantage de ce qui mortifiait sa patrie. Mais Goethe restait ébloui (et comment ne pas l'être?) par ce rêve qui semblait en passe de se réaliser, d'une unification pacifiée, glorieuse, de l'Europe entière, qui eût laissé, sinon à tous les petits États leur autonomie, leur raison d'être, du moins à Weimar, du moins à lui, Goethe, une importance encore accrue et, pensait-il, toute sa liberté de pensée" (AQ 123).

102. Gide's contemporaries seized on the parallel. Playing on Napoleon's "You are a man, Monsieur Goethe" (I.I. 98) ("Vous êtes un homme, Monsieur Goethe")— a statement that Gide quotes in his "Introduction au Théâtre de Goethe" (AQ 123)— Jean Paulhan joked: "Hitler said to Gide: 'Monsieur Gide, you are a man'" ("Hitler a dit à Gide: 'Monsieur Gide, vous êtes un homme'") (Grenier 156). Maurice Nadeau's post-Liberation review of Gide's wartime diary makes a similar comparison: "This temptation to make Hitler an instrument of fate, destined moreover to correct our mistakes and curb our weaknesses [. . .] is it not the yellowed copy of a very old image: that of Goethe shaking hands with Napoleon?" ("Cette tentation de faire de Hitler un instrument du destin, destiné en outre à corriger nos erreurs et à suspendre le cours de nos faiblesses [. . .] n'est-elle pas la copie jaunie d'une très vieille image: celle de Goethe serrant la main de Napoléon?") (Nadeau, Rev. of *Pages de Journal*).

103. Stanislas Fumet's *Temps Nouveaux* was shut down by Vichy authorities in July 1941, Emmanuel Mounier's *Esprit* in August of that year (J 4: 85; Winock, *Histoire* 223).

104. Justin O'Brien offers this translation, indicating that the phrase is "inspired by Virgil's *Vires acquirit eundo*" in the *Aeneid* (J 4: 85).

105. "Après *Temps nouveaux*, *Esprit* est réduit au silence. (Je propose comme devise à Mounier, à propos de sa revue et du groupement de ses amis: *Vires acquirit tacendo*.) [. . .] pour un peu, je dirais: c'est bien fait. Nous avons d'abord besoin d'ordre, de discipline, tout comme un grand blessé a besoin de tranquillité pour se remettre" (J II: 783). Gide's views on the benefits of silence are politically ambiguous: as William Kidd explains, "the need for a period of 'silence' and reflexion as a precondition of the rediscovery of the 'permanent' values inherent in French civilisation" was among the ideas common to both resistance and collaborationist discourse (47). Gide's near-approval of the newspaper shutdowns hardly suggests a dissident stance, however.

106. "[Q]ui présentement se taisent et laissent leur pensée, leur vertu, se fortifier peu à peu dans la retraite et le silence"; "Ceux sur qui nous pouvons compter le plus, [. . .] ce sont ceux qui savent attendre, qui mûrissent en attendant. *Vires acquirit tacendo* c'est aujourd'hui la meilleure devise" (AQ 65, 163).

107. "*L'art vit de contrainte et meurt de liberté*—dans un moment où, dans ce domaine, la censure sévissait"; "la contrainte dont je me châtie m'amènera, si j'ai du talent, à une certaine perfection; celle qu'on m'impose me contraindra à inventer les moyens de la déjouer. [. . . Les] deux contraintes [. . . se] combineront [. . . en] une *combine*, pour faire la nique à cette chose bête et basse: le pouvoir" (Herbart, *Inédits* 90–91).

CHAPTER FOUR. BATTLES ON THE HOME FRONT: DOMESTIC ALLEGORY IN THE TUNIS *JOURNAL*

1. "Ici, me dit-il, je ne me sens plus en sûreté. La presse continue à se déchaîner contre moi; on m'accuse d'avoir perverti la jeunesse"; "Vous me promettez qu'au moins il sera sage!" (Tournier and Tournier 466).

2. "[C]e dernier carnet diffère des précédents, que je n'ouvrais que par intermittences et lorsque l'esprit m'y poussait. Ce dernier carnet devenait pour moi la bouée où le naufragé se raccroche. L'on y sent cet effort quotidien pour se maintenir à flot" (J II: 909). Two weeks earlier, Gide had said of his work on the preface to his *Anthologie de la poésie française*: "I greatly need this semblance of activity to bind me to life, and this is likewise why I cling to this *Journal*" (J 4: 169) ("j'ai grand besoin de ce semblant d'activité pour me rattacher à la vie; et c'est aussi pourquoi je me cramponne à ce *Journal*") (J II: 898).

3. "À trois reprises, j'ai, de la fenêtre du salon, contemplé longuement les étranges illuminations du ciel" (J II: 854); "[Un] splendide feu d'artifice" (J II: 855); "Exaltation sauvage, élémentaire, à la fois irrépressible et inavouable, causée par le saccage" (J II: 854).

4. "Parfois, mais pas toujours, je maudis la fichue idée que j'ai eue de venir ici; je songe alors avec angoisse à ceux que j'ai laissés en France et que je ne retrouverai peut-être pas; je m'inquiète de cette obscurité grandissante qui les enveloppe, qui les cache, qui nous étouffe. [. . .] Mais parfois aussi je me félicite de me trouver en un point où se joue, ou va se jouer, une partie peut-être décisive" (J II: 908). In a June 1942 letter to Dorothy Bussy, Gide had expressed his regrets about living far from the center of action (CAG 11: 207). Within months, however, the tables had turned: Gide, "who thought he had found peace and security [. . .] has simply placed himself [. . .] in the lion's den" ("qui croyait avoir trouvé la paix et la sécurité [. . .] a été simplement se mettre [. . .] dans la gueule du loup"), Roger Martin du Gard wrote in his journal (542). Paul Léautaud was more catty, claiming that Gide had left France "in order to be able to eat well [. . . and] to flee the war" ("pour pouvoir bien manger [. . . et] pour fuir la guerre") but now faced stringent rationing and heavy Allied bombardments (15: 72).

5. In January 1943, Gide turned down a seat on an airplane repatriating several officers and civilians, citing his curiosity about the unfolding events and solidarity with his new friends. Three months later, he declined a second opportunity for fear that he would not be allowed to take his manuscripts with him (J II: 886, 928). Though Gide was firm in his decision to remain in Tunis, rumors to the contrary circulated in Paris. In January 1943, Paul Léautaud reported that Gide had asked a group of writers to compose a petition requesting his repatriation from Tunisia. Roger Martin du Gard set the record straight: while a group of writers at *Le Figaro* had indeed mooted the idea of engineering Gide's return to France, their consultations with Gide's closest friends and family convinced them that the writer had no desire to leave Tunisia (15: 72, 106).

6. "Je me penche jusqu'à six fois par jour sur la radio, avec cette enfantine illusion que l'excès de mon attention va pouvoir faire avancer les événements" (J II: 883).

7. During the Axis occupation, Tunis's three papers were replaced by a single French-language daily, *Tunis-Journal*, whose assurances of German victory Gide read with a great deal of skepticism (Boretz 22; J II: 905).

8. "Cette atmosphère de mensonge organisé" (J II: 853).

9. "Victor se plaît à empoisonner cette vie en commun, qui pourrait être presque charmante, en dépit des privations, si chacun y mettait un peu du sien"; "son égoïsme est déclaré, résolu, cynique"; "[il] empoiss[e] de sa fiente le siège des cabinets"; "[il] semble n'avoir d'autre souci que de rendre flagrant son mépris" (J II: 859, 877, 927, 896).

Gide reacts to Victor much as he did to his daughter Catherine, another teenager with whom he spent a portion of the war years. In January 1942, Gide expressed deep disappointment that Catherine, an aspiring actress, no longer had time for the elocution lessons he longed to give her. Feeling rejected, he harshly characterized his daughter as selfish and unloving: "up to now she has shown no love or persistent attention but for herself" (J 4: 96) ("jusqu'à présent elle n'a d'amour et d'attention assidue que pour elle") (J II: 797). Twelve months later, he censured young François Reymond in nearly identical terms: "he has never felt any real affection for anyone up to now" (J 4: 137) ("jusqu'à présent, il n'a ressenti de réelle affection pour personne") (J II: 851).

10. Gide refers to the boy as "François" in his correspondence with Martin du Gard and in the *Journal* manuscript. Published versions of the diary have the pseudonym "Victor."

11. "[I]l est très réussi le portrait du François! Et ça va *beaucoup plus loin* qu'un cas individuel. C'est un des types [. . .] de cette 'jeunesse' devant laquelle tous les dirigeants du monde dansent le pas de la séduction et déploient tous les machiavélismes de leurs propagandes." Martin du Gard again underscored the timeliness of the portrait in his letter of 6 October 1942: "This portrait could turn out to be very revealing, very timely" ("Ce portrait pourrait être bien révélateur, bien actuel"); (G/MG 271, 273–74).

12. "[V]os compliments m'ont gentiment encouragé et [. . .] j'ai rouvert (éperonné par vous) mon *Journal*" (G/MG 274).

13. The Axis occupation of Tunis actually began on 9 November 1942, when German forces captured the Tunis-El Aouina airfield, but many of the city's inhabitants expected speedy deliverance by Allied forces. On 29 November, when fighting in the surrounding area was audible in downtown Tunis, liberation seemed imminent. The Anglo-American offensive was unsuccessful, however (Boretz 10, 15–16). On 30 November 1942, the day after this military and psychological turning point, Gide began his diary entry by stating: "The German and Italian forces are occupying Tunis" (J 4: 134) ("Les forces allemandes et italiennes occupent Tunis") (J II: 847).

14. Five Victor entries follow days when Gide made no entry in his *Journal* (7 December 1942, 22 January, 19 March, 31 March, and 10 April 1943); three were made on days when electrical outages silenced the radio (2 and 5 January and 3 February 1943); two follow entries about propaganda and the unreliability of information (29 January and 27 March 1943). In addition, Gide turned his thoughts to his domes-

tic situation in times of discouragement and uncertainty, as when Allied bombings were temporarily suspended (16–17 January 1943) and especially following Allied setbacks: after the American retreat near Tebourba, which Gide noted on 12 January 1943, there follow three days of journal entries on Victor (13, 14, and 15 January 1943). One Victor entry comes right after Gide's realization that he would be in Tunis for quite some time (25 December 1942); two are juxtaposed with reflections on the offers of repatriation that Gide rejected (20 January and 19 March 1943). Realizing he was stuck for the duration seemed to bring out Gide's impatience with his young host.

15. "Hier, Victor a consenti à sortir un instant de son mutisme pour nous annoncer l'occupation de Gabès" (J II: 933). General Montgomery and the Eighth Army broke through the German-controlled Mareth line to conquer Gabès on 28 March 1943 (Kassab 438).

16. "Nous n'aurions pas dû gagner l'autre guerre. Cette fausse victoire nous a trompés. Nous n'avons pu la supporter. Le relâchement qui l'a suivie nous a perdus"; "il eût bien mieux valu pour [. . . la France] qu'elle fût vaincue en 1918, plutôt que de remporter alors ce faux triomphe qui acheva de l'aveugler et l'endormit dans la décadence" (J II: 702, 718).

17. "J'ai toujours pensé qu'en France nous élevons mal les enfants. [. . .] Est-ce affaire du tempérament français ou simplement (je préférerais) d'éducation? Peuple indigne de la liberté qu'il revendique" (J II: 807).

18. The familiar Gidian preoccupation with discipline pervades the wartime writings, though the political message varies: in certain *Journal* passages, Gide suggests that German discipline and the rigors of occupation will be beneficial for France; in the "Interviews imaginaires," on the other hand, he presents discipline as an attribute of successful resistance (AQ 145).

19. "C'est ce besoin constant [. . .] de redresser, de réformer aussi bien autrui que moi-même, qui m'a souvent rendu si insupportable [. . .] mais qui me ferait, je crois, si bon sujet d'une vraie république" (J II: 931).

20. "Son comportement envers moi est, je le jurerais, dicté par le camarade Lévy, qui circule quotidiennement ou presque, dans l'appartement, sans saluer personne; qui lui inculque des principes de marxisme, l'entête dans son égoïsme et fournit des bases solides à sa goujaterie spontanée." On 13 and 15 January as well, Gide states that Lévy indoctrinates Victor with communist thought (J II: 910–11, 880, 882).

21. "Ce grand bourgeois bolchévisant" (Mauclair 7).

22. "[V]ous savez sans doute les pogromes qui terrifient la Côte, chasse aux Juifs étrangers, déportements brutaux, massifs, enfants séparés de leurs parents, etc., sous les yeux d'une population indignée, mais impuissante et passive" (G/MG 264).

23. "[C]omme aide aux victimes des bombardements anglo-américains *dont ils sont responsables*, 'la juiverie internationale' ayant, comme chacun le sait depuis longtemps, 'voulu et préparé la guerre'" (J II: 859).

24. "[I]l y a en France une littérature juive, qui n'est pas la littérature française"; "l'apport des qualités juives dans la littérature [. . .] apporte moins d'éléments nou-

veaux [. . .] qu'elle ne coupe la parole à la lente explication d'une race et n'en fausse gravement, intolérablement, la signification" (J I: 763).

25. Gide's anxiety about Lévy's ostensible rudeness and influence on François recalls his assertion, in the 1914 diary entry condemning Jewish authors' contributions to French literature, that: "It would be far better, whenever the Frenchman comes to lack sufficient strength, for him to disappear rather than to let an uncouth person play his part in his stead and in his name" (J 2: 5) ("Mieux vaudrait, le jour où le Français n'aurait plus force suffisante, disparaître, plutôt que de laisser un malappris jouer son rôle à sa place, en son nom") (J I: 764).

26. "[L]e jeune V., dont il est si fâcheusement question dans le dernier volume du *Journal* [. . .] est fou de rage et jure de se venger" (CAG 7: 175). Postwar attacks by communist writers and politicians left Gide in a shaky position for years after the Liberation. The gravity of the accusations in *L'Envers du Journal* was exacerbated by the fact that "the troublesome V. is a communist" ("le fâcheux V. est communiste") (CAG 7: 175).

27. The pseudonym "Derais" evokes Gilles de Rais, the historical Bluebeard—a fifteenth-century nobleman who confessed to raping and murdering hundreds of children. Thus, the book's title page holds a suggestion of sexual violence.

28. "[M]aître de la place" (J II: 887; DR 177).

29. "[T]erriblement averti" (G/MG 270).

30. "[C]ertains regards, certaines allusions que j'interprétais comme de discrètes invites"; "[ils] avaient toujours eu à mon égard une attitude de parfaite correction"; "un vieillard prestigieux, que son grand âge ne pouvait que rendre inoffensif sur le terrain des bassesses charnelles"; "vous vous placiez derrière lui, [. . .] la main sur l'épaule [. . .] votre main [. . .] allait et venait, et tantôt pétrissait, tantôt attirait brusquement l'enfant à vous, tantôt au contraire se relâchait pour n'être plus qu'un frôlement sur la pointe de ses seins" (DR 131, 134, 135).

31. "[L]e visage encore enfantin, parfois presque charmant" (J II: 874).

32. "[U]ne proie de choix" (DR 136).

33. "[V]ous m'avez trouvé en train de lire, allongé sur le divan du living-room, vêtu seulement d'une chemisette et d'un short très court. [. . .] Sous le prétexte bien faux de vous intéresser à ma lecture, vous rappelez-vous ce que vous avez fait? Nous étions presque seuls, alors dans la grande maison, et il ne s'agissait plus seulement d'épaule. [. . .] J'aurais hurlé, si la honte ne m'en avait empêché. [. . .] Seule m'a retenu la pensée que ma mère apprenne tout cela, me questionne, que je doive lui parler de ce qu'une immense pudeur [. . .] m'ordonnai[t] de taire. Je parvins enfin à me dégager sans scandale; il n'était que temps à voir votre visage et votre agitation extrême! [. . .] Le soir, je n'osai regarder personne en face" (DR 137).

34. Though he rejected Gide's advances, Reymond acknowledges the possibility that he might have been persuaded to accept: on the two occasions when Gide approached him, he reminds the author, "you said absolutely nothing, which is very regrettable. Maybe, who knows, I might have let myself get carried away by your eloquence" ("vous ne disiez absolument rien, ce qui est bien regrettable. Peut-être, qui

sait, me serais-je laissé emporter par votre éloquence"). In many respects, Reymond is extremely honest about his adolescent interactions with other men: he tells of his sexual experimentation with a male classmate and acknowledges feeling "a certain pleasure [. . .] oh! completely momentary, in being courted" ("un certain plaisir [. . .] oh! tout momentané, à être courtisé") by an Arab doctor. Nevertheless, he takes pains to surround these admissions with extensive anecdotes about his adolescent crushes on young girls, and he emphatically proclaims his heterosexual identity (DR 141, 238–39, 133, 247).

35. "[J]e vous fuyais très soigneusement"; "je craignais fort de vous voir renouveler vos essais" (DR 141, 177).

36. Reymond also expressed his views on Gide in a letter to Armand Guibert: "I spent a very painful wartime winter; the bombings, rationing, etc., were less of a problem than what I had to put up with from that pain in the a . . . Chacha and that old a . . . hole Gide" ("j'ai passé un hiver de guerre bien pénible; les bombardements, les restrictions, etc., étaient un moindre mal à côté de ce que me valurent cette emm . . . de Chacha et ce vieux c . . . de Gide"), adding other unpleasant remarks about the elderly author (qtd. in Schveitzer 68).

37. After reading the manuscript, Gide wrote a letter addressed to Jean Amrouche but apparently intended for François Reymond's eyes. The substance of this as yet unpublished letter can be surmised from Reymond's reply (published as an appendix in *L'Envers du Journal*) and from *Ainsi soit-il*, the final volume of memoirs into which Gide apparently incorporated his message to Reymond. Gide's letter to Amrouche, as quoted by Reymond, declares: "I cannot remember ever having 'panted' after anyone" (adapted from SBI 162) ("Je n'ai pas souvenir d'avoir jamais 'brâmé' après quelqu'un")—to which Reymond replies: "That's news to me" ("Voilà ce que j'ignorais") (DR 259). Gide repeats this assertion in *Ainsi soit-il*, adding that throughout his life he immediately ceased his attentions when he realized that his feelings were not reciprocated (SV 1070). If this were the case, Reymond concedes, the entire quarrel grew out of a misunderstanding (DR 259).

38. "[L]'attachement passionné d'un aîné, ou d'un ami du même âge [. . .] peut être pour l'enfant l'invitation la meilleure au courage, au travail, à la vertu"; "sans prétendre avec Lycurgue [. . .] qu'un citoyen ne pouvait être vraiment honnête et utile à la République s'il n'avait un ami, je prétends que l'uranisme n'est en lui-même nullement néfaste au bon ordre de la société, de l'État; tout au contraire" (Gide, *Corydon* [Fr.] 126–27, 122).

39. In October 1942, while living in the Reymond household and developing his portrait of young François, Gide reaffirmed the importance of the 1924 treatise: "*Corydon* remains in my opinion the most important of my books" (J 4: 130) ("*Corydon* reste à mes yeux le plus important de mes livres") (J II: 842).

40. "[P]elotage raté" (DR 201).

41. "[Des] ragots rassemblés [. . .] entre deux couvertures" (Guibert 349).

42. "[H]ostilités," "combats," "lutte," "notre bataille," "l'adversaire," "l'ennemi habile" (DR 185; 178, 189, 205; 178, 181; 183; 205; 180). In *André Gide: Pedagogy and Pederasty*, one of the few exceptions to the generalized critical neglect of *L'Envers du*

Journal, Naomi Segal argues that "[w]arfare was an easier [. . .] substitute for a negotiated settlement because neither was able to say a word about what had happened between their bodies" (340).

43. Reymond claims that he attacked Gide only in self-defense: "I rarely took the first step on the path of new hostilities, but satisfied myself with fiercely counterattacking on the battlefields where you pursued me" ("je faisais rarement le premier pas dans la voie d'hostilités nouvelles, me contentant de contre-attaquer férocement sur les terrains où vous me poursuiviez") (DR 185).

44. "[T]out au long de votre séjour [. . .] je n'ai cessé un instant de vous considérer comme un intrus et un parasite"; "vos amis [. . .] nous avaient envahi[s]" (DR 175, 170–71).

45. Whether or not the dog was named "Tommy" with British soldiers in mind, his name fits neatly with the political allegory Reymond is developing.

46. "[U]ne somme dérisoire" (DR 172–73).

47. In his *Journal*, Gide leads readers to believe that he made a substantial contribution to household expenses: "[Victor] was very much amazed to learn that I share with [Chacha] the daily expenses of the house" (J 4: 194) ("[Victor] s'est montré fort étonné en apprenant que je faisais avec [Chacha], pour les frais quotidiens de la maison, bourse commune") (J II: 930). This claim does not appear in the *Journal* manuscript (ms. γ1642: 29).

48. "[E]ntièrement à la charge de mes parents, et vous avec!"; "tout en n'ignorant pas que Chacha n'avait aucune qualité pour disposer de l'appartement"; "je pardonnais mal à ma grand'mère de trahir un peu la famille" (DR 174, 166, 208).

49. "[É]pouvantée à l'idée de devoir demeurer seule avec son terrible petit-fils" (J II: 908).

50. Reymond adds that Gide came back to the avenue Roustan apartment "the very day of the liberation" ("le jour même de la libération") (DR 172).

51. "Les Français de quelque réflexion, durant ces années, auront plus ou moins couché avec l'Allemagne" (qtd. in Veillon 189).

52. "On relèvera partout dans les articles de Chateaubriant, de Drieu, de Brazillach (sic) de curieuses métaphores qui présentent les relations de la France et de l'Allemagne sous l'aspect d'une union sexuelle où la France joue le rôle de la femme. Et très certainement la liaison féodale du collaborateur à son maître, a un aspect sexuel. Pour autant qu'on puisse concevoir l'état d'esprit de la collaboration, on y devine comme un climat de féminité. [. . .] Il me paraît qu'il y a là un curieux mélange de masochisme et d'homosexualité. Les milieux homosexuels parisiens, d'ailleurs, ont fourni de nombreuses et brillantes recrues" (Sartre, *Situations* 58).

53. "J'appartenais au mouvement de jeunesse vichyste des 'Compagnons de France', mais j'étais porté à abandonner ces idées et à me joindre à l'opposition au régime alors régnant; le goût du risque, l'attrait de l'inconnu, et aussi, quoi que vous puissiez en penser, les idées généreuses de justice sociale que l'on me présentait, me décidèrent à cette totale volte-face" (DR 216).

54. "[Des] mots d'ordre incisifs sur les occupants et leurs valets" (DR 218–19).

55. Whereas Eugène Boretz emphasizes the danger faced by the communist *résistants* who mimeographed and distributed the slim monthly newsletter, Reymond considered his role in the paper's circulation to be relatively risk-free (Boretz 22; DR 219–20).

56. When his offer to procure André Gide's identity papers was rejected as impractical because of the writer's fame and advanced age, François stole the card belonging to Jean Amrouche's wife Suzanne. When he later admitted the theft, Jean and Suzanne replied: "Why didn't you ask us for it? We would have been glad to give it to you" ("Pourquoi ne nous l'as-tu pas demandée? Nous te l'aurions volontiers donnée") (DR 220–21).

57. "[S]éparée en deux camps"; "espionner l'adversaire"; "pour lire votre *Journal* en cachette et avoir ainsi, sur le moral de l'ennemi, quelques renseignements" (DR 156, 180).

58. "[V]ous modifiez un peu votre journal après coup, ainsi que j'ai pu m'en rendre compte par comparaison avec le souvenir de ce que j'en lus furtivement à l'époque" (DR 124). Reymond cites an incident involving the six-volume Larousse dictionary as evidence of Gide's alterations to the original diary. On 8 March 1943, Gide accused François of locking the dictionary in his room. Reymond claims that Gide later withdrew his accusation, but omitted the retraction from the published version of his *Journal*. The 9 March entry—in which Gide admits he had falsely accused the boy—was indeed absent from published versions of the *Journal* until 1997 (J II: 919, 920; DR 184–85).

59. "Je ne doute pas que votre renom et votre grand âge ne vous aient habitué à plus de docilité chez les jeunes sujets que le hasard met sous votre main"; "vous [avez] trompé indignement mes parents, abusé de ma confiance en votre prestige de vieillard 'auréolé de gloire'" (DR 141, 137).

Roger Martin du Gard makes similar charges in his journal entry for 9 November 1940. Recording Gide's indignant reaction—"This is odious!" ("C'est odieux!")—when a teacher sexually harassed Gide's seventeen-year-old daughter Catherine, Martin du Gard deems the teacher's behavior less reprehensible than Gide's own:

> Now, dear old Gide has spent his life committing far more serious breaches of trust! How many times has he insinuated himself into a family of friends, increasing his kindness toward the parents with the sole intent of approaching the young son of the household, sometimes a schoolboy only thirteen years old, joining him in his bedroom, awakening his sexual curiosity, and teaching him about sexual pleasure! More clever than Catherine's teacher, more diabolical in his temptations, more daring, too; how many times has he been able to fool the parents, obtain the child's complicity, and engage him in tender and perverse games? Back then he did not find anything "odious" about the extensive, premeditated corruption of a young boy whose parents had naïvely entrusted him to their friend Gide!

> [Or, ce bon Gide a passé sa vie à commettre de bien plus graves abus de confiance! Combien de fois s'est-il introduit dans une famille amie, multipliant

les amabilités avec les parents, dans le seul but d'approcher le jeune fils de
la maison, parfois un écolier de treize ans, de le rejoindre dans sa chambre,
d'éveiller ses curiosités sexuelles, de lui apprendre le plaisir! Plus malin que
le professeur de Catherine, plus diabolique dans ses tentations, plus hardi
aussi, combien de fois a-t-il su embobiner les parents, s'assurer la complicité
d'un enfant, et se livrer avec lui à des jeux tendres et pervers? Il ne trouvait
alors rien d'"'odieux" dans le détournement prémédité et poussé aussi loin
que possible du jeune garçon, que ses parents confiaient ingénument à l'ami
Gide!] (361–62)

60. "[L]e choix même de ses petits complices (enfants du peuple, ne parlant pas
sa langue, nègres) avec lesquels aucun échange n'est possible que physique, rétrécit le
champ de l'éventuelle déception" (Herbart, *Recherche* 23).

61. "[A]u long de ce travail, j'ai senti à chaque instant tout ce que mes pensées,
mes réactions, vous devaient, tant à vous-même qu'à votre œuvre. Pourquoi le nier?
Ceux que ma jeunesse a respectés, ceux auxquels je dois quelque part de ma formation
présente, étaient vos disciples" (DR 255).

62. "Ma première démarche fut de porter dans ma chambre deux ou trois de vos
livres [. . .] que je me mis à lire ou à relire, voulant d'abord ainsi profiter de votre
présence"; "Eugène K. [. . .] m'avait demandé avec une curieuse insistance de la voix
et des yeux si j'avais lu ses livres, ce que j'en pensais, etc." (DR 127, 131).

63. "[T]out désir de le peloter a vite cédé au désir de le calotter en entendant ses
insolences" (G/MG 270).

64. "Ah, vous n'avez jamais su comment je me suis précipité dans la salle de
bains, savonné, frotté avec une brosse à laver à m'en faire saigner, de quelle manière,
tant j'étais fébrile, je me heurtais aux robinets et aux parois de la baignoire!"; "'elle
attire contre le sien mon visage, passe autour de mon cou son bras nu, descend sa main
dans ma chemise entr'ouverte, demande en riant si je suis chatouilleux, pousse plus
avant. [. . . J]e m'enfuis; je courus jusqu'au fond du jardin; là, dans un petit citerneau
du potager, je trempai mon mouchoir, l'appliquai sur mon front, lavai, frottai mes
joues, mon cou, tout ce que cette femme avait touché!' On ne saurait mieux dire,
Jérôme . . . sauf que vous n'étiez pas une jeune et jolie tante" (DR 137, 138–39).

65. "[Chacha] parle de 'son petit cagibi' où elle s'enferme, comme faisait la
Séquestrée de Poitiers de son 'cher grand-fond Malampia'" (J II: 881). The sequestered
woman, Blanche Monnier (whom Gide called Mélanie Bastian), referred to her quarters as "my dear little grotto" ("ma chère petite grotte") and "my dear big black
Malampia" ("mon cher grand fond Malampia") (*Ne jugez pas* 215, 227).

66. "[R]ien n'est plus banal et plus facile à inventer que les traits de cynisme
égoïste" (G/MG 274).

67. "L'eussé-je connu plus tôt, j'aurais enrichi de ses traits le Strouvilhou de mes
Faux-Monnayeurs" (J II: 878).

68. "Pour la première fois peut-être, un de vos personnages, en partie réel et en
partie composé, a pris la parole pour vous répondre, et raconter lui-même son histoire"
(DR 257).

69. "J'ai connu à Tunis, en juin dernier, deux nuits de plaisir comme je ne pensais plus en pouvoir connaître de telles à mon âge"; "Tout son être chantait merci"; "Il semblait si peu se soucier de mon âge que j'en venais à l'oublier moi-même" (J II: 826–27).

70. "Ah, j'en connais un autre qui s'en est soucié" (DR 134).

71. In an appendix to the second edition of *L'Envers du Journal*, Reymond's co-author Henri Rambaud rehearses the debate about the veracity of the "June nights" passage. While an anonymous source has confirmed the existence of "F.," Rambaud concludes that the passage was written after the fact (DR 262). He calls the reader's attention to the date of the journal entry: 3 August 1942, "only nine days after his failure with François!" ("juste neuf jours après l'échec avec François!"). Rambaud suggests that Reymond's rejection prompted Gide to transcribe his memory of "those luminous hours" ("ces heures lumineuses") in order to convince himself that his days of seducing young boys were not behind him "[de] peur que l'heure de séduire ne fût, déjà, derrière lui" (DR 92).

72. "Fâcheuse coïncidence, l'initiale de son prénom est aussi celle du mien; et même est-ce seulement une coïncidence?" (DR 134). At least one reader apparently assimilated the initial "F." and the name "François": among the *Journal*'s many references to young boys, Gide's biographer Justin O'Brien lists "'François' at Tunis in June 1942" (*Portrait* 263).

73. "De mon attitude odieuse, de ce que j'ai été avec vous insolent, égoïste, menteur, vous donnez diverses explications bien fantaisistes" (DR 202).

74. "[J]e me persuade qu'il ne faut voir là qu'un effet de sa goujaterie naturelle"; "Comment Victor, qui ressemble tant à son père, supporte-t-il d'être à ce point captif de son hérédité? Il y a peut-être, dans son mutisme envers moi, moins de résolution que de laisser-aller à sa pente" (J II: 896, 937). The manuscript has "hostile resolve" ("résolution hostile") (ms. γ1642: 8).

75. "He does not yet seem very developed, sexually speaking" ("Il ne semble pas encore très développé, sexuellement parlant"); "curious to know whether puberty, which is slow in coming to him, will awaken any feelings [in him]" ("curieux de savoir si la puberté, qui chez lui se fait attendre, éveillera quelques sentiments affectifs") (J II: 930, 876).

76. "Si je ne veux pas coucher avec vous, ce n'est pas, bien sûr, parce que cela ne me dit rien du tout, mais parce que je suis impubère!" (DR 250).

77. Gérard Boutelleau was the son of Jacques Chardonne, the writer whose pro-German *Chronique privée de l'an 1940* had jarred Gide out of his *attentiste* position. On learning of his son's arrest, Chardonne contacted Gerhard Heller, head of the literary section of the Propaganda-Staffel in Paris. Trading on the extent to which Chardonne had "compromised himself" ("combien celui-ci s'est compromis") with the Germans, Heller managed to obtain Gérard's release from the Sachsenhausen-Oranienburg concentration camp to which he had been deported (Heller 87).

78. The confiscated notebook contained Gide's diary entries from January through April 1942. Hope Boutelleau managed to conceal a second notebook con-

taining the still untranscribed diary for May to December 1942. Gide feared that the first notebook would prompt the Italians to seize the second—not because of the manuscript's content, but because of its commercial value (J II: 916).

79. "[L]e manuscrit ayant trait à Em."; "les cahiers confidentiels de Louksor" (J II: 917).

80. "[C]omme témoin susceptible de parler et que l'on préfère ne pas céder aux Anglais"; "Encore que j'aie du mal à me convaincre que [. . .] ma personne ou ma voix puisse être de quelque importance, mieux valait ne pas courir la chance d'un voyage et séjour contraints en Allemagne ou en Italie" (J II: 943).

81. "[C]ompagnons de captivité" (J II: 943). Duché's guests were among the estimated five to six thousand people living in hiding by the end of the Tunisian occupation. These thousands included Jews, who had been called up for work details beginning in December 1942, as well as socialists, communists, Freemasons, and Spanish Republican fighters who had sought refuge in Tunis after the Spanish Civil War. During the final weeks of the Tunisian occupation, the ranks of the clandestine grew considerably, for the Service du Travail Obligatoire was instituted in Tunis on 20 April 1943: all men aged eighteen to forty-eight were subject to conscription for work in Germany, but few responded to the call-up (Boretz 74; J II: 857; Kassab 440–41).

82. "[J]'attends, pour me raser à neuf, la délivrance"; "Nous vivons, ici, sans électricité et, partant, sans nouvelles de la radio; souvent sans eau, sans presque plus d'alcool, ni de gaz, ni d'huile, sur un reste de provisions presque épuisé, mal soutenus par des repas chaque jour plus insuffisants" (J II: 946, 945).

83. "Aucun plaisir; content de rentrer dans ma grotte" (J II: 949).

84. When she was discovered after twenty-five years of confinement, her body emaciated and her hair excessively long, Blanche Monnier begged not to be removed from her "dear little grotto" ("chère petite grotte") (Gide, *Ne jugez pas* 223–24, 215).

85. "[L]a ville en délire" (J II: 951).

86. "[D]ébouche sur la délivrance, lorsque l'intime et le public fêtent la même libération" (Sagaert, Introduction xxv).

87. According to Éric Marty, the battle of Tunis "acquires meaning only retrospectively [in Gide's *Journal*]; yet while it was *taking place*, it was [. . .] almost meaningless, ambiguous, unreal, and, as always, mingled with the most deeply private aspects of Gide's life" ("La bataille de Tunis [. . .] ne prendra de sens que rétrospectivement, alors que, tant qu'elle *avait lieu*, elle était [. . .] pauvre de sens, ambiguë, sans réalité, et mêlée comme toujours à la plus profonde intimité gidienne") (31).

88. "Tandis qu'hier, j'écrivais ces lignes, les Alliés entraient déjà dans la ville. [. . .] On comprend encore à peine que ce que l'on attendait depuis si longtemps a eu lieu; qu'*ils* sont là; on n'ose encore y croire" (J II: 950–51).

89. "[J]e n'ai pas à noter ici ce qui ressortit à l'histoire" (J II: 952).

90. "[M]épris [. . .] à l'égard de l'Histoire" (Marty 25).

91. "Les Alliés ne seraient nullement pressés de vaincre, et, tandis que leur écrasante supériorité numérique leur permettrait depuis longtemps le triomphe, ils

préfèrent attendre"; "savante stratégie, ou maladresse; prudente patience, ou impéritie timorée?"; "De tous côtés, il nous revient que les troupes américaines, tout autant que les forces anglaises ou françaises, se sont admirablement battues. Les lenteurs qu'on put leur reprocher d'abord, n'étaient que mesures de prudence, aussi longtemps qu'insuffisamment munies. Il importait de n'engager le combat qu'avec l'assurance de le pouvoir mener jusqu'à la victoire. L'événement a levé ce qu'il pouvait rester de doutes et montré la sagesse de cet atermoiement, alors que la précipitation risquait de tout compromettre" (J II: 929, 885, 956).

Having changed his views on the American army, Gide subsequently worried about publishing the *Journal*'s many criticisms of the Americans' supposed inactivity. "Several times in recent years," reports Justin O'Brien, "André Gide has expressed the desire for simultaneous publication of [. . . his Tunis *Journal*] in French and English, in the naïve hope, unshared by his French publisher, that such a delicate attention would somewhat mitigate the sting of his remarks about the American forces in Tunisia." However, says O'Brien, "the men who took part in the North African campaign should be interested in the way they looked to those they were about to liberate, especially as that view changed so drastically upon contact" (Introduction vii).

92. "[T]ous les peuples conquis et sous le joug allemand, vont puiser dans cet immense revers de l'oppresseur, un extraordinaire encouragement à la résistance. On peut y entendre l'annonce d'un effondrement général" (J II: 955).

93. "Je n'ai rien écrit de plus plat; et jamais aucun texte de moi ne rencontra pareil accueil; il ne reste plus qu'à le servir dans les 'Morceaux Choisis' pour lycées!"; "avec force éloges absurdes" (CAG 11: 603).

94. The editor of *Combat* acknowledged that the paper was reprinting "La Libération de Tunis" without Gide's authorization (Gide, "Libération" [*Combat*] 8).

95. "[D]'énormes contresens" (CAG 11: 603).

96. "Vite, avant de quitter ma retraite, je rase une barbe de *quatre semaines* et descends avec mes compagnons de captivité dans la rue, où *eux* n'avaient pas reparu depuis exactement six mois" (J II: 951, emphasis added); "je rase hâtivement ma barbe fournie et puis, avec mes compagnons de captivité, je descends dans la rue où *nous* ne nous sommes pas aventurés pendant exactement six mois" (Gide, "Libération" [*Combat*] 8, emphasis added). Étienne Lalou rectifies the misapprehension occasioned by this double translation in a May 1945 article in the resistance-oriented paper *Gavroche*: "Let's set the record straight [. . .] he was not imprisoned for six months in Tunis, but simply had to hide during the few weeks preceding the city's liberation" ("Précisons [. . .] qu'il ne fut pas emprisonné pendant six mois à Tunis, mais qu'il dut simplement se cacher pendant les quelques semaines qui précédèrent la délivrance de la ville") (3).

97. An editor's note states: "The printing of this volume [*Chroniques interdites II*], published at the expense of a few patriotic intellectuals, was completed under [German] oppression in Paris on 14 July 1944" ("Ce volume publié au dépens de quelques lettrés patriotes a été achevé d'imprimer sous l'oppression à Paris le 14 juillet 1944") (*Chroniques* 94).

98. The telegraphic entry of 6 June 1944—"ALLIED LANDING IN NORMANDY" (J 4: 242) ("DÉBARQUEMENT DES ALLIÉS EN NORMANDIE") (J II: 991)—is one of Gide's few references to the war after May 1943.

99. "[E]n ces temps encore tout déchirés de misères et de catastrophes, ce journal intime risque d'impatienter le lecteur" (CAG 6: 329).

100. "C'est si maladroit, en ce moment où tous les 'héros' racontent leur odyssée, et où tant de gens, confrères et lecteurs, ont des souvenirs 'héroïques', de publier ce texte d'actualité, ce 'journal de guerre' qui ne peut servir qu'à mettre en évidence la différence qu'il y a entre la façon dont Gide a souffert de la guerre, et celle de la majorité des Français!" (R. Martin du Gard 725).

101. "Il se soumit à la dure discipline que connaissent tous ceux qui, en Europe occupée, vivent en marge des lois allemandes" (Amrouche).

102. "[F]aute de mieux et incapable d'écrire quoi que ce soit de neuf 'ad hoc'"; "fort déprimé par un mois de claustration avec nourriture tout juste suffisante [. . .] et défense non seulement de sortir, mais même de mettre le nez à la fenêtre à cause des gens de la maison d'en face"; "l'extrême dévouement des amis communistes qui m'hébergeaient et m'apportaient pitance" (CAG 11: 602–03).

103. As late as 1947, in fact, Gide's supporter Jacques Galland felt the need to reiterate this point: "[Gide] was taken to safety, to a place where several political notables of the Regency, whose notoriety had made their disappearance desirable, had already found refuge. This is where he spent the last days of the occupation, cloistered in the company of socialists, communists, and trade unionists" ("[Gide] fut mis en sécurité dans un lieu où plusieurs personnalités politiques de la Régence, dont la notoriété avait rendu l'éclipse désirable, avaient déjà trouvé refuge. C'est là qu'il passa les derniers temps de l'occupation, cloîtré en compagnie de socialistes, de communistes et de syndicalistes") (8).

104. "Mise en abyme" denotes the embedded structure of images duplicated within images, or stories within stories. Gide coined the term, derived from the language of heraldry, in an 1893 *Journal* entry (J I: 171).

CHAPTER FIVE. REPOSITIONINGS:
PAGES DE JOURNAL AND *THÉSÉE*

1. Gide's hostess Anne Heurgon-Desjardins was the daughter of Paul Desjardins, founder of the intellectual *décades* at Pontigny.

2. "Il est certainement appelé à jouer un grand rôle et semble 'à la hauteur'. [. . .] Je ne ferai pas de difficulté pour raccrocher à lui mes espoirs" (J II: 965).

3. Friends in France had their first news of Gide from English and Algerian radio stations, which announced in mid-May that the writer had safely survived the occupation of Tunis (CAG 6: 309, 310).

4. I am indebted to Michael Tilby, who guided me to the Foreign Office files concerning Gide.

5. "Espère joindre prochainement votre belle-famille" (CAG 11: 264).

6. "[L]'opportunité de créer une nouvelle revue qui groupât les forces intellectuelles et morales de la France libre ou combattant pour l'être" (J II: 965).

7. "[L]es choses à sauver ne manquent pas!" (CAG 6: 313). Like the Biblical ark, *L'Arche* offered a temporary refuge. Gide clearly saw his participation—as well as the publication of his *Attendu que . . .* and *Pages de Journal* by the Algiers firm Charlot—as temporary: "I have merely *lent myself* (circumstances having forced me to do so) to *L'Arche* and Charlot [. . . and] my heart and mind remain devoted to the *N.R.F.* and to *our* old group" ("je n'ai fait que *me prêter* (les circonstances m'y forçant) à *L'Arche* et à Charlot [. . . et] je reste acquis de cœur et d'esprit à la *N.R.F.* et à *notre* ancien groupement"), he wrote to Jean Schlumberger in October 1944. After relocating to Paris, Gide and his associates planned, "*L'Arche* would continue to appear so long as the *N.R.F.* lay dormant, then it could announce the resumption of the *N.R.F.* and its own reabsorption [into the *N.R.F.*]" ("*L'Arche* continuerait de paraître tant que *La N.R.F.* sommeillerait, puis pourrait annoncer sa reprise et sa propre résorption") (G/Sch 959–60). Thus, the "ark" was not only a refuge: it was also a vessel to help Gide and his colleagues return "home" to the *N.R.F.* Unfortunately, this plan failed: although *L'Arche* transferred to Paris in 1945 and continued to appear there until 1947 (J 4: 231), the *Nouvelle Revue Française* was not authorized to resume publication during Gide's lifetime.

8. "Le rôle de l'*Arche* [. . .] est de rallier et de grouper les Résistants [. . .] disséminés aujourd'hui en Amérique, en Angleterre, dans l'Afrique du Nord et les colonies, en attendant le jour où nous pourrons rallier aussi ceux de France" (Gide, "Appel" 14).

9. The "Manifeste" and Gide's "Appel" agree on the need for preserving diversity in postwar France and express this thought in identical terms: "France [. . .] desires not Unison but Harmony" ("la France [. . .] veut non l'Unisson, mais l'Harmonie") ("Appel" 14); "A totalitarian France would no longer be France. [. . .] Far from forcing its diverse voices to sing in unison [. . .] French genius [. . .] blends them into a superior harmony" ("Une France totalitaire ne serait plus la France. [. . .] Loin d'imposer l'unisson aux voix diverses [. . .] le génie français [. . .] en compose une harmonie supérieure") ("Manifeste" 8).

In fact, the manifesto's resonance with Gide's oeuvre goes back as far as the 1897 *Nourritures terrestres*, in which Gide wrote: "ASSUME AS MUCH HUMANITY AS POSSIBLE—let this be your motto" (*Fruits* 17) ("ASSUMER LE PLUS POSSIBLE D'HUMANITÉ, voilà la bonne formule") (R 158). The manifesto of *L'Arche* echoes this notion: "a work is truly French only insofar as 'it assumes as much humanity as possible'" ("une œuvre n'est vraiment française que dans la mesure où 'elle assume le plus d'humanité possible'") ("Manifeste" 6). In *Les Nouvelles Nourritures*, the 1935 work addressed to the youth of the Soviet Union, Gide argued that "[i]t is not only the world that must change, but man" (*Fruits* 277) ("Ce n'est pas seulement le monde qu'il s'agit de changer; mais l'homme") (R 292). In a similar vein, the 1944 "Manifeste" evokes the need to "transform the outside world, improve the conditions of men's existence, indeed, but much more is at stake: [we must] build man, obtain man, against *nature* and against *his nature*" ("Transformer le monde extérieur, améliorer les conditions d'existence de l'homme, certes, mais il s'agit de bien plus: de construire l'homme, d'obtenir l'homme, contre *la* nature et contre *sa* nature") ("Manifeste" 9).

10. "La France se glorifie d'avoir 'dépassé la guerre'" ("Manifeste" 6).

11. The manifesto's disapproval of Vichy was nevertheless explicit: "France must define, manifest, and illustrate [. . .] the human values to which French genius has given perfect form. [. . .] No need to add that we refuse to recognize these values [. . .] in certain sacrilegious parodies that we have been shown" ("[La France] doit définir, manifester, illustrer [. . .] les valeurs humaines auxquelles le génie français a donné une forme accomplie. [. . .] Inutile sans doute d'ajouter que ces valeurs [. . .], nous refusons de les reconnaître en certaines parodies sacrilèges qu'on s'efforça de nous en offrir") ("Manifeste" 7, 8).

12. Ehrenburg declared that the manifesto "insulted the U.S.S.R. by its statement that the Russian Revolution had contributed towards the establishment of fascist régimes in Germany and Italy" ("Criticism" 112). This rather tendentious interpretation of the manifesto is difficult to defend: although the "Manifeste" refers to pre-1939 revolutions in Germany, Italy, and the Soviet Union, it does so to valorize France's revolutionary contribution—"the universal principles of 1789" ("les principes universels de 1789") ("Manifeste" 10–11).

13. "[U]ne loi historique donne tort aux émigrés et raison à ceux qui sont demeurés sur le sol de leur patrie" ("Texte radiodiffusé"; "La France"). Étienne Lalou rectified this erroneous claim in a May 1945 article in *Gavroche*, stating categorically that Gide had never written that "an emigrant is always in the wrong" ("un émigré a toujours tort") (3).

14. Several papers reported that Gide was working for resistance or Allied propaganda services in North Africa ("André Gide, arrêté"; "Gide à Alger"; Dyssord 7). Others claimed, incorrectly, that he had been arrested (or threatened with arrest) on the orders of General Giraud: the communist-instigated arrest was supposed to be revenge for Gide's *Retour de l'U.R.S.S.* ("Gide en prison"; "André Gide, arrêté"; "Gide à Alger"; "Les Mésaventures"). Literary chronicler Paul Léautaud joined a handful of journalists in reporting that Gide had fled to London (16: 25), either to escape his communist enemies or, according to a spurious article in *L'Écho*, to avoid Jewish intellectuals' requests for political and financial support ("Échos des lettres").

15. "Les enjuivés d'Alger peuvent se réjouir de l'arrivée d'André Gide" ("Dans le jardin").

16. "[E]uropéanisme"; "[les] adversaires de l'Europe" (Fernand-Demeure).

17. "Quel motif d'exaltation autrement grand [. . .] André Gide eût pu trouver dans l'idéal national-socialiste auquel l'avait préparé sa connaissance de Nietzsche! Comme cet esprit communautaire, respectueux des indispensables hiérarchies, eût satisfait davantage son esprit que la basse démagogie du communisme" (Dyssord 7).

18. "Le 'gaullisme' de Gide n'est plus vraiment qu'un épisode bien négligeable parmi ces variations infinies"; "la quasi-totalité de 'l'intelligence française'" (Rebatet, "L'Académie" 6, 1).

19. "I should like to cry aloud my affection for Russia; and that my cry should be heard, should have importance" (J 3: 179–80) ("je voudrais crier très haut ma sympathie pour l'U.R.S.S.; et que mon cri soit entendu; ait de l'importance"), Gide wrote in 1931 (*Pages de Journal [1929–1932]* 115; J II: 296).

20. "Je voudrais donc qu'on n'accordât à aucune de ces pages, et particulièrement à celles du début, d'autre valeur que relative: si leur suite peut instruire, c'est à la manière d'un itinéraire intellectuel, en marquant, au sortir d'une ombre épaisse, les étapes d'un lent acheminement vers la lumière" (PJ [A] 9; J II: 1104). Without naming names, Gide also uses the "Avant-propos" to register his support for de Gaulle: "Blessed be he who permitted and favored the restoration of our dignity" (J 4: 307) ("Béni soit celui qui permit et favorisa la restauration de notre dignité") (J II: 1104).

21. "C'est [. . .] pourquoi, vers la fin de ma vie, et durant cette année tragique, me touche si particulièrement tout ce qui vient de cette autre France, et que je souris avec tant de joie à ce bel éveil de jeunesse, de l'est à l'ouest de notre Afrique du Nord, si ardente, si préservée, et sur qui nous fondons tant d'espoirs" (Gide, "Notre" 276). "In the cryptic language of the period, these lines signified a great deal (or at least we endowed them with a great deal of meaning)" ("Dans la langue cryptique de l'époque, ces lignes signifiaient beaucoup (ou du moins, nous leur donnions beaucoup de sens)"), explains *Fontaine*'s founder Max-Pol Fouchet (125).

22. "La France, hélas! depuis des mois, des années, ne nous a guère donné de motifs d'être fiers" (PJ [A] 90; J II: 768); "ne va certes pas toujours dans le sens que les mots d'ordre de Vichy proposent" (PJ [A] 92; J II: 775); "cette singerie de 'Révolution Nationale'" (PJ [A] 100; J II: 796).

23. "[E]nseignement et réconfort à considérer le chemin parcouru" (CAG 11: 312).

24. As Minister of the Interior, Pucheu had ordered the executions of many members of the communist resistance. Attempting to change sides once Germany's defeat seemed inevitable, Pucheu traveled to Morocco in February 1943 under the protection of General Giraud. He was soon arrested, however, and an Algiers tribunal eventually condemned him to death. General de Gaulle, under pressure from the resistance, refused a plea for leniency, and Pucheu was executed on 20 March 1944 (Rousso 154–55).

25. "[M]alaise indicible"; "son crime essentiel: il a cru à la victoire allemande" (qtd. in J II: 986).

26. "Est-il possible qu'on puisse imprimer à Alger des phrases comme celles-ci"; "Aujourd'hui, la littérature est une arme de guerre. C'est pourquoi je réclame la prison pour André Gide et des poursuites contre le gérant de l'"Arche'" (qtd. in J II: 1104, 1105).

"If Clemenceau were here, the author of these foul writings would be already arrested, brought before the military court under the law that punishes traitors with death in wartime" (qtd. in J 4: 308) ("Si Clemenceau était là, l'auteur de ces écrits infâmes serait déjà arrêté, déféré au Tribunal militaire avec l'article du Code qui punit de mort les traîtres en temps de guerre") (qtd. in J II: 1105), Giovoni further declared. Berthe Zuckerkandl, sister-in-law of the late radical statesman, protested Giovoni's reference to Clemenceau in a 9 July 1944 letter to Gide. Despite his love of the earth and those who cultivate it, she stated, Clemenceau would have agreed with Gide's assessment of the peasant character. Above all, she denounced Giovoni's "false patriotism and his totalitarian attack on intellectual freedom" (qtd. in J 4: 310) ("son faux patriotisme et son attaque totalitaire contre la liberté de l'esprit") (qtd. in J II: 1106).

27. "[A]ux rares journaux et revues patriotiques d'Alger" (qtd. in J II: 1105). Shortly after Giovoni's speech in the Assemblée Consultative, *La Liberté* published additional inflammatory remarks made by the *député*. Dramatically subtitled "Mort aux traîtres!" (Death to traitors!), the article claimed that Gide advocated working for Pétain and Hitler. It further alleged that Gide's manuscript diary declared: "That which is called collaboration and treason today may be called good sense tomorrow" ("Ce qu'on nomme aujourd'hui collaboration et trahison pourrait s'appelait (sic) demain bon sens") ("Les Insultes").

28. Clearly working from the manuscript, the undoubtedly pseudonymous Mémoire echoes Gide's argument then cites Gide's withdrawal from the *N.R.F.* and his transparently oppositional articles in *Le Figaro* as instances of great courage. He further praises Gide for not publishing only those *Journal* entries that, "read in isolation, would have allowed him to lay claim to the title of Gaullist from the very beginning" ("lus isolément, lui eussent permis de revendiquer le titre de gaulliste de première heure"). Mémoire concludes by declaring the publication of the *Pages de Journal* a public service: "By publishing this diary which, like any other diary, is a confession, Gide [. . .] meant to serve the nation" ("En publiant ce journal qui, comme tout autre, est une confession, Gide [. . .] a voulu servir l'État") (Mémoire).

29. The similarity between Giovoni's tactics and those of the Légion was a common theme in newspaper articles defending Gide after the *député*'s attack, and the reminder that Gide had been no friend of Vichy helped undermine Giovoni's allegations (Celio 1; Després; Jaques).

30. "[A]lors que notre pays semblait définitivement écrasé, qu'il était abandonné à lui-même, en une effroyable solitude, et que tout espoir paraissait de la démence" (qtd. in Gide, "Rester" 1).

31. In his diary and correspondence, Gide repeatedly states that his opinions have changed since 1940 and explains that he published the early *Journal* entries to show how far he had come (J II: 1002; G/Sch 967; CAG 11: 311–12).

32. "Vous demandez ma mort. [. . .] Or je ne connais pas de fin plus belle que de mourir pour la liberté de l'esprit; et c'est dire aussi: pour la France. Tout à votre disposition. Je préfèrerais (sic), il est vrai, que la coupe de cigüe (sic) me fût tendue par nos ennemis communs, contre lesquels il me semble que devraient rester unies toutes les forces de la Résistance" (Gide, "Rester" 3).

33. "[Je trouve] inopportun tout prétexte à division entre Français"; "non par frousse [. . .] mais par décence" (CAG 11: 284; G/MG 321).

34. In his diary entry of 2 October 1944, Gide combines a call for French unity with praise for de Gaulle: "It is good, it is indispensable, for the French to put up a united, unanimous front in their love of the country they share and in their joy at their deliverance; also in their hatred of their former oppressor and all those who abetted the oppressor. Only this degree of unanimity can make possible the task of reconstruction and restoration undertaken so gloriously by de Gaulle; each of us must help in that task and, as far as I am concerned, I will go about it wholeheartedly" ("Il est bon, il est indispensable, que les Français se montrent unis, unanimes, dans leur amour pour la patrie commune et la joie de la délivrance; dans leur haine également de l'op-

presseur d'hier et de tous ceux qui l'ont favorisé. Cette unanimité seule peut permettre le travail de reconstruction et reconstitution entrepris si glorieusement par de Gaulle; chacun de nous doit y aider et, pour ma part, je m'y emploierai de tout cœur") (J II: 999).

35. "[Q]ue l'on ne vienne point arguer de division entre Français. La seule division aujourd'hui dont nous ayions à tenir compte est discorde entre ceux qui *consentent* et ceux qui *résistent*" (Gide, "Appel" 14).

36. "Il n'est que de se soumettre, d'accepter, hélas! l'inévitable, et contre quoi toute révolte ne peut réussir qu'à diviser entre eux les Français" (J II: 705).

37. Gide repeatedly emphasized this entry, as in his 3 February 1945 letter to Claude Mauriac: "how happy it makes me to have written in my Journal for the 24th of June, 1940: 'How could anyone refuse to agree with the Declaration of General de Gaulle?'" (qtd. in *Conversations* [Eng.] 224) ("combien heureux d'avoir écrit dans mon Journal à la date du 24 juin 1940: 'Comment ne pas donner de tout cœur son adhésion à la déclaration du général de Gaulle?'") (qtd. in *Conversations* [Fr.] 266).

38. "[S]'assure et s'affirme dans la résistance" (J II: 741).

39. "Gide never had any qualms about correcting and selectively editing his texts" ("Gide a toujours corrigé son texte, sans scrupules, et fait un choix"), contends José Cabanis (v).

40. "[E]n dehors des notes sur Madeleine, *je n'ai jamais rien supprimé* de mon Journal" (CAG 7: 133).

41. "[A]pprêté [. . .] corrigé" (Julia); "truqué [. . .] gommé" (Marty 55); "maquill[é]" (Guillemin 212).

42. "[P]etit volume tout mince et réduit" (G/MG 282).

43. The first extensive comparison of alterations to Gide's wartime *Journal* can be found in a 1956 essay by Henri Guillemin. Guillemin calls attention to the *Journal 1939–1942*'s preamble, which lists previous publications of material from the wartime diary. Although Gide mentions the New York and Algiers editions of *Pages de Journal* and the serialization in *L'Arche*, Guillemin points out, he fails to mention the publication of early diary excerpts in Drieu La Rochelle's collaborationist *N.R.F.* (J 39–42: 7; Guillemin 211).

44. "Ces pages du *Journal* que je tenais [. . .] au cours des sombres mois qui suivirent notre défaite, je ne me reconnais le droit d'y rien changer" (PJ [A] 9; J II: 1103); "pas même celui de choisir seulement les moins sombres, d'exclure celles qui peignent un accablement que je ne reconnais plus aujourd'hui" (Gide, "Pages" [*L'Arche*] 3). Even in his final years, Gide maintained that his wartime *Pages de Journal* were unaltered and unexpurgated: "a diary which permits of touching up and tries to color the past loses its interest, its reason for existence" (AL 249) ("perd son intérêt, sa raison d'être, le journal de qui s'y permet des retouches et cherche à farder le passé"), he wrote in 1948 (FA 239).

45. "[J]e vais jusqu'à croire préférable, pour un temps, la sujétion allemande, avec ses pénibles humiliations, moins préjudiciable pour nous, moins dégradante, que la *stupide* discipline que nous propose aujourd'hui Vichy" (PJ [A] 86, emphasis added; see

also J II: 760). This entry cannot be verified against the *Journal* manuscript because the notebook for December 1940 through December 1941 is unavailable for consultation. The Pléiade edition is based on typescripts and page proofs of this portion of the diary (Sagaert, Note 1123).

46. "Je laisse d'autres s'en étonner. J'ai l'esprit si peu porté à l'insoumission, à la rouspétance . . . pour un peu, je dirais: c'est bien fait" (J II: 783).

47. "Ce devrait pouvoir être la devise de tous ceux que l'on bâillonne. J'espère du moins qu'elle est vraie pour beaucoup" (PJ [A] 99). As with the previous reference to Vichy's "stupid" discipline, this variant cannot be checked against the diary manuscript (see note 45).

48. See in particular the *Journal* entries for 17 and 19 July and 29 September 1940, all omitted from the Algiers volume (J II: 716, 736, 774).

49. "[D]éplaisir" (J II: 741); "Auprès des gaillardes pages qui l'environnent, de Drieu ou de Petitjean, on dirait les ratiocinations d'un vieillard" (PJ [NY] 88). The sentence in question also appeared in the "Nouvelles Pages de Journal" published in the Buenos Aires journal *Les Lettres Françaises* in 1944 (2).

50. The Algiers *Pages de Journal* omits reflections on dictatorship dated 10 July 1940, 12 January, 10 May, and 7 June 1941, and 10 April 1942 (J II: 711–12, 746, 761, 763, 807). Among the deleted passages is the diary entry in which Gide develops his Hitler fantasies at great length (J II: 748).

Gide's friends and sympathetic critics believed that recontextualizing the wartime diary fragments in the "monumental whole of the *Journal*" ("ensemble monumental du 'Journal'") would give a more favorable impression of Gide's opinions and political evolution (G/MG 320). However, the complete text sometimes has the opposite effect, showing that Gide held certain views over a considerable period of time.

51. "J'aurais dû pour le moins dater (et laisser dans leur ordre chronologique) ces *Feuillets*, extraits de mon *Journal* (F 2: 350; J II: 741).

52. "Il y a quelque . . . romantisme à se désoler que les choses ne soient pas autrement qu'elles ne sont" (J II: 691). The following passage lambastes "[t]hose few intellectuals who today beat their breast and accuse themselves of having 'loved literature too much'" (J 4: 22) ("[c]es quelques intellectuels, qui font aujourd'hui leur *mea culpa* et s'accusent d'avoir 'trop aimé la littérature'") (F 1: 78; J II: 700). Written on 11 June 1940, this entry prefigures the post-Armistice debates blaming literature for the fall of France (F 1: 78; J II: 700).

53. Whereas the "Feuillets" criticize Vichy's "return to the soil" in mild terms, *Pages de Journal* deems it a "withdrawal [that] plays into Hitler's hands" (J 4: 47) ("[un] repliement [qui] fait le jeu de Hitler") (PJ [A] 70).

54. Reinstated entries on the wisdom of coming to terms with one's former enemy and Frenchmen's supposed willingness to accept German domination if it meant abundance would become the most sharply criticized passages from Gide's wartime diary (PJ [A] 68, 45).

55. There is no entry for 13 April 1942 in the manuscript diary: notebook 72 ends with 11 April 1942, and notebook 73 begins with 5 May 1942 (Sagaert, Annexes

1133). The composite entry combines apolitical remarks from 11 April with political criticisms from 22 May and 12 June 1942 (J II: 809, 817, 819).

56. "Est-il encore quelqu'un avec qui je prenne réel plaisir à causer? Je ne puis plus rien affirmer sans qu'aussitôt mon affirmation ne me paraisse forcer un peu ma pensée. Plus aucune de mes convictions n'est solide suffisamment pour que la moindre objection aussitôt ne l'ébranle. [. . .] De plus en plus je crains qu'une idée ne me paraisse juste, simplement parce qu'elle est bien formulée" (PJ [A] 37; J II: 705).

57. "[E]xpliquent et [. . .] corrigent" (G/Sch 967).

58. *Les Lettres Françaises* reprinted excerpts from the *Pages de Journal* with Gide's permission ("Nouvelles" 1); *Le Figaro*'s editor Pierre Brisson selected the excerpts published in that paper ("Pages" [*Le Figaro*] 1).

59. Thanks to director Pierre Brisson's involvement in the clandestine Comité National des Journalistes, *Le Figaro* was the only Occupation–era newspaper authorized to resume publication in Paris on the first day of the Liberation (Aron 174–75). Gide congratulated Brisson on the paper's revival in a letter published as "Un Message d'André Gide" in September 1944. Expressing his joy at France's newly regained freedom of speech, Gide implies universal—if silent—opposition to the oppressive wartime regime: "Despite our silence, we still remained united in our hearts and minds, I know" ("De cœur et d'esprit, bien qu'en silence, nous restions unis cependant, je le sais") (1).

60. "That we now look to the U.S.S.R., even more than to America, for our salvation, this is only right!" ("Que ce soit de l'U.R.S.S. à présent, plus que de l'Amérique encore, que nous attendions le secours, c'est bien fait!") (Gide, "Fragments" 30).

61. "À quoi bon rédiger des 'Feuilles de route' si du départ à l'arrivée il ne se passe rien, si tout est prévu d'avance. [. . .] Le 'Journal' de Gide est un acheminement" (Després).

62. In their negative reviews of Gide's *Journal 1939–1942*, Robert Kanters and Maurice Nadeau both associate Gide's political vacillations with the value of *disponibilité* (openness), which Gide had long championed. "What I sense here [. . .] is the excessive desire to come across as an unbiased thinker: [Gide's] complete openness begins to look coquettish" ("Ce que je sens trop ici [. . .] c'est la volonté de faire figure d'esprit non prévenu: la parfaite disponibilité tourne à la coquetterie"), writes Robert Kanters, highlighting Gide's successive approval of Pétain, then de Gaulle, the theory of the "double jeu" (double game) (the notion that Pétain was duping the Germans) and then support for the resistance (Kanters). Maurice Nadeau declares that Gide's "vagaries [. . . are] the fruit of the values with which he has identified himself. In openness and the refusal to choose, there existed a fault through which his entire being has slipped" ("[ses] errements [. . . sont] le fruit des valeurs auxquelles il s'est identifié. Il existait dans la disponibilité et le refus du choix une faille par laquelle son être entier a passé") ("Gide, victime").

63. "[L]'incidence paralysante des événements" (Durosay, "Thésée" 205).

64. "[D]ans un état de ferveur joyeuse que je ne connaissais plus depuis longtemps et pensais ne plus jamais connaître. [. . .] Au surplus, exalté par les événements et le relèvement de la France" (J II: 989–90). In his correspondence as well, Gide reports

composing the *récit* "in a state of indescribable joy" ("dans un état de joie indicible") (G/MG 281; CAG 11: 273). Significantly, joy is one of Thésée's salient characteristics (R 1431).

65. "Je n'écrivis jamais rien de bon, que dans la joie; et par instants je doute s'il en reste encore une seule paillette en mon cœur" (F 2: 342).

66. "[M]aints tyrans, bandits et monstres" (R 1417).

67. "[J]e lui demandai comment et quand à son avis, un officier pouvait et devait prendre sur lui de passer outre. Il répondit fort bien que ce ne pouvait être que lors de grands événements et lorsque le sentiment du devoir entrait en opposition avec un ordre reçu" (J II: 964).

68. "Il siégeait sur un trône que dominait la double hache et tenait de la main droite [. . .] un sceptre d'or [. . .]; de l'autre une fleur trilobée" (R 1420).

69. "Le roi [. . .] avait pour insignes le sceptre et la double hache, la labrys" (Glotz, *La Civilisation* 173).

70. "Deux mille ans avant de devenir le symbole de l'autorité à Rome, la hache l'est déjà dans le palais du labyrinthe" (Glotz, *La Civilisation* 173).

71. "[A]ntique tribu dont les 'bons' Français du régime de Vichy étaient censés descendre" (Drevet-Benatti).

72. "Rencontre bien extraordinaire" (Glotz, *La Civilisation* 173).

73. "[V]aillant rassembleur de cités"; "petites cours de justice locale"; "salles de conseil régional" (R 1437, 1446).

74. "[G]ouvernement populaire"; "chaque citoyen de l'État aura droit égal au Conseil" (R 1446).

75. "[L]es mêmes droits que les aborigènes et que les citoyens précédemment établis dans la ville" (R 1447).

76. "[C]urieux mélange d'individualisme aristocratique et de socialisme" (Renauld 103).

77. The standard edition of *Thésée*, published by Gallimard in 1946, omits the New York edition's ninth chapter and contains a number of stylistic changes (R 1608; Étiemble 43–45).

78. Étiemble supports his assertion with a quotation from the New York edition of *Thésée*: "It is a good thing that the superior men should rise above the vulgar mass to the full height of their personality" (adapted from TL 105) ("Il est bon que les meilleurs dominent la masse vulgaire de toute la hauteur de leur personnalité") (Gide, *Thésée* 107). The term "personnalité" is replaced by "vertu" (virtue) in the Gallimard edition (Étiemble 45; R 1446). Daniel Durosay disagrees with Étiemble's judgment, interpreting the original text as "simply a reaffirmation of Gide's individualism and his constant tendency toward elitism" ("simplement une réaffirmation de l'individualisme gidien et de sa constante tentation élitiste") ("Thésée" 218).

79. "Je ne puis me défendre d'avoir pour Hitler une admiration pleine d'angoisse, de crainte et de stupeur; une admiration hébétée. [. . .] L'horreur, la terreur n'y peu-

vent mais; mon admiration *passe outre* et, de même que Hitler lui-même, n'en tient compte" (J II: 723, emphasis added).

80. "Ce qui m'inquiéterait, moi, c'est qu'il ne le fût pas assez, autoritaire" (Fouchet 134).

81. "J'ai eu 'la main forcée' par *l'Arche* à qui je n'avais rien d'autre à donner" (CAG 11: 311–12).

82. "Minos [. . .] supporte tout. Il tient que le plus sage est d'admettre ce que l'on ne peut pas empêcher" (R 1430).

83. "[N]ullement enclin à la révolte" (J II: 732; F 1: 85).

84. "[À] ce point alourdis par l'ivresse qu'incapables de résister"; "J'insistai, dis que je leur apportais la délivrance. 'La délivrance de quoi?' s'écrièrent-ils" (R 1440).

85. "Entrer dans le labyrinthe est facile. Rien de plus malaisé que d'en sortir. Nul ne s'y retrouve qu'il ne s'y soit perdu d'abord" (R 1437).

86. "[U]ne ascension sage et continue vers le triomphe. [. . .] Au lieu d'une existence ambiguë, [. . .] Gide oppose une victoire sans équivoque, stabilisée dans une sagesse finale" (Durosay, "Thésée" 213).

87. "[D]urant un long temps d'exil" (R 1414).

88. "Certains faits controuvés ont défrayé la légende. [. . .] Je me gardais de démentir ces bruits d'où je tirais un surcroît de prestige; et même renchérissais sur les racontars" (R 1445).

89. "Ce fil sera ton attachement au passé. Reviens à lui. Reviens à toi. Car rien ne part de rien, et c'est sur ton passé, sur ce que tu es à présent, que tout ce que tu seras prend appui" (R 1433).

90. "Il n'y a pas de rattachement au passé qui tienne. J'aime et j'admire ce que la France était, le rôle qu'elle a su jouer dans l'Histoire. Mais c'est de son avenir que je m'éprends" (Gide, "Appel" 13). The forward-looking attitude of the "Appel" and the "Manifeste" is consistent with Gide's long-standing disagreement with Vichy's plan to restore the values of the past.

CHAPTER SIX. COMING HOME: THE PURGE AND THE AFTERMATH

1. "[V]énérable institution"; "Quant à l'Académie . . . *quae te dementia cepit?*"; "On apporterait sous mes fesses le fauteuil, que je ne m'y assiérais point" (G/Sch 958).

2. Louis Aragon, Julien Benda, Albert Camus, Georges Duhamel, François Mauriac, Jean Paulhan, Jean-Paul Sartre, Jean Schlumberger, and Vercors were among the members of the C.N.E. (Lottman, *Purge* 234, 240).

3. "[É]crivains indésirables"; "dont l'attitude ou les écrits pendant l'Occupation ont apporté une aide morale ou matérielle à l'oppresseur" (Assouline, *L'Épuration* 161, 163).

4. "[L]e calme courage français"; "je ne demande pas qu'on fusille M. Gide; je demande qu'on ne le publie [. . . pas] dans les *Lettres Françaises*" (Aragon, "Retour" 1, 5).

5. "[Le] prédécesseur en antibolchevisme"; "une pièce majeure dans la main de la propagande ennemie" (Aragon, "Retour" 1). "Presumably Aragon did not know, or did not care to remind readers, that Gide's *Retour de l'U.R.S.S.* [. . .] had been banned by the Germans in occupied Paris," Herbert Lottman remarks (*Left* 229).

6. "[L]a subite application dont ce *Journal* témoigne dès la fin de juin 40, que M. Gide apporte à l'étude de la langue allemande" (Aragon, "Retour" 1). Here Aragon echoes Lucien Barrucand, whose article in the Algiers paper *Les Dernières Nouvelles* just days after Giovoni's attack declared that Gide could not possibly have been in touch with the French people, "occupied, as he was at the time, with perfecting his knowledge of the German language" ("occupé, comme il l'était à l'époque, à parfaire sa connaissance de la langue allemande"). Implying that shifting objects of study reveal changing political affiliations, the critic acknowledges that Gide later left off his study of German and concentrated instead on English literature (Barrucand).

7. Ehrenburg's *Pravda* article quotes the *Journal* entries in which Gide expresses grudging admiration for Hitler, describes memorizing German verbs, and laments that nine Frenchmen out of ten would accept German domination if it ensured prosperity (3).

8. "L'exercice de la vie au mépris de toutes les considérations morales qui pourraient le limiter a été prêché à l'individu; en Allemagne, par Nietzsche avec sa volonté de puissance; en France, par Gide avec l'*Immoraliste* et 'l'acte gratuit'" (Benda, *Byzantine* 255). Benda paints with too broad a brush: at the war's outset, Gide clearly delineated the differences between Hitler's doctrines, which promoted uniformity and "systematic disindividualization" ("désindividualisation systématique") and Nietzsche's philosophy, which he understood as favoring "strongly differentiated characters" ("des caractères fortement différenciés") (J 4: 19; J II: 696).

9. "[U]n inverti notoire, théoricien de son cas"; "entouré de stupéfiants dans une chambre aux volets clos"; "[si] cette carence d'idéal moral chez les chefs littéraires [. . .] n'a pas été pour quelque chose dans les récents malheurs de la France" (Benda, *Byzantine* 254).

10. Communist *député* Giovoni described Gide with rhetoric one might expect from right-wing Vichy supporters: "this artificial writer who has exercised such a murky influence over young minds indulges in defeatism in the midst of the war. His craze for originality and exoticism, his immoralism and his perversity make him a dangerous individual" (qtd. in J 4: 309) ("cet écrivain frelaté, qui a exercé une trouble influence sur les jeunes esprits, fait du défaitisme en pleine guerre. Sa manie de l'originalité et de l'exotique, son immoralisme et sa perversité en font un individu dangereux") (qtd. in J II: 1105).

11. "[T]rès délicat, car, s'il est tendancieux, le relevé de ce qu'on laisse tomber peut susciter des commentaires" (G/Sch 973).

12. "[S]implifient la question à l'excès" (Eubé 108).

13. "Vive la pensée comprimée!" (J II: 734).

14. "[E]n septembre 1940 on n'avait encore qu'une très faible idée de ce que le nazisme réaliserait dans les pays occupés"; "sous les espèces en vérité bénignes d'une censure" (Marcel 136).

15. "Il fallut qu'il assimilât superficiellement aux contraintes qu'impose l'écriture à l'homme de lettres la contrainte sociale pour se persuader que l'oppression n'avilit pas les hommes vraiment libres" (Nadeau, Rev. of *Pages de Journal*).

16. The uneven quality of the "Interviews" and the chronic paper shortage had initially caused Roger Martin du Gard to question the wisdom of publishing the *Figaro* essays in book form. After the Aragon affair, he discovered that the "Interviews" provided Gide's best defense, as reviewers publicly acknowledged the essays' coded messages of opposition (560).

17. "[D]issidence dans l'incidente"; "audacieux"; "voilà [. . .] M. Gide querellé par d'anciens amis, menacé même d'interdit. Ce n'est pas la première fois qu'on veut l'empêcher de parler. Il me semble bien me souvenir que cela lui est déjà arrivé, à Nice ou à Cannes, sous Vichy" (Henriot 1).

18. Maurice Noël and F. Després reminded readers of threats against Gide by the Légion and Vichy press (M. N. 2), and Després said wryly: "André Gide resisted in the literary domain. Is it fair to blame him for not joining the guerilla fighters?" ("André Gide résista sur le plan littéraire. Veut-on lui faire grief de n'avoir pas pris le maquis?") (Després).

19. Gide's disgust with the abuses of the purge was so strong that he was momentarily tempted to subscribe to the opinions of Vichy apologist Alfred Fabre-Luce, who called the resistance "a Terror, a Ku Klux Klan" ("une Terreur, un Ku-Klux-Klan") in his 1945 brochure *Opposition*. Gide was impressed by Fabre-Luce's arguments—if only because "refusing to echo the majority opinion is almost always enough to impress him" ("il suffit presque toujours de ne pas faire chorus avec tout le monde pour l'impressionner") (CAG 6: 355)—but he soon recovered from his transitory approbation: while Fabre-Luce shared Gide's loathing for the injustices of the purge, he also denounced de Gaulle, upheld Pétain, and admired Laval (Lecache 2).

20. "[C]oiffée d'un bonnet rouge" (G/Sch 975).

21. "[L]'oppression de la pensée [. . .] commence de s'exercer, à l'instar de l'U.R.S.S., en France. Toute pensée non conforme devient suspecte et est aussitôt dénoncée" (J II: 1009).

22. "La liberté de pensée est en plus grand péril encore que du temps de Vichy et de l'occupation allemande" (CAG 11: 297). References to oppression and terror are as numerous in the postwar *Journal* as in the wartime diary; remarks on totalitarianism are in fact far more frequent in reference to the purge than to the Occupation.

23. "[U]n totalitarisme anti-nazi" (J II: 1010); "le Nazisme remporte ainsi une de ses plus indirectes et perfides victoires" (G/MG 302). Condemning Aragon's attack on Gide, Henri Marnier called the postwar insistence on conformity of thought "one of the vestiges of the totalitarian spirit [. . .] that so gravely threatens our future freedom" ("une de ces survivances de l'esprit totalitaire [. . .] qui menace si gravement la liberté de demain") (Marnier).

24. "[M]algré le violent désir que j'ai de vous retrouver, je ne vous conseillerai pas de rentrer tout de suite: les passions sont à leur comble" (Mauriac, *Conversations* [Fr.] 263).

25. "Diverses raisons, dont ma non-résistance . . . au froid, m'ont engagé à remettre à plus tard mon retour" (Gide, "Deux autres" 3).

26. "[J]e pense, sans plaisanterie, que ce serait tout simplement *risquer votre peau,* que d'affronter, avant que la belle saison ne soit solidement installée en France, la vie qui est faite actuellement aux Français!" (G/MG 303).

27. "[A]ttendant que la température, matérielle et morale, se soit faite un peu plus clémente" (Mauriac, *Conversations* [Fr.] 261). Even after returning to France, Martin du Gard cautioned, Gide would have to watch his step: "Bear this in mind when you arrive in Paris: it is a minefield!" ("Songez-y en débarquant à Paris: le sol est miné!") (G/MG 320).

28. "German oppression, by its very horror, has restored patriotic feeling through shared suffering. Since it began, the peasants of all our provinces have felt solidarity, and gradually even the most selfish elements have linked up with the noblest elements of the Resistance" ("L'oppression allemande a, par son horreur même, restauré dans une souffrance commune le sentiment de la patrie. Les paysans de toutes nos provinces se sont dès lors sentis solidaires et, peu à peu, même les plus égoïstes intérêts se sont rattachés aux plus nobles éléments de la Résistance") (Gide, "Réponse" [*L'Arche*] 129–30).

29. "[Un] rôle important dans l'Europe de demain, aux côtés de l'immense et glorieuse Russie" (Gide, "D'une France" 1).

30. "[P]hrase malheureuse [. . .] qui semble vouloir faire oublier le *Retour de l'U.R.S.S.*" (G/Sch 968).

31. "Il importe que, non seulement [. . . l'Allemagne] soit vaincue, mais qu'elle *se sente* vaincue; et que nous ne recommencions pas cette grave erreur de la guerre précédente, de ne point pousser la victoire jusqu'au cœur du pays, jusqu'à Berlin" (Gide, "D'une France" 1).

32. "Mais sur le sol enfin reconquis, la passion doit céder la place, non point à des sentiments édulcorés—et Benda fait fort bien de rappeler ici la parole de Malebranche: 'Il faut toujours rendre justice, avant que d'exercer la charité'—mais c'est précisément à la raison que doit faire appel la justice; mais c'est sur la raison que devra se fonder et prendre appui l'État nouveau" (Gide, "La Justice avant la charité" 1).

33. "[L]a patrie et [. . .] tout ce qui nous y rattache"; "donner le pas [. . .] à l'idéal tout humain et approximatif de la justice, sur celui, si évidemment supérieur, mais ruineux, de la charité" (Gide, "Justice ou charité?" 1–2).

34. "[P]rotestations violentes"; "approbation enthousiaste" (G/MG 318).

35. "[M]e voici faisant, aux yeux de ces zélotes d'une juste charité, ou d'une charitable justice, figure d'épurateur féroce et impie" (CAG 11: 336).

36. Gide decries the disproportion between wartime crimes and their punishments:

what relationship, what comparison between the fact of having, for so many years, poisoned public opinion in the *Action française, Je suis partout* or *Gringoire,* and confinement, even if perpetual, or death? And what is more, is it just that the poisoner should pay no more than the poisoned, and those whose sole crime will be not to have thought afterwards "as one should" ("commerce with the enemy" is often reduced to that, if at least no shameful profit was obtained by that commerce). (AL 242)

[quel rapport, quelle proportion entre le fait d'avoir empoisonné durant tant d'années l'opinion publique dans l'*Action française, Je Suis Partout* ou *Gringoire*, et la détention, fût-elle perpétuelle, ou la mort? Et surtout est-il équitable que l'empoisonneur ne paie pas plus que tels empoisonnés, que ceux dont le seul crime sera de n'avoir pas, par la suite, pensé 'comme il fallait' (car c'est à cela que se réduit souvent l'inculpation de 'commerce avec l'ennemi', si du moins l'on n'a pas tiré profit honteux de ce commerce)]. (Gide, "Justice ou charité?" 1)

37. Like his former assistant Lucien Combelle, Gide's future secretary and editor Yvonne Davet made misguided choices. In 1943, the young woman went to Jena as part of the *relève*, the scheme that liberated one French prisoner of war for every three French workers who volunteered to work in Germany. Though friends tried to dissuade her, she insisted on going—"just one week before the fall of Stalingrad, when a child could have predicted what was going to happen" ("et cela huit jours avant la chute de Stalingrad, quand un enfant aurait pu prédire ce qui allait arriver"), according to Dorothy Bussy. Bussy reports that Davet was "completely seduced" ("complètement séduite") by Nazi propaganda and believed the Germans' promises of good treatment: an apartment, an eight-hour work day, plus time to learn German and write a book about Gide's *Journal*. Instead, she was housed in prison-like quarters, subjected to forced labor like a criminal, paid starvation wages, and forbidden to return to France at the end of her contract. To Gide's way of thinking, Davet's "absurd" decision was the equivalent of "a slow suicide" ("un lent suicide") (CAG 11: 263, 267; 288–89; 298, 343; 282).

38. The petition was unsuccessful: de Gaulle declined clemency and Brasillach was executed on 6 February 1945 (Rousso 44).

39. Despite Jean Paulhan's urgings, Gide declined to write a letter in support of C.N.E.-blacklisted writer Marcel Jouhandeau, who had attended the October 1941 Weimar conference promoting intellectual and cultural collaboration among European nations. Whereas the majority of the French delegation were already committed to the principle of collaboration and some were avowed fascists, Paulhan believed that Jouhandeau had accepted the conference invitation out of curiosity and a desire to help French prisoners of war. He added that Jouhandeau's intervention had kept the German authorities from arresting Bernard Groethuysen and himself in 1943 (G/P 279–80). Paulhan's opinions notwithstanding, Gide chose not to support Jouhandeau.

40. "Je ne connais Brasillach que par ses articles, qui, dans le temps, m'ont indigné. Gracier de tels empoisonneurs, c'est tenir en réserve un danger public" (CAG 11: 321). References to such "empoisonneurs" (poisoners) abound in Gide's correspondence from January 1945 (G/S 975; G/MG 308; CAG 11: 321).

41. "[M]y former accusers suddenly and all together turned up on the wrong side: Béraud, Massis, Mauclair, Maurice Martin du Gard . . . without a single exception so

far as I know" (J 4: 256) ("mes accusateurs d'hier se trouvèrent tous et d'un coup du mauvais côté: Béraud, Massis, Mauclair, Maurice Martin du Gard, sans exception que je sache"), Gide wrote in January 1946 (J II: 1017). He makes a similar observation in *Ainsi soit-il*: "Time often helped me out, and in many disputes my opponent withdrew without my needing to record his collapse. This is what took place for Maurras, for Massis, for Béraud, and for Montfort" (SBI 27) ("Le temps m'a souvent apporté son concours et, dans maintes contestes, l'opposant s'est retiré sans qu'il me fût besoin de marquer sa déconfiture. C'est ce qui a eu lieu pour Maurras, pour Massis, pour Béraud, pour Montfort") (SV 1004).

42. Mauriac's defense of accused collaborators earned him the sobriquet "Saint Francis of the Assize Court" ("saint François des Assises") (G/MG 308).

43. "[D]onner à Aragon ce triomphe" (G/P 303).

44. "Il n'était certes besoin d'aucun courage pour les écrire; il en fallait peut-être pour les publier au moment où elles pouvaient me faire le plus de tort"; "j'étais en droit d'espérer que ces pages tempéreraient la furie des accusations portées contre les Giono, les Jouhandeau, les Montherlant, contre tous ceux qui se trompèrent. Cette erreur de jugement, ç'avait également été la mienne: on pouvait me la reprocher comme à eux. [. . .] Si vous les condamnez, condamnez-moi de même" (FA 239–40).

45. In naming himself as an example, Gide echoes a similar 1948 statement by his friend Jean Paulhan. In *De la paille et du grain*, Paulhan explains that he wanted the C.N.E.'s charter to include an article "acknowledging the writer's right to be mistaken. I would have gladly cited my own name as an example" ("qui reconnût à l'écrivain le droit à l'erreur. J'aurais volontiers donné mon propre exemple") (68). Paulhan's wartime publishing activities were indeed paradoxical. Like many of the Gallimard writers, he contributed regularly to *Comoedia*, whose harmless, apolitical articles on the arts helped the Germans project their desired image of occupied France as an unchanged cultural capital—while its "Page européenne" dished out German propaganda (G/P 258; Assouline, *Gallimard* 315–16; Assouline, *L'Épuration* 109). His participation in this venture may have served as cover for more subversive activities, however. Paulhan was involved in resistance groups from July 1940 on: he cofounded the clandestine resistance paper *Les Lettres Françaises* in 1941 and was a "pivotal contact for the editors of the then clandestine *Éditions de Minuit* and for *Messages*, a literary review banned by the Nazis" (Syrotinski 110).

46. "[Le] sinistre et, pour lui, glorieux procès de Riom"; "Je lui sais grand gré de ne me tenir pas grief des passages assez durs de mon *Journal* au sujet des Juifs et de lui-même (que, du reste, je ne puis renier car je continue de les croire parfaitement exacts)" (J II: 1054).

47. "[C]'est l'antisémite qui *fait* le Juif" (Sartre, *Réflexions* 84).

48. "[I]l y a tout de même une 'question juive', angoissante, obsédante, et qui n'est pas près d'être résolue" (J II: 1055).

49. "La persécution venant à cesser, ce sont eux qui, de droit, occuperont les plus hauts postes; et les antisémites auront beau jeu, de nouvelles occasions de protester, de s'écrier: Vous voyez bien que nous avions raison de les exclure"; "[Je] me méfie beaucoup des précocités" (J II: 856, 1055).

50. "[C]hargés comme des ânes [. . .], nous devions avoir l'air de deux vieux provinciaux qui débarquaient à Paris et n'avaient jamais pris le métro depuis la guerre"; "instant grave et bouleversant" (CAG 6: 353, 354).

51. "[L]a nouvelle se propage, court de bouche en bouche et, toute la nuit, des avions pacifiques ont survolé la ville, laissant tomber des étoiles; des fusées partaient dans le ciel, du Sacré-Cœur et du Trocadéro, préparant le feu d'artifice de ce soir" (La N.R.F., *Lettres* 133).

52. "[M]alséant"; "dilettante et [. . .] rentier" (G/Sch 975, 972).

53. Because both literature and politics were off-limits, Gide was somewhat stymied by *Le Figaro* editor Pierre Brisson's pressing demands for copy. In January 1945, he hit on a compromise: "Rencontre à Sorrente," originally published in the October–November 1944 issue of *L'Arche*, tells of Gide's chance meeting with a University of Naples professor during a 1937 journey through Italy. The professor confesses his difficulty in communicating with his students: "They only have ears for watchwords. The slogan 'Credere–Obbedire–Combattere' [Believe–Obey–Fight] excuses and releases them from any reflection, inquiry, or effort" ("Ils n'ont d'oreille que pour des mots d'ordre. Le slogan 'Credere–Obbedire–Combattere' les dispense et tient quittes de toute réflexion, de toute recherche, de tout effort") (134). By linking fascism with intellectual laziness, this anecdote implicitly underscores the antitotalitarian nature of Gide's lifelong emphasis on critical thinking. Though *Le Figaro* never published "Rencontre à Sorrente," Gide's desire to have it reprinted reflects his effort to find some acceptable mode of expression.

54. De Gaulle's list of potential *Immortels*—André Gide, Paul Claudel, Roger Martin du Gard, Jules Romains, Louis Aragon, Jean Paulhan, Paul Éluard, and André Malraux—blended the old and the new guard, writers with low political profiles and those strongly associated with the resistance (CAG 7: 18–19).

55. Friends persuaded Gide that there were better ways of honoring Valéry. Gide paid tribute to the poet in both *Le Figaro* ("Le Rayonnement de Paul Valéry") and *L'Arche* ("Paul Valéry").

56. "[D]éclarant que je considère ce livre comme le plus important et le plus *serviceable* [. . .] de mes écrits" (J II: 1017).

57. "[T]outes les forces du fascisme et du mensonge" (Gide, "Avant-propos" 1). Gide's warning against postwar totalitarianism was prescient: Herbart eventually shut down *Terre des Hommes* "when I realized that it would cease to be free" ("lorsque je me rendis compte qu'il cesserait d'être libre") (Herbart, *La Ligne* 150).

58. "[D]es pages de vous, qui vous soient [. . .] particulièrement précieuses." In comparing *Thésée* to Mallarmé's last, great work, *Un Coup de dés*, Gide characterizes the *récit* as his literary swan song (G/P 275, 276).

59. "[J]e crains que [. . .] la barbarie [. . .] s'introduise dans vos rangs [. . .] camouflée en liberté" (Gide, "Existentialisme" 6). Gide, who was "impervious to [Sartre's] new philosophy" ("[t]rès rebelle à cette nouvelle philosophie"), quipped: "I consent to be an existentialist provided that I don't know it" ("Je consens à être existentialiste à la condition de ne pas le savoir") (CAG 6: 372).

60. "[C]eux-là qui n'ont que le mot 'Liberté' dans la bouche" (CAG 11: 297).

61. "On découvrait partout tricherie, exploitation, abus, et les mots mêmes avaient perdu le sens authentique autour desquels on eût voulu pouvoir se rallier" (SV 1062).

62. The similarity is reinforced by the postwar essays' indirectness of expression: while linguistic issues are important, Gide states, there are other, more urgent questions "which it is not my place to address" ("sur lesquelles pourtant je n'ai pas à me prononcer") ("Défense II" 1). As during the war, Gide implies that he is not entirely free to speak his mind on political matters.

63. "Un peuple qui tient à sa langue tient bon" (AQ 47).

64. "[É]tait-il plus belle occasion de prononcer l'h à la manière forte, que le nom même de *Hitler*?" (Gide, "Défense V" 2).

65. Repeated references to current events in Gide's grammatical examples point to a keen and critical attention to politics. In another "Défense" installment, Gide obliquely raises questions about purge-era justice and the former resistance's legitimacy as a postwar power. Citing an article on the trial of René Hardy, a *résistant* convicted of leading to resistance leader Jean Moulin's capture, Gide calls his readers' attention to a glaring grammatical error: "What [*Que*] will weigh heavier on the scales of justice: the government commissioner's conclusions or Hardy's denials and personality?" ("*Que* pèsera le plus dans la balance de la justice: les conclusions du commissaire du gouvernement ou les dénégations et la personnalité même de Hardy?") (qtd. in "Défense IV" 1). (The sentence should read "qu'est-ce qui pèsera le plus . . . ?") Though the topic is ostensibly faulty grammar, one wonders whether Gide is thinking about other types of fallibility as well, especially since the Hardy scandal combined with "the iniquities of the *épuration* [. . .] to tarnish the image of the Resistance" (Rioux 123).

66. The transient nature of Gide's initially punitive stance toward Germany is underscored by his enthusiastic speculation, within weeks of the Reich's surrender, about a visit to Berlin—the "gay capital" of Europe that he had often visited during the interwar years. "I must go there" ("il faut y aller"), he told Roger Stéphane in June 1945: "just imagine: two million people are living in cellars. I must see this subterranean city, this underground life" ("pensez donc que deux millions d'êtres vivent dans des caves. Il faut voir cette ville souterraine, cette vie souterraine") (Stéphane 84). Here, as so often during the war, Gide seems blithely unaware of the potential political ramifications of his actions. Pierre Herbart's eyes were open, however, and his words of caution won out against Gide's curiosity (CAG 6: 358). Having abandoned his travel plans in 1945, Gide hoped to visit Berlin after the 1947 Munich youth conference. His plans were again frustrated—this time by the fear that the Russians might arrest him and his traveling companions Jef Last and Pierre Herbart (Lambert 112–13).

67. "[P]lus sainement éduquée"; "travail patient de rééducation" (Gide, "D'une France" 1). As Yaffa Wolfman has observed, the "pedagogical principal of punishment" ("principe pédagogique du châtiment") that Gide proposes for Germany echoes his 1942 remarks about France's unreadiness for self-governance (168; J II: 807).

68. Gide raised similar issues in his August 1946 "Allocution de Pertisau," delivered at a youth conference in the Austrian Tyrol (Foucart, *Gadouille* 150; CAG 7: 262). There he quoted a letter from Bernd Schmeier, a young German he had met in Berlin in 1928. While in Paris in 1940 as a member of the occupying forces—"in Paris 'as a conqueror' (but with tears in my eyes)" ("'comme vainqueur' (les larmes aux yeux) à Paris")—the young officer sent Gide a letter vigorously denouncing Hitler and National Socialism, a letter that would forever prevent the writer from making a global judgment about the Germans (qtd. in Foucart, "Sémélé" 10–11, 22–23; "Allocution" 2–3).

69. "[N]ouveaux maîtres" (J II: 1025; Sagaert, Notes [J II] 1491–92). Exhausted by the war, many young people welcomed the "tranquillity, certainty, and intellectual comfort" ("repos, assurance, et confort intellectuels") offered by submission to Catholic and communist doctrines. Gide feared disastrous consequences, however: "through abnegation or laziness, they are going to contribute to the defeat, to the retreat, to the rout of the spirit; to the establishment of some form or other of 'totalitarianism' which will be hardly any better than the Nazism they were fighting" (J 4: 263) ("par dévouement—ou par paresse—ils vont concourir à la défaite, à la retraite, à la déroute de l'esprit; à l'établissement de je ne sais quelle forme de 'totalitarisme' qui ne vaudra guère mieux que le nazisme qu'ils combattent") (J II: 1026).

70. "[I]nquiétude perpétuelle et vivifiante" (FA 204–05).

71. "Le monde ne sera sauvé, s'il peut l'être, que par des *insoumis*" (J II: 1026).

72. In "Souvenirs littéraires et problèmes actuels," "La Justice avant la charité," and the November 1945 essay "Les Deux Cortèges," Gide is responding in part to Julien Benda's 1944 article "Une Nouvelle Idole: le dynamisme." Benda claims that Gide—"whose thought has such an affinity with German thought" ("dont la pensée a tant d'affinité avec celle d'outre-Rhin")—is responsible for promulgating a dangerous denial of absolute truths and abstract justice in favor of ideals that change to fit the circumstances. By associating Gide with this "justice *of the moment*" ("justice *du moment*"), Benda attempts to link him with the anti-Dreyfus camp, Action Française, and Nazi Germany (1). Benda has completely misunderstood him, Gide asserts: he has always opposed the "theories of expedient truth" ("théories de la vérité opportune") upheld by Maurras and Barrès and has worked all his life for "a restoration of true, permanent values" ("une restauration des vraies valeurs permanentes") ("Les Deux Cortèges" 1).

73. "[S]ous forme de *littérature engagée*" (FA 189). In a 1948 *Journal* entry, Gide identifies himself with those writers of his generation—Valéry, Proust, Suarès, and Claudel—who, though profoundly different, were all marked by Mallarmé's influence. These writers believed that "art operates in the eternal and debases itself by trying to serve even the noblest causes. [. . .] Consequently nothing seems to me at once more absurd and more justified than the reproach that is directed at me today of never having managed to *commit myself*" (J 4: 287–88) ("l'art opère dans l'éternel et s'avilit en cherchant à servir, fût-ce les plus nobles causes. [. . .] Aussi rien ne me paraît plus absurde à la fois et plus justifié que ce reproche que l'on me fait aujourd'hui de n'avoir jamais su *m'engager*") (J II: 1057).

74. "[C]'est aujourd'hui dans le camp adverse, c'est chez les communistes, que se font sentir à présent les ravages des doctrines relativistes, de 'la fin qui justifie les moyens'" (FA 195).

75. "L'effrayante absurdité des Sartre et des Camus [. . .] n'ouvre que des horizons de suicide" (qtd. in J II: 1025).

76. "[L]'univers et notre existence sont des tumultes insensés" (qtd. in FA 203).

77. "[Le] désuet bréviaire d'une génération qui s'en va" (AP 41).

78. The existentialists exemplified this trend: "Existentialism turns up its nose at permanence" ("L'existentialisme fait fi de la durée") (Gide, "Existentialisme" 6).

79. "[I]l n'est plus question aujourd'hui de *durée*. L'inconfiance en l'avenir a développé chez les nouveaux venus le goût excessif du présent, de l'immédiat. [. . .] L'ancien système poétique de naguère, si savamment établi [. . .] pour permettre à la mémoire de retenir les traits où s'inscrit l'émotion, la beauté; ce nombre régulier, ce retour des rimes et leur alternance, ces temps forts marquant les césures, toutes ces règles enfin, si profondément en nous inculquées qu'elles nous paraissaient fatales, naturelles et indispensables; tout cela n'a plus raison d'être, dès l'instant que l'instant seul compte et qu'il n'y a plus d'*avenir*" (AP 39).

Gide had developed this line of thinking in his 1947 address to the Munich youth conference, stating that European youth shared "a lack of faith in the future (it is, alas, only too justified), that causes them to place everything on the present. Literature and art no longer concern themselves with permanence" ("ein Mangel an Vertrauen in die Zukunft (er ist, ach! nur zu berechtigt), der sie alles auf die Gegenwart setzen läßt. In der Literatur und Kunst ist nicht mehr die Rede von *Dauer*") ("Nicht" 34). He explored the connection between the historic and the aesthetic in his "Défense de la langue française," as well, lamenting that the postwar generation was characterized by "a lack of confidence in the future and, consequently, a lack of caring about permanence. The most recent poetry has no interest in remembering or being remembered; and hence it abandons everything that might aid memory, everything on which yesterday's poetics was based" ("l'inconfiance en l'avenir et, partant, le non-souci de la durée. La poésie la plus récente n'a nul souci de retenir, de se faire retenir; et de là l'abandon de tout ce qui pourrait apporter aide à la mémoire, sur quoi la poétique d'hier était basée") ("Défense V" 2).

80. "J'écrivais, avant la guerre: 'Je ne gagnerai mon procès qu'en appel', ou: 'J'écris pour être *relu*'—et cela ne signifie plus rien, du moment qu'il n'y a plus d'appel et qu'il n'est plus question de *relire*"; "c'en sera fait de notre culture et de cette tradition que nous avons tant lutté pour maintenir" (AP 40, 41).

81. "[T]out cela pourrait bien disparaître, cet effort de culture qui nous paraissait admirable" (J II: 677–78).

82. "Quand la violence eut renouvelé le lit des hommes sur la terre,/ Un très vieil arbre, à sec de feuilles reprit le fil de ses maximes . . . / Et un autre arbre de haut rang montait déjà des grandes Indes souterraines/ Avec sa feuille magnétique et son chargement de fruits nouveaux" (qtd. in AP 41).

83. "Pourront-ils citer un seul de mes amis [. . .] qui ne se soit très bien tenu durant ces années tragiques et comporté, les jeunes surtout, de manière souvent

admirable. [. . .] C'est, en revanche, de l'autre côté qu'il faut chercher ceux qui s'é-
taient déclarés contre moi" (J II: 1002).

84. "[U]n de ses fervents les plus fidèles"; "entre lui et moi la communion d'idées
était parfaite" (Gide, "Un Serviteur" 231). Gide was a guest in the home of Viénot's
mother-in-law Loup Mayrisch for several months early in the war.

85. "[S]e croyait ou se voulait gaulliste" (Heurgon-Desjardins 6).

86. Gide's failure to name the mutual friend rather weakens this assertion. Moreover, a letter Saint-Exupéry wrote on the eve of his death calls the credibility of Gide's
claim into question. Describing the Algiers Gaullist milieu as a "factory generating
hatred and disrespect" ("usine à haine, à irrespect"), Saint-Exupéry declared: "I don't
give a damn. They can all go to hell" ("moi je m'en fous. Je les emmerde") (979).

87. "Or nombreux sont les opposants d'hier, ralliés ou non à la néfaste politique
de Vichy (et Saint-Exupéry ne le fut en aucun temps ni d'aucune manière), qui
doivent reconnaître aujourd'hui [. . .] que de Gaulle est en train de sauver la France"
(Gide, "Saint-Exupéry" 2).

88. Before his arrest, Paulhan managed to take the mimeograph machine apart
and dispose of it, piece by piece, in the Seine (Heller 48). At Drieu La Rochelle's
request, Paulhan was released from prison after a week of confinement (Syrotinski
110; G/P 250).

89. Suffering from typhus, Martin-Chauffier was repatriated with other sick ex-
prisoners in late May 1945 (CAG 6: 356; Martin-Chauffier, *L'Homme* 225). Two
weeks later, Maria Van Rysselberghe recorded the "moving visit with Martin-
Chauffier. This is the first time we have seen someone we know well come back from
the hell of the German camps" ("visite émouvante de Martin-Chauffier. C'est la première fois que nous voyons un être que nous connaissons bien revenir de l'enfer des
camps allemands") (CAG 6: 358). Gide, Van Rysselberghe, and Dorothy Bussy heard
similarly horrifying tales from Thea Sternheim's daughter Mopse, who had been
arrested for resistance activities in 1943 and held in the Ravensbrück concentration
camp until April 1945 (CAG 6: 364; G/Ster lxxvi).

90. Confused by his title of "délégué 'général'" of the Mouvement de la Libération Nationale, Van Rysselberghe erroneously reported that Herbart had held the
rank of general in the resistance (Delarue 479; CAG 6: 319).

91. "Il tournerait le film *Malraux* qu'il ne jouerait pas mieux" (CAG 6: 314).

92. "[C]onciliabules, entrevues, allées et venues, tout cela très secret comme il sied
à des conspirateurs"; "Ah! si Gide était là! combien tout ceci l'exciterait, et combien
sa seule présence ajouterait au pathétique de la situation" (CAG 6: 314–15). Van Rysselberghe's daughter Élisabeth echoed this sentiment in a September 1944 letter to her
mother: "You can't imagine what your Vaneau is like since Pierre came back: our guests
are all lieutenants and abbots! Machine guns clutter up the office, cars roar at the gate,
and we really need a telephone operator (and I constantly say to myself [. . .]: to think
that Gide isn't here!)" ("Tu n'imagines pas ton Vaneau depuis le retour de Pierre, on
n'y reçoit que lieutenants et abbés! et les mitraillettes encombrent le bureau, les
voitures ronflent à la porte, et il faudrait un standardiste au téléphone (et je pense tout
le temps [. . .]: et dire que Gide n'est pas là!)") (qtd. in CAG 6: 318).

93. "[U]ne extraordinaire réserve de feuilles [. . .] et des cachets, et des tampons, de quoi nantir de fausses identités toute une armée; de quoi faire fusiller ceux qui avaient assumé la téméraire mission de les répartir" (SV 1061–62).

94. I am grateful to Christine Latrouitte Armstrong and Walter Putnam for pointing out this connection with *Les Faux-Monnayeurs*.

95. "[D]éfaillances"; "rien ne m'autorisait à supposer la moindre ébauche de résistance. Plus chimérique encore me paraissait une organisation de celle-ci" (SV 1060).

96. The visitor designated as "X." may have been André Calas, a young student who visited Gide in December 1940 (Sagaert, Notes [*Ainsi*] 1436; CAG 6: 216).

97. Born in St. Petersburg in 1908, Boris Vildé lived and studied in Germany during the early 1930s. Gide first met Vildé while delivering a lecture in Berlin and invited the young "Nordic god" ("dieu nordique") to his home in Paris (Aveline 1). After a brief infatuation with National Socialism, Vildé soon became an ardent opponent of Nazism and emigrated to France in September 1932 (Le Témoin des martyrs 25, 27). He spent his first year in Paris living in one of the mansards at 1 *bis*, rue Vaneau, where he "spent much of his time in Gide's library, studying and reading French" (Blumenson 62).

98. Gide exaggerates his own role in the young man's life. Although he implies that "Boris Wilde, whom I had been lodging for months in a vacant room above mine on the sixth floor" (SBI 147) ("Boris Wildé, que, depuis des mois, j'hébergeais dans une chambre dont je disposais au-dessus de la mienne, au sixième") (SV 1061) was his tenant at the time of the 1941 encounter, the young man's stay in the rue Vaneau actually dated back to his 1932 arrival in France (CAG 6: 227; Blumenson 62).

99. "[J]e l'avais chaleureusement recommandé à Paul Rivet qui dirigeait alors le Musée de l'Homme au Trocadéro" (SV 1061).

100. "[J]e n'hésitai pas à le mettre en rapport avec Pierre Viénot qui dormait [. . .] dans la chambre voisine de la mienne"; "Leur conversation se prolongea jusqu'au matin" (SV 1061).

101. The *Journal* has "Wilde" (J II: 995; ms. γ1646: 35); *Ainsi soit-il* has "Wildé" (SV 1061; *Ainsi soit-il*, ms.). I am deeply indebted to Catherine Gide and Martine Sagaert for providing access to these manuscripts.

102. "*Dear*, vous voulez le petit musicien?" (SV 307).

103. "[M]émorable soirée" (SV 312).

104. "C'est peu de jours après cette rencontre de Cabris que Wildé, circonvenu, fut fusillé à Saint-Étienne" (SV 1061). Gide has his dates wrong: Vildé was arrested shortly after his trip to Cabris, but the Musée de l'Homme resisters were not executed until February 1942, after a year of imprisonment and torture (Blumenson 165–66, 250; Le Témoin des martyrs 20). Gide's error merely serves to heighten the drama, however.

105. "Ah! de quel enfer je sortais! Et pas un ami à qui pouvoir parler, pas un conseil; pour avoir cru tout accommodement impossible et n'avoir rien voulu céder d'abord, je sombrais" (SV 309).

106. "[T]out mon ciel en fut illuminé" (SV 1061).

107. "[D]ès l'instant que cette résistance paraît possible, devient possible, il va sans dire que j'en suis" (J II: 1003).

108. "Esprit d'insoumission, de révolte; ou même d'abord et simplement: esprit d'examen"; "Cet esprit (ce mauvais esprit) qu'ils blâmaient en moi, fut celui qui sauva la France" (J II: 1017).

EPILOGUE. WHAT HAPPENED TO ANDRÉ GIDE

1. Television character Archie Bunker's question "'What's the difference' did not ask for difference but means instead 'I don't give a damn what the difference is,'" de Man explained in his illustration of the notion that "[t]he same grammatical pattern engenders two meanings that are mutually exclusive" (*Allegories* 9).

2. "It was Sartre, and not writers who had been far more active in the Resistance [. . .] who took the leading role in postwar French letters," explains Alice Kaplan. Because his ethic of engagement "offered a future for literature," Kaplan surmises, it was Sartre who "came to stand in the public mind for the antifascist cure" ("Literature" 970).

3. "On le croyait sacré et embaumé: il meurt et l'on découvre combien il restait vivant"; "il a su réaliser contre lui l'union des bien-pensants de droite et de gauche"; "toute démarche de l'esprit nous rapprochait ou nous éloignait *aussi* de Gide" (Sartre, "Gide vivant" 150).

4. "Mes soirées, je les passais pour la plupart au Flore: jamais un occupant n'y mettait les pieds" (Beauvoir, *La Force* 488). "Most histories of this period contradict her statement," reports biographer Deirdre Bair (636).

5. Whereas Gide's wealth and fame spared him the financial urgency described by Beauvoir, he did sign an "Aryan declaration" by proxy: in order to keep the N.R.F. firm open for business, Gaston Gallimard and Jean Schlumberger had to declare that its four directors, including Gide, were neither Jewish nor dependent on the firm's recently purged Jewish directors and stockholders (Fouché I: 151–52).

6. "[L]a première règle sur laquelle s'accordèrent les intellectuels résistants, c'est qu'ils ne devaient pas écrire dans les journaux de la zone occupée" (Beauvoir, *La Force* 498).

7. "C'est dans *Comoedia* que les écrits de Sartre et Beauvoir trouvent le meilleur accueil et la plus prompte promotion" (Assouline, *Gallimard* 318).

8. "Les écrivains de notre bord avaient tacitement adopté certaines règles. On ne devait pas écrire dans les journaux et les revues de zone occupée, ni parler à Radio-Paris" (Beauvoir, *La Force* 528).

9. "[S]ur mon refus, elle m'accusa de détournement de mineure. Avant guerre, l'affaire n'eût pas eu de suite" (Beauvoir, *La Force* 554).

10. "Je ne sais par quel truchement j'obtins une situation de 'metteuse en ondes' à la radio nationale" (Beauvoir, *La Force* 554–55).

11. "Radio-Paris ment, Radio-Paris ment, Radio-Paris est allemand" was sung to the tune of "La Cucaracha" (Bair 640).

12. Because Beauvoir's work consisted primarily of research conducted in various Paris libraries, she was largely able to avoid the radio station's "controversial offices" (Bair 279).

13. "[D]'après notre code, on avait le droit d'y travailler: tout dépendait de ce qu'on y faisait. Je proposai un programme incolore: des reconstitutions parlées, chantées, bruitées de fêtes anciennes, du Moyen Age à nos jours" (Beauvoir, *La Force* 555).

14. "C'est seulement dans ce qu'elle a d'inactuel que la pensée peut demeurer valable"; "Mes pensées intempestives, en attendant des jours meilleurs, je les veux engranger dans ce carnet" (J II: 731; 680–81).

15. While Beauvoir and Sartre's "record is not scrupulously clean," concludes biographer Bair, "neither is it clearly soiled" (296).

16. "L'antisémitisme vulgaire se plaît volontiers à considérer les phénomènes culturels de l'après-guerre (d'après la guerre de 14–18) comme dégénérés et décadents, parce que enjuivés"; "il a suffi qu'on découvre quelques écrivains juifs sous des pseudonymes latinisés pour que toute la production contemporaine soit considérée comme polluée et néfaste" (de Man, *Wartime* 45).

17. Alice Kaplan points out that "claims of Jewish mediocrity and insignificance" are also present in "the 'irrational' anti-Semitism of a Céline," whose *Bagatelles pour un massacre* may well have been the exemplar of "vulgar anti-Semitism" from which de Man wished to distance himself ("Paul de Man" 274). Moreover, argues Jeffrey Mehlman, de Man's perception of negligible influence is a double-edged sword, for "the author maintains that modern literature—*unlike the modern world*—has not been contaminated (or 'polluted') by Jewish influence" ("Perspectives" 325).

18. De Man's charge of mediocrity seems to be reserved for Jewish authors from French-speaking countries, since he lists Franz Kafka among the great writers of the 1920s (*Wartime* 45).

19. "En gardant, malgré l'ingérance (sic) sémite dans tous les aspects de la vie européenne, une originalité et un caractère intacts, elle a montré que sa nature profonde était saine" (de Man, *Wartime* 45).

20. "[L]'apport des qualités juives dans la littérature [. . .] apporte moins d'éléments nouveaux [. . .] qu'elle ne coupe la parole à la lente explication d'une race et n'en fausse gravement, intolérablement, la signification" (J I: 763).

21. "[C]ombien les admirerais-je de cœur plus léger si elles ne venaient à nous que traduites!" (J I: 764).

22. "[O]n voit donc qu'une solution du problème juif qui viserait à la création d'une colonie juive isolée de l'Europe, n'entraînerait pas, pour la vie littéraire de l'Occident, de conséquences déplorables. Celle-ci perdrait, en tout et pour tout, quelques personnalités de médiocre valeur et continuerait, comme par le passé, à se développer selon ses grandes lois évolutives" (de Man, *Wartime* 45).

23. Significantly, Gide's own references to Nietzsche's *Untimely Meditations* in the wartime diary emphasize not the forgetting of the past but the past's lessons for the

present. He repeatedly mentions Nietzsche's commentary on the Franco-Prussian War when arguing that France was ruined by its World War I victory (J II: 702, 735; J 4: 23, 49).

24. De Man concludes his examination of Nietzsche by asserting that: "the bases for historical knowledge are not empirical facts but written texts, even if these texts masquerade in the guise of wars or revolutions" (*Blindness* 165).

25. "Jeffrey Mehlman went so far as to surmise that deconstruction in America was really nothing more than an elaborate cover-up campaign, an 'amnesty' organized by literary intellectuals who could find no other means to evade or excuse their burden of collective guilt," reports Christopher Norris (178–79).

26. De Man also praised Alfred Fabre-Luce's openly collaborationist *Anthologie de la nouvelle Europe* (Mehlman, "Perspectives" 325).

27. "[L']anti-historicité de mon esprit" (J II: 736).

Works Cited

Amrouche, Jean. "André Gide à Tunis." *Vaincre* 18 Jun. 1943: N. pag. Dossier II. 17, item 11. Fonds André Gide, Bibliothèque Littéraire Jacques Doucet, Paris.

"André Gide, arrêté par Giraud est remis en liberté." *Le Courrier du Pas-de-Calais* 1 Sep. 1943: N. pag. Dossier II. 17, item 16. Fonds André Gide, Bibliothèque Littéraire Jacques Doucet, Paris.

"André Gide's Proposed Visit to the U. K." 11 Aug. 1943. Foreign Office file FO 371/ 36287–Z8576. Public Record Office, Kew, England.

"L'Anti-Littré ou les mauvais exemples." *Le Figaro* 17 May 1941: 3.

Aragon, Louis. *La Diane française.* Paris: Seghers, 1946.

————. "Retour d'André Gide." *Les Lettres Françaises* 25 Nov. 1944: 1+.

Arendt, Hannah. *The Origins of Totalitarianism.* Rev. ed. New York: Harcourt Brace Jovanovitch, 1973.

Aron, Robert. *Histoire de l'épuration.* Vol. 3, part 2: *Le Monde de la presse, des arts, des lettres . . . 1944–1953.* Paris: Fayard, 1975.

Assouline, Pierre. *L'Épuration des intellectuels.* Paris: Éditions Complexe, 1996.

————. *Gaston Gallimard: un demi-siècle d'édition française.* Paris: Balland, 1984.

Atlas, James. "The Case of Paul de Man." *The New York Times Sunday Magazine* 28 Aug. 1988: 36+.

"Auspices Under Which André Gide Should Visit the U. K." 4 Aug. 1943. Foreign Office file FO 371/ 36287–Z8538. Public Record Office, Kew, England.

"Aux quatre vents." *Le Figaro* 12 Apr. 1941: 3.

Aveline, Claude. "L'Affaire du Musée de l'Homme." *Les Lettres Françaises* 24 Feb. 1945: 1.

Bair, Deirdre. *Simone de Beauvoir: A Biography.* New York: Simon and Schuster, 1990.

Barrucand, Lucien. Rev. of "Pages de Journal," by André Gide. *Les Dernières Nouvelles* 12 Jul. 1944: N. pag. Dossier II. 42, item 7. Fonds André Gide, Bibliothèque Littéraire Jacques Doucet, Paris.

Beauce, Jacques. Rev. of *Attendu que . . .* , by André Gide. *La Marseillaise* n. d.: N. pag. Dossier II. 18, item 7. Fonds André Gide, Bibliothèque Littéraire Jacques Doucet, Paris.

Beauvoir, Simone de. *La Force de l'âge*. Paris: Gallimard, 1960.

———. *The Prime of Life*. Trans. Peter Green. 1962. New York: Harper and Row, 1976.

Béguin, Albert. "Le Dialogue d'Œdipe et Thésée." *Une Semaine dans le Monde* 31 Aug. 1946: N. pag. Dossier III. 7, item 25. Fonds André Gide, Bibliothèque Littéraire Jacques Doucet, Paris.

Benda, Julien. *La France byzantine ou le triomphe de la littérature pure*. Paris: Gallimard, 1945.

———. "Une Nouvelle Idole: le dynamisme." *Les Lettres Françaises* 23 Dec. 1944: 1.

Benjamin, Walter. *The Correspondence of Walter Benjamin*. Ed. Gershom Scholem and Theodor W. Adorno. Trans. Manfred R. Jacobson and Evelyn M. Jacobson. Chicago: U of Chicago P, 1994.

Billy, André. "Sur la responsabilité des écrivains et sur l'avenir du roman." *Le Figaro Littéraire* 31 Aug. 1940: 2.

Blumenson, Martin. *The Vildé Affair*. Boston: Houghton Mifflin, 1977.

Bobin, Robert. "Plaindre Gide? S'agit de s'entendre. . . ." *Le Rassemblement* 15 Jun. 1941: N. pag. Dossier II. 40, item 11. Fonds André Gide, Bibliothèque Littéraire Jacques Doucet, Paris.

Boretz, Eugène. *Tunis sous la croix gammée*. N. p.: Office Français d'Édition, 1944.

Brasillach, Robert. *Les Quatre Jeudis: images d'avant-guerre*. Paris: Les Sept Couleurs, 1951.

Buenzod, Janine. "Thomas Mann et André Gide." *Thomas Mann*. Ed. Frédérick Tristan. Paris: Éditions de l'Herne, 1973. 242–52.

Cabanis, José. "Un Résistant?" *Le Monde des Livres* 22 Nov. 1969: v.

"Le Cas Gide." *Les Lettres Françaises* 2 Dec. 1944: 2.

Cate, Curtis. *Antoine de Saint-Exupéry*. New York: G. P. Putnam's Sons, 1970.

Céline, Louis-Ferdinand. *Bagatelles pour un massacre*. Paris: Éditions Denoël, 1937.

Celio [Jacques Arnault]. "Les Clercs qui n'ont pas trahi: André Gide." *La Fraternité* 24 Oct. 1944: 1. Dossier II. 42, item 16. Fonds André Gide, Bibliothèque Littéraire Jacques Doucet, Paris.

Chardonne, Jacques [Jacques Boutelleau]. *Chronique privée de l'an 1940*. Paris: Éditions Stock, 1940.

———. "L'Été à La Maurie." *La Nouvelle Revue Française* 322 (Dec. 1940): 7–16.

———. *Voir la figure: réflexions sur ce temps*. Paris: Grasset, 1941.

Chroniques interdites II. Paris: Éditions de Minuit, 1944.

Churchill, Winston S. *Winston S. Churchill: His Complete Speeches 1897–1963*. Vol. 6. Ed. Robert Rhodes James. New York: Chelsea House, 1974.

Cohen-Solal, Annie. *Sartre, 1905–1980*. Paris: Gallimard, 1985.

Combelle, Lucien. *Je dois à André Gide*. Paris: F. Chambriand, 1951.

Copley, Antony. *Sexual Moralities in France, 1780–1980: New Ideas on the Family, Divorce, and Homosexuality*. London and New York: Routledge, 1989.

Cornick, Martyn. *The* Nouvelle Revue Française *Under Jean Paulhan, 1925–1940*. Amsterdam: Rodopi, 1995.

Cowley, Malcolm. Introduction. *Imaginary Interviews*. By André Gide. Trans. Malcolm Cowley. New York: Alfred A. Knopf, 1944. vii–xvii.

"Criticism of *L'Arche*." *Review of the Foreign Press* 7 Aug. 1944: 112.

"Dans le jardin des lettres." *L'Union Française* 3 Jul. 1943: N. pag. Dossier V, item 332ZO. Fonds André Gide, Bibliothèque Littéraire Jacques Doucet, Paris.

Daudet, Alphonse. *Contes du lundi*. Paris: Henri Cyral, Éditeur, 1930.

———. *Monday Tales*. Freeport, NY: Books for Libraries Press, 1970.

Debû-Bridel, Jacques. "Éloquence du silence." *Domaine Français. Messages 1943*. Geneva: Éditions des Trois Collines, 1943. 93–99.

de Gaulle, Charles. *Œuvres complètes. Discours et Messages. Pendant la guerre, juin 1940–janvier 1946*. Paris: Cercle du Bibliophile, 1970.

"De jour en jour." *Le Figaro* 15 Nov. 1941: 3.

Delarue, Maurice. "Pierre Herbart, 'pseudo' Le Vigan, à Rennes, été 44." *Bulletin des Amis d'André Gide* 96 (1992): 469–80.

de Magne, S. "Le Nouveau Livre d'André Gide: 'Attendu que. . . .'" *Paris* 21 Jan. 1944: N. pag. Dossier II. 18, item 6. Fonds André Gide, Bibliothèque Littéraire Jacques Doucet, Paris.

de Man, Paul. *Allegories of Reading: Figural Language in Rouseau, Nietzsche, Rilke, and Proust*. New Haven: Yale UP, 1979.

———. *Blindness and Insight: Essays in the Rhetoric of Contemporary Criticism*. 2nd ed. Minneapolis: U of Minnesota P, 1983.

———. *Critical Writings, 1953–1978*. Ed. Lindsay Waters. Minneapolis: U of Minnesota P, 1989.

———. *Wartime Journalism, 1939–1943*. Ed. Werner Hamacher et al. Lincoln: U of Nebraska P, 1988.

Derais, François [François Reymond], and Henri Rambaud. *L'Envers du Journal de Gide: Tunis 1942–43*. 2nd ed. Paris: Le Nouveau Portique, 1952.

Deschodt, Éric. *Gide, le contemporain capital*. Paris: Perrin, 1991.

Després, F. "Le Combat de l'esprit." *Combat* [Algiers] 24 Dec. 1944: N. pag. Dossier II. 42, item 1. Fonds André Gide, Bibliothèque Littéraire Jacques Doucet, Paris.

Dhérin, Céline, Henri Heinemann, Pierre Masson, and Claude Martin. "Varia." *Bulletin des Amis d'André Gide* 106 (Apr. 1995): 367–71.

Dimaras, C[onstantin]. "Gide et la Grèce." *Bulletin des Amis d'André Gide* 90/91 (Apr.–Jul. 1991): 290–92.

Domaine Français. Messages 1943. Geneva: Éditions des Trois Collines, 1943.

Drevet-Benatti, Valentine. E-mail to the author. 13 Feb. 1997.

Drieu La Rochelle, Pierre. "Bilan." *La Nouvelle Revue Française* 347 (Jan. 1943): 103–11.

———. *Journal 1939–1945.* Ed. Julien Hervier. Paris: Gallimard, 1992.

Duché, Jean. "Jean Paulhan et Vercors disputent de l'épuration chez les écrivains." *Le Littéraire* 29 Mar. 1947: 1–2.

Durosay, Daniel. "Thésée roi: essai sur le discours politique dans le *Thésée* de Gide." *Bulletin des Amis d'André Gide* 106 (Apr. 1995): 201–21.

———. "*Voyage au Congo, Le Retour du Tchad.* Notice." *Souvenirs et voyages.* By André Gide. Paris: Gallimard, Bibliothèque de la Pléiade, 2001. 1194–1211.

Dyssord, Jacques. "Les Aventures d'André Gide: aux quatre vents de l'esprit." *Pariser Zeitung* 5 Mar. 1944: 7.

"Échos des lettres." *L'Écho* 8 Apr. 1944: N. pag. Dossier V, item 346ZO. Fonds André Gide, Bibliothèque Littéraire Jacques Doucet, Paris.

Ehrenburg, Ilya. "A Chain of Evil." Foreign Office file FO 371/ 42149–Z6790. Public Record Office, Kew, England.

Epting, Karl. Préface. *Anthologie de la poésie allemande des origines à nos jours.* Ed. René Lasne and Georg Rabuse. Paris: Stock, 1943. ix–xv.

Étiemble, René. *C'est le bouquet! (1940–1967).* Paris: Gallimard, 1967.

Eubé, Charles. "Pages d'introspection." *Poésie 45* 24 (Apr.–May 1945): 108. Dossier III. 7, item 4. Fonds André Gide, Bibliothèque Littéraire Jacques Doucet, Paris.

Fabrègues, Jean de. "À la recherche des valeurs françaises." *Demain* 20 Sep. 1942: 1, 6.

Fabre-Luce, Alfred, ed. *Anthologie de la nouvelle Europe.* Paris: Librairie Plon, 1942.

———. "Lettre à un Américain." *La Nouvelle Revue Française* 322 (Dec. 1940): 64–72.

Fernand-Demeure. "André Gide et l'Allemagne." *L'Écho* 12 May 1944: N. pag. Dossier V, item 347ZO. Fonds André Gide, Bibliothèque Littéraire Jacques Doucet, Paris.

Ferro, Marc. *Questions sur la IIe guerre mondiale.* Florence: Casterman, 1993.

Le Figaro. 21 Nov. 1942: 1.

Forster, E. M. "Homage to André Gide," ts. Foreign Office file FO 371/ 36287–Z8538. Public Record Office, Kew, England.

Foucart, Claude. "'Dans les années sans nom': Sémélé et Jupiter (Correspondance André Gide–Bernd Schmeier)." *Bulletin des Amis d'André Gide* 70 (Apr. 1986): 9–39.

———. *Le Temps de la "gadouille" ou le dernier rendez-vous d'André Gide avec l'Allemagne (1933–1951).* Bern: Peter Lang, 1997.

Fouché, Pascal. *L'Édition française sous l'Occupation, 1940–1944.* 2 vols. Paris: Bibliothèque de Littérature Française Contemporaine de l'Université Paris 7, 1987.

Fouchet, Max-Pol. *Un Jour, je m'en souviens.* . . . Paris: Mercure de France, 1968.

"La France ne peut durer qu'en France." *Le Petit Niçois* 24 Jul. 1944: N. pag. Dossier II. 42, item 13. Fonds André Gide, Bibliothèque Littéraire Jacques Doucet, Paris.

Fraysse, Louis. "André Gide et la question des réfugiés." *Le Petit Niçois* 19 Oct. 1939: N. pag. Dossier II. 17, item 4. Fonds André Gide, Bibliothèque Littéraire Jacques Doucet, Paris.

Fry, Varian. *Assignment: Rescue. An Autobiography.* New York: Scholastic, 1945.

Galland, Jacques. "André Gide en Afrique du Nord." *Paru* 27 (Feb. 1947): 5–9. Dossier II. 17, item 9. Fonds André Gide, Bibliothèque Littéraire Jacques Doucet, Paris.

Gerber, François. *Saint-Exupéry: de la rive gauche à la guerre.* Paris: Denoël, 2000.

Gide, André. *Ainsi soit-il.* Ms. Private collection of Catherine Gide. N. pag.

———. *Allocution prononcée à Pertisau le 18 août 1946.* [Austria]: Imprimerie Nationale de France en Autriche, [1946].

———. *Anthologie de la poésie française.* Paris: Gallimard, Bibliothèque de la Pléiade, 1949.

———. "Appel." *L'Arche* 1 (Feb. 1944): 13–15.

———. *Attendu que.* . . . Algiers: Charlot, 1943.

———. "Auguste Bréal." *Le Figaro* 22 Feb. 1941: 3.

———. *Autumn Leaves.* Trans. Elsie Pell. New York: Philosophical Library, 1950.

———. "Avant-propos." *Terre des Hommes* 29 Sep. 1945: 1.

———. *Corydon.* Paris: Gallimard, 1924.

———. *Corydon.* Trans. Richard Howard. Urbana: U of Illinois P, 1983.

———. Déclaration d'André Gide devant la salle comble du Ruhl, à Nice. Ts. γ1467–2. Bibliothèque Littéraire Jacques Doucet, Paris.

———. "Déclaration de M. André Gide." *La Revue Juive de Genève* 63 (Dec. 1938): 105.

———. *Découvrons Henri Michaux.* [Paris]: Gallimard, 1941.

———. "Défense de la langue française II." *Le Littéraire* 28 Dec. 1946: 1.

———. "Défense de la langue française IV." *Le Littéraire* 8 Feb. 1947: 1.

———. "Défense de la langue française V." *Le Littéraire* 29 Mar. 1947: 1–2.

———. "La Délivrance de Tunis." *Les Lettres Françaises* 18 Nov. 1944: 1+.

———. "La Délivrance de Tunis." *La Syrie et l'Orient* Aug. 1943: N. pag.

———. "Deux autres lettres inédites d'André Gide à Jean Denoël." *Bulletin des Amis d'André Gide* 17 (Oct. 1972): 3–6.

———. "Les Deux Cortèges." *Terre des Hommes* 3 Nov. 1945: 1.

———. "Don d'un arbre." *Cahiers de la Pléiade* (Summer–Fall 1950): 23–27.

———. "Du classicisme." *Domaine Français. Messages 1943*. Geneva: Éditions des Trois Collines, 1943. 259–63.

———. "D'une France nouvelle." *Combat* 23 Dec. 1944: 1.

———. "Éloge de la Suisse." *Images de la Suisse*. Spec. issue of *Cahiers du Sud* (Jun. 1943): 15–17.

———. "Existentialisme." *Terre des Hommes* 17 Nov. 1945: 6.

———. *Experiences in the Congo: France's Inefficiency as a Colonial Power*. Berlin: n. p., 1940.

———. "Feuillets." *La Nouvelle Revue Française* 322 (Dec. 1940): 76–86.

———. "Feuillets." *La Nouvelle Revue Française* 324 (Feb. 1941): 342–51.

———. *Feuillets d'automne*. Paris: Mercure de France, 1949.

———. "Fragments d'un journal, 1942 et 1943." *Chroniques interdites II*. Paris: Éditions de Minuit, 1944.

———. *The Fruits of the Earth*. Trans. Dorothy Bussy. New York: Alfred A. Knopf, 1949.

———. *If It Die*. Trans. Dorothy Bussy. New York: Vintage Books, 1935.

———. *Imaginary Interviews*. Trans. Malcolm Cowley. New York: Alfred A. Knopf, 1944.

———. *Interviews imaginaires*. Ms. γ890. Bibliothèque Littéraire Jacques Doucet, Paris.

———. *Interviews imaginaires*. [Paris]: Gallimard, [1943].

———. Introduction. *Théâtre*. By Johann Wolfgang von Goethe. Paris: Gallimard, Bibliothèque de la Pléiade, 1942. ix–xxiv.

———. "Introduction au Théâtre de Goethe (suite et fin)." *Le Figaro* 7 Feb. 1942: 3.

———. *Journal*. Mss. γ1638, 1639, 1642, 1646. Bibliothèque Littéraire Jacques Doucet, Paris.

———. *Journal I, 1887–1925*. Ed. Éric Marty. Paris: Gallimard, Bibliothèque de la Pléiade, 1996.

———. *Journal II, 1926–1950*. Ed. Martine Sagaert. Paris: Gallimard, Bibliothèque de la Pléiade, 1997.

———. *Journal, 1939–1942*. Paris: Gallimard, 1946.

———. *Journal, 1942–1949*. Paris: Gallimard, 1950.

———. *The Journals of André Gide*. Ed. and trans. Justin O'Brien. 4 vols. New York: Alfred A. Knopf, 1948–51.

———. "Les Juifs, Céline et Maritain." *La Nouvelle Revue Française* 295 (Apr. 1938): 630–36.

———. "La Justice avant la charité." *Combat* 7 and 8 Jan. 1945: 1.

———. "Justice ou charité?" *Le Figaro* 25 Feb. 1945: 1–2.

———. Letter to George Seferis. 10 June 1943. *Bulletin des Amis d'André Gide* 90/91 (Apr.–Jul. 1991): 296.

———. "La Libération de Tunis." *Combat* [Algiers] 9 Jan. 1944: 8.

———. "La Libération de Tunis." *La France Nouvelle* 15 Oct. 1943: 7.

———. *Littérature engagée*. Ed. Yvonne Davet. Paris: Gallimard, 1950.

———. "Un Message d'André Gide." *Le Figaro* 10 Sep. 1944: 1.

———. *Ne jugez pas*. Paris: Gallimard, 1930.

———. "Nicht Gleichheit, sondern Harmonie." *Ruf an die deutsche Jugend*. Ed. Gerhard Fauth. Munich: Verlag der Zwölf, 1947. 33–34.

———. "Notre 'Afrique intérieure.'" *Fontaine* 13 (Mar. 1941): 274–76.

———. "Nouvelles pages de journal." *Les Lettres Françaises* [Buenos Aires] 12 (1944): 1–6.

———. *Œuvres complètes d'André Gide*. Ed. Louis Martin-Chauffier. 15 vols. Paris: N.R.F., 1932–1939.

———. "Pages de Journal." *L'Arche* 2 (Mar. 1944): 3–23.

———. "Pages de Journal." *Le Figaro* 23 Sep. 1944: 1+.

———. "Pages de Journal." *Fontaine* 31 (1943): 8–13.

———. *Pages de Journal (1929–1932)*. Paris: Gallimard, 1934.

———. *Pages de Journal, 1939–1941*. Algiers: Charlot, 1944.

———. *Pages de Journal, 1939–1942*. Ed. Jacques Shiffrin. New York: Pantheon, 1944.

———. "Paul Valéry." *L'Arche* 10 (Oct. 1945): 4–17.

———. "Peuple et poésie." *Le Figaro* 13 Dec. 1941: 3.

———. *Prétextes*. Paris: Mercure de France, 1947.

———. "Que serait-il advenu si la France n'avait pas résisté à l'Allemagne?" *Anthologie de la nouvelle Europe*. Ed. Alfred Fabre-Luce. Paris: Librairie Plon, 1942. 266–67.

———. "Le Rayonnement de Paul Valéry." *Le Figaro* 25 Jul. 1945: N. pag.

———. "Reconnaissance à la Grèce." *Bulletin des Amis d'André Gide* 90/91 (Apr.–Jul. 1991): 303–04.

———. "Réflexions sur l'Allemagne." *La Nouvelle Revue Française* 69 (1919): 35–46.

———. "Rencontre à Sorrente." *L'Arche* 6 (Oct.–Nov. 1944): 133–35.

———. "Réponse à une enquête." *L'Arche* 6 (Oct.–Nov. 1944): 129–32.

———. "Réponse à une enquête." *Le Figaro* 12 Oct. 1940: 3.

———. "Rester unis." Ts. γ1174–2. Bibliothèque Littéraire Jacques Doucet, Paris.

———. *Return from the U.S.S.R.* Trans. Dorothy Bussy. New York: McGraw-Hill, 1964.

———. *Romans, récits et soties, œuvres lyriques*. Paris: Gallimard, Bibliothèque de la Pléiade, 1958.

———. "Saint-Exupéry." *Le Figaro* 1 Feb. 1945: 1+.

———. "Un Serviteur de la France nouvelle: Pierre Viénot." *La France Libre* VIII. 46 (15 Aug. 1944): 231.

———. *So Be It, or The Chips Are Down*. Trans. Justin O'Brien. London: Chatto & Windus, 1960.

———. *Souvenirs et voyages*. Ed. Pierre Masson, Daniel Durosay, and Martine Sagaert. Paris: Gallimard, Bibliothèque de la Pléiade, 2001.

———. *Strait Is the Gate*. Trans. Dorothy Bussy. New York: Alfred A. Knopf, 1959.

———. "Texte de Gide sans titre ni date." *Bulletin des Amis d'André Gide* 90/91 (Apr.–Jul. 1991): 293–94.

———. "Le Théâtre de Goethe." Dossier II. 18, item 2. Fonds André Gide, Bibliothèque Littéraire Jacques Doucet, Paris.

———. *Thésée*. New York: Pantheon Books, 1946.

———. *Two Legends: Œdipus and Theseus*. Trans. John Russell. New York: Alfred A. Knopf, 1950.

Gide, André, and François-Paul Alibert. *Correspondance 1907–1950*. Lyon: Presses Universitaires de Lyon, 1982.

Gide, André, and Dorothy Bussy. *Correspondance André Gide–Dorothy Bussy III: janvier 1937–janvier 1951*. Ed. Jean Lambert. Notes by Richard Tedeschi. *Cahiers André Gide* 11. Paris: Gallimard, 1982.

———. *Selected Letters of André Gide and Dorothy Bussy*. Ed. Richard Tedeschi. Oxford: Oxford UP, 1983.

Gide, André, and Jacques Copeau. *Correspondance André Gide–Jacques Copeau*. Ed. Jean Claude. Vol. II. *Cahiers André Gide* 13. Paris: Gallimard, 1988.

Gide, André, and Jef Last. *Correspondance 1934–1950*. Ed. C. J. Greshoff. Lyon: Presses Universitaires de Lyon, 1985.

Gide, André, and Jean Malaquais. *Correspondance: 1935–1950*. Ed. Pierre Masson and Geneviève Millot-Nakach. Paris: Phébus, 2000.

Gide, André, and Roger Martin du Gard. *Correspondance 1935–1951*. Vol. 2. Paris: Gallimard, 1968.

Gide, André, and Jean Paulhan. *Correspondance 1918–1951*. Ed. Frédéric Grover and Pierrette Schartenberg-Winter. Paris: Gallimard, 1998.

Gide, André, and Jules Romains. *Correspondance André Gide–Jules Romains: l'individu et l'unanime*. Ed. Claude Martin. *Cahiers Jules Romains* 1. Paris: Flammarion, 1976.

Gide, André, and Jean Schlumberger. *Correspondance 1901–1950*. Ed. Pascal Mercier and Peter Fawcett. Paris: Gallimard, 1993.

Gide, André, and Thea Sternheim. *Correspondance 1927–1950.* Ed. Claude Foucart. Lyon: Centre d'Études Gidiennes, 1986.

Gide, André, and Paul Valéry. *Correspondance 1890–1942.* Ed. Robert Mallet. Paris: Gallimard, 1955.

——— . *Self-Portraits: The Gide/Valéry Letters, 1890–1942.* Ed. Robert Mallet. Trans. June Guicharnaud. Chicago: U of Chicago P, 1966.

"Gide à Alger." *Le Pays Libre* 6 Feb. 1944: N. pag. Dossier V, unnumbered item. Fonds André Gide, Bibliothèque Littéraire Jacques Doucet, Paris.

"Gide en prison." *Er Rachid* 25 Oct. 1943: N. pag. Dossier II. 17, item 16. Fonds André Gide, Bibliothèque Littéraire Jacques Doucet, Paris.

"Le Gide et son . . . Michaux." *L'Appel* 12 Jun. 1941: N. pag. Dossier II. 40, item 12. Fonds André Gide, Bibliothèque Littéraire Jacques Doucet, Paris.

Gillouin, René. "Responsabilité des écrivains et des artistes." *Le Journal de Genève* 33, 7 and 8 Feb. 1942: 3.

Glotz, Gustave. *The Aegean Civilization.* Trans. M. R. Dobie and E. M. Riley. New York: Barnes & Noble, Inc., 1968.

——— . *La Civilisation égéenne.* Paris: Éditions Albin Michel, 1952.

Goethe, Johann Wolfgang von. "Faust et Chiron." Trans. André Gide. *Anthologie de la poésie allemande des origines à nos jours.* Ed. René Lasne and Georg Rabuse. Paris: Stock, 1943. 150–55.

Grenier, Jean. *Sous l'Occupation.* Ed. Claire Paulhan and Gisèle Sapiro. Paris: Éditions Claire Paulhan, 1997.

Guibert, Armand. "Avec André Gide en Tunisie." *Bulletin des Amis d'André Gide* 116 (Oct. 1997): 347–53.

Guillemin, Henri. *À vrai dire.* Paris: Gallimard, 1956.

Guitard-Auviste, Ginette. *Jacques Chardonne ou l'incandescence sous le givre.* Paris: Éditions Olivier Orban, 1984.

Hallett, Ronald A. *A Translation, with Introduction and Notes, of the* Délie *of Maurice Scève.* Diss. Pennsylvania State University, 1973. Ann Arbor: UMI, 1973. 7324009.

Halls, W. D. *The Youth of Vichy France.* Oxford: Clarendon Press, 1981.

Handourtzel, Rémy. "La Politique scolaire de Vichy (1940–1944)." *Sources* 1 (1985): 53–63.

Hanna, Martha. "What Did André Gide See in the Action Française?" *Historical Reflections; Réflexions Historiques* 17.1 (1991): 1–22.

Hebey, Pierre. *La NRF des années sombres, juin 1940–juin 1941: des intellectuels à la dérive.* Paris: Gallimard, 1992.

Heller, Gerhard, and Jean Grand. *Un Allemand à Paris, 1940–1944.* Paris: Éditions du Seuil, 1981.

Henriot, Émile. "Le Dernier Gide." *Le Monde* 27 Dec. 1944: 1.

Herbart, Pierre. À *la recherche d'André Gide*. Paris: Gallimard, 1952.

———. *Inédits*. Paris: Le Tout sur le Tout, 1981.

———. *La Ligne de force*. Paris: Gallimard, 1958.

Heurgon-Desjardins, Anne. "Introduction—Gide à Alger." *Entretiens sur André Gide*. Ed. Marcel Arland and Jean Mouton. Paris: Mouton & Co., 1967.

Hoog, Armand. "Gide, ou la présence d'un absent." *Carrefour* 23 Dec. 1944: 5.

Hugo, Victor. *Les Contemplations*. Ed. L. Cellier. Paris: Garnier, 1969.

———. *L'Œuvre de Victor Hugo: poésie, prose, théâtre*. Ed. Maurice Levaillant. Paris: Librairie Delagrave, 1931.

———. *Selected Poems*. Vol. 1. Philadelphia: George Barrie & Son, 1897.

"Les Insultes d'André Gide au sentiment patriotique français." *La Liberté* 12 Jul. 1944: N. pag. Dossier II. 42, item 6. Fonds André Gide, Bibliothèque Littéraire Jacques Doucet, Paris.

Jackson, Julian. *France: The Dark Years, 1940–1944*. Oxford: Oxford UP, 2001.

Janvier, A. "Pour l'épuration du livre." *Le Cri du Peuple* 21 Nov. 1940: N. pag. Dossier V, item 301ZO. Fonds André Gide, Bibliothèque Littéraire Jacques Doucet, Paris.

Jaques, Claudine. "Littérature ou politique? Faut-il fusiller Gide?" *La Quatrième République* 22 Jul. 1944: N. pag. Dossier II. 42, item 11. Fonds André Gide, Bibliothèque Littéraire Jacques Doucet, Paris.

"La Jeunesse de France." *Le Temps* 9 Jul. 1940: 1.

Julia, Louis. "À propos de 'Pages de Journal' d'André Gide." *Alger Républicain* 2 Jan. 1944: N. pag. Dossier II. 42, item 9. Fonds André Gide, Bibliothèque Littéraire Jacques Doucet, Paris.

Kanters, Robert. "Rien qu'un homme." *Le Spectateur* 27 Aug. 1946: N. pag. Dossier III. 7, item 21. Fonds André Gide, Bibliothèque Littéraire Jacques Doucet, Paris.

Kaplan, Alice Yaeger. *The Collaborator: The Trial and Execution of Robert Brasillach*. Chicago: U of Chicago P, 2000.

———. "Literature and Collaboration." *A New History of French Literature*. Ed. Denis Hollier. Cambridge: Harvard UP, 1989. 966–71.

———. "Paul de Man, *Le Soir*, and the Francophone Collaboration (1940–1942)." *Responses: On Paul de Man's Wartime Journalism*. Ed. Werner Hamacher et al. Lincoln: U of Nebraska P, 1989. 266–84.

———. *Reproductions of Banality: Fascism, Literature, and French Intellectual Life*. Minneapolis: U of Minnesota P, 1986.

Kassab, Ahmed. *Histoire de la Tunisie. L'Époque contemporaine*. Tunis: Société Tunisienne de Diffusion, 1976.

Kidd, William. "French Literature and World War II: Vercors and Chardonne." *Forum for Modern Language Studies* 23.1 (1987): 38–47.

Koffeman, Maaike. "André Gide et l'évolution de la première *NRF*, ou la stratégie des satellites." *Bulletin des Amis d'André Gide* 131/132 (Jul.–Oct. 2001): 437–45.

Krauss, Kenneth. *The Drama of Fallen France: Reading* la Comédie sans Tickets. Albany: State University of New York Press, 2004.

La Bruyère, Jean de. *Œuvres complètes*. Paris: Gallimard, Bibliothèque de la Pléiade, 1951.

Lalou, Étienne. "Interview non imaginaire: André Gide." *Gavroche* 24 May 1945: 3.

Lambert, Jean. *Gide familier*. Paris: Julliard, 1958.

Larnac, Jean. "Les Interviews imaginaires d'André Gide." *L'Université Libre* 20 Nov. 1944: N. pag. Dossier V, item 353. Fonds André Gide, Bibliothèque Littéraire Jacques Doucet, Paris.

Lasne, René, and Georg Rabuse. *Anthologie de la poésie allemande des origines à nos jours*. Paris: Stock, 1943.

Léautaud, Paul. *Journal littéraire*. 19 vols. Paris: Mercure de France, 1954–66.

Lecache, Bernard. "Fabre-Luce ou le Juvénal clandestin." *Les Lettres Françaises* 11 Aug. 1945: 2.

Léger, François. "Les Relations de Gide et de Maurras." *Écrits de Paris* 431 (Jan. 1983): 61–68.

Lepape, Pierre. *André Gide le messager*. Paris: Éditions du Seuil, 1997.

Lévy, Yves. "André Gide a bouclé la boucle. . . ." *Volontés* 6 Dec. 1944: 4.

Lottman, Herbert R. *The Left Bank: Writers, Artists, and Politics from the Popular Front to the Cold War*. San Francisco: Halo Books, 1991.

———. *The Purge*. New York: William Morrow, 1986.

Lucey, Michael. *Gide's Bent: Sexuality, Politics, Writing*. New York, Oxford: Oxford UP, 1995.

Macmillan, Harold. Memo to the Foreign Office. 6 July 1943. Foreign Office file FO 371/ 36287–Z7591. Public Record Office, Kew, England.

———. Memo to the Foreign Office. 15 July 1943. Foreign Office file FO 371/ 36287–Z7931. Public Record Office, Kew, England.

Malaquais, Jean. *Journal de guerre, suivi de Journal du métèque*. Paris: Phébus, 1997.

Mallarmé, Stéphane. *Collected Poems*. Trans. Henry Weinfield. Berkeley: U of California P, 1994.

"Manifeste." *L'Arche* 1 (1944): 5–11.

Marcel, Gabriel. Rev. of *Pages de Journal (1939–1942)*, by André Gide. *La Nef* May 1945: 135–36. Dossier III. 7, item 5. Fonds André Gide, Bibliothèque Littéraire Jacques Doucet, Paris.

Maritain, Jacques. *Les Juifs parmi les nations*. Paris: Les Éditions du Cerf, 1938.

———. "Réponse à André Gide sur les Juifs." *La Nouvelle Revue Française* (Jun. 1938): 1020–22.

Marnier, Henri. "Aragon contre André Gide." *Paris* 15 Dec. 1944: N. pag. Dossier II. 43, item 4. Fonds André Gide, Bibliothèque Littéraire Jacques Doucet, Paris.

Marrus, Michael R., and Robert O. Paxton. *Vichy France and the Jews.* New York: Basic Books, 1981.

Martin, Claude. "'Ce fou de Jef . . .': André Gide et Munich." *Revue des Sciences Humaines* 137 (Jan.–Mar. 1970): 119–25.

———. *La* Nouvelle Revue Française *1940–1943.* Lyon: Centre d'Études Gidiennes, 1975.

Martin-Chauffier, Louis. *L'Homme et la bête.* Paris: Gallimard, 1947.

———. "Ma patrie, la langue française." *Domaine Français. Messages 1943.* Geneva: Éditions des Trois Collines, 1943. 63–70.

Martin du Gard, Maurice. "La Méprise de M. Gide." *Voir la figure.* By Jacques Chardonne. Paris: Grasset, 1941. 117–23.

Martin du Gard, Roger. *Journal III, 1937–1949. Textes autobiographiques 1950–1958.* Paris: Gallimard, 1993.

Marty, Éric. *L'Écriture du jour: le* Journal d'André Gide. Paris: Éditions du Seuil, 1985.

Marx, Karl. *The Eighteenth Brumaire of Louis Bonaparte.* New York: International Publishers, 1963.

Masson, Pierre. "Gide et l'Espagne: de la quête égotiste à la solidarité politique." *Bulletin des Amis d'André Gide* 119/120 (Jul.–Oct. 1998): 307–21.

Mattingly, H[arold]. Introduction. *Tacitus on Britain and Germany.* Trans. H. Mattingly. Hammondsworth, Eng.: Penguin Books, 1948. 7–49.

Mauclair, Camille. "Pour un assainissement littéraire." *La Gerbe* 2 Jan. 1941: 7.

Maulnier, Thierry [Jacques Talagrand]. "Controverse à propos des anthologies." *Le Figaro* 23 Dec. 1941: 3+.

Mauriac, Claude. *Conversations avec André Gide.* Paris: Éditions Albin Michel, 1951.

———. *Conversations with André Gide.* Trans. Michel Lebeck. New York: George Braziller, 1965.

———. "La Décade des réfugiés." *La Flèche* 25 Aug. 1939: N. pag. Dossier V, item 293. Fonds André Gide, Bibliothèque Littéraire Jacques Doucet, Paris.

M. C. "L'Arche d'alliance." *Le Cri du Peuple* 25 Oct. 1943: N. pag. Dossier V, item 337ZO. Fonds André Gide, Bibliothèque Littéraire Jacques Doucet, Paris.

McLeod, Enid. Memo to R. L. Speaight. 2 August 1943. Foreign Office file FO 371/36287–Z8538. Public Record Office, Kew, England.

Mégret, Fred. "André Gide à Alger." *La Gazette des Lettres* 16 Feb. 1946: 3. Dossier II. 17, item 14. Fonds André Gide, Bibliothèque Littéraire Jacques Doucet, Paris.

Mehlman, Jeffrey. *Legacies of Anti-Semitism in France.* Minneapolis: U of Minnesota P, 1983.

———. "Perspectives: On De Man and *Le Soir.*" *Responses: On Paul de Man's Wartime Journalism.* Ed. Werner Hamacher et al. Lincoln: U of Nebraska P, 1989. 324–33.

Mémoire, Guy. "Offensive contre Gide." Dossier II. 42, item 10. Fonds André Gide, Bibliothèque Littéraire Jacques Doucet, Paris.

"Les Mésaventures de Corydon." *L'Essor* 1 May 1944: N. pag. Dossier V, item 346ZO. Fonds André Gide, Bibliothèque Littéraire Jacques Doucet, Paris.

"Mise au point." *L'Éclaireur* 26 May 1941: N. pag. Dossier II. 40, item 8. Fonds André Gide, Bibliothèque Littéraire Jacques Doucet, Paris.

M[aurice]. N[oël]. "Quelques nouvelles des Lettres." *Le Figaro* 2 Dec. 1944: 2.

Mortimer, Raymond. Letter to Oliver Harvey. 19 June 1943. Foreign Office file FO 371/ 36287–Z7234. Public Record Office, Kew, England.

Mounier, Emmanuel. "Sur l'intelligence en temps de crise." *Esprit* 97 (Feb. 1941): 201–15.

Moutote, Daniel. *André Gide: l'engagement (1926–1939)*. Paris: SEDES, 1991.

Nadeau, Maurice. "Gide, victime de lui-même." *Gavroche* 1 Aug. 1946: N. pag. Dossier III. 7, item 18. Fonds André Gide, Bibliothèque Littéraire Jacques Doucet, Paris.

———. Rev. of *Pages de Journal (1939–1942)*, by André Gide. *Combat* 19 Jul. 1946: N. pag. Dossier III. 7, item 11. Fonds André Gide, Bibliothèque Littéraire Jacques Doucet, Paris.

Norris, Christopher. *Paul de Man: Deconstruction and the Critique of Aesthetic Ideology*. New York: Routledge, 1988.

Noulet, E. Rev. of *Interviews imaginaires*, by André Gide. *Les Lettres Françaises* [Buenos Aires] (Oct. 1944): N. pag. Dossier II. 18, item 13. Fonds André Gide, Bibliothèque Littéraire Jacques Doucet, Paris.

La Nouvelle Revue Française. *Cent dix-huit lettres inédites*. Paris: [N.R.F.], 1976.

Novick, Peter. *The Resistance Versus Vichy: The Purge of Collaborators in Liberated France*. New York: Columbia UP, 1968.

O'Brien, Justin. Introduction. *The Journals of André Gide*. By André Gide. Trans. Justin O'Brien. Vol. 4. New York: Alfred A. Knopf, 1951. v–x.

———. *Portrait of André Gide: A Critical Biography*. New York: McGraw-Hill, 1953.

Painter, George D. *André Gide, A Critical Biography*. London: Weidenfeld and Nicolson, 1968.

Patri, A[imé]. Rev. of *Attendu que . . .*, by André Gide. *La Tunisie Française* 23 Jan. 1944: 1. Dossier II. 18, item 8. Fonds André Gide, Bibliothèque Littéraire Jacques Doucet, Paris.

"Le Patriotisme de M. Gide." *La Liberté* 6 Jul. 1944: N. pag. Dossier II. 42, item 2. Fonds André Gide, Bibliothèque Littéraire Jacques Doucet, Paris.

Paulhan, Jean. *De la paille et du grain*. Paris: Gallimard, 1948.

Paxton, Robert O. *Vichy France: Old Guard and New Order, 1940–1944*. New York: Columbia UP, 1972.

Peake, Charles. Memo to Mack. 28 July 1943. Foreign Office file FO 371/ 36287–Z8375. Public Record Office, Kew, England.

Pétain, Philippe. *Actes et écrits*. Ed. Jacques Isorni. Paris: Flammarion, 1974.

———. *Discours aux Français. 17 juin 1940–20 août 1944*. Ed. Jean-Claude Barbas. Paris: Albin Michel, 1989.

Poliakov, Léon. *Histoire de l'antisémitisme*. 4 vols. Paris: Calmann-Lévy, 1955–77.

Pollard, Patrick. "The Sources of André Gide's 'Thésée.'" *The Modern Language Review* 65.2 (1970): 290–97.

Prévost, Jean. *Les Caractères*. Paris: Éditions Albin Michel, 1948.

Price, Roger. *A Concise History of France*. Cambridge, Eng.: Cambridge UP, 1993.

Privaz, Étienne. *Un Malfaiteur: André Gide*. Paris: Albert Messein, Éditeur, 1931.

Putnam, Walter. "Writing the Wrongs of French Colonial Africa: *Voyage au Congo* and *Le Retour du Tchad*." *André Gide's Politics: Rebellion and Ambivalence*. Ed. Tom Conner. New York: Palgrave, 2000. 89–110.

Rebatet, Lucien. "L'Académie de la dissidence ou la trahison prosaïque." *Je Suis Partout* 10 Mar. 1944: 1, 6.

———. *Les Tribus du cinéma et du théâtre*. Paris: Nouvelles Éditions Françaises, 1941.

Renan, Ernest. *La Réforme intellectuelle et morale*. 3rd ed. Paris: Michel Lévy Frères, 1872.

Renauld, Pierre. "Le Mythe de Thésée." *Trames, Mythes, Images, Représentations*. Proc. of the XIVᵉ Congrès de la Société Française de Littérature Générale et Comparée, 1977, Limoges. Ed. Jean-Marie Grassin. N. p.: n. p., 1977. 99–104.

Richard, Lionel. "Drieu La Rochelle et la *Nouvelle Revue Française* des années noires." *Revue d'Histoire de la Deuxième Guerre Mondiale* 97 (Jan. 1975): 67–84.

Riche, Paul [Jean Mamy]. "Gallimard et sa 'belle' équipe." *Au Pilori* 18 Oct. 1940: N. pag. Dossier V, item 299ZO. Fonds André Gide, Bibliothèque Littéraire Jacques Doucet, Paris.

Rioux, Jean-Pierre. *The Fourth Republic, 1944–1958*. Trans. Godfrey Rogers. Cambridge, Eng.: Cambridge UP, 1987.

Romains, Jules. *Les Hauts et les bas de la liberté*. Paris: Flammarion, 1960.

Rousso, Henry. *La Collaboration*. Paris: M. A. Éditions, 1987.

Rubenstein, Joshua. *Tangled Loyalties: The Life and Times of Ilya Ehrenburg*. New York: Basic Books, 1996.

Sadoul, Georges, ed. *Aragon*. Paris: Éditions Seghers, 1967.

Sagaert, Martine. Annexes. *Journal II, 1926–1950*. By André Gide. Paris: Gallimard, Bibliothèque de la Pléiade, 1997. 1129–42.

———. Introduction. *Journal II, 1926–1950*. By André Gide. Paris: Gallimard, Bibliothèque de la Pléiade, 1997. ix–xxxiii.

———. Note sur le texte. *Journal II, 1926–1950*. By André Gide. Paris: Gallimard, Bibliothèque de la Pléiade, 1997. 1122–29.

———. Notes [*Ainsi soit-il*]. *Souvenirs et voyages.* By André Gide. Paris: Gallimard, Bibliothèque de la Pléiade, 2001. 1424–38.

———. Notes et variantes. *Journal II, 1926–1950.* By André Gide. Paris: Gallimard, Bibliothèque de la Pléiade, 1997. 1142–1515.

———. Notice. *Journal II, 1926–1950.* By André Gide. Paris: Gallimard, Bibliothèque de la Pléiade, 1997. 1109–22.

Saint-Exupéry, Antoine de. *Œuvres complètes II.* Ed. Michel Autrand et al. Paris: Gallimard, Bibliothèque de la Pléiade, 1999.

Saint-John Perse [Alexis Léger]. *Winds.* Trans. Hugh Chisholm. New York: Pantheon Books, 1953.

Sartre, Jean-Paul. *Anti-Semite and Jew.* Trans. George J. Becker. New York: Schocken Books, 1995.

———. "Gide vivant." *Les Critiques de notre temps et Gide.* Ed. Michel Raimond. Paris: Éditions Garnier Frères, 1971. 150–53.

———. "New Writing in France." *Vogue* (Jul. 1945): 84–85.

———. *Réflexions sur la question juive.* Paris: Gallimard, 1954.

———. *Situations III.* Paris: Gallimard, 1949.

Scève, Maurice. *The 'Délie' of Maurice Scève.* Ed. I. D. McFarlane. Cambridge, Eng.: Cambridge UP, 1966.

Schlumberger, Jean. "Propos sur le langage." *Domaine Français. Messages 1943.* Geneva: Éditions des Trois Collines, 1943. 107–14.

Schveitzer, Marcelle. *Gide aux oasis.* N. p.: Éditions de la Francité, 1971.

Segal, Naomi. *André Gide: Pederasty and Pedagogy.* Oxford: Clarendon Press, 1998.

Sérant, Paul. *Les Dissidents de l'Action Française.* Paris: Copernic, 1978.

Sheridan, Alan. *André Gide: A Life in the Present.* London: Hamish Hamilton, 1998.

Sipriot, Pierre. Préface. *Henry de Montherlant—Roger Peyrefitte: Correspondance.* Ed. Roger Peyrefitte and Pierre Sipriot. Paris: Éditions Robert Laffont, 1983. 11–27.

Snyder, Louis. *The War: A Concise History, 1939–1945.* New York: Julian Messner, Inc., 1960.

Soria, Georges. "Dans les ruines de la Chancellerie, j'ai découvert des dossiers, des diplômes estranges. . . ." *Ce Soir* 18 Jun. 1945: N. pag. Dossier V, item 378. Fonds André Gide, Bibliothèque Littéraire Jacques Doucet, Paris.

Starkie, Enid. *André Gide.* Cambridge, Eng.: Bowes and Bowes, 1953.

Stéphane, Roger. *Fin d'une jeunesse.* Paris: La Table Ronde, 1954.

Stewart, W. Memo to R. L. Speaight. 10 May 1943. Foreign Office file FO 371/36287–Z5519. Public Record Office, Kew, England.

Strauss, Leo. *Persecution and the Art of Writing.* Glencoe, IL: The Free Press, 1952.

Syrotinski, Michael. *Defying Gravity: Jean Paulhan's Interventions in Twentieth-Century French Intellectual History.* Albany: State University of New York Press, 1998.

Tacitus, Cornelius. *Tacitus on Britain and Germany*. Trans. H. Mattingly. Hammondsworth, Eng.: Penguin Books, 1948.

Tatsopoulos-Polychronopoulos, Hélène. "André Gide en Grèce." *Bulletin des Amis d'André Gide* 90/91 (Apr.–Jul. 1991): 199–244.

Le Témoin des martyrs [Louis Aragon]. *Le Crime contre l'esprit*. Paris: Éditions de Minuit, 1944.

Terdiman, Richard. "Bonapartism." *A New History of French Literature*. Ed. Denis Hollier. Cambridge: Harvard UP, 1989. 717–22.

"Texte radiodiffusé par la radio ennemie." 21 July 1944. Dossier II. 42, item 14 bis. Fonds André Gide, Bibliothèque Littéraire Jacques Doucet, Paris.

Thierry, Jean-Jacques. *André Gide*. Paris: Hachette, 1986.

Tilby, Michael. "Image and Counter-Image: André Gide and the Occupation." *France 1940: Literary and Historical Reactions to Defeat*. Ed. Anthony Cheal Pugh. Durham French Colloquies No. 3. Durham, Eng.: U of Durham, 1991.

Tournier, Paul, and Robert Tournier. "André Gide en Tunisie." *Bulletin des Amis d'André Gide* 96 (Oct. 1992): 453–68.

Van Rysselberghe, Maria. *Les Cahiers de la Petite Dame: notes pour l'histoire authentique d'André Gide. Cahiers André Gide* 4–7. Paris: Gallimard, 1973–77.

Veillon, Dominique. *La Collaboration*. Paris: Livre de Poche, 1984.

Vercors [Jean Bruller]. *Le Silence de la mer*. Paris: Albin Michel, 1951.

Verdès-Leroux, Jeannine. *Refus et violences: politique et littérature à l'extrême droite des années trente aux retombées de la Libération*. Paris: Gallimard, 1996.

Waters, Lindsay. "Introduction. Paul de Man: Life and Works." *Critical Writings, 1953–1978*. By Paul de Man. Ed. Lindsay Waters. Minneapolis: U of Minnesota P, 1989. ix–lxxiii.

Watson-Williams, Helen. *André Gide and the Greek Myth*. Oxford: Clarendon Press, 1967.

Werth, Léon. *Déposition. Journal 1940–1944*. Ed. Lucien Febvre and Jean-Pierre Azéma. [France]: Viviane Hamy, 1992.

Wiener, Jon. "Deconstructing de Man." *The Nation* 9 Jan. 1988: 22–24.

Winock, Michel. *Histoire politique de la revue* Esprit, *1930–1950*. Paris: Éditions du Seuil, 1975.

———. *Le Siècle des intellectuels*. Paris: Éditions du Seuil, 1997.

Wolfman, Yaffa. *Engagement et écriture chez André Gide*. Paris: Nizet, 1996.

"Yale Scholar Wrote for Pro-Nazi Newspaper." *New York Times* 1 Dec. 1987, B1+.

Index